# Hands-On Full-Stack Development with Swift

Develop full-stack web and native mobile applications using Swift and Vapor

**Ankur Patel**

**BIRMINGHAM - MUMBAI**

# Hands-On Full-Stack Development with Swift

Copyright © 2018 Packt Publishing

All rights reserved. No part of this book may be reproduced, stored in a retrieval system, or transmitted in any form or by any means, without the prior written permission of the publisher, except in the case of brief quotations embedded in critical articles or reviews.

Every effort has been made in the preparation of this book to ensure the accuracy of the information presented. However, the information contained in this book is sold without warranty, either express or implied. Neither the author, nor Packt Publishing or its dealers and distributors, will be held liable for any damages caused or alleged to have been caused directly or indirectly by this book.

Packt Publishing has endeavored to provide trademark information about all of the companies and products mentioned in this book by the appropriate use of capitals. However, Packt Publishing cannot guarantee the accuracy of this information.

**Commissioning Editor:** Kunal Chaudhari
**Acquisition Editor:** Siddharth Mandal
**Content Development Editor:** Onkar Wani
**Technical Editor:** Akhil Nair
**Copy Editor:** Safis Editing
**Project Coordinator:** Devanshi Doshi
**Proofreader:** Safis Editing
**Indexer:** Pratik Shirodkar
**Graphics:** Jason Monteiro
**Production Coordinator:** Shantanu Zagade

First published: March 2018

Production reference: 1270318

Published by Packt Publishing Ltd.
Livery Place
35 Livery Street
Birmingham
B3 2PB, UK.

ISBN 978-1-78862-524-1

www.packtpub.com

*To my parents, Girish and Jagruti Patel, and my sister, Reena, for their sacrifices and for supporting me throughout my career.*

*To my wife, Nirali, for being my loving partner and standing beside me, without whose support this book would not have been completed.*

*To my soon to be born child, whom my wife and I are excited to welcome into our life.*

mapt.io

Mapt is an online digital library that gives you full access to over 5,000 books and videos, as well as industry leading tools to help you plan your personal development and advance your career. For more information, please visit our website.

# Why subscribe?

- Spend less time learning and more time coding with practical eBooks and Videos from over 4,000 industry professionals

- Improve your learning with Skill Plans built especially for you

- Get a free eBook or video every month

- Mapt is fully searchable

- Copy and paste, print, and bookmark content

# PacktPub.com

Did you know that Packt offers eBook versions of every book published, with PDF and ePub files available? You can upgrade to the eBook version at www.PacktPub.com and as a print book customer, you are entitled to a discount on the eBook copy. Get in touch with us at service@packtpub.com for more details.

At www.PacktPub.com, you can also read a collection of free technical articles, sign up for a range of free newsletters, and receive exclusive discounts and offers on Packt books and eBooks.

# Contributors

## About the author

**Ankur Patel** is a web and mobile application developer specializing in iOS, with a passion for making innovative consumer applications. Ankur is a generalist who has worked with a variety of programming languages, such as Objective-C, Ruby, JavaScript, Swift, Java, and C. He has held multiple roles in firms both big and small, including IBM, Oracle, Goldman Sachs, Bloomberg, Shutterstock, and MyTime. He is also the author of the book *Learning Swift - Building an iOS Game*, which teaches readers how to build an iOS game and publish it to the App Store.

> *I am grateful to Packt Publishing for offering me the opportunity to write this book. Thank you Onkar, Siddharth, and the reviewers, for your support and guidance. I would also like to thank my parents and my wife for being by my side through the nights and weekends. Lastly, I am grateful to God for blessing my wife and I with a child, as thoughts of being a father gave me hope and joy on my journey writing this book.*

# About the reviewers

**Albert Wold** lives in Tempe, Arizona, with his wife and two children. He has always had an enthusiasm for programming and was initially attracted to it at the age of eight while wanting to learn to build a game. He has spent the last few years focusing on iOS development and is a big fan of the Swift programming language.

**Vinod Madigeri** is a curious software engineer with a particular interest in app design and development. He has worked in several industries (telecommunication, game technologies, and consumer electronics) as a developer, team leader, and mentor, writing software in C, C++, C#, Objective-C, and Swift.

Vinod has been doing this professionally for 8 years and had been goofing with computers for 12 years before that. Vinod was also a technical reviewer of *Object–Oriented Programming with Swift* and *Multiplayer Game Development with HTML5*.

> *I'd like to thank my lovely wife, Shruti, for her constant support, encouragement, and vanguard thoughts.*

# Packt is searching for authors like you

If you're interested in becoming an author for Packt, please visit `authors.packtpub.com` and apply today. We have worked with thousands of developers and tech professionals, just like you, to help them share their insight with the global tech community. You can make a general application, apply for a specific hot topic that we are recruiting an author for, or submit your own idea.

# Table of Contents

**Preface**   1

**Chapter 1: Getting Started with Server Swift**   7
  **Modern app development**   8
  **Swift's evolution**   8
    Open source   9
    Server-side Swift   9
  **Benefits of server-side Swift**   10
  **Getting started with Swift package manager**   11
    Building a Swift package   12
    Publishing a Swift package   15
    Consuming a Swift package   16
    Installing the package's executable   19
  **How do the web servers work?**   19
    User requesting a web page   19
    Mobile application requesting data   21
    HTTP request and response   21
  **Building a web server in Swift**   24
  **Server-side web frameworks**   28
    Vapor   29
  **Book roadmap**   31
  **Summary**   31

**Chapter 2: Creating the Native App**   33
  **Features of our Shopping List app**   33
  **Creating an app**   34
  **Blueprinting the Shopping List Item model**   37
    Exercise   39
      Exercise answer   39
  **Controlling the flow of our application using View Controller**   39
  **Wiring up the view**   42
    Table View Controller   47
  **Adding items to the list**   51
  **Editing the list**   55
  **Loading and auto-saving the Shopping List**   60
  **Multiple lists**   62
    Refactoring to share code   62
    Blueprinting the Shopping List Model   63
    The Shopping List Table View Controller   66

| Summary | 74 |
|---|---|
| **Chapter 3: Getting Started with Vapor** | **75** |
| What is Vapor? | 76 |
| Building servers using Vapor's engine | 77 |
| Building a basic HTTP server | 78 |
| Building a static file server | 80 |
| Building a WebSocket server | 82 |
| Building a Vapor application from scratch | 85 |
| Vapor toolbox | 87 |
| Installing the Vapor toolbox | 87 |
| Vapor toolbox commands | 88 |
| Creating a Vapor application using the toolbox | 90 |
| Vapor folder structure | 93 |
| Vapor config | 94 |
| Vapor droplet | 96 |
| Views | 98 |
| Controllers | 99 |
| Summary | 100 |
| **Chapter 4: Configuring Providers, Fluent, and Databases** | **101** |
| Shopping List API Vapor app | 102 |
| What are Providers? | 104 |
| Building your first Provider | 104 |
| Exercise time | 109 |
| Adding a Provider | 110 |
| Getting started with databases | 112 |
| What is MongoDB? | 113 |
| How to install and run MongoDB | 113 |
| What are ORM and Fluent? | 114 |
| Fluent in action | 115 |
| Creating an item | 118 |
| Updating an item | 119 |
| Getting all items | 119 |
| Finding an item | 119 |
| Finding items using filter | 119 |
| Deleting an item | 120 |
| Counting items | 120 |
| Relations in Fluent | 120 |
| One to one (parent-child relation) | 121 |
| One to many | 122 |
| Many to many | 123 |
| Connecting with MongoDB | 125 |
| Configuring Fluent config | 125 |
| Mongo config - mongo.json | 126 |
| Adding MongoProvider | 127 |

| | |
|---|---|
| Summary | 132 |
| **Chapter 5: Building a REST API using Vapor** | **133** |
| Routing in Vapor | 134 |
| HTTP methods | 134 |
| Routers | 135 |
| Nested routing | 138 |
| Dynamic routing | 138 |
| Wildcard routing | 140 |
| Routing parameters | 140 |
| Vapor Models | 141 |
| The Shopping List Model | 142 |
| Preparation protocol | 144 |
| JSONConvertible protocol | 145 |
| ResponseRepresentable protocol | 146 |
| Updateable protocol | 146 |
| Item Model | 147 |
| Controllers in Vapor | 150 |
| RESTful Controller | 150 |
| Shopping List controller | 154 |
| REST API in action | 156 |
| Creating the Shopping List | 156 |
| Getting the Shopping List | 157 |
| Updating the Shopping List | 159 |
| Deleting the Shopping List | 160 |
| Creating items | 160 |
| Exercise | 162 |
| Summary | 163 |
| **Chapter 6: Consuming API in App** | **165** |
| Xcode Workspace | 166 |
| Making network requests | 173 |
| Network configuration | 174 |
| Request helper | 175 |
| Fetching data from the server | 177 |
| Debugging the app and server side by side | 182 |
| Adding a Shopping List | 186 |
| Deleting a Shopping List | 190 |
| Exercise | 192 |
| Adding a Shopping List Item | 192 |
| Deleting an item | 195 |
| Checking and unchecking an item | 196 |
| Summary | 198 |
| **Chapter 7: Creating Web Views and Middleware** | **199** |

[ iii ]

## View rendering in Vapor app — 200
### What is Leaf? — 200
## Adding Leaf Provider — 204
## Serving JSON and HTML formats — 209
### Creating a middleware — 209
### Creating a BaseResourceController — 213
## Adding JavaScript — 219
### Creating a new Shopping List — 220
### Deleting a Shopping List — 221
### Adding an Item — 221
### Deleting an Item — 222
### Checking and unchecking an Item — 223
## Summary — 224

# Chapter 8: Testing and CI — 225
## Testing the Vapor application — 226
### Setting up the test environment — 226
### Running tests — 227
## Testing RESTful routes — 231
### Fetching all Shopping Lists — 232
### Creating a Shopping List — 233
### Deleting the Shopping List — 234
### Updating the Shopping List — 235
## Exercise — 236
## Automated testing pipeline — 237
### Enabling Travis build check on Pull request — 244
## Summary — 246

# Chapter 9: Deploying the App — 247
## Where can we deploy a Vapor App? — 247
## Deploying to Heroku — 248
### Priming the app for deployment — 251
### Configuring and deploying Vapor to Heroku — 251
### Adding the MongoDB Heroku addon — 255
## Setting up Continuous Deployment — 257
## Exercise — 259
## Summary — 259

# Chapter 10: Adding Authentication — 261
## Creating a User model — 262
### Best practices for storing password — 262
### Getting started with the User model — 264
## User has many Shopping Lists — 268
## Adding Registration and Login — 270
## Showing user specific Shopping Lists — 275

| | |
|---|---:|
| **Adding token-based authentication for app** | 276 |
| Testing the token-based authentication | 281 |
| **Adding authentication flow to iOS app** | 281 |
| Bringing it all together in the Storyboard | 285 |
| **Summary** | 300 |
| **Chapter 11: Building a tvOS App** | 301 |
| **Shopping List app on tvOS** | 301 |
| **Sharing code between iOS and tvOS** | 307 |
| Making code work with both iOS and tvOS apps | 309 |
| **Configuring the tvOS storyboard** | 311 |
| **Summary** | 332 |
| **Other Books You May Enjoy** | 335 |
| **Index** | 339 |

# Preface

This book is about building cross-platform software solution using Swift. The book will take the reader on a journey of building an app for iOS and extending the app to a different platform, such as the web and tvOS. The app will start out simple, but get more and more complex as it progresses. Toward the end, we will have a product that will work on iOS, tvOS, and in the browser and have a server component, all written entirely in Swift.

Through this journey, we will learn how Swift has progressed from a language used just for iOS to a language that can be used on the server side. We will also learn how to build server-side packages using Swift and Vapor, which is one of the most popular Swift packages for building web servers. Using Vapor, we will build a full-stack web application that will act as an API server for our iOS and tvOS app, and will also be our web server, which will render a web view of our app. Several technologies will be covered while building the backend, including MongoDB, which is a non-relational database.

We will be using Swift 4 throughout the book and will cover new features introduced in this version of Swift. We will use Xcode 9 as our IDE to build for these different platforms, and readers will learn how to share code and development tools to make development fun and productive. We will also use Vapor 2.0 to build our server in Swift, and learn how the framework makes it easy to build rich backends for our application.

I hope that on this journey, you will learn how to write code in these different application stacks. By the end of this book, you should feel comfortable building your next product using Swift. From building a native app, to the backend, to a marketing page, or web app, you will have the knowledge to get hands-on with Swift to build your next big idea.

## Who this book is for

This book is intended for developers familiar with Swift and web development on the client side who want to build both a full-stack web application and a native mobile application using the Swift and Vapor framework. An understanding of how HTML and CSS work and knowledge of JavaScript will be helpful when building server-rendered pages with Vapor.

*Preface*

# What this book covers

Chapter 1, *Getting Started with Server Swift*, dives into the world of server-side Swift and shows you how to build and use Swift packages, and how to build a simple HTTP server using pure Swift.

Chapter 2, *Creating the Native App*, explains how to build a Shopping List app in pure Swift, using Xcode and Storyboard. At the end of this chapter, you will have a fully-functioning app that persists data offline on the iPhone in a secure way.

Chapter 3, *Getting Started with Vapor*, delves deep into Vapor features and packages and shows how to get started with using Vapor to start building rich web applications.

Chapter 4, *Configuring Providers, Fluent, and Databases*, provides a solid background on ORM for Swift and shows how to set up a database for a Vapor app using Fluent and Providers.

Chapter 5, *Building REST API Using Vapor*, explores how to build a RESTful API using Vapor for our Shopping List app and goes into detail about how to create RESTful routes and controllers.

Chapter 6, *Consuming API in App*, contains details on how to refactor our iOS app to consume the RESTful API we built in Chapter 5, *Building REST API using Vapor*, and how to make network requests to our API when creating, reading, updating, and deleting data from our iOS app.

Chapter 7, *Creating Web Views and Middleware*, shows how to create HTML views in our Vapor app and demonstrates the use of Middleware to conditionally load HTML views for a browser and a render view as JSON for an API request from the iOS app.

Chapter 8, *Testing and CI*, contains information on how to test a Vapor app and how to set up a Continuous Integration pipeline to automatically run tests before code is merged using Travis CI.

Chapter 9, *Deploying the App*, contains deployment options for a Vapor app and shows how to deploy a Vapor app to Heroku and set up an automated deployment pipeline when code is merged into the Git repo.

Chapter 10, *Adding Authentication*, demonstrates how to add authentication to a Vapor app so that users can log in or register and own the Shopping List that they create. This chapter also demonstrates how an iOS app is updated to support token-based authentication implemented in the Vapor app.

Chapter 11, *Building a tvOS App*, wraps up the book by demonstrating how easy it is to build for another platform with maximum code shareability between the iOS and tvOS apps and how a small team of Swift developers can build a multiplatform full-stack application using Swift.

# To get the most out of this book

You should have basic knowledge of the following topics:

1. Swift
2. Xcode
3. Storyboard and Autolayout
4. HTML
5. JavaScript
6. CSS
7. Terminal/Command Line Tools

You should also use macOS as we will be using Xcode to build our native apps and our server app.

# Download the example code files

You can download the example code files for this book from your account at www.packtpub.com. If you purchased this book elsewhere, you can visit www.packtpub.com/support and register to have the files emailed directly to you.

You can download the code files by following these steps:

1. Log in or register at www.packtpub.com.
2. Select the **SUPPORT** tab.
3. Click on **Code Downloads & Errata**.
4. Enter the name of the book in the **Search** box and follow the onscreen instructions.

[ 3 ]

*Preface*

Once the file is downloaded, please make sure that you unzip or extract the folder using the latest version of:

- WinRAR/7-Zip for Windows
- Zipeg/iZip/UnRarX for Mac
- 7-Zip/PeaZip for Linux

The code bundle for the book is also hosted on GitHub at https://github.com/PacktPublishing/Hands-On-Full-Stack-Development-with-Swift. In case there's an update to the code, it will be updated on the existing GitHub repository.

We also have other code bundles from our rich catalog of books and videos available at https://github.com/PacktPublishing/. Check them out!

# Conventions used

There are a number of text conventions used throughout this book.

`CodeInText`: Indicates code words in text, database table names, folder names, filenames, file extensions, pathnames, dummy URLs, user input, and Twitter handles. Here is an example: "Go to our `ShoppingListTableViewController.swift` file and update one line inside the `didSelectAdd` method."

A block of code is set as follows:

```
html, body, #map {
  height: 100%;
  margin: 0;
  padding: 0
}
```

When we wish to draw your attention to a particular part of a code block, the relevant lines or items are set in bold:

```
@IBAction func didSelectAdd(_ sender: UIBarButtonItem) {
  requestInput(title: "Shopping list name",
    message: "Enter name for the new shopping list:",
    handler: { listName in
      let listCount = self.lists.count
      ShoppingList(name: listName).save() { list in
        self.lists.append(list)
        self.tableView.insertRows(at: [IndexPath(row: listCount, section: 0)], with: .top)
      }
```

# Preface

```
            })
        }
```

Any command-line input or output is written as follows:

```
~ $ mongod --config /usr/local/etc/mongod.conf
```

**Bold**: Indicates a new term, an important word, or words that you see onscreen. For example, words in menus or dialog boxes appear in the text like this. Here is an example: "Build and run the **Run** Scheme on the **My Mac** platform"

Warnings or important notes appear like this.

Tips and tricks appear like this.

# Get in touch

Feedback from our readers is always welcome.

**General feedback**: Email feedback@packtpub.com and mention the book title in the subject of your message. If you have questions about any aspect of this book, please email us at questions@packtpub.com.

**Errata**: Although we have taken every care to ensure the accuracy of our content, mistakes do happen. If you have found a mistake in this book, we would be grateful if you would report this to us. Please visit www.packtpub.com/submit-errata, selecting your book, clicking on the Errata Submission Form link, and entering the details.

**Piracy**: If you come across any illegal copies of our works in any form on the Internet, we would be grateful if you would provide us with the location address or website name. Please contact us at copyright@packtpub.com with a link to the material.

**If you are interested in becoming an author**: If there is a topic that you have expertise in and you are interested in either writing or contributing to a book, please visit authors.packtpub.com.

# Reviews

Please leave a review. Once you have read and used this book, why not leave a review on the site that you purchased it from? Potential readers can then see and use your unbiased opinion to make purchase decisions, we at Packt can understand what you think about our products, and our authors can see your feedback on their book. Thank you!

For more information about Packt, please visit `packtpub.com`.

# 1
# Getting Started with Server Swift

Swift is yet another programming language, introduced in 2014 by Apple. According to them, Swift is a general-purpose programming language, built using a modern approach to safety, performance, and software design patterns. They created the language to help make development on their platform more fun and productive as their flagship language Objective-C is bit dated and has a very distinct syntax that makes it hard for anyone to quickly get started.

A few years ago, Swift was open sourced and the Swift community has pushed the language forward by trying to build server components using Swift. This has led to the creation of the term server-side Swift. So what is server-side Swift? What are the benefits of using it on the server? Can it be used to build different stacks of your application?

In this chapter, we will answer those questions while getting our feet wet in the world of server-side Swift. We'll cover the following:

- Learning about modern app development
- Seeing how Swift has evolved
- Looking at the benefits of server-side Swift
- Learning about the Swift package manager and its CLI
- Building a simple library and an executable Swift package
- Learning how web servers work and building a simple web server in pure Swift
- Discovering server-side web frameworks for Swift and Swift package catalog
- Learning about Vapor, one of the most used server-side web frameworks for Swift
- Going over the idea for the apps we will be building in the book

# Modern app development

Application development in today's world is not just about building for one platform. Modern applications have an ecosystem of apps that run on multiple devices and platforms. In order for these apps to run on the multiple platforms they also need a server-side component to be able to seamlessly save and retrieve data so that a user can switch between them and start using the app from where they left off on another platform. To make these modern applications possible, developers write code on the different technology stacks that have different programming languages and frameworks/libraries. This makes the job of the developer especially difficult due to the context switching between programming languages when building the application.

In the world of the web, developers have enjoyed working on the frontend web applications using JavaScript but after the introduction of Node.js, web developers who were mainly focused on the frontend could finally work on the backend in a language that feels familiar. Web developers have embraced the idea of working across different technology stacks as part of their app development because they can now write the frontend in JavaScript and use the same language to build server-side components.

Similarly, Swift, which is popular in the world of iOS, tvOS, and macOS for building rich client-facing applications, is now available on server-side thanks to Apple. Like JavaScript developers, Swift developers can now finally build server-side components in a language that is familiar to them while they continue to build frontend applications for different platforms, such as mobile, watch, TV, or desktop. Currently Swift is gaining popularity on the server-side, and it has never been a good time to be Swift developers. We can now engage ourselves in true full stack app development by working on different platforms using the same language and standard libraries that we are familiar with when building iOS, tvOS, watchOS, and macOS applications.

# Swift's evolution

Swift started out as a general-purpose programming language, intended to replace Objective-C as the default language for building iOS, tvOS, watchOS, and macOS applications. Swift is a compiled language that compiles down to **Low Level Virtual Machine** (**LLVM**) bytecode and is **Just-In-Time** (**JIT**) compiled to native code of the architecture on its first run making Swift a very fast language. Swift also uses **Automatic Reference Counting** (**ARC**) to manage memory, making it simple to write applications especially for iOS where memory management is critical.

With all of these features, Swift definitely stands out from the rest of the languages popular during that time, which included Scala, Rust, Elixir, Kotlin, and C#. With growing popularity, all it needed was more platforms to run on and that is what Apple did when they open sourced it in late 2015.

# Open source

In December 2015, Apple announced that it would open source Swift; this opened up the possibility of writing applications in Swift on other platforms, especially Linux. Open sourcing Swift meant that anyone could take the Swift code base and build a Swift compiler and toolset on their host **operating system** (**OS**) where LLVM is supported. This is exactly what Apple did soon after Swift was open sourced by creating Swift toolset that worked on Ubuntu, a popular distribution of Linux. Apple kept its promise of truly open sourcing Swift by also porting its libraries and frameworks, including `Foundation`, which is used extensively in iOS and macOS platforms, and made them work on Ubuntu. Without these frameworks, it would be hard to build cross-platform applications in Swift that work on both Apple's OS and Linux with same feature parity since `Foundation` is the standard library that contains access to essential data types, collections, and operating system services to define the base layer of functionality for any application.

# Server-side Swift

Since Swift is a language that is elegant and expressive while being performant, it was about time that it would be ported to run on a server-side platform. Building command-line tools with Swift become popular on the macOS platform soon after Apple made it easy to use Swift for general purpose programming outside of iOS app development with the use of the Hash Bang, `#!`, syntax specified on top of the Swift file just like in a scripting language such as Perl, Ruby, or Python. This made it very easy for anyone to write and run Swift code without having to compile it. The same technique works on Linux platform; so, let's see how it works:

1. Creating a Swift file called `hello.swift`
2. Adding the following code to the file:

   ```
   #!/usr/bin/swift
   print("Hello World from Swift!")
   ```

3. Making the file an executable by changing the permission on the file using `chmod`:

   ```
   $ chmod +x hello.swift
   ```

4. Running the Swift code by typing the filename in the Terminal:

   ```
   $ ./hello.swift
   ```

You should see **Hello World from Swift!** printed on the command line. This shows you how easy it is to create an executable in Swift without even having to compile it ahead of time; you can quickly test Swift code from the command line.

# Benefits of server-side Swift

There are several benefits of using Swift on the server side. Some of them include:

- **Being able to work on a feature as a whole**: Being able to work on an entire feature helps deliver the feature on time and as expected. Traditionally, teams are divided into frontend and backend teams but if you have the same language used for both front and backend then it will help developers contribute to the entire stack. Developers working on building the app can create the API endpoints needed to avoid the unnecessary back and forth between developers and prevent an app developer from being blocked by the backend engineer and move the feature development forward.
- **Working with familiar language and tools**: Working with a familiar language reduces the biggest hurdle to working across different stacks. You can build both mobile and server-side components using the same language and tools. Swift developers can use their favorite IDE, Xcode, to build their backend server and do not have to learn new tools or install different IDEs.
- **Sharing code base**: Code shareability is another big win for using Swift as you can share models, validations, and business logic easily across platforms. Not having to rewrite the same logic in different languages saves times and helps avoid expensive bugs caused by inconsistencies introduced by different developers who might have worked on rewriting the business logic on a different stack.
- **Leveraging great APIs**: Apple did a great job building easy-to-use APIs on their platform and now being able to use those APIs server-side is a big benefit for developers as they do not have to learn new standard libraries or reinvent them on the Linux platform.

# Getting started with Swift package manager

Mastering the command line is important, especially when trying to build and deploy Swift on a production Linux machine or in the Cloud. Since Xcode will not be available on those hosts, Apple has provided us with an easy-to-use command-line tool to help create, build, and distribute our Swift code. This tool is called the **Swift package manager** and it is useful for managing the distribution of Swift code while integrating with the Swift build system to automate the process of downloading, compiling, and linking dependencies. The following are some of the useful commands provided by the package manager to quickly get you started:

- `swift package init`: This will create a Swift package or module that is an easy portable way to share code. It will create a package using the name of the folder you are currently in. Passing a `--type executable` option will make an executable package where the product of the build will be an executable program such as a web server or a command-line program. Think of this as gems for Ruby or node modules for Node.js.
- `swift build`: This builds the Swift package you currently are in by compiling Swift code in your `Sources` folder. If your package is an executable, then it will generate a binary in the `.build/debug` folder. If you pass a release configuration using the `--configuration` release option, then it will build a highly optimized binary and place it in `.build/release`. The same output is generated for non-executable binary but generate Swift modules instead to be imported by whoever wants to use this module.
- `swift run`: A quick way to run a Swift executable package from the command line. This command builds the Swift code if it is not built already and runs the binary. You can pass the `-c` release option to build and run the optimized version of the binary.
- `swift test`: To run tests written in the `Test` folder of your package.
- `swift package generate-xcodeproj`: This command generates an Xcode project file so that you can work on the package in Xcode instead of a plain text editor.

These are some of the more important commands that will come in handy when trying to build and test your web server in Swift and also when deploying and running your web application in production. There are a lot more commands and you can learn about them by running `swift package` in the Terminal:

```
~/W/WebServer $ swift package
OVERVIEW: Perform operations on Swift packages

USAGE: swift package [options] subcommand

OPTIONS:
  --build-path              Specify build/cache directory [default: ./.build]
  --configuration, -c       Build with configuration (debug|release) [default: debug]
  --disable-prefetching
  --disable-sandbox         Disable using the sandbox when executing subprocesses
  --enable-prefetching
  --no-static-swift-stdlib
                            Do not link Swift stdlib statically
  --package-path            Change working directory before any other operation
  --static-swift-stdlib     Link Swift stdlib statically
  --verbose, -v             Increase verbosity of informational output
  -Xcc                      Pass flag through to all C compiler invocations
  -Xcxx                     Pass flag through to all C++ compiler invocations
  -Xlinker                  Pass flag through to all linker invocations
  -Xswiftc                  Pass flag through to all Swift compiler invocations
  --help                    Display available options

SUBCOMMANDS:
  clean                     Delete build artifacts
  describe                  Describe the current package
  dump-package              Print parsed Package.swift as JSON
  edit                      Put a package in editable mode
  generate-completion-script
                            Generate completion script (Bash or ZSH)
  generate-xcodeproj        Generates an Xcode project
  init                      Initialize a new package
  reset                     Reset the complete cache/build directory
  resolve                   Resolve package dependencies
  show-dependencies         Print the resolved dependency graph
  tools-version             Manipulate tools version of the current package
  unedit                    Remove a package from editable mode
  update                    Update package dependencies
~/W/WebServer $ _
```

# Building a Swift package

Right now, we will go through an exercise to build a simple Swift package and learn about the important files and folders. We will also publish this package and consume it in another Swift package to show how we can publish packages and import them as dependencies. For our exercise, we will create a simple `cat` command-line tool which will concatenate and print the contents of the files specify relative to the current directory.

In order for us to do so we will first build a package called `FileReader` which will read and return the contents of the file. To build this Swift package, we need to do the following:

1. Create a folder called `FileReader` (`mkdir FileReader`) and change directory (`cd`) into that folder
2. Run `Swift package init` and it will generate files and folders for the package

Let's inspect the contents of the package. The following is the file and folder structure inside of `FileReader`:

```
~/W/FileReader $ tree .
.
├── Package.swift
├── README.md
├── Sources
│   └── FileReader
│       └── FileReader.swift
├── Tests
    ├── FileReaderTests
    │   └── FileReaderTests.swift
    └── LinuxMain.swift
4 directories, 5 files
```

- `Package.swift`: This file is where you describe meta-information about the package, including dependencies of the package.
- `Sources`: This is where you place your Swift code that will get built by the Swift package manager when you run the `swift build` command. It can contain multiple folders if you want to build multiple products or targets in your package.
- `Tests`: This is where you place your test files and that get run when `swift test` is run from the command line.

Now that we know the basic file and folder structure, we can start writing our Swift code to read files from disk inside of the `FileReader.swift` file. By default, it will contain boilerplate code which we can remove and replace with this:

```
import Foundation
class FileReader {
 static func read(fileName: String) -> String? {
    let fileManager = FileManager.default
    let currentDirectoryURL = URL(fileURLWithPath:
                        fileManager.currentDirectoryPath)
    let fileURL = currentDirectoryURL.appendingPathComponent(fileName)
    return try? String(contentsOf: fileURL, encoding: .utf8)
```

```
    }
}
```

In this file, we import `Foundation`, which is a standard library available in macOS and Linux and it provides us with the standard library to read from a file path using the `FileManager`. After that, we define the `FileReader` class and create one static function in it, called `read`, that takes a filename and this function will return the contents of the file if the file exists. The code inside the function does the following:

1. Gets a singleton `FileManager` object:

   ```
   let fileManager = FileManager.default
   ```

2. Creates a URL pointing to the current directory. The current directory is set to the directory from which the OS Process using this library was called from:

   ```
   let currentDirectoryURL = URL(fileURLWithPath: fileManager.currentDirectoryPath)
   ```

3. Appends the filename passed to this function to the current directory:

   ```
   let fileURL = currentDirectoryURL.appendingPathComponent(fileName)
   ```

4. Tries to read contents of the file if it exists and return it:

   ```
   return try? String(contentsOf: fileURL, encoding: .utf8)
   ```

Now that we have the code, we can build it using Swift build. To test that our code is working, we need to write a test for it and we can do so by taking the following steps:

1. Editing the `FileReaderTests.swift` file and replacing the body of `testExample` function block with the following:

   ```
   XCTAssertEqual(FileReader.read(fileName: "hello.txt"), "Hello World")
   ```

2. Running the following command to create a `hello.txt` file in the root directory of the package with the contents `Hello World`:

   ```
   printf "Hello World" > hello.txt
   ```

*Chapter 1*

3. Run the test for your package using the `swift test` command. You should see the test pass and print as such:

```
~/W/FileReader $ swift test
Compile Swift Module 'FileReaderTests' (1 sources)
Linking ./.build/x86_64-apple-
macosx10.10/debug/FileReaderPackageTests.xctest/Contents/MacOS/File
ReaderPackageTests
Test Suite 'All tests' started at 2017-09-29 12:14:57.278
Test Suite 'FileReaderPackageTests.xctest' started at 2017-09-29
12:14:57.278
Test Suite 'FileReaderTests' started at 2017-09-29 12:14:57.278
Test Case '-[FileReaderTests.FileReaderTests testExample]' started.
Test Case '-[FileReaderTests.FileReaderTests testExample]' passed
(0.094 seconds).
Test Suite 'FileReaderTests' passed at 2017-09-29 12:14:57.372.
	 Executed 1 test, with 0 failures (0 unexpected) in 0.094 (0.094)
seconds
Test Suite 'FileReaderPackageTests.xctest' passed at 2017-09-29
12:14:57.372.
	 Executed 1 test, with 0 failures (0 unexpected) in 0.094 (0.094)
seconds
Test Suite 'All tests' passed at 2017-09-29 12:14:57.372.
	 Executed 1 test, with 0 failures (0 unexpected) in 0.094 (0.094)
seconds
```

Now that we have a working Swift package, we can publish it.

## Publishing a Swift package

Publishing a Swift package is as simple as committing code, tagging it, and pushing it up to a git repository. To publish the package, perform the following steps:

1. Create a public git repository on `github.com`.
2. Open the Terminal and change your directory to your package's path, `cd /path/to/your/swift/package`. Then initialize the git repository by running the `git init` command.
3. Add a remote origin to the local git repo by running this command:

    ```
    git remote add origin git@github.com:<repoaccount>/<reponame>.git
    ```

4. Make sure to replace the repo account and repo name with the one you created in Step 1.

[ 15 ]

5. Add all files to this repo using `git add .` and commit them using `git commit -m "Initial Commit"`.
6. Tag it with a version. Since it is our first package we will tag it 1.0.0, `git tag 1.0.0`.
7. Publish it by pushing it up to the repo along with the tag:

   ```
   git push origin master --tags
   ```

It is that easy to make a Swift package and publish it. All you need is a git repository to push your code to and tag your code appropriately so that whoever uses your package as a dependency can point to a specific version.

## Consuming a Swift package

Next, we will try to use this package to create an executable package called `cat` that concatenates and prints the contents of the files passed in as arguments to the command. This executable will work like the built-in-system `cat` command found in most Unix based operating systems. To do so, we need to perform the following steps:

1. Open the Terminal and create a directory called `cat` (`mkdir cat`) and change the directory into it (`cd cat`).
2. Initialize the package by running `swift package init --type executable`. This will generate a `main.swift`, which is the entry point for the executable and the code will start executing line by line starting from that file.
3. Add the URL to your GitHub repo that contains the `FileReader` package and add the following line in your `Package.swift` under dependencies:

   ```
   .package(url: "https://github.com/<repoaccount>/<reponame>", from: "1.0.0"),
   ```

4. Add your `FileReader` package to the dependencies under the targets section in `Package.swift`:

   ```
   import PackageDescription

   let package = Package(
     name: "cat",
     dependencies: [
       .package(url: "https://github.com/ankurp/FileReader", from: "1.0.0"),
     ],
     targets: [
   ```

```
        .target(
          name: "cat",
          dependencies: ["FileReader"]),
      ]
    )
```

5. Add the following code to `main.swift`:

   ```
   import FileReader
   
   for argument in CommandLine.arguments {
     guard argument != "arg1" else { continue }
   
     if let fileContents = FileReader.read(fileName: argument) {
       print(fileContents)
     }
   }
   ```

Let's try to understand what we have done in the preceding code:

1. Import the `FileReader` package:

   ```
   import FileReader
   ```

2. Iterate over the command-line arguments:

   ```
   for argument in CommandLine.arguments {
   ```

3. We ignore the first argument using the `guard` clause in Swift because it is the command name `cat`:

   ```
   guard argument != "arg1" else { continue }
   ```

4. Print the contents of the file by printing it in the console:

   ```
   if let fileContents = FileReader.read(fileName: argument) {
     print(fileContents)
   }
   ```

Now that we have understood the code, let's build and run it to see whether it works. To build and run, just type the following command in the Terminal:

```
$ swift run cat Package.swift Sources/cat/main.swift
```

# Getting Started with Server Swift

You should see the contents of both the files, `Package.swift` and `Sources/cat/main.swift`, printed in the console. Great job! We have a working command line tool written in Swift using one of our published Swift packages:

```
~/W/cat (master|+1) $ swift run cat Package.swift Sources/cat/main.swift
Compile Swift Module 'cat' (1 sources)
Linking ./.build/x86_64-apple-macosx10.10/debug/cat
// swift-tools-version:4.0
// The swift-tools-version declares the minimum version of Swift required to build t
his package.

import PackageDescription

let package = Package(
    name: "cat",
    dependencies: [
        // Dependencies declare other packages that this package depends on.
        .package(url: "https://github.com/ankurp/FileReader", from: "1.0.0"),
    ],
    targets: [
        // Targets are the basic building blocks of a package. A target can define a
 module or a test suite.
        // Targets can depend on other targets in this package, and on products in p
ackages which this package depends on.
        .target(
            name: "cat",
            dependencies: ["FileReader"]),
    ]
)

import FileReader

for argument in CommandLine.arguments {
  guard argument != "arg1" else {
    continue
  }

  if let fileContents = FileReader.read(fileName: argument) {
    print(fileContents)
  }
}
~/W/cat (master|+1) $ _
```

## Installing the package's executable

How do we install the command line tool we just created? Don't worry, it's simple too. All you need to do is build it with the release configuration, so that it builds a highly optimized binary and also add flags to statically link the Swift standard library. This means that the executable can work even when Swift versions change on your operating system, or if you plan on distributing it on another platform, such as Linux. The following is the command to build the executable command with the release configuration:

```
$ swift build -c release -Xswiftc -static-stdlib
```

Once you have the binary built, you need to copy it to one of the directories where binaries are stored in your user path. One such place is `/usr/local/bin`. To copy it, just run the following command and call your binary file whatever you want. In my case, I chose to rename my command to `swiftycat`:

```
$ cp -f .build/release/cat /usr/local/bin/swiftycat
```

Now, try it out in the Terminal by running the following command:

```
$ swiftycat Package.swift Sources/cat/main.swift
```

# How do the web servers work?

Before we start building web applications or web servers using Swift, it's a good idea to understand the basics of how they work. What is HTTP? What is a request and a response? What does it look like? These are some of the questions that will be answered in this section. To reinforce the concepts, we will try to go through the steps of what happens when a user types a URL in the browser.

## User requesting a web page

When a user goes to the browser and types a URL, what exactly is happening?

1. The browser tries to look up the IP address of the domain name in the URL by getting it from the DNS Server. Think of DNS as a directory mapping the domain name to the IP Address.

2. Once the browser has the IP Address, it sends a HTTP request to that IP Address on port 80. If the URL is secure (HTTPS), then the request is sent to port 443. A simple HTTP request that is sent in plain text format looks like this:
   `GET /hello.html HTTP/1.1`.
3. The request also contains headers that are shared to pass additional information about the request, such as authentication information, cookies, or the type of the browser making the request.
4. The request is routed through all of the routers to the final destination, which is an application or web server serving web pages.
5. The server looks at the request and figures out what type of request it is. In our simple example, we made a `GET` request. The following types of request are supported by the web/application server: `GET`, `POST`, `PUT`, `PATCH`, `DELETE`, and `HEAD`.
6. The server also looks at the request and figures out what path is being requested. In our example, we are requesting a web page at the `/hello.html` path.
7. In the request, we specify the protocol we are using, which is the `HTTP/1.1` protocol. Currently `HTTP/2` is also available and certain browsers that support it will make a request with it.
8. The request can also contain headers that contain extra information from the browser for the server to figure out how to respond. After the header section, the request is followed by two empty new lines that tell the server that it has received the entire request message and now it is time for the server to respond.
9. The server then will either generate the `hello.html` page or serve it from disk. The web servers that serve HTML pages from disk are called static web servers while the web servers that dynamically generate content are called application servers as they have some business logic to generate the HTML content dynamically based on the type and the user requesting it.
10. The server replies back to the request with a response. The response format is similar to the request where the first few lines are called the response headers and they are key value pairs of metadata, followed by two new lines, and then followed by the HTML response or plain text response from the server.
11. The server closes the connection, which tells the browser that it has received all of the response and then it renders the HTML or plain text in the browser.

## Mobile application requesting data

Similar to how the browser requests a web page from the web server, a mobile application can request data in JSON or XML format from the application server via HTTP or HTTPS. It uses the same protocol to send similar types of requests with headers followed by two new line characters and gets a reply back in the same format with headers followed by two new lines and data as plain text in JSON format.

> JSON is a lightweight data format used to exchange data on the web by mobile, desktop, and web applications. It stands for JavaScript Object Notation and is easy to read and write as it is in plain text. It has become the *de facto* format for exchanging data on the web and for mobile applications, and has quickly replaced XML as a medium for exchanging data.

## HTTP request and response

To see all of this in action, let's make all of the requests that the browser does behind the scenes using `telnet`, which is a command-line tool used to connect to a host, and send messages to it on a port, which is exactly what the browser does. We will do the following in the Terminal:

1. Connect to a host called `httpbin.org`, which is a free HTTP server sending back fake data for testing and learning purpose. To make a HTTP request via `telnet`, we need to connect on port `80` using the following command. If you do not have the `telnet` command installed locally on your macOS, install it using the brew package manager:

   ```
   $ telnet httpbin.org 80
   ```

2. This should print out the following, saying it is trying to connect to an IP address, which is the IP it got from the DNS server for this domain, `httpbin.org`:

   ```
   Trying 54.243.145.223...
   Connected to httpbin.org.
   Escape character is '^]'.
   ```

*Getting Started with Server Swift*

3. Enter the HTTP request followed by the header(s) to get our IP address as the response from the server. We need to type the following in the Terminal in our `telnet` session. Make sure to add two new lines at the end that will mark the end of our request to the server:

   ```
   GET /ip HTTP/1.1
   Host: httpbin.org
   ```

4. After you enter the second new line, you will get back a response which is an HTTP response from the application server. The format is similar to the request where the headers are followed by the two new lines and then by the content, as follows:

   ```
   HTTP/1.1 200 OK
   Connection: keep-alive
   Server: meinheld/0.6.1
   Date: Tue, 03 Oct 2017 21:26:23 GMT
   Content-Type: application/json
   Access-Control-Allow-Origin: *
   Access-Control-Allow-Credentials: true
   X-Powered-By: Flask
   X-Processed-Time: 0.000671863555908
   Content-Length: 30
   Via: 1.1 vegur

   {
     "origin": "73.80.254.5"
   }
   ```

Servers can pass back a header value of `Connection: keep-alive`, which keeps the `telnet` client connected to the server even after it prints the response. Without this header line, the `telnet` client would disconnect after printing to the console. Browsers also obey this and reuse the live connection to send other HTTP requests via the same connection.

To verify this, we can send another `GET` request to `/ip` by passing the same request and header value followed by two new lines:

```
~ $ telnet httpbin.org 80
Trying 204.236.236.192...
Connected to httpbin.org.
Escape character is '^]'.
GET /ip HTTP/1.1
Host: httpbin.org

HTTP/1.1 200 OK
Connection: keep-alive
Server: meinheld/0.6.1
Date: Tue, 03 Oct 2017 21:26:23 GMT
Content-Type: application/json
Access-Control-Allow-Origin: *
Access-Control-Allow-Credentials: true
X-Powered-By: Flask
X-Processed-Time: 0.000671863555908
Content-Length: 30
Via: 1.1 vegur

{
  "origin": "73.80.254.5"
}
GET /ip HTTP/1.1
Host: httpbin.org

HTTP/1.1 200 OK
Connection: keep-alive
Server: meinheld/0.6.1
Date: Tue, 03 Oct 2017 21:27:02 GMT
Content-Type: application/json
Access-Control-Allow-Origin: *
Access-Control-Allow-Credentials: true
X-Powered-By: Flask
X-Processed-Time: 0.000478029251099
Content-Length: 30
Via: 1.1 vegur

{
  "origin": "73.80.254.5"
}
^]
telnet> Connection closed.
~ $
```

This exercise was designed to show you how HTTP works behind the scenes. You should now have a better understanding of how the browser or mobile applications make the request to our server and how we can respond back so that the browser or applications can accept and understand the web page or data passed back. It also touched on different parts of the HTTP request and response, such as the request signature, which contains the headers followed by two new lines and the response signature, which contains the headers followed by the two new lines, and finally followed by the text (for HTML/XML or JSON) or binary content (for images or videos).

I hope this gives you a better understanding of the request response cycle and how the server can deliver a better network performance by keeping the connection alive via the keep-alive header. The following diagram shows how a persistent connection with keep-alive can help make the web application or transfer data quickly, as it does not need to establish a connection every time:

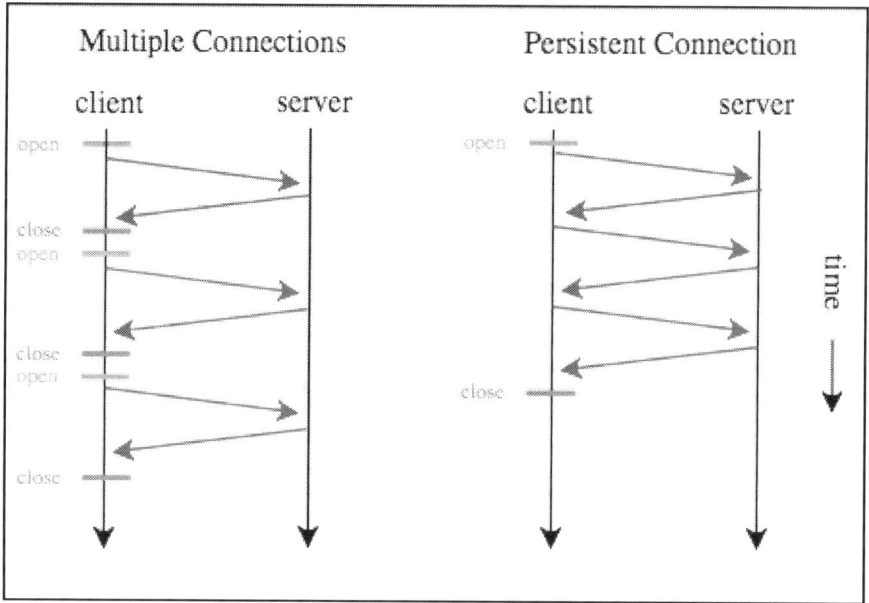

## Building a web server in Swift

Now that we have a little background on HTTP and formats for its request and response payloads, let's try to build an HTTP server from scratch using Swift and some C libraries that we can access via Swift. The point of this exercise is to learn how to build a very basic HTTP web server so we have a better understanding of how all of these web servers are built using sockets. Getting a full stack view is helpful in case you need to dive into low-level code to debug an issue or fix a bug in a package or library you might be using to build our web server. You might also be curious on how to code your own simple web servers, it's actually fairly easy. To create a web server, let's try the following steps:

1. Import the C libraries in Swift:

   ```
   import Darwin.C
   ```

2. Create a `socket` using the `socket` system call. Sockets are a way for other hosts on the network to connect to this process:

   ```
   let sock = socket(AF_INET, SOCK_STREAM, 0)
   ```

3. Create a `socket` address structure and initialize it with host and port information. Then call the `bind` system call with the `socket` address structure and bind the server to the localhost on the port specified:

   ```
   bind(sock, sockaddrPtr, socklen_t(socklen))
   ```

4. Listen for incoming requests by calling `listen` and specifying the max number of requests to be added to the queue to be served by our process:

   ```
   listen(sock, 5)
   ```

5. Now, we can accept incoming connections by calling `accept` with the `socket` file descriptor for our `socket` that clients connect to. It will remove requests from the listen queue and return a new client `socket` connection:

   ```
   let client = accept(sock, nil, nil)
   ```

6. We can `read` from the new client socket connection and `send` data to it using HTTP Protocol:

   ```
   let html = "<!DOCTYPE html><html><body><h1>Hello from Swift Web Server.</h1></body></html>"
   let httpResponse: String = """
     HTTP/1.1 200 OK
     server: simple-swift-server
     content-length: \(html.count)

     \(html)
     """
   httpResponse.withCString { bytes in
     send(client, bytes, Int(strlen(bytes)), 0)
   }
   ```

7. Close the connection using the `close` system call:

   ```
   close(client)
   ```

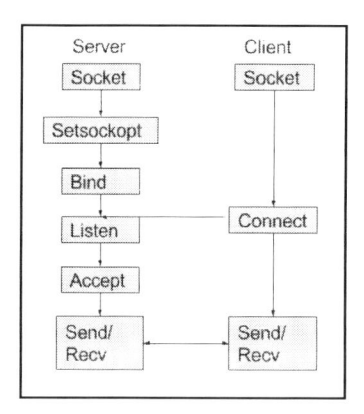

[Diagram: Server/Client socket flow — Server: Socket → Setsockopt → Bind → Listen → Accept → Send/Recv; Client: Socket → Connect → Send/Recv]

That was a quick overview of how network-based programs work and how our web server will work as well. Now, let's look at the code as a whole:

```
import Darwin.C
let zero = Int8(0)
let transportLayerType = SOCK_STREAM // TCP
let internetLayerProtocol = AF_INET // IPv4
let sock = socket(internetLayerProtocol, Int32(transportLayerType), 0)
let portNumber = UInt16(4000)
let socklen = UInt8(socklen_t(MemoryLayout<sockaddr_in>.size))
var serveraddr = sockaddr_in()
serveraddr.sin_family = sa_family_t(AF_INET)
serveraddr.sin_port = in_port_t((portNumber << 8) + (portNumber >> 8))
serveraddr.sin_addr = in_addr(s_addr: in_addr_t(0))
serveraddr.sin_zero = (zero, zero, zero, zero, zero, zero, zero, zero)
withUnsafePointer(to: &serveraddr) { sockaddrInPtr in
  let sockaddrPtr = UnsafeRawPointer(sockaddrInPtr).assumingMemoryBound(to: sockaddr.self)
  bind(sock, sockaddrPtr, socklen_t(socklen))
}
listen(sock, 5)
print("Server listening on port \(portNumber)")
repeat {
  let client = accept(sock, nil, nil)
  let html = "<!DOCTYPE html><html><body style='text-align:center;'><h1>Hello from <a href='https://swift.org'>Swift</a> Web Server.</h1></body></html>"
  let httpResponse: String = """
    HTTP/1.1 200 OK
```

```
      server: simple-swift-server
      content-length: \(html.count)

      \(html)
      """
    httpResponse.withCString { bytes in
      send(client, bytes, Int(strlen(bytes)), 0)
      close(client)
    }
  } while sock > -1
```

To run our server, let's take look at the following steps:

1. Create a Swift file and call it `simple-server.swift`.
2. Copy the preceding code into the file.
3. Run the code using the Swift command and pass the file name as the first argument, as follows:

   ```
   $ swift simple-server.swift
   ```

4. The Swift compiler will try to compile the contents of `simple-server.swift` and run it in one command. You should see the following printed in the Terminal when the server has started:

   ```
   Server listening on port 4000
   ```

5. Open the browser and go to `http://localhost:4000`. You will see the response from our Swift simple HTTP server replying back with HTML content:

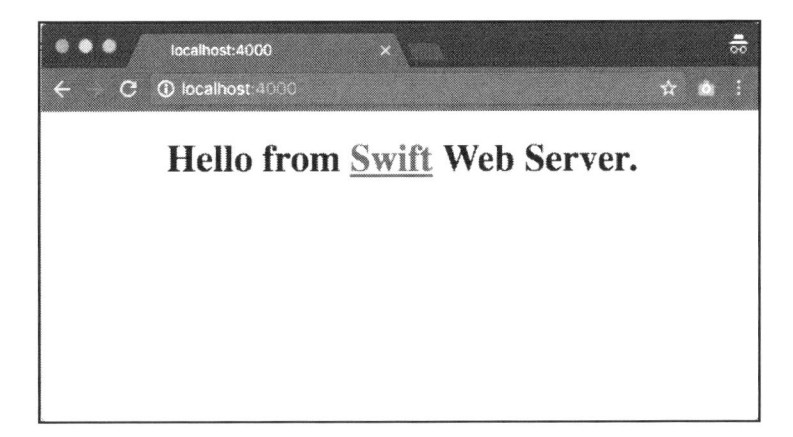

**Hello from Swift Web Server.**

The example code works only on **macOS** but you can easily make it work in Linux by using `import Glibc` instead of `import Darwin.C` and changing some of the datatypes that are passed in creation of a socket. Swift supports some of the C directives, such as `#if`, `#elsif`, `#else`, and `#endif`, to help include or skip code blocks before compiling on certain platforms, such as Linux or macOS, where a certain feature or API usage may be different. In our case, since we depend on C-based libraries, we'd need to `import Glibc` when OS is Linux or `import Darwin.C` and also set different types for two variables we use in our code, as follows:

```
#if os(Linux)

import Glibc
let zero = UInt8(0)
let transportLayerType = SOCK_STREAM.rawValue // TCP

#else

import Darwin.C
let zero = Int8(0)
let transportLayerType = SOCK_STREAM // TCP

#endif
```

> **Directives** are a way to let the compiler know how to process the source code before compiling. There are specific language constructs that let the compiler preprocess the source code and this comes in handy when we want to build a server-side Swift web applications where we need to ignore certain code blocks in Linux that are specific to macOS and vice versa so that the compiler does not fail to compile the code because certain standard libraries are missing or do not exist on certain platforms.

## Server-side web frameworks

Building a web server like we just did is tedious and not scalable. There are a lot of things we need to implement, from routing to persisting data to rendering views. For such use cases, it's best to use a framework that can provide us with all the bells and whistles needed to quickly get started so we can focus on the application logic rather than spending time configuring and reinventing what others have already built.

Developers and even giant corporations, such as IBM, are betting that server-side Swift is the future by building frameworks in the form of Swift packages that make it very easy to build a web application. A few months after Swift was open sourced, one startup created a server-side framework called **Perfect**, which is very popular for building an entire server backend in Swift. IBM has spent a lot of effort creating **Kitura**, which is their take on a server-side swift framework that is lightweight and customizable, similar to express in Node.js or Sinatra in Ruby. **Vapor** is also a very popular framework with a lot of features.

# Vapor

**Vapor** (https://vapor.codes/) is the Swiss Army knife of the web frameworks in Swift. It is a framework to get developers building modern web apps, sites, APIs, and even real-time web apps, using web sockets. It is currently the most used package in Swift (https://packagecatalog.com/browse?chart=mostessentialpage=1), more used than Kitura and Perfect, which are the other two popular server-side frameworks for Swift. Vapor has a strong and vibrant developer community where developers from different companies, including Apple, are contributing to the framework to make Vapor fast, stable, and extensible so that it is easy to use and build large-scale web apps with. Swift is the next big platform for web and backend development, and Vapor is the framework that will help Swift get there. Vapor is the future of web development on the server platform. Here are some reasons to get excited about Vapor:

- It has an amazing CLI tool that helps you create, build, run, and even deploy a Vapor app.
- It is very fast compared to other frameworks, such as Kitura or Perfect, based on independent benchmark tests. It is especially fast when compared to other languages, such as Ruby, PHP, or Node.js.
- It is secure from the beginning and has trusted encryption and TLS from OpenSSL and BCrypt hashing included by default to make security easy.
- It is very extensible as it is very easy to add middleware and even create extensions for both the framework and CLI tools to customize the developer experience. Vapor is also modular, so you can use parts of Vapor, such as the Vapor Engine, to build your HTTP Server. Vapor is more than just an HTTP Server with Routing, and you can substitute a Kitura HTTP Server in place of Vapor's default HTTP Server while using other parts of the framework, such as its powerful Object-relational mapping engine, database migrations, and the view rendering engine.

- It is heavily configurable via the config files that are in JSON format. The configurations allow for environment variable substitution, so you can easily swap out database URLs or other configurations for different environments using only environment variables.
- It uses the model-view-controller architectural pattern, popularized by Rails, making it easy to create and debug apps.
- It is resourceful by default, and has great APIs to build RESTful web applications. It is also resourceful in the sense that you can serve static assets such as CSS, JS, and even render views in different formats, such as HTML or JSON, depending on who is requesting a resource and with which format.
- It is expressive where you write less code to do more, making Vapor apps more concise and powerful.
- Vapor Apps are easy to deploy thanks to its cloud service, which is similar to Heroku, but you can also deploy the Vapor app to your cloud or data center if you like:

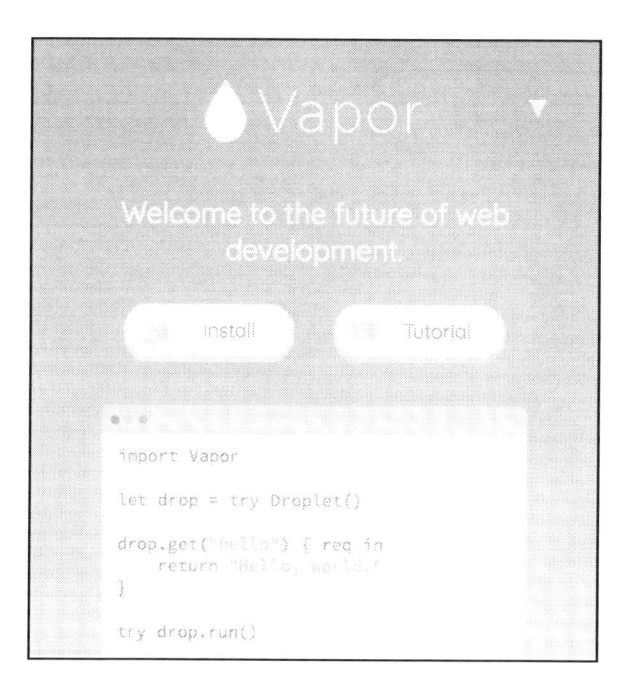

Considering that Vapor is more than just a simple HTTP server with routing like other server-side Swift frameworks and has all the bells and whistles of a full stack web application framework, it's an obvious choice that allows us to focus on writing the business logic for our application. We will be using Vapor to build our server-side component for the iOS apps that we'll be creating throughout this book.

# Book roadmap

The goal of the book is to try to help guide you into the world of full stack Swift development by building a frontend in both a mobile and browser app. Throughout this book, we will try to work on building a Shopping List App. The final product will consist of the following components:

- Native mobile app written in Swift for iOS
- API backend written in Swift using Vapor
- Frontend web app built using HTML rendered by Vapor, along with JavaScript and CSS for client-side interaction and styling

We will begin by building out the native application, and then proceed to building the backend for the app and integrate the app with the API. Then we will focus on rendering web views and adding authentication for both the API and the web app. Toward the end of the book, we will look at how to add real-time updates using web sockets in these apps and also try to build a simple chat application using Swift and Vapor.

# Summary

I hope by now you have a better understanding of the state of Swift and where it is heading. Swift, which was once a language for mobile app development, can now be used on the server to build server-side web applications. By now, you should have the following:

- An understanding of how Swift has evolved and is being used for web development
- An idea of how you can use Swift for full stack app development and reuse the tooling and knowledge of the language to build backends in Swift
- Knowledge about the Swift package manager and how to use its CLI

- Built and published a Swift package and know how to share code and import dependencies into your Swift package
- An understanding of how web servers are built and work under the hood using sockets
- Some knowledge of the server-side Swift frameworks that can help you build a full stack web application
- Familiarity with Vapor, which we will be using throughout the book
- A mental model of what we are trying to build throughout the book to learn how to build full stack native apps using Swift

In the next chapter, we will dive into building an actual native iOS app in Swift and flesh out the features of the app.

# Creating the Native App

In the previous chapter, we got a little preview of server-side Swift. Now, we will switch gears, and start working with Swift on a platform that it was originally designed for: Apple's iOS. Swift is currently a very popular language for app development, not only for iOS, but also for tvOS and macOS platforms. In this chapter, we will focus on iOS and build our first iOS app in pure Swift using Xcode. We will be following the model-view-controller architectural pattern popular for building apps in iOS. In the chapter, we will cover the following:

- The features of our Shopping List app
- Walk through how to create a new app project using Xcode
- The structure of an app and its Models, Views, and View Controllers
- Learn how to use the storyboard to create and link View Controllers
- Wire up the Table View Controllers to show Shopping List Items in our Shopping List and learn how to update the view when items are added, rearranged, and deleted in our controller
- Learn how to save and load data for our app

## Features of our Shopping List app

The app we will be building is a simple Shopping List app. It is a general-purpose Shopping List app that allows users to add items to their list and check items from the list. The following is the full list of features for our app:

- Users will be able to add Shopping List Items
- They will be able to enter details about the items, such as the item name
- The item can be checked to mark it as bought

*Creating the Native App*

- Users will be able to view all of the items entered in the Shopping List, rearrange them, and even delete them
- Users will be able to have more than one Shopping List and move items between Shopping Lists
- The app will persist the data and load the Shopping Lists and their items whenever the app starts
- Users will be able to filter the Shopping List based on items that are not checked and also be able to search for items in the list based on their names
- Users can update the list from any device and it will get synced

# Creating an app

To create an app, you will need to have Xcode installed. You can get it from Apple's App Store. Once you open Xcode, you will be greeted with the Welcome to Xcode modal. This is where you will see your most recent projects:

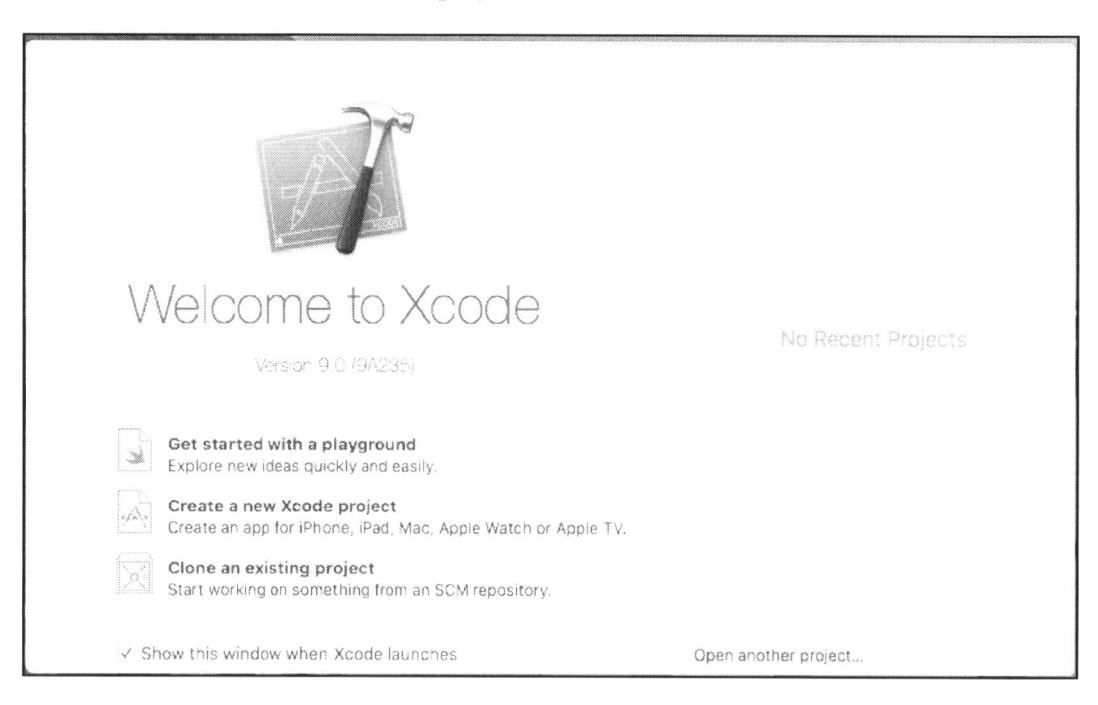

*Chapter 2*

We will get started by selecting the **Create a new Xcode project** option from the dialog. If you want to just explore Swift language, you can select **Get started with a playground**.

> **TIP**: Playgrounds are a hybrid between a text editor for Swift code and a code runner where you can see the result of your code as you type, making it easy to learn the language or try out something quickly.

This will open another dialog where we will be prompted to select the template for our project. There are several templates to choose from, but for our app, the **Single View App** is a good template to begin with:

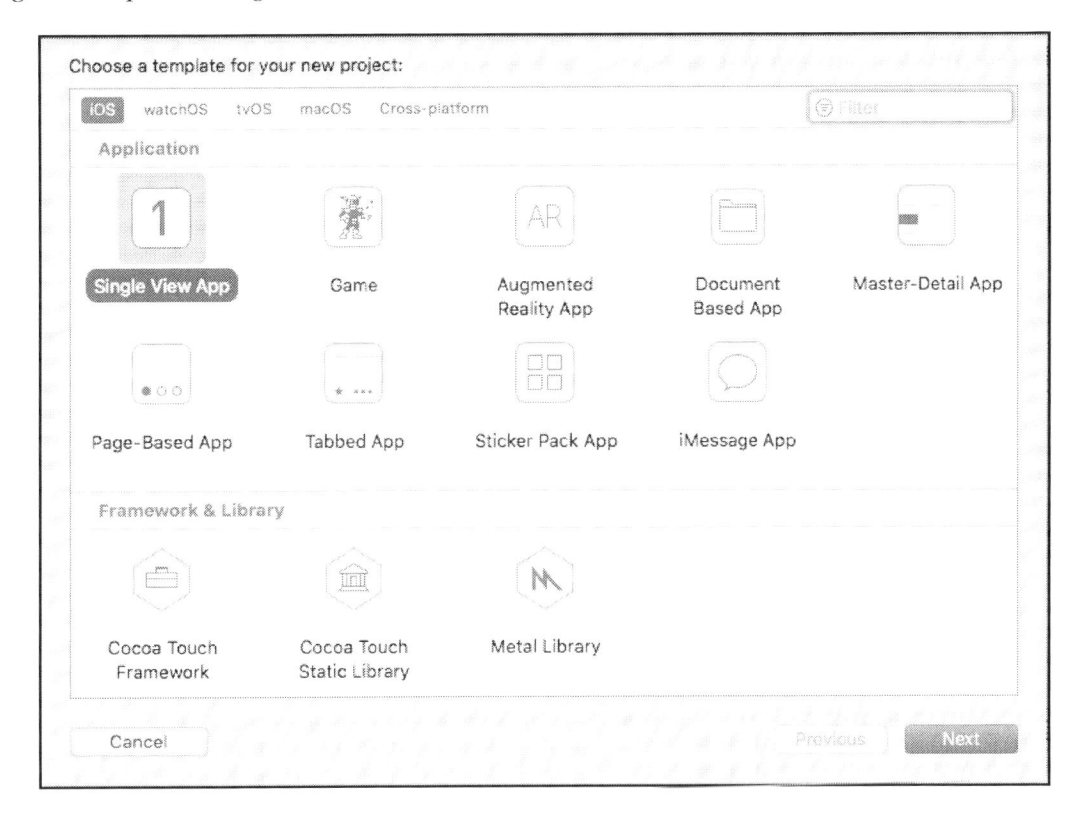

[ 35 ]

*Creating the Native App*

Give your app a name and make sure the language selected is Swift (we will not check core data or other test options) and click **Next**:

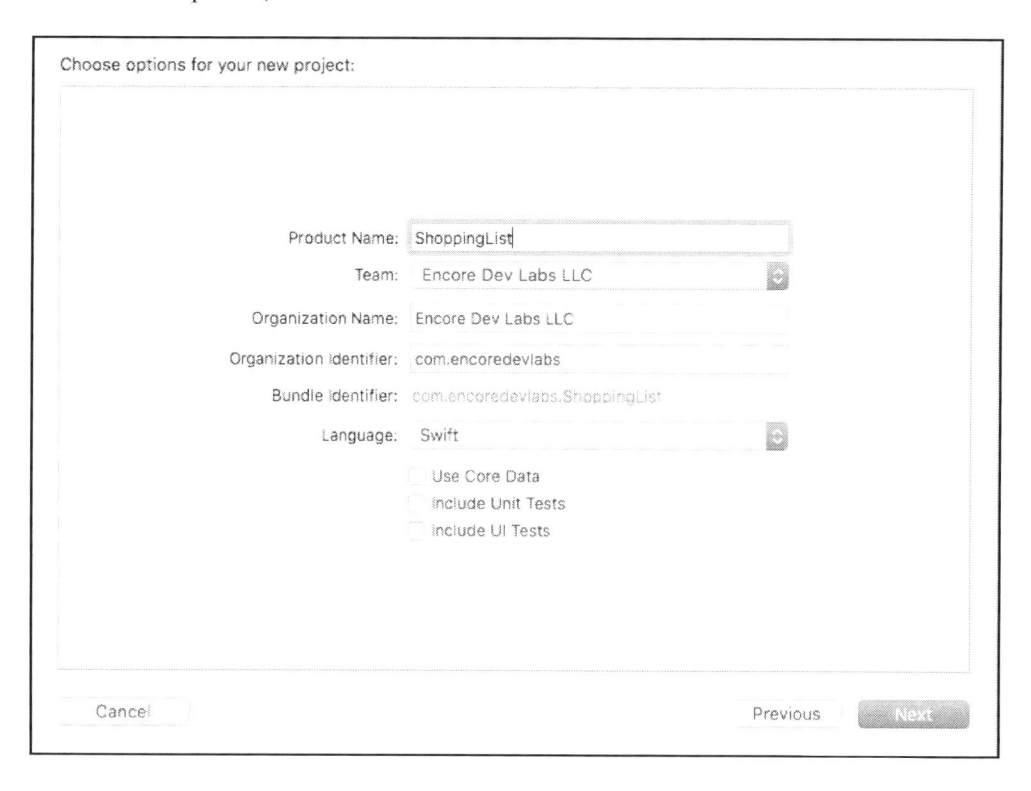

It will prompt you to select a folder where this project will be created. Select a folder, click **Create**, and Xcode will generate the project and open it.

The generated project will contain two Swift files, two storyboards, an `Assets` folder, and `Info.plist`. Let's explore each of these files in detail:

- `AppDelegate.swift`: This is the entry point of our app and where we have some callback functions that get called when the app gets started, goes in the background, or becomes active. This is a good file where we perform any actions we want to do before the app becomes inactive or becomes active again, such as loading and saving the state of the app.
- `ViewController.swift`: This is the default and first View Controller that is created by our app. View controllers are in charge of handling the state of the view and reacting on actions by the user, such as a button tap or refreshing the view when the network request is completed.

- `Main.storyboard`: This is the main file that contains the visual representation of the app. It shows and defines how the app progresses from one view to another. You can get the full picture of all of the states in the app by viewing the Storyboard in a simple iOS application.
- `LaunchScreen.storyboard`: This is the storyboard file that contains the view that is shown when the app starts up.
- `Assets.xcassets`: This is a folder where you place all of your image assets, including app icon images.
- `Info.plist`: This is the config file in XML format that contains the configuration for your app and also contains settings to request permission for certain capabilities of the phone, such as user location:

```
▼ ShoppingList
    ▼ ShoppingList
        AppDelegate.swift
        ViewController.swift
        Main.storyboard
        Assets.xcassets
        LaunchScreen.storyboard
        Info.plist
    ▶ Products
```

# Blueprinting the Shopping List Item model

Now that we understand the files and folders in our projects a little bit, let's start writing some code. We will begin by writing code for our first model, the Shopping List Item. To do so, perform the following steps:

1. Create a new group called `Models` under the `ShoppingList` folder in your project.
2. Then right-click and click on **New File...** under the `Models` folder and select a Swift file from the iOS template. Call this new file `Item.swift` and click **Create**.

3. Copy the following code into the `Item.swift` file:

```swift
import UIKit
class Item {
    var name: String
    var isChecked: Bool
    init(name: String, isChecked: Bool = false) {
        self.name = name
        self.isChecked = isChecked
    }
}
```

Let's go over the code in more detail:

We define a class called `Item` which will serve as a blueprint for our Shopping List Items:

```swift
class Item {
```

We then define two properties to store a name for the item and the state of the item on whether it is checked or unchecked. These two properties are called `name` and `isChecked` and their types are `String` and `Bool`, respectively:

```swift
var name: String
var isChecked: Bool
```

Lastly, we define a construction that takes in one require argument, which is name, and the second optional argument, which is the property value for `isChecked` that defaults to `false`:

```swift
init(name: String, isChecked: Bool = false) {
    self.name = name
    self.isChecked = isChecked
}
```

That is our model to store the data of our Shopping List Item. We will look at how we can create an instance of our model in the controller and then show them in the table view. Before we do, it's time for a short exercise. The solution of this exercise will be used later in the app to generate fake items to show some data in the app when it launches, instead of seeing an empty table view on launch.

## Exercise

Create a class level method in our `Item` model that can generate and return fake Shopping List Items. This method will take one argument, which will be the number of fake items to create and return. You can give your items random names or append the item name with a counter. You can also mark your items checked or unchecked if you like. The following is the method that you need to fill out by adding your code inside the function block:

```
static func fake(_ count: Int) -> [Item] {
  // Your code goes here
}
```

## Exercise answer

The following is the answer to generating fake items. Copy this code if you were not able to create your own version of generating fake items as we will need this later in our app:

```
static func fake(_ count: Int) -> [Item] {
  var items = [Item]()
  for i in 0...count {
    let item = Item(name: "Item \(i)", isChecked: i % 2 == 0)
    items.append(item)
  }
  return items
}
```

# Controlling the flow of our application using View Controller

iOS apps have a controller file, which as the name implies, controls the flow of your application. It's one file that's responsible for keeping track of data that will be used to render the view. It also listens to triggers from the user and reacts to them by modifying the data if needed, and re-rendering the view with the modified data. There are a few kinds of View Controllers, but the one that is most commonly used is a **Table View Controller**.

*Creating the Native App*

Table View Controllers are specialized View Controllers that are used when you want to show a list of data. It can also be used in creative ways to make more complex user interfaces, such as an image reel or a carousel. For our app, we'll use the Table View Controller to list our Shopping List Items one by one, and the View Controller will be responsible for keeping the entire list in memory.

Before we dive into the code for our Table View Controller, we need to understand a few concepts about the life cycle events of a View Controller. Let's look at the life cycle:

- All View Controllers start out by having the `viewDidLoad` method invoked. This method is only called if the View Controller has not loaded before. This is a good place to load data for our application by generating fake Shopping List Items or by reading a Shopping List from disk. We can also make a network request to get the Shopping List Items.
- After this, the `viewWillAppear` method is called on our View Controller. This gets called every time the view is going to appear but is not 100% visible to the user yet. This is another good place to refresh our data so that the user sees the most up-to-date Shopping List as the user switches between View Controllers.
- Then, `viewDidAppear` will get called when the view is visible to the user. This is a good place to end any animation or stop a spinner in case data is being loaded over the network and taking some time to load.
- The same methods exist when the view is removed, first by getting a call to the `viewWillDisappear` method. And finally, by getting a call to `viewDidDisappear`. These are good methods to save data or they can be ignored, if you prefer that the data for the Shopping List is saved on every change.

*Chapter 2*

Table View Controller, which is a subclass of View Controllers, inherit the following life cycle methods. We can override these methods as needed to fetch and save data. Table View Controllers also have a few more methods that we will examine by first creating a new Table View Controller file in our project. Like we did for the model, we need to do the following:

1. Create a new group called `Controllers` under the `ShoppingList` folder in your project

2. Then create a **New File...** under the `Controllers` folder, select a **Cocoa Touch Class** from the iOS template, and click **Next**:

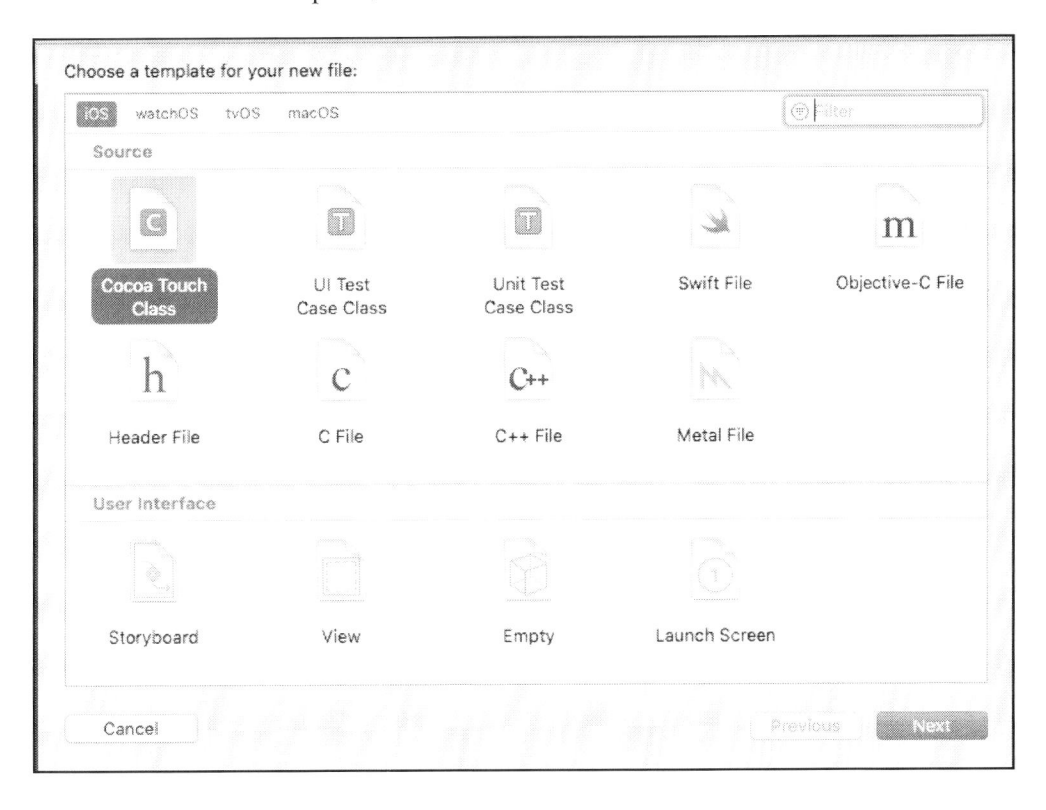

3. Under Subclass of type select **UITableViewController**, name the file `ItemTableViewController`, and make sure Language is set to **Swift**. Click **Next** and then click **Create** in the next dialog:

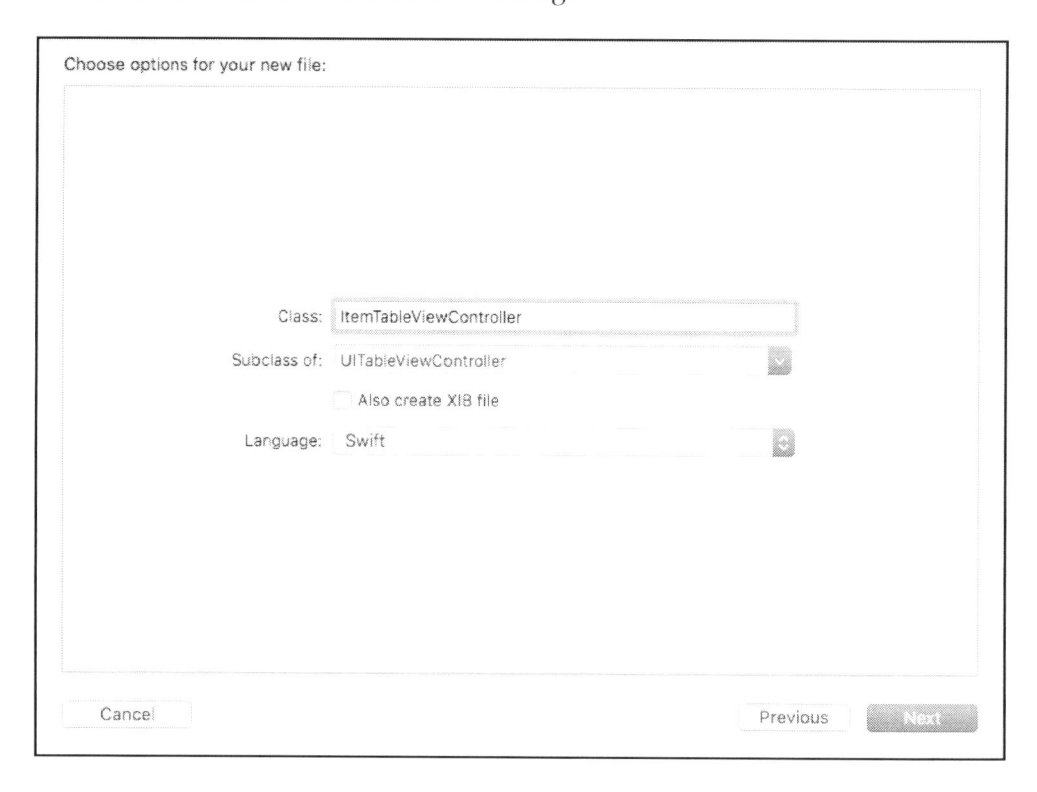

Xcode should generate the file and it will have some code commented out. We will fill out this class shortly. Now, we will switch files and jump to the `Main.storyboard`.

# Wiring up the view

Storyboard is where you define the flow of your application. It's where the initial View Controller is defined and also the place where you can set up other View Controllers and connect them. Configuring our app's UI is done using Xcode, but all of these configurations can be programmatically done by writing additional code.

*Chapter 2*

To use our new `TableViewController` file in our application, we need to edit our main storyboard. To do so, we need to perform the following steps:

1. Delete the `ViewController.swift` file in our project as we will not be using it. You can do so by right-clicking on the file, selecting **Delete**, and then in the modal selecting **Move to Trash**.
2. Open the `Main.storyboard`. We will click on **View Controller Scene** in the left pane of our storyboard file and delete it:

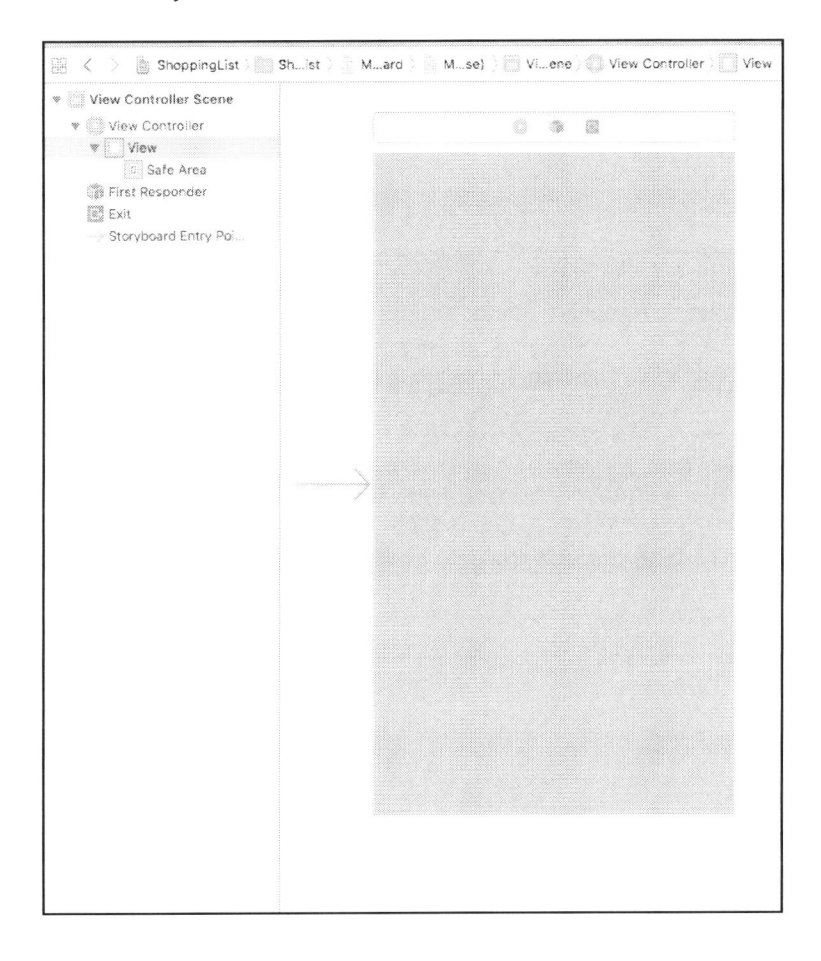

3. Drag the **Navigation Controller** from the **Object Library** on the bottom right-hand corner of Xcode. You can filter for it by typing `Navigation Controller` in the filter field. Navigation Controller comes with a Table View Controller when you drag it into the storyboard and it will be set as the **Root View Controller**:

4. Click on the **Root View Controller** and then go to the **Identify Inspector** which is on the top right corner of Xcode. In **Class** field, type `ItemTableViewController`, our newly created controller:

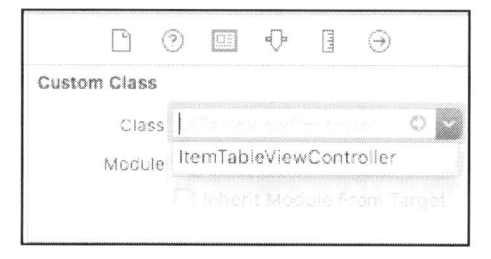

5. Tell storyboard that the **Navigation Controller** is our **Initial View Controller** and to start the app from there. We can do so by first selecting **Navigation Controller**, then selecting the **Attributes Inspector** tab in the top-right corner and checking the **Is Initial View Controller** checkbox. As a confirmation, we will not see an arrow to the left of our **Navigation Controller** in the storyboard:

[ 44 ]

*Chapter 2*

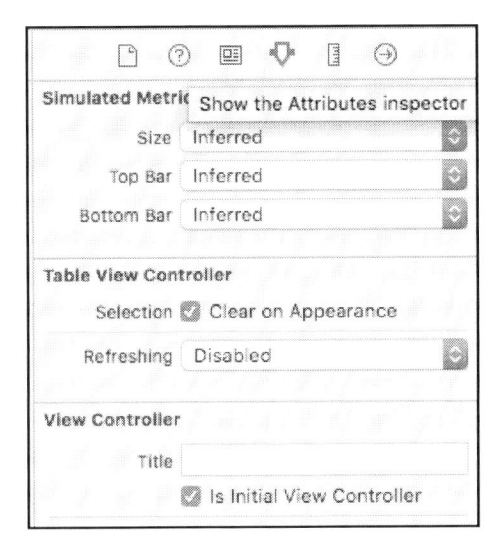

6. Run the app by clicking on the play button on the top-left corner of Xcode to make sure we have wired everything correctly and the app runs:

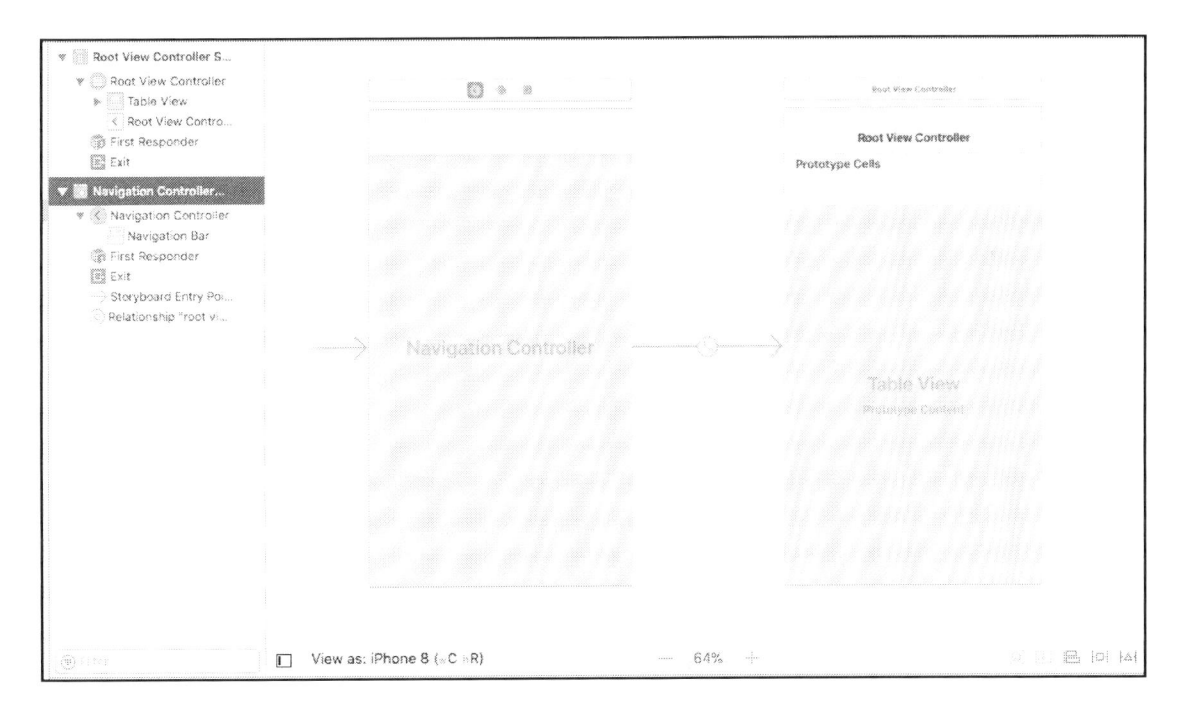

[ 45 ]

The app will not do anything exciting, but in the next section we will write code in our Table View Controller to start creating, editing, and deleting our Shopping List Items:

# Table View Controller

To get our app to do something interesting, we will now need to write some code. We begin with our `ItemTableViewController`. Opening the file, you will see there is some template code already and some code that has been commented. We will fill out these code blocks one by one to understand what each of these methods does. In our controller, we need to do the following:

1. Define a controller instance property called `item`, which will be an array of `Item` objects. This is the same `Item` class we created earlier in this chapter. We will set items to default to the fake items that we will get from the `fake` method defined on `Item` class that you created in the earlier exercise:

    ```
    class ItemTableViewController: UITableViewController {
        var items: [Item] = Item.fake(10)
    ```

2. In our `viewDidLoad` method, which we touched upon earlier in the View Controller life cycle, we will add the following code. In this code block, we are first calling `viewDidLoad`, defined in our parent class using `super`. Then we set the title that is shown in the navigation bar. Finally, starting in iOS 11, the navigation bar can have a large title which we set to `true`:

    ```
    super.viewDidLoad()

    self.title = "Shopping List Items"

    self.navigationController?.navigationBar.prefersLargeTitles = true
    ```

3. We need to tell the app how many sections to render. By default, the `numberOfSections` method returns 0 but we need to change this by removing the warning and change the return value to 1. Sections are a way to split apart a `tableView`, but in our app we just need one to list all of the items:

    ```
    override func numberOfSections(in tableView: UITableView) -> Int {
      return 1
    }
    ```

# Creating the Native App

4. The next method we need to update
   is `tableView(_:numberOfRowsInSection:)`. This method is called for each section in your `tableView` and you are passed the section number to figure out how many rows you want to display in each section. In our app, we will have one row for each item, so we need to return the size of our items array:

   ```
   override func tableView(_ tableView: UITableView,
   numberOfRowsInSection section: Int) -> Int {
     return items.count
   }
   ```

5. The next method we need to fill out is `tableView(_:cellForRowAt:)`. This method is called with an `indexPath` that contains the section and row in that section. Using this, we need to return a cell view that is displayed in that section and row. In iOS, there is a convention to reuse cells instead of creating new ones for each row, as there can be a lot or an infinite number or rows that can be generated and, hence, a cell is reused and the subviews in the cells are rendered with the data for cell of that specific row. In our case, we will get the item for the row it is being requested for, then get a reusable cell, and set the value on the subviews of that reusable cell:

   ```
   let cell = tableView.dequeueReusableCell(withIdentifier:
   "ItemCell", for: indexPath)

   let item = items[indexPath.row]
   cell.textLabel?.text = item.name

   if item.isChecked {
       cell.accessoryType = .checkmark
   } else {
       cell.accessoryType = .none
   }

   return cell
   ```

6. In the previous code block, we get the cell from the table view using `tableView.dequeueReusableCell(withIdentifier: "ItemCell", for: indexPath)`. We need to define `ItemCell` in our storyboard inside the Table View for it to return the cell. We do this by going to our `Main.storyboard` and selecting our **Table View** from the **Root View Controller** and selecting the **Table View Cell**. Then, we go to the attributes Inspector on the right and add `ItemCell` to the **Identifier** field, which will change the name of the cell to `ItemCell` in the storyboard. Finally, change the **Style** to **Basic** from the Attribute Inspector for this cell:

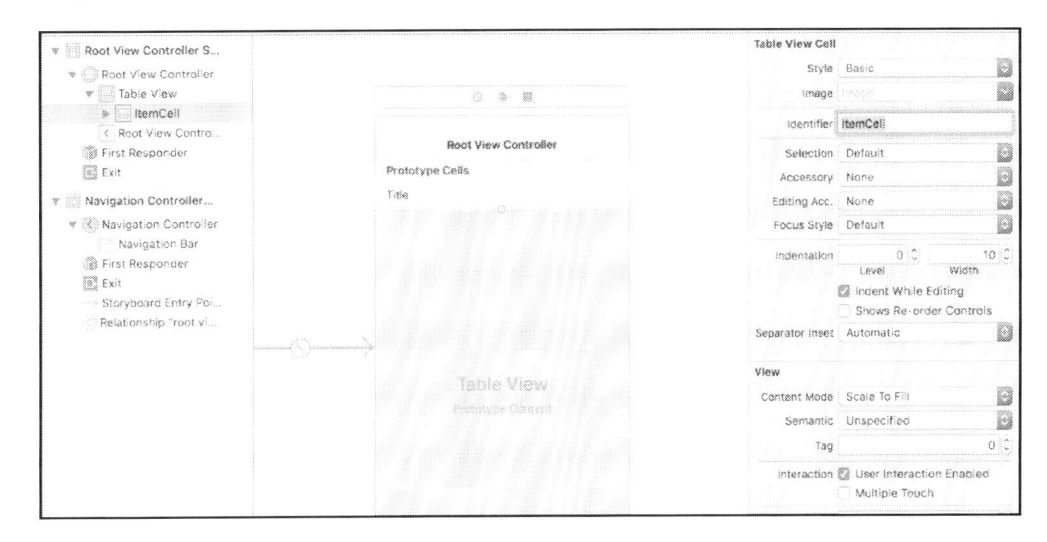

7. Let's run our app and see how it looks. Hit the play button or press on *command + R* to run the app:

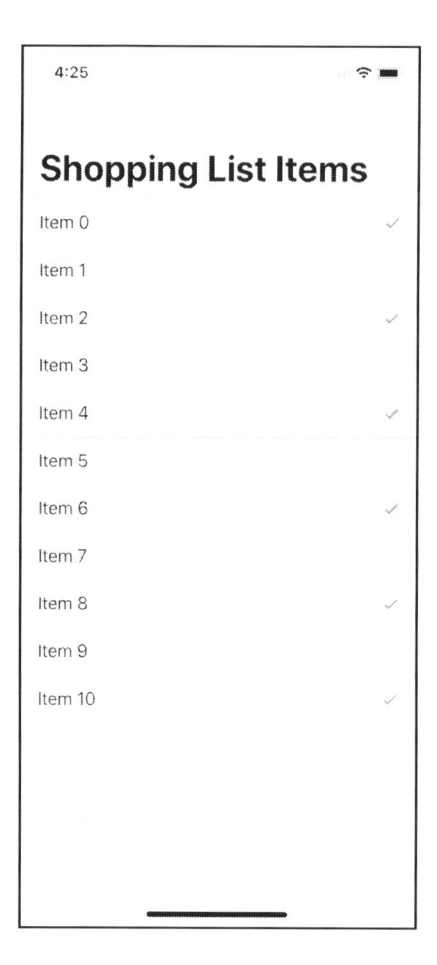

```
4:25

Shopping List Items
Item 0                    ✓
Item 1
Item 2                    ✓
Item 3
Item 4                    ✓
Item 5
Item 6                    ✓
Item 7
Item 8                    ✓
Item 9
Item 10                   ✓
```

Much better. Now we can see the list of items on our Shopping List. Let's now add the ability to add new items to our list.

# Adding items to the list

To add items, we will need to add a new bar button to our navigation bar and set up a tap handler on the button so that we can respond to it by showing an input dialog to the user to enter the name of the item they want to add. To do so, we need to perform the following steps:

1. Open up our `Main.storyboard`, search for **Bar Button Item** from the Object library, and drag it to the right-hand side of the navigation bar:

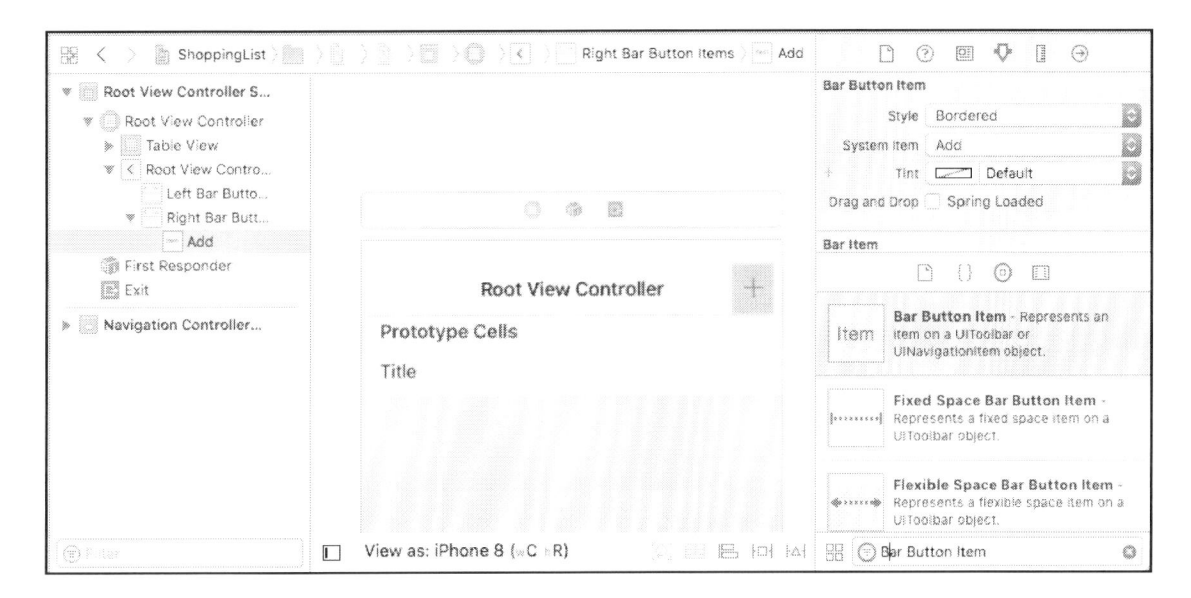

2. Select the **Bar Button Item** and change the **System Item** to **Add**:

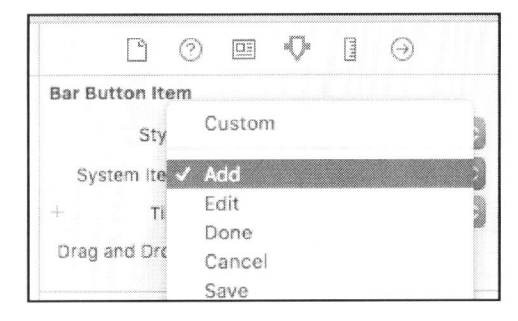

*Creating the Native App*

3. Click the **Assistant Editor** to open the source code for our Table View Controller side-by-side with the storyboard:

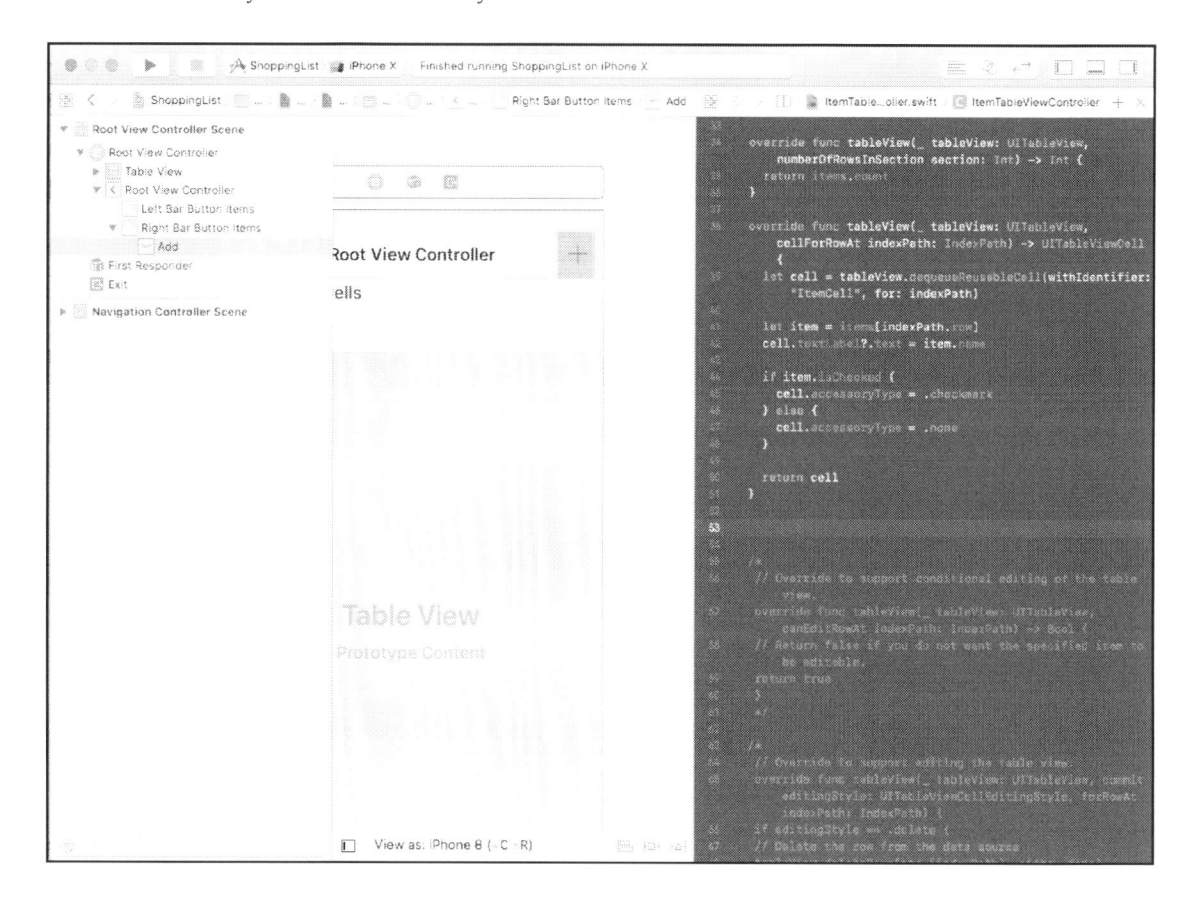

4. *Control* click on the add button (+) and drag into into your source code file where there is a blank line outside of any method and leave it:

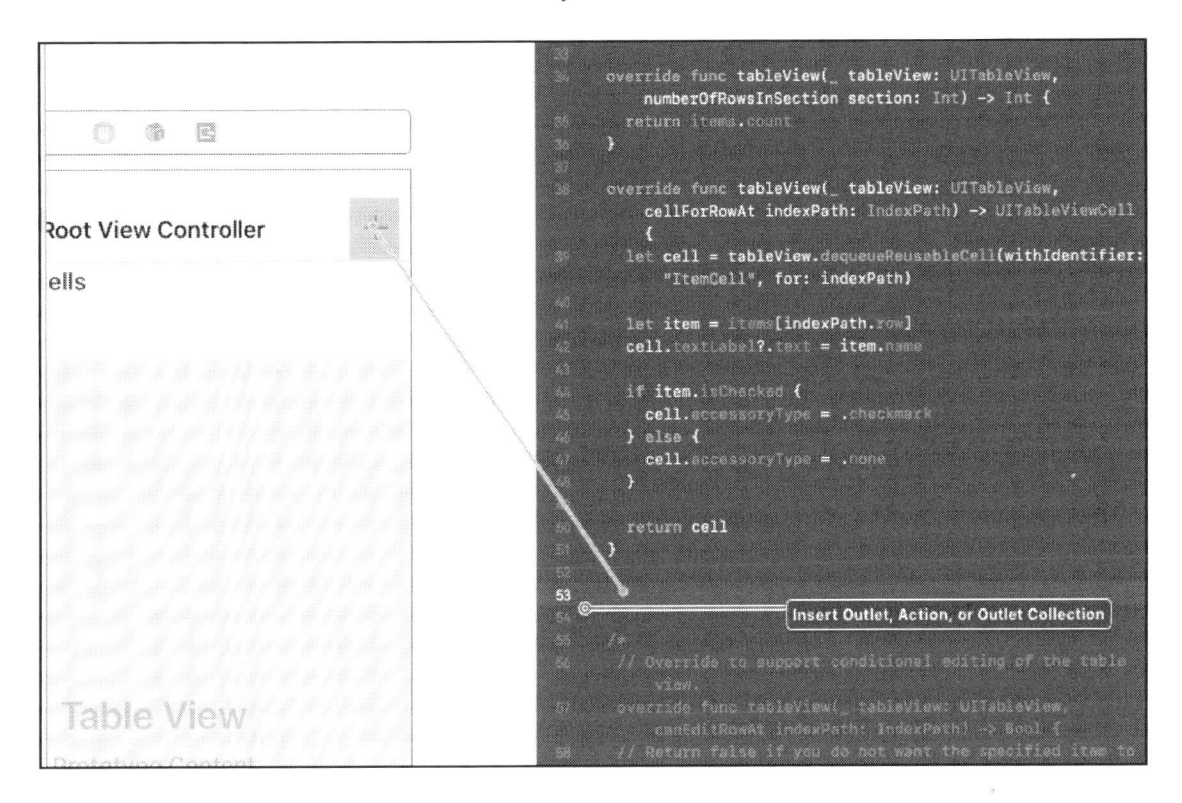

5. You will then see a modal where you need to change the **Connection** to **Action** and **Type** to **UIBarButtonItem**. In the **Name** field, give your method a name. I called mine `didSelectAdd`:

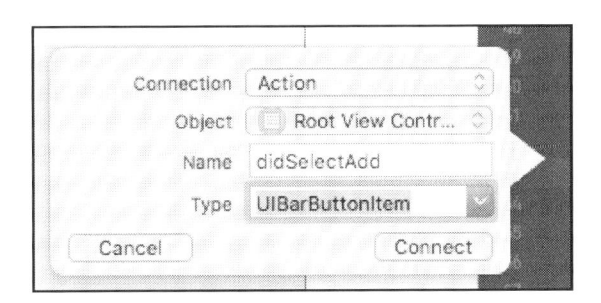

# Creating the Native App

This will add a method to your controller with the following signature:

```
@IBAction func didSelectAdd(_ sender: UIBarButtonItem)
```

6. Inside of this method, we need to add the following code to create an alert dialog, present it, ask the user for the input, handle the input by creating a new Item, append the new item to our items array, and then refresh the table view to show the new item:

```
let alert = UIAlertController(title: "New shopping list item",
  message: "Enter item to add to the shopping list:",
  preferredStyle: .alert)

alert.addTextField(configurationHandler: nil)

alert.addAction(UIAlertAction(title: "Cancel", style: .cancel,
handler: nil))

alert.addAction(UIAlertAction(title: "Add", style: .default,
handler: { (_) in
  if let itemName = alert.textFields?[0].text {
    let itemCount = self.items.count;
    let item = Item(name: itemName)
    self.items.append(item)
    self.tableView.insertRows(at: [IndexPath(row: itemCount,
section: 0)], with: .top)
  }
}))

self.present(alert, animated: true, completion: nil)
```

[ 54 ]

7. Let's run this to see how it looks:

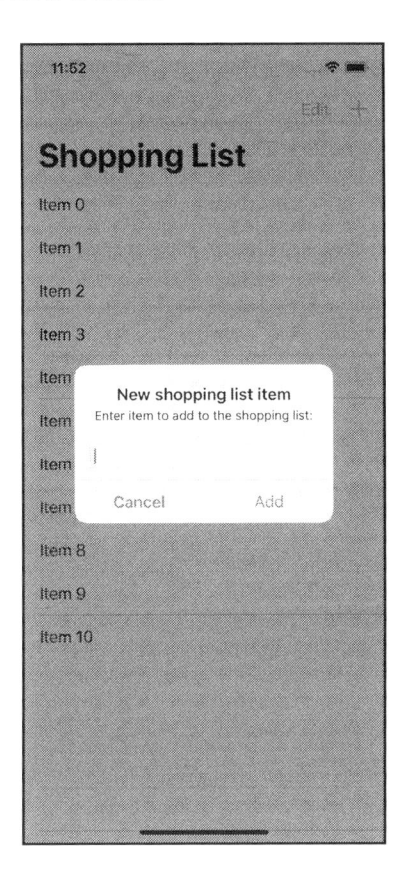

![Screenshot of Shopping List app with New shopping list item dialog]

Great! Now we are able to add an item to our app. Let's look at how to edit it.

# Editing the list

Adding the ability to edit the list of items by either deleting them or rearranging them is easy as well. All we need to do is implement few more methods to let our `ItemTableViewController` know that we want to delete certain rows or rearrange them and write code to update our model representing the list, which is our array of items.

First, let's implement deleting. To turn on deleting, we need to perform the following steps:

1. Implement the `tableView(_:canEditRowAt:)` method. In this method, we need to return true and it will allow deleting of all rows and hence all Shopping List Items. Setting this to `true` will allow users to swipe the cell to the left to reveal the **Delete** button, or it can be swiped all the way to the left to trigger a delete:

    ```
    override func tableView(_ tableView: UITableView, canEditRowAt
    indexPath: IndexPath) -> Bool {
      return true
    }
    ```

2. Implement `tableView(_:commit:forRowAt:)`. In this method, we need to delete the row from the table and also remove the item from our array of items. In the following code, we are checking whether the `editingStyle` is `delete` and if it is, then we remove the item from the array and, also delete the row from the `tableView` with a fade animation:

    ```
    override func tableView(_ tableView: UITableView, commit
    editingStyle: UITableViewCellEditingStyle, forRowAt indexPath:
    IndexPath) {
      if editingStyle == .delete {
        items.remove(at: indexPath.row)
        tableView.deleteRows(at: [indexPath], with: .fade)
      }
    }
    ```

3. Add an edit button to the navigation bar, which is another way to indicate to the user that the cell is editable and can be deleted. To add the edit button, all we need to do is add the following code to the `viewDidLoad` method:

    ```
    self.navigationItem.rightBarButtonItems?.append(editButtonItem)
    ```

Let's try this out by running the app. You should see the edit button and also swiping to the left will reveal a **Delete** option below the cell, swiping all the way to the left will delete the row and the item. Cool!:

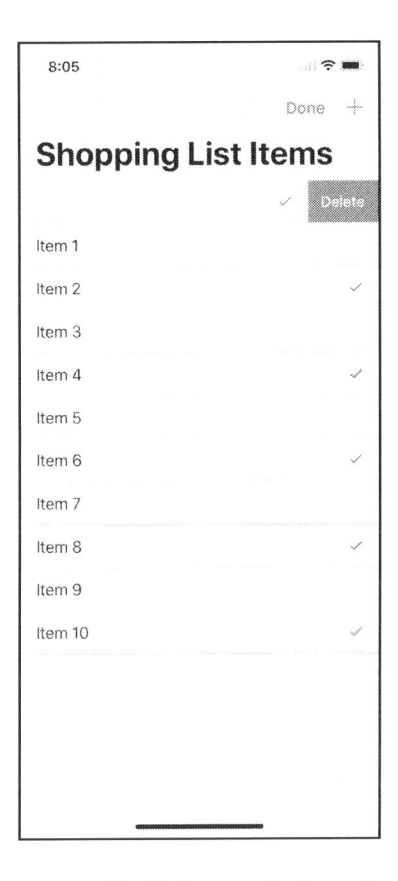

Now, let's add the ability to rearrange the list as part of our feature to edit the list. To do so again, we need to implement two more methods:

1. Add the `tableView(_:canMoveRowAt:)` method and return `true` for all rows:

   ```
   override func tableView(_ tableView: UITableView, canMoveRowAt
   indexPath: IndexPath) -> Bool {
     return true
   }
   ```

*Creating the Native App*

2. Implement the rearranging logic to update our model. It's as easy as removing an item from our array and inserting it into a new index:

```
override func tableView(_ tableView: UITableView, moveRowAt
fromIndexPath: IndexPath, to: IndexPath) {
  let item = items.remove(at: fromIndexPath.row)
  items.insert(item, at: to.row)
}
```

Run the app again. Now, when we tap on the `Edit` button, you will now see three horizontal bars next to each cell indicating that it can be rearranged. Moving one cell to another will also update our model behind the scenes:

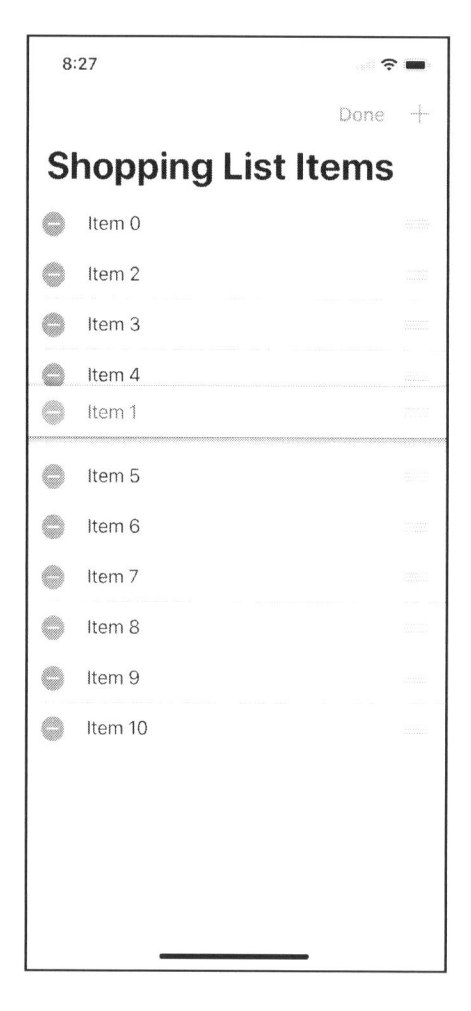

*Chapter 2*

Only one thing is left now in terms of editing items our list, and that's checking and unchecking the items. We can do so by listening for the selection of a cell as an indicator to toggle an item between the checked and unchecked state. To achieve this, we need to do the following:

1. Add the `tableView(_:didSelectRowAt:)` method to our `ItemTableViewController.swift` file. This method is called every time user selects a cell via a tap. The `indexPath`, which contains the section and row information, is passed in the argument, which we can use to figure out which item was selected.
2. Using the `indexPath`, we figure out that it's the following item:

   ```
   let item = items[indexPath.row]
   ```
3. Toggle the `isChecked` state:

   ```
   item.isChecked = !item.isChecked
   ```
4. Tell `tableView` to reload the cell whose model was just edited and it will cause the cell to refresh:

   ```
   tableView.reloadRows(at: [indexPath], with: .middle)
   ```

So the entire method block would look like this

```
override func tableView(_ tableView: UITableView, didSelectRowAt indexPath: IndexPath) {
  let item = items[indexPath.row]
  item.isChecked = !item.isChecked
  tableView.reloadRows(at: [indexPath], with: .middle)
}
```

Try it out by running the app and it will toggle the check mark next to the right of the cell and animate it.

# Loading and auto-saving the Shopping List

Now that we have the app working the way we want, there is one thing missing: the app doesn't save our Shopping List every time we make changes to our list. Also, we do not want to show the fake items. So let's see how we can persist the Shopping List and save it every time we make changes. For this we will need to:

1. Switch to `Item.swift` and first import the core `Foundation` framework as we will be using `UserDefaults`, `PropertyListEncoder`, and `PropertyListDecoder` class objects to save our items. Add the following line to the top of the file:

    ```
    import Foundation
    ```

2. Have the `Item` class implement the `Codable` protocol, which will allow our item to be encoded and decoded to be stored in `UserDefaults`. `UserDefaults` is a quick and easy way to save user settings or data that is application-specific:

    ```
    class Item: Codable {
    ```

3. Add a new instance method called `toggleCheck`, which will return a new item with the same name, but with its `isChecked` value toggled. We will use this new item and update our item in the Table View Controller with this new item rather than mutating the item itself:

    ```
    func toggleCheck() -> Item {
      return Item(name: name, isChecked: !isChecked)
    }
    ```

4. Use extensions in Swift to extend the `Array` class to add a save method and a class level load method to save and load the items from `UserDefaults`:

    ```
    extension Array where Element == Item {
      func save() {
        let data = try? PropertyListEncoder().encode(self)
        UserDefaults.standard.set(data, forKey: String(describing:
                                                Element.self))
        UserDefaults.standard.synchronize()
      }
      static func load() -> [Element] {
        if let data = UserDefaults.standard.value(forKey:
            String(describing: Element.self)) as? Data,
          let items = try?
    PropertyListDecoder().decode([Element].self,
                                                from: data){
    ```

*Chapter 2*

```
            return items
        }
        return []
    }
}
```

5. Switch to the `ItemTableViewController` file and update the `items` instance variable that is defaulting to fake items, to actually load from `UserDefaults`. We can do so by updating it to this:

    ```
    var items: [Item] = [Item].load() {
      didSet {
        items.save()
      }
    }
    ```

6. In the preceding code block, we are setting items array to default to items loaded from the `UserDefaults` storage. This is done by calling `[Item].load()`. We also have a `didSet` block defined that gets called every time the items array is modified. We need to save the items to `UserDefaults` again when that happens by calling the `save` method on the items array.

7. Update the `tableView(_:didSelectRowAt:)` method again and replace it with this and use the `toggleCheck` method that we just created instead to trigger the `didSet` method to automatically save our items:

    ```
    override func tableView(_ tableView: UITableView, didSelectRowAt indexPath: IndexPath) {
      items[indexPath.row] = items[indexPath.row].toggleCheck()
      tableView.reloadRows(at: [indexPath], with: .middle)
    }
    ```

Let's run the app now and you should not see any items at first but if you add few items, check some items, close the app, and start it up again, you will see the items will load in the state they were before closing the app.

# Multiple lists

Now that we have items created for one list, let's see how we can add multiple Shopping Lists to our app. It's quite similar to what we just did for Items, but before we get started, let's refactor our code so that it becomes easier to add a new Shopping List View Controller.

## Refactoring to share code

Perform the following steps:

1. Create a new empty Swift file in our `Controllers` folder and call it `BaseTableViewController.swift`.
2. Inside of our `BaseTableViewController.swift` file, create a new class that inherits from the `UITableViewController` and has a `requestInput` method:

    ```
    import UIKit
    class BaseTableViewController: UITableViewController {
      func requestInput(title: String, message: String, handler:
          @escaping (String) -> ()) {
        let alert = UIAlertController(title: title,
                                      message: message,
                                      preferredStyle: .alert)
        alert.addTextField(configurationHandler: nil)
        alert.addAction(UIAlertAction(title: "Cancel", style: .cancel,
                    handler: nil))
        alert.addAction(UIAlertAction(title: "Add", style: .default,
                    handler: { (_) in
          if let listName = alert.textFields?[0].text {
            handler(listName)
          }
        }))
        self.present(alert, animated: true, completion: nil)
      }
    }
    ```

3. We've created a `BaseTableViewController` class so that we can subclass our View Controllers from `BaseTableViewController` and share the `requestInput` method, which will do all of the heavy lifting of creating an `UIAlertController` and presenting to get user input. All we have to do now is call this method in our `ItemTableViewController` and pass it a title, a message, and a handler, which will return us the text that was entered as input by the user in our handler.
4. Switch the files and in our `ItemTableViewController` and change the class inheritance from `UITableViewController` to `BaseTableViewController`:

   ```
   class ItemTableViewController: BaseTableViewController {
   ```

5. Update the `didSelectAdd` method to use the inherited `requestInput` method by updating the body of the method to this:

   ```
   @IBAction func didSelectAdd(_ sender: UIBarButtonItem) {
     requestInput(title: "New shopping list item",
                 message: "Enter item to add to the shopping list:",
                 handler: { (itemName) in
       let itemCount = self.items.count;
       let item = Item(name: itemName)
       self.items.append(item)
       self.tableView.insertRows(at: [IndexPath(row: itemCount, section: 0)], with: .top)
     })
   }
   ```

Now run the app and it should work as before, but we've refactored it to be able to share the code to get input from the user and inherit any new View Controllers from `BaseTableViewController` that require an easy way to get input from users using `UIAlertView`.

## Blueprinting the Shopping List Model

We need to create and refactor our model so that we can create a relationship between the Shopping List and items:

1. Create a new Swift file and call it `ShoppingList.swift` file in our `Models` folder

2. Copy the following code, which lets us create a Shopping List Model with an array of items and also a callback handler that gets invoked when the items in the list are modified:

```swift
import Foundation
class ShoppingList: Codable {
  var name: String
  var items: [Item] {
    didSet {
      onUpdate()
    }
  }
  var onUpdate: () -> () = {}

  init(name: String, items: [Item] = []) {
    self.name = name
    self.items = items
  }
  convenience init(name: String, items: [Item], onUpdate: @escaping () -> ()) {
    self.init(name: name, items: items)
    self.onUpdate = onUpdate
  }
  func add(_ item: Item) {
    self.items.append(item)
  }
  func remove(at index: Int) {
    self.items.remove(at: index)
  }
  func swapItem(_ fromIndex: Int, _ toIndex: Int) {
    self.items.swapAt(fromIndex, toIndex)
  }
  func toggleCheckItem(atIndex index: Int) {
    items[index] = items[index].toggleCheck()
  }
  private enum CodingKeys: String, CodingKey {
    case name
    case items
  }
}
```

3. Go to our Item model and update the extension we have on `Array` and change the `Element` type from Item to Shopping List:

   ```
   extension Array where Element == ShoppingList {
   ```

4. Update the load method in this extension of the `Array` class to load the Shopping List elements now and the `onUpdate` trigger save on the list with the following code:

   ```
   static func load() -> [Element] {
      if let data = UserDefaults.standard.value(forKey: String(describing: Element.self)) as? Data,
         let elements = try? PropertyListDecoder().decode([Element].self, from: data){
         for element in elements {
            element.onUpdate = elements.save
         }
         return elements
      }
      return []
   }
   ```

We now have all of our Models set up correctly, but the code will break and not compile as our `ItemTableViewController` is trying to load the items. It will not be able to as we change the extension of the `Array` element type from Item to `ShoppingList`. We need to update our `ItemTableViewController` now:

1. Switch to `ItemTableViewController.swift` and replace the instance variable items with Shopping List and create a new computed items property:

   ```
   var list: ShoppingList!
   var items: [Item] {
     get {
        return list.items
     }
   }
   ```

*Creating the Native App*

2. In our `viewDidLoad` method, we need to change the title from always being set to `title = "Shopping List Items"` to be set to the name of our list `title = list.name`
3. Inside `didSelectAdd`, we need to replace the `self.items.append(item)` line with `self.list.add(item: item)`
4. Update the line where we remove the item from the item's `items.remove(at: indexPath.row)` array and replace it with `list.remove(at: indexPath.row)`
5. Where we swap items using `items.swapAt(fromIndexPath.row, to.row)`, we need to replace it with `list.swapItem(fromIndexPath.row, to.row)`
6. Where we toggle the item using `items[indexPath.row] = items[indexPath.row].toggleCheck()`, we need to replace it with `list.toggleCheckItem(atIndex: indexPath.row)`

At this point, the project will compile and you should not have any compiler errors. However, we are not done yet, the app won't work and will crash since we don't have a list that the `ItemTableViewController` requires to load.

## The Shopping List Table View Controller

As you may have guessed, we need a new View Controller to get our app to work. This will be called `ShoppingListTableViewController` and it will be very similar to `ItemTableViewController`. This new Shopping List View Controller will be our Root View Controller and it will list all of our Shopping Lists. On tapping one of those lists, it will push a new Item View Controller into the navigation and list all of the items in that shopping list. To get started:

1. Create a new Table View Controller file in the `Controllers` folder by right-clicking on the folder and selecting **New File...**.
2. Select **Cocoa Touch Class** and Subclass it from `BaseTableViewController`, then call the `ShoppingListTableViewController` file.
3. Copy the following code into the new `ShoppingListTableViewController.swift` file. This file has the same methods defined as in `ItemTableViewController`, but it also has few extra methods to pass the selected list to `ItemTableViewController` on selection of a list:

    ```
    import UIKit
    class ShoppingListTableViewController: BaseTableViewController {
    ```

[ 66 ]

```swift
  var lists: [ShoppingList] = [ShoppingList].load() {
    didSet {
      lists.save()
    }
  }
  override func viewDidLoad() {
    super.viewDidLoad()
    title = "Shopping Lists"
    navigationController?.navigationBar.prefersLargeTitles = true
navigationItem.rightBarButtonItems?.append(editButtonItem)
  }
  override func didReceiveMemoryWarning() {
    super.didReceiveMemoryWarning()
  }
  @IBAction func didSelectAdd(_ sender: UIBarButtonItem) {
    requestInput(title: "Shopping list name",
                 message: "Enter name for the new shopping list:",
                 handler: { (listName) in
      let listCount = self.lists.count;
      let list = ShoppingList(name: listName, items: [], onUpdate: self.lists.save)
      self.lists.append(list)
      self.tableView.insertRows(at: [IndexPath(row: listCount, section: 0)], with: .top)
    })
  }

  // MARK: - Table view data source

  override func numberOfSections(in tableView: UITableView) -> Int {
    return 1
  }

  override func tableView(_ tableView: UITableView,
numberOfRowsInSection section: Int) -> Int {
    return lists.count
  }
  override func tableView(_ tableView: UITableView, cellForRowAt indexPath: IndexPath) -> UITableViewCell {
    let cell = tableView.dequeueReusableCell(withIdentifier: "ListCell", for: indexPath)
    let list = lists[indexPath.row]
    cell.textLabel?.text = list.name

    return cell
  }
  override func tableView(_ tableView: UITableView, canEditRowAt
```

# Creating the Native App

```
    indexPath: IndexPath) -> Bool {
      return true
    }
    override func tableView(_ tableView: UITableView, commit
editingStyle: UITableViewCellEditingStyle, forRowAt indexPath:
IndexPath) {
      if editingStyle == .delete {
        lists.remove(at: indexPath.row)
        tableView.deleteRows(at: [indexPath], with: .fade)
      }
    }
    override func tableView(_ tableView: UITableView, moveRowAt
fromIndexPath: IndexPath, to: IndexPath) {
      lists.swapAt(fromIndexPath.row, to.row)
    }
    override func tableView(_ tableView: UITableView, canMoveRowAt
indexPath: IndexPath) -> Bool {
      return true
    }

    override func prepare(for segue: UIStoryboardSegue, sender: Any?)
{
      if let destinationViewController = segue.destination as?
ItemTableViewController {
        if let indexPath = self.tableView.indexPathForSelectedRow {
          let list = lists[indexPath.row]
          destinationViewController.list = list
        }
      }
    }
}
```

If we build our app, it should compile without any errors, but it will not work and that's because we haven't updated our storyboard to start our application with the `ShoppingListTableViewController`. This is fairly easy to do. All we need to do is take the following steps:

1. Open `Main.storyboard` and drag a new Table View Controller into the board:

*Chapter 2*

2. Select the new Table View Controller. Under **Custom Class**, change the **Class** to `ShoppingListTableViewController`:

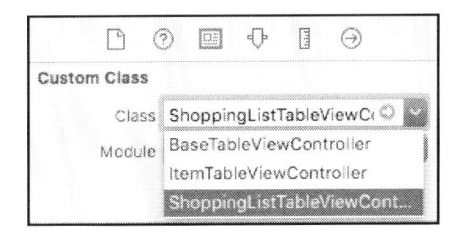

[ 69 ]

*Creating the Native App*

3. Press Control and drag it from the Navigation Controller to the Shopping List Table View Controller and select the **Relationship Segue** as the **Root View Controller**:

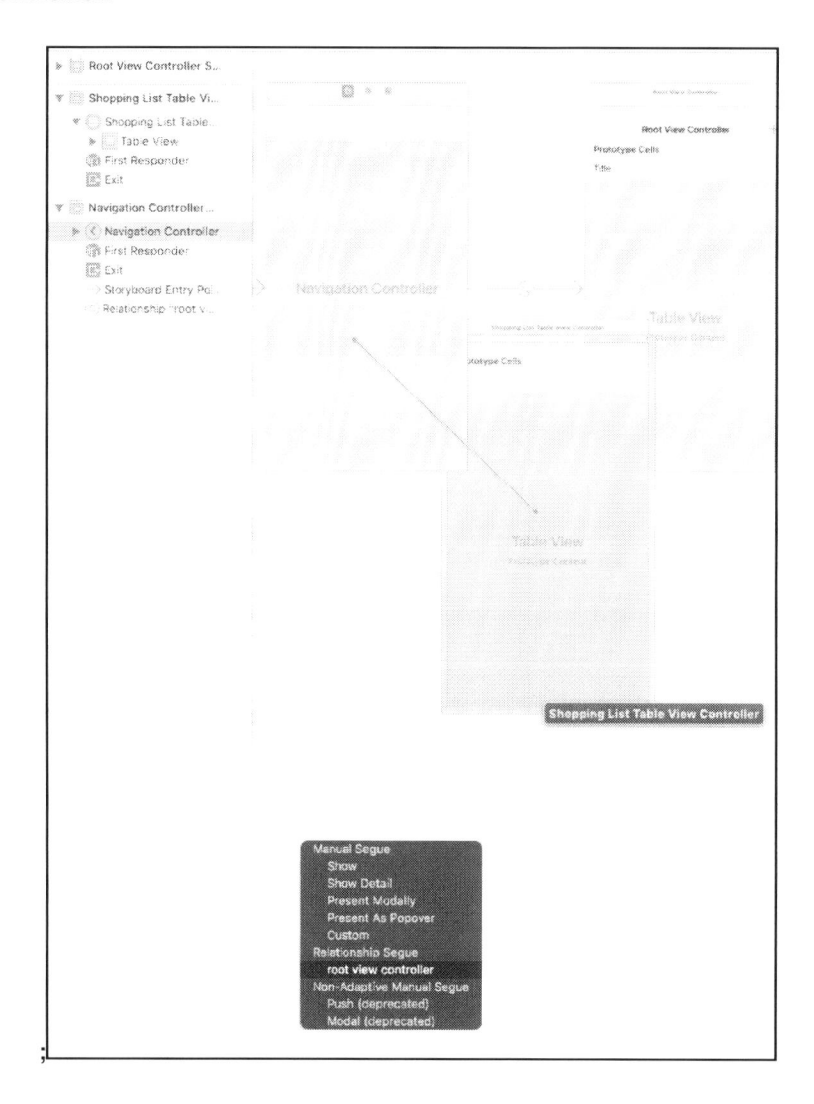

4. Inside the Shopping List Table View Controller, click on the **Table View Cell**, change the **Style** under **Attribute Inspector** to **Basic**, **Accessory** to **Disclosure Indicator**, and in the **Identifier** field, enter `ListCell`:

*Chapter 2*

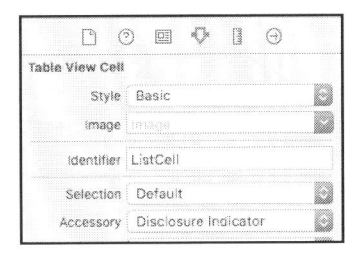

5. Press *control* again and now drag from the Table View Cell of the Shopping List Controller to the Root View Controller, which is our Item View Controller, and select **Show** from the **Selection Segue**:

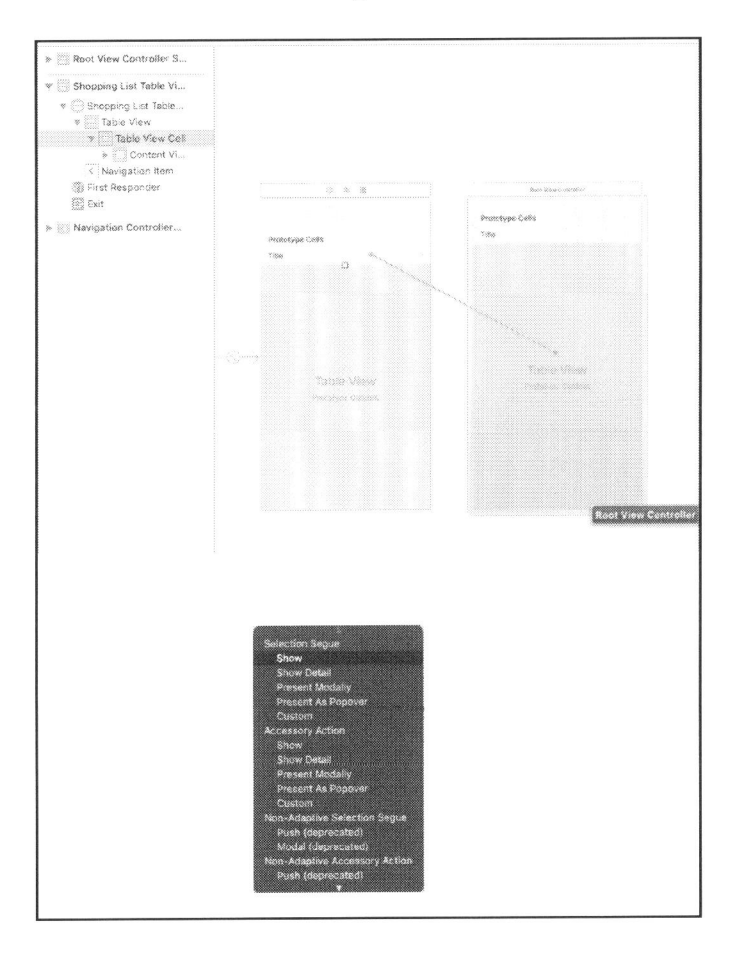

*Creating the Native App*

6. Just like the Item View Controller, drag the **Bar Button Item**, add it to the right side of the Shopping List Controller's navigation bar, and change the **System Item** to **Add**:

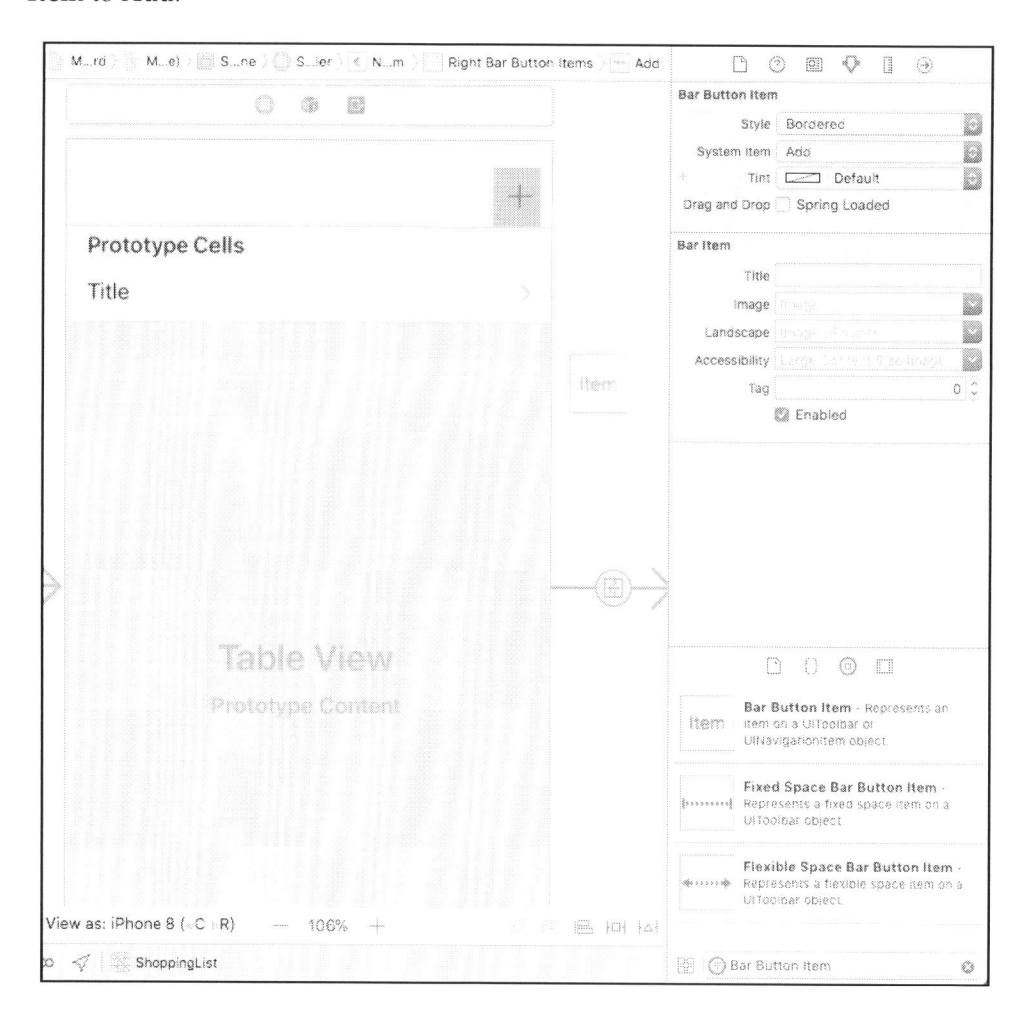

7. Press *control* and drag the Add (+) Bar Button from the navigation bar of the Shopping List Controller and drag it to the **Shopping List Table View Controller**, on the left side of the Storyboard and under **Sent Actions** select `didSelectAdd`:

[ 72 ]

*Chapter 2*

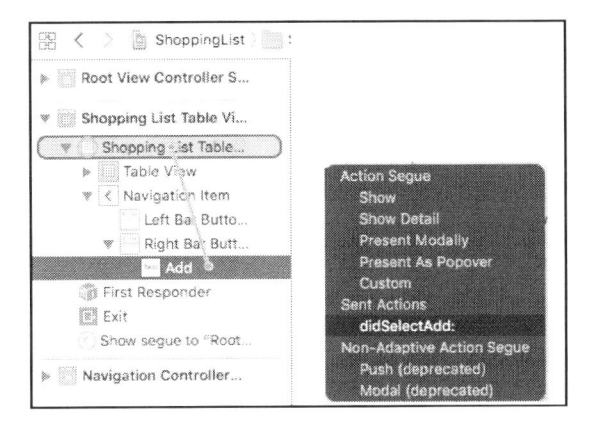

Run the app and everything should work, now we have multiple Shopping Lists in our application. We can dive into one of these Shopping Lists and add, delete, rearrange the items in that Shopping List and even delete the entire Shopping List itself. Modifying any of the Shopping Lists should save them in our app:

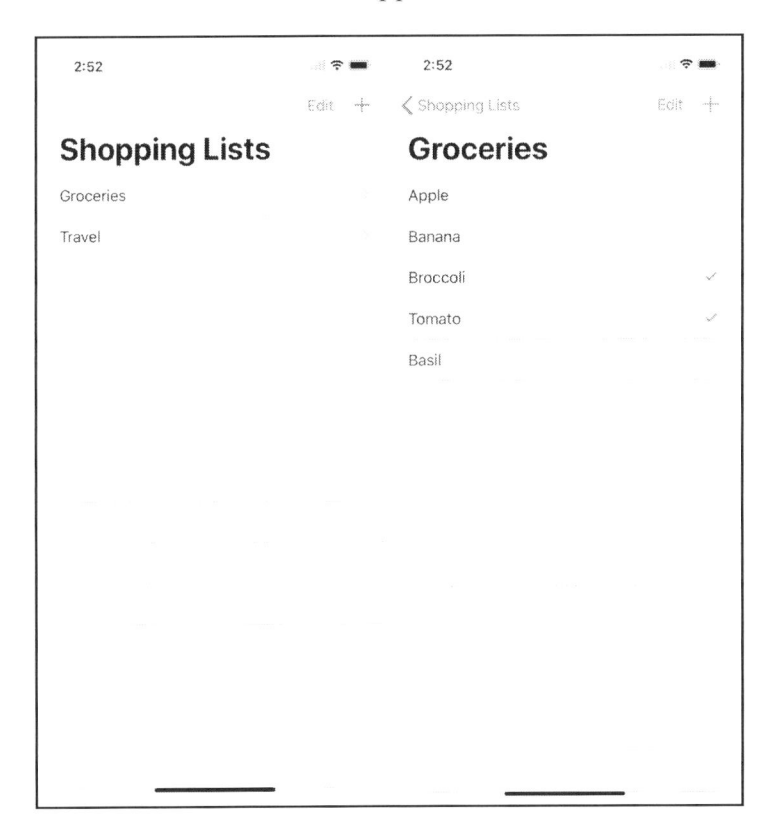

## Summary

In this chapter, we learned the basics of how to create a new app project using Xcode and Swift. We went over the structure of the generated project and how to structure out app into Models, Views, and Controllers. We touched on how to use storyboard to create and link actions triggered by those Views into our View Controller. You should now understand how to wire up the Table View Controller and shop Shopping List Items in the Shopping List app and update them, rearrange then, delete them, and properly save our Shopping List on the app. Lastly, we went through how to add a new Shopping List View Controller, so that we can create and manage multiple Shopping Lists and transition from the Shopping List view to the items view of a specific Shopping List.

In the next chapter, we will go over Swift on server side by exploring Vapor and creating a server-side Shopping List project. This server-side project will act as an API server for our app and also serve as a web application serving a responsive web view of the Shopping List that is accessible via the web browser.

# Getting Started with Vapor 3

In the previous chapter, we went over how to make an iOS app using Xcode in pure Swift. We also covered different concepts in iOS development such as **Model View Controller** (**MVC**) pattern and how to build iOS apps using the models which contain the state of our app. We also went over how to use the controller to control the flow of our app, to add, delete, and rearrange items and shopping lists. We also covered how to configure the views in storyboard to define the look and feel of the app, such as the navigation bar to table view cells. We also used some of the elegant syntax provided by Swift to help us aggregate all of the changes to our models and use a consistent method to save the state of the application, so that it can be easily restored using extensions built in the `Array` class, codable protocol, `UserDefaults`, and Swift's `didSet` callback methods.

In this chapter, we will put our server-side engineering hat on and explore Swift on the server side, using Vapor framework. We will see how we can use Vapor to build an API server for the iOS app we just built. We will also explore the modularity of the framework, as Vapor is made up of multiple Swift packages built using the Swift package manager that we went over in `Chapter 1`, *Getting Started with Server Swift*, it is a framework built purely in Swift, with performance in mind. More specifically, in this chapter, we will cover the following topics:

- What is Vapor, and what Swift packages make up Vapor? What functionality do these Swift packages provide?
- How can these Swift packages be used to build a simple HTTP server or your own web framework?
- What is the Vapor toolbox, and how do you use it to start building Vapor apps?
- How can you create and run a simple Vapor application server?
- How is our Vapor app structured?

# What is Vapor?

**Vapor** is a Swift package that provides the APIs to build a web application. It consists of several Swift packages, and, contrary to what most people might think, Vapor is not a monolithic Swift package. It is rather small and modular, consisting of several Swift packages that are stitched together to create a very rich web framework. The Swift packages it depends on are created by the Vapor team and grouped together based on their functionality. So, anyone who wants to build their own web framework in Swift can do so by consuming these packages. Vapor is broken down into the following packages:

- `core`: The core package contains core extensions, type-aliases, and functions that facilitate common tasks
- `bits`: This is a small package to help deal with bytes
- `debugging`: This package aids Vapor users in better debugging around the framework
- `random`: This package is useful for generating random bytes and numbers
- `bcrypt`: This package contains Swift implementation of the BCrypt password hashing function
- `crypto`: This package contains Swift implementation of cryptography functions
- `tls`: This package is a wrapper for OpenSSL and TLS
- `sockets`: This package provides a pure Swift (POSIX) TCP and UDP non-blocking socket layer, with event-driven server and client
- `node`: This package is a formatted data encapsulation, meant to facilitate the transformation from one object to another
- `json`: This package is a convenience wrapper for `Foundation` JSON
- `console`: This package is the good wrapper around console I/O
- `engine`: This package provides non-blocking networking for Swift (HTTP and WebSockets)
- `routing`: This package provides type-safe generic HTTP routing
- `multipart`: This package contains modules that parse and serialize multi-part/mixed and multi-part/form-data content types
- `sqlite`: This package is a Swift wrapper for SQLite 3
- `fluent`: This package is a Swift ORM (queries, models, and relations) for NoSQL and SQL databases
- `vapor`: This is a server-side Swift web framework that builds on top of all of the preceding packages

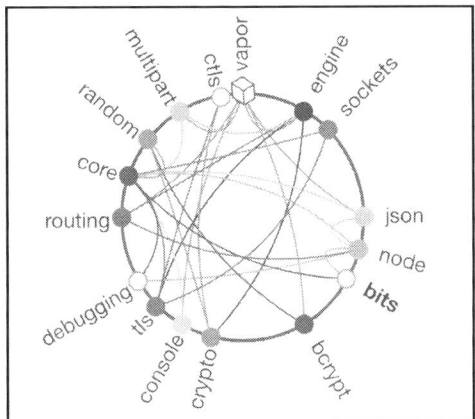

Here is a visualization of these packages and their relationships to each other:

# Building servers using Vapor's engine

Before we start using Vapor, let's see how the Vapor package is built on top of its engine package. This will give us a better understanding of what, exactly, Vapor provides, and what is provided by the dependencies that it consumes, in case you need to build a lightweight server or want to embrace building your own variation of a web framework. We will do the following:

1. First, build a basic web server that returns `Hello World`
2. Then, modify our `Hello World` server to serve file content, making a static file server similar to Apache or Nginx
3. Lastly, we will build a web socket server that will accept connections and echo back the message sent via the web socket connection

Going through the exercise of building these different kinds of servers using Vapor's engine will help us understand how Vapor works under the hood. It will also help us realize that building a large scale web application requires a lot of features, such as routing, persisting to the database, migrations, rendering HTML templates, and much more, which Vapor provides via its other Swift packages. This makes Vapor very modular, and anyone who wants to build something lightweight can pick and choose the modules they want, or they can use the Vapor Swift package to get the entire bundle pre-configured, making it easy to build large-scale web applications quickly.

# Building a basic HTTP server

To get started with building a basic HTTP server using Vapor's engine, we need to follow these steps:

1. Create an empty folder, call it `Server`, and open the folder in the Terminal.
2. Then, within this folder in the Terminal, let's create an executable Swift package by running the following command:

    ```
    swift package init --type executable
    ```

3. In `Package.swift`, we need to specify the dependencies by adding them to the `dependencies` section:

    ```
    dependencies: [
      .package(url: "https://github.com/vapor/engine.git", from: "2.2.1"),
      .package(url: "https://github.com/vapor/sockets.git", from: "2.2.1"),
    ],
    ```

4. We also need to specify the following two modules in our target's dependencies:

    ```
    .target(
      name: "Server",
      dependencies: ["Transport", "HTTP"]),
    ```

5. Then, we need to switch to our `main.swift` file under `Sources/Server` and update it to the following code:

    ```
    import Transport
    import HTTP

    class Hello: Responder {
      func respond(to request: Request) throws -> Response {
        return "Hello World".makeResponse()
      }
    }

    let PORT = Port(5000)
    let server = try BasicServer(scheme: "http", hostname: "0.0.0.0", port: PORT)

    print("Started on port \(PORT)")
    try server.start(Hello()) { error in
      print(error)
    ```

[ 78 ]

*Chapter 3*

```
}
```

In this code, we import `Transport` and `HTTP` modules as part of Engine. We then create a class, `Hello`, which is a subclass of `Responder` and has a `respond` method that returns a `Response` object. We then create a `BasicServer` and specify the protocol, hostname, and port number to run on, and start it up by calling `start` on our server, with an instance of the `Hello` responder class.

6. Now, we can start the server by running `swift run` in the Terminal. It will first install all of the dependencies by downloading them from GitHub, and will then build the modules and run our executable. You should see the following output:

```
~/W/Server $ swift run
Fetching https://github.com/vapor/engine.git
Fetching https://github.com/vapor/sockets.git
Fetching https://github.com/vapor/tls.git
Fetching https://github.com/vapor/crypto.git
Fetching https://github.com/vapor/core.git
Fetching https://github.com/vapor/random.git
Fetching https://github.com/vapor/ctls.git
Fetching https://github.com/vapor/bits.git
Fetching https://github.com/vapor/debugging.git
Cloning https://github.com/vapor/random.git
Resolving https://github.com/vapor/random.git at 1.2.0
Cloning https://github.com/vapor/core.git
Resolving https://github.com/vapor/core.git at 2.1.2
Cloning https://github.com/vapor/debugging.git
Resolving https://github.com/vapor/debugging.git at 1.1.0
Cloning https://github.com/vapor/ctls.git
Resolving https://github.com/vapor/ctls.git at 1.1.2
Cloning https://github.com/vapor/engine.git
Resolving https://github.com/vapor/engine.git at 2.2.1
Cloning https://github.com/vapor/crypto.git
Resolving https://github.com/vapor/crypto.git at 2.1.1
Cloning https://github.com/vapor/sockets.git
Resolving https://github.com/vapor/sockets.git at 2.2.1
Cloning https://github.com/vapor/tls.git
Resolving https://github.com/vapor/tls.git at 2.1.1
Cloning https://github.com/vapor/bits.git
Resolving https://github.com/vapor/bits.git at 1.1.0
Compile CHTTP http_parser.c
Compile Swift Module 'libc' (1 sources)
Compile Swift Module 'Bits' (19 sources)
Compile Swift Module 'Debugging' (1 sources)
Compile Swift Module 'Core' (23 sources)
Compile Swift Module 'Random' (6 sources)
Compile Swift Module 'Transport' (10 sources)
Compile Swift Module 'URI' (6 sources)
Compile Swift Module 'Sockets' (22 sources)
Compile Swift Module 'TLS' (12 sources)
Compile Swift Module 'HTTP' (45 sources)
Compile Swift Module 'Server' (1 sources)
Linking ./.build/x86_64-apple-macosx10.10/debug/Server
Started on port 5000
```

7. Open the web browser and go to `http://localhost:5000`, and you should see **Hello World** on the web page.

Great! We now have a basic server that we built using Vapor's engine package. Vapor uses the same `BasicServer` under the hood with the Vapor package, but this server is a lot more robust and performant than the basic HTTP server we built in Chapter 1, *Getting Started with Server Swift*, in pure Swift using sockets.

## Building a static file server

If you need to create a very basic static file server, that is easy to do, as well. The static file server we will create will serve the contents of the file specified in the URL path, relative to where the server was started from the Terminal. This is very similar to starting a basic HTTP file server in Python using the following command:

```
python -m SimpleHTTPServer 8080
```

To get started with building a basic file server, we will need to follow these steps in our existing `Basic Server` package:

1. First, import `Foundation` into `main.swift` by adding it to the top of the file. We will need this to use the `NSData` type provided by `Foundation`, to read the contents of a file in raw data format:

    ```
    import Foundation
    ```

2. Next, we need to figure out the directory from which the server was started so that we can serve files relative to that folder:

    ```
    let currentDirectoryURL = URL(fileURLWithPath: FileManager.default.currentDirectoryPath)
    ```

3. Next, we will create an extension on the `NSData` class and add a computed property called `toBytes`, which will return data as the `Bytes` type. `Bytes` is an alias type of `[UInt8]`, and we use this type as it is used to represent both textual data and binary data, such as images, PDFs, and so on:

    ```
    extension NSData {
      var toBytes: Bytes {
        get {
          return Bytes(UnsafeBufferPointer(start: bytes.assumingMemoryBound(to: UInt8.self), count: length))
        }
      }
    }
    ```

*Chapter 3*

4. Lastly, we will update the `respond` method in the `Hello` class to the following code block, so that it returns the raw contents of the file instead of `Hello World`:

   ```
   let fileURL =
   currentDirectoryURL.appendingPathComponent(request.uri.path)
   if let data = NSData(contentsOf: fileURL) {
      return Response(status: .ok, body: data.toBytes)
   }
   return Response(status: .notFound)
   ```

5. Now, compile and run the server from the Terminal using the `swift run` command and open the browser to `http://localhost:5000/Package.swift`.

Great! We just created a static file server, and you should see the contents of the `Package.swift` file in the browser. If you add an image or an HTML file in our `Server` directory, then you can view it in the browser by specifying the relative path to that image or HTML page in the URL.

The entire code for our static file server is shown as follows. For a better naming convention, the `Hello` class has been renamed `FileResponder`:

```
import Transport
import HTTP
import Foundation

let currentDirectoryURL = URL(fileURLWithPath:
FileManager.default.currentDirectoryPath)

extension NSData {
  var toBytes: Bytes {
    get {
      return Bytes(UnsafeBufferPointer(start: bytes.assumingMemoryBound(to:
UInt8.self), count: length))
    }
  }
}

class FileResponder: Responder {
  func respond(to request: Request) throws -> Response {
    let fileURL =
currentDirectoryURL.appendingPathComponent(request.uri.path)
    if let data = NSData(contentsOf: fileURL) {
      return Response(status: .ok, body: data.toBytes)
    }
    return Response(status: .notFound)
  }
```

```
}

let PORT = Port(5000)
let server = try BasicServer(scheme: "http", hostname: "0.0.0.0", port:
PORT)

print("Started on port \(PORT)")
try server.start(FileResponder()) { error in
  print(error)
}
```

## Building a WebSocket server

We will end our exploration of the engine package by creating a WebSocket server that echoes our message back. We will learn how to accept a WebSocket connection, how to receive messages from a WebSocket connection, and how to reply back with a message. To get started, we will create a new package and follow these steps:

1. Create a new folder, call it `WebSocket`, and open that folder in the Terminal.
2. Then, within this folder in the Terminal, let's create an executable Swift package by running the following command:

    **swift package init --type executable**

3. In `Package.swift`, specify the following dependencies by adding them to the `dependencies` section:

    ```
    dependencies: [
      .package(url: "https://github.com/vapor/engine.git", from:
    "2.2.1"),
      .package(url: "https://github.com/vapor/sockets.git", from:
    "2.2.1"),
    ],
    ```

4. We also need to specify the following modules in our target's dependencies:

```
.target(
  name: "WebSocket",
  dependencies: ["Transport", "HTTP", "WebSockets"]),
```

5. We then need to switch to our `main.swift` file under `Sources/Server` and update it to the following code:

```
import Transport
import HTTP
import WebSockets

class WebSocketResponder: Responder {
  func respond(to request: Request) throws -> Response {
    return try request.upgradeToWebSocket { ws in
      try ws.send("Hello from web socket!")
      ws.onText = { ws, text in
        try ws.send("Got message: \(text)")
      }
    }
  }
}

let PORT = Port(5000)
let server = try BasicServer(scheme: "http", hostname: "0.0.0.0", port: PORT)

print("Started on port \(PORT)")
try server.start(WebSocketResponder()) { error in
  print(error)
}
```

6. Now we can start the server by running `swift run` in the Terminal. It will first install all of the dependencies by downloading them from GitHub, and will then build the modules and run our executable.

7. Connect to the server via a web socket client. You might want to use the simple WebSocket client Chrome extension. Connect to `ws://localhost:5000`, and you should see a **Hello from web socket!** message; sending any message will echo it back from our WebSocket server:

```
Server Location
URL: ws://localhost:5000                Close
Status: OPENED

Request
Hi from websocket client
Send   [Shortcut] Ctr + Enter

Message Log   Clear
Hello from web socket!
Hi from websocket client
Got message: Hi from websocket client
```

Great! You have just created a WebSocket server from scratch, using Vapor's engine package. We hope this gives you a better understanding of the building blocks that Vapor uses and gives you an alternative for building a very simple web or WebSocket server that responds to requests, instead of using Vapor, which gives you a lot more out of the box.

# Building a Vapor application from scratch

Before we start creating Vapor applications using the Vapor toolbox, which is an awesome tool provided by the Vapor team, let's see the minimal amount of code needed to create a Vapor application from scratch using the Vapor package. To do so, we need to follow the following steps:

1. Create a new `Hello` folder and open it in the Terminal.
2. Then, initialize the Swift package by running the `init` command, and make it an executable type. This should generate the `Sources` folder and `Test` folder, and also create a `Package.swift` file:

   ```
   $ swift package init --type executable
   ```

3. Update the dependencies section in `Package.swift` to include Vapor as a dependency, and also include Vapor in the target dependency for the `Hello` target:

   ```
   let package = Package(
     name: "Hello",
     dependencies: [
       .package(url: "https://github.com/vapor/vapor.git",
   .upToNextMajor(from: "2.4.4")),
     ],
     targets: [
       .target(
         name: "Hello",
         dependencies: ["Vapor"]),
     ]
   )
   ```

4. Now, we need to update the `main.swift` file under `Sources/Hello` folder with the example code on the `vapor.code` website by first importing Vapor:

   ```
   import Vapor
   ```

5. Next, we create a `Droplet`, which is a service container that gives you access to many of Vapor's facilities. It is responsible for registering routes, starting the server, appending middleware, and more:

   ```
   let drop = try Droplet()
   ```

*Getting Started with Vapor*

6. Then, we define the `GET` route on `/hello` and respond to all requests with `"Hello.world."`:

   ```
   drop.get("hello") { req in
     return "Hello, world."
   }
   ```

7. Finally, we start the app run, which will start our Vapor application on the default port, 8080. Because the server can throw an error when starting up, we need to catch the error using `try`:

   ```
   try drop.run()
   ```

8. Now that we have all of our code in `main.swift`, we are ready to build our code in the Terminal using the `swift build` command.

9. Then, run the application using the `swift run` command, and you will see the server started on port 8080, as printed on the console:

   ```
   $ swift run
   Could not load config files from:
   /Users/apatel/Downloads/Hello/Config/
   Try using the configDir flag
   ex: .build/debug/Run --configDir=/absolute/path/to/configs
   The default hash should be replaced before using in production.
   The default cipher should be replaced before using in production.
   No command supplied, defaulting to serve...
   Starting server on 0.0.0.0:8080
   ```

10. Open the browser and go to `http://localhost:8080/hello`, and you should see **Hello, world**.

That's it; you have built a bare-bones Vapor app that prints **Hello World**. Because we are using Vapor, we get a few more things out of the box for free; one is the **404 Not Found** page when you go to any URL other than `/hello`. It also prints warnings that the `configDir` is missing because, by default, application specific configurations are in the `Config` folder.

# Vapor toolbox

So far, we have learned how to build web servers and a lightweight Vapor application using the `swift package` command. This is good for small-scale projects, but when we embark on building a production-ready application, we need more powerful tools that can generate, build, and run our server-side web application. Luckily, Vapor provides us with a command-line tool that makes it easy to create a new server-side web application by generating the files and folders needed for the Vapor application. This command-line tool can also build our Vapor application by installing our dependencies and then compiling our application, and can also run our application. This tool is also capable of deploying to the server. In short, the command-line interface provides shortcuts and assistance for common tasks with our Vapor application. This command-line tool is called the **Vapor toolbox**.

## Installing the Vapor toolbox

To install the Vapor toolbox on macOS, all we need to do is follow these steps:

1. First, verify that you have the right version of Xcode, and whether it is compatible with Vapor, by running the following command in the Terminal:

    ```
    eval "$(curl -sL check.vapor.sh)"
    ```

2. You should see the following output if everything is compatible:

    ```
    bash-3.2$ eval "$(curl -sL check.vapor.sh)"
    ✓ Compatible Xcode
    ✓ Compatible with Vapor 2
    bash-3.2$
    ```

*Getting Started with Vapor*

3. Next, we need to install `brew`, if you do not have it installed already on your mac OS. `brew` is a package manager similar to `apt-get` in Debian based Linux OS. You can install it by following the instructions on the Homebrew website, `https://brew.sh`, or by running the following command in the Terminal:

   ```
   $ /usr/bin/ruby -e "$(curl -fsSL https://raw.githubusercontent.com/Homebrew/install/master/install)"
   ```

4. Once we have `brew` installed, we need to run these two commands to add the Vapor repository and update the list of packages available for installing `brew` locally:

   ```
   $ brew tap vapor/homebrew-tap
   $ brew update
   ```

5. Finally, we can install Vapor using the `brew install` command:

   ```
   $ brew install vapor
   ```

Once you are done, you can verify that you have the Vapor toolbox installed by running the `vapor version` command in the Terminal, and it will print the version of the Vapor toolbox that was just installed on your system.

# Vapor toolbox commands

Vapor toolbox is a versatile tool. It provides commands for a lot of things that you might want to do, from installing dependencies and building the application to deploying it in the cloud. To see a list of helpful commands, we need to type `vapor --help` in the Terminal:

```
$ vapor --help
Usage: vapor command

Join our Slack if you have questions, need help,
or want to contribute: http://vapor.team

Commands:
      new Creates a new Vapor application from a template.
          Use --template=repo/template for github templates
          Use --template=full-url-here.git for non github templates
          Use --web to create a new web app
          Use --auth to create a new authenticated API app
          Use --api (default) to create a new API
    build Compiles the application.
```

*Chapter 3*

```
        run Runs the compiled application.
      fetch Fetches the application's dependencies.
     update Updates your dependencies.
      clean Cleans temporary files--usually fixes
            a plethora of bizarre build errors.
       test Runs the application's tests.
      xcode Generates an Xcode project for development.
            Additionally links commonly used libraries.
    version Displays Vapor CLI version
      cloud Commands for interacting with Vapor Cloud.
     heroku Commands to help deploy to Heroku.
   provider Commands to help manage providers.

Use `vapor command --help` for more information on a command.
```

The following are the most commonly used commands:

- `vapor new AppName`: This is used to create a new Vapor application. It will create a new folder called `AppName` and generate project files and folders in it. Replace `AppName` with the name of the application you want to create. The new command also gives options to specify the template to clone from bypassing the `--template=` option, followed by the repository URL (`http://example.com/git-repo.git`) or GitHub path (`vapor/api-template`), which will create a new project based on the clone of that repo. You can also pass three options (`api`, `web`, `auth`) in the template option to create a new project based on three official templates provided by Vapor. As the names imply, these three templates are for making API based apps, web apps which render HTML, and auth based apps that support session based and token-based authentication, respectively.
- `vapor build`: This will download the dependencies from the git repo and also build them, and will build the Vapor application by compiling all of the code.
- `vapor run`: This will run the Vapor application.
- `vapor fetch`: This will fetch all of the application's dependencies from the git repo.
- `vapor update`: This will update your application specific dependencies.

[ 89 ]

- `vapor clean`: This will remove the `.build` folder, and also remove all of the dependencies, along with any temporary files.
- `vapor test`: This will run application-specific tests.
- `vapor xcode`: This will generate an Xcode project for the Vapor application, and will link all of the dependencies so that Xcode can build the application along with its dependencies.
- `vapor cloud`: This command will deploy the application to Vapor's own cloud service. It will ask a series of question to set up the cloud deployment account and to create the project and its dependencies, all from the command line.
- `vapor heroku`: This will configure your git repo to be able to push to Heroku for deployment and link the appropriate build pack, so that Heroku can build and run the Vapor application.
- `vapor provider`: This command manages the providers and makes it easy to add providers to your application.

## Creating a Vapor application using the toolbox

Now that we have the Vapor toolbox installed, we are ready to create our first Vapor application using the toolbox. You will find out how easy it is to create an app using the toolbox, as it scaffolds the files and folders needed to quickly get started. We will examine the files and folders and the application structure of our Vapor application to get a better understanding of how Vapor applications work. To get started, let's first create a Vapor application using the toolbox by following these steps:

1. Create a new application using the `vapor new` command in the Terminal. By default, the `vapor new` command uses the API template, but we will use the web template to create a `Greeter` example app that greets the user by dynamically generating a page based on the name passed in the URL:

   ```
   $ vapor new Greeter --template=ankurp/web-template
   ```

## Chapter 3

2. This will generate a `Greeter` folder and print the following in the console. Now, go into the folder in the Terminal:

   ```
   $ vapor new Greeter --template=ankurp/web-template
   Cloning Template [Done]
   Updating Package Name [Done]
   Initializing git repository [Done]
   ```

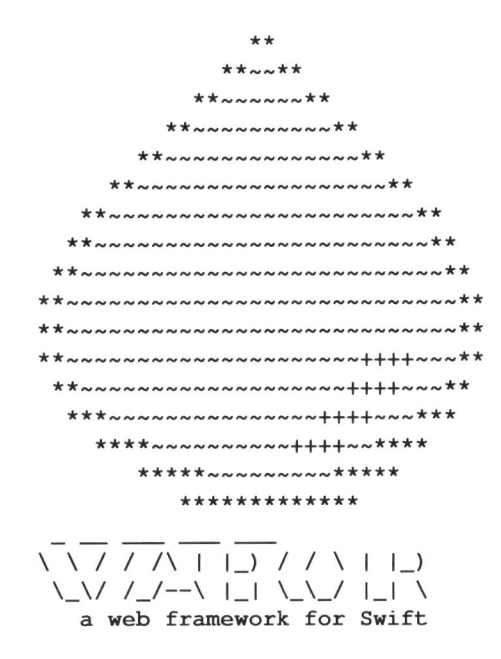

   ```
                          **
                        **~~**
                      **~~~~~~**
                    **~~~~~~~~~~**
                  **~~~~~~~~~~~~~~**
                **~~~~~~~~~~~~~~~~~~**
              **~~~~~~~~~~~~~~~~~~~~~~**
            **~~~~~~~~~~~~~~~~~~~~~~~~~~**
          **~~~~~~~~~~~~~~~~~~~~~~~~~~~~~~**
        **~~~~~~~~~~~~~~~~~~~~~~~~~~~~~~~~~~**
      **~~~~~~~~~~~~~~~~~~~~~~~~~~~~~~~~~~~~~~**
      **~~~~~~~~~~~~~~~~~~~~~~~~~~~~~~~~~~~~~~**
      **~~~~~~~~~~~~~~~~~~~~~~~~~~~++++~~~~**
        **~~~~~~~~~~~~~~~~~~~~~~~++++~~~**
         ***~~~~~~~~~~~~~~~~~~~++++~~~***
          ****~~~~~~~~~~~~~++++~~****
            *****~~~~~~~~~~*****
              *************

        _   __    ___   ___    ___
        \ \ / /  / _ \ | _ \  / _ \ | _ \
         \ V /  / /_\ \|  _/ | | | ||   /
          \_/  /_/ \_\|_|    \___/ |_|_\
               a web framework for Swift

            Project "Greeter" has been created.
        Type `cd Greeter` to enter the project directory.
    Use `vapor cloud deploy` to host your project for free!
                       Enjoy!
   ```

3. Now, we need to build the project before running it, which we can do by running the `build` command. This might take some time, as it will download the dependencies and compile all of the code:

   ```
   $ vapor build
   No .build folder, fetch may take a while...
   Fetching Dependencies [Done]
   Building Project [Done]
   ```

*Getting Started with Vapor*

4. Finally, we can start our Vapor application by running it using the `run` command. Do not worry about the warnings; they are there to let us know that we need to update the `crypto.json` config to make our Vapor application more secure, by specifying a custom cipher key:

```
$ vapor run
Running Greeter ...
The current hash key "0000000000000000" is not secure.
Update hash.key in Config/crypto.json before using in production.
Use `openssl rand -base64 <length>` to generate a random string.
The current cipher key
"AAAAAAAAAAAAAAAAAAAAAAAAAAAAAAAAAAAAAAAAAAA=" is not secure.
Update cipher.key in Config/crypto.json before using in production.
Use `openssl rand -base64 32` to generate a random string.
No command supplied, defaulting to serve...
Starting server on 0.0.0.0:8080
```

5. Now, open your browser and go to `http://localhost:8080/`, and you should be greeted by Vapor with a message saying **It Works;**.

Cool! We have built and run our first Vapor app. It was easy, thanks to Vapor's toolbox, as it handled the redundant task of making a folder and cloning a base repo to start from. You may have noticed that Vapor has commands similar to those we ran when building Swift packages from scratch using the Swift CLI. This is because the Vapor toolbox invokes the underlying Swift commands for some commands, and is a light wrapper for those commands.

This web template does more than just serve an **It Works** page. If you go to `http://localhost:8080/hello`, you will be greeted with a standard **Hello, World!** message, and if you add your name at the end of the URL (`http://localhost:8080/hello/John`), then you will be greeted with **Hello, John!** in your browser. Its's very interesting; so, let's dive into the project to see how it works.

# Vapor folder structure

The following is the list of files and folders generated by the Vapor toolbox. There are several files and folders, but the Vapor team has done a good job organizing them. The structure is similar to a Swift package, but there are some extra folders that help to organize the code, to make it easier to build features and debug issues:

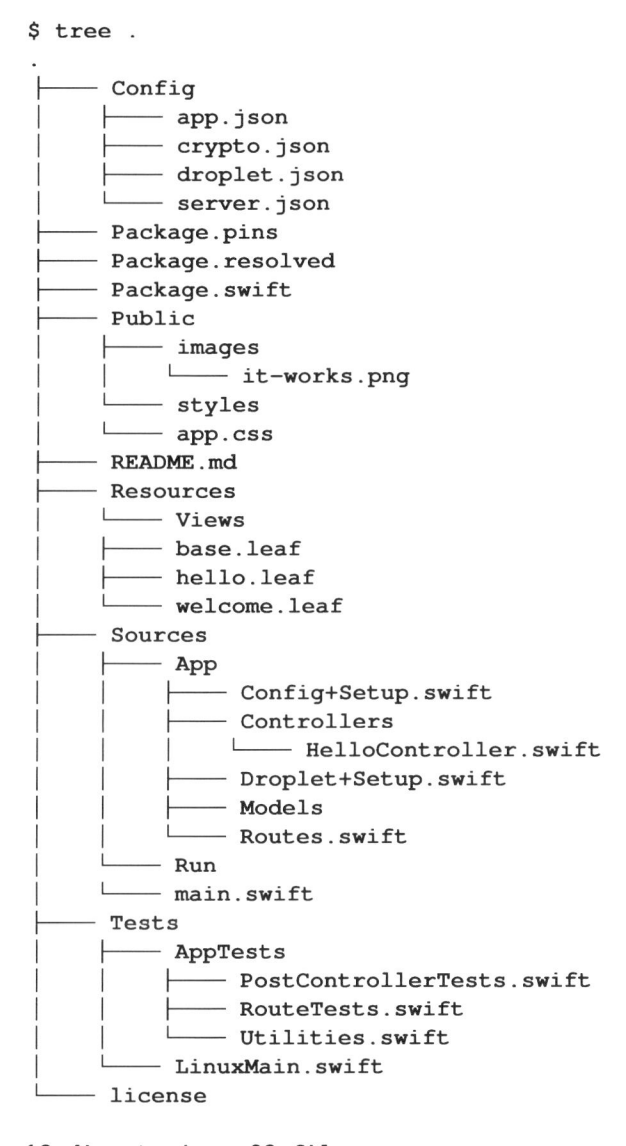

```
$ tree .
.
├── Config
│   ├── app.json
│   ├── crypto.json
│   ├── droplet.json
│   └── server.json
├── Package.pins
├── Package.resolved
├── Package.swift
├── Public
│   ├── images
│   │   └── it-works.png
│   ├── styles
│   └── app.css
├── README.md
├── Resources
│   └── Views
│       ├── base.leaf
│       ├── hello.leaf
│       └── welcome.leaf
├── Sources
│   ├── App
│   │   ├── Config+Setup.swift
│   │   ├── Controllers
│   │   │   └── HelloController.swift
│   │   ├── Droplet+Setup.swift
│   │   ├── Models
│   │   └── Routes.swift
│   └── Run
│       └── main.swift
├── Tests
│   ├── AppTests
│   │   ├── PostControllerTests.swift
│   │   ├── RouteTests.swift
│   │   └── Utilities.swift
│   └── LinuxMain.swift
└── license

13 directories, 23 files
```

## Vapor config

Vapor has a sophisticated configuration system that consists of configurations stored in the JSON file format. The configuration files are specified in the `Config` folder, and you can use these config files to set the server hostname or port, or even to configure the database you might be using. Vapor also supports environment specific configuration files, where you can have the application run on a different port in production than in development (locally), or specify different secrets, such as the database username and password for production environment for that development. By default, the Vapor template we cloned came with four config files:

- `app.json`
- `crypto.json`
- `droplet.json`
- `server.json`

`app.json` is a good place to specify any custom configurations you might want to use in your application. Vapor will not be using any of the configurations specified in this file, and is intended for specifying custom config values that are application specific. You can use this config to store a default shopping list for your API server, for users who are new to the app and do not have any `shopping-list` setup. Using the configuration, you can generate fake items for the default `shopping-list`, and the information about the items is now transferred into the config, which is easier to maintain and update than updating it in the code. A sample `app.json` config that contains the config for generating a shopping list may look like this:

```
{
  "shopping-list": {
    "name": "Groceries",
    "items": [{
      "name": "Apple"
    }, {
      "name": "Tomato"
    }]
  }
}
```

*Chapter 3*

The `crypto.json` config file contains the configuration for the type of hash function that is used by Vapor, or can be used by our application to generate a fixed sized token. These tokens cannot be mapped back to their original value, and are great for storing as passwords, as they cannot be mapped back to the actual password the user types. There are different kinds of hash functions, and to make them more secure, you want to specify a key that is unique for your application and will randomize the generated hash value even more, making your application secure. The `crypto.json` config also has a cipher config, which is useful for converting a value into an obfuscated value that makes it hard to map back to the original value without knowing the key and the method used to generated it. The configurations for the cipher can also be modified in this file. A sample config looks like this:

```
{
  "hash": {
    "method": "sha256",
    "encoding": "hex",
    "key": "0000000000000000"
  },
  "cipher": {
    "method": "aes256",
    "encoding": "base64",
    "key": "AAAAAAAAAAAAAAAAAAAAAAAAAAAAAAAAAAAAAAAAAAA="
  }
}
```

The configurations specific to the Vapor framework can be found in `droplet.json`. This file contains configs for the following:

- What kind of server to use. It defaults to using the server found in Vapor's Engine.
- What kind of request client to use. It defaults to using the client provided in Vapor's Engine.
- Where to log output. It defaults to printing in the console.
- Where the config for the hash function is. It uses `crypto.json` by default.
- Where the config for the cipher function is. It uses `crypto.json` by default.
- What view engine to use. For our web template, it defaults to Leaf.
- What middleware to use.
- What custom commands can be used as part of the Vapor toolbox.

*Getting Started with Vapor*

Lastly, there is `server.json`, which contains configurations for the server, such as what host to run on and where to start the server. You can also specify whether you want to use SSL for a secure connection to your server via HTTPS, instead of HTTP protocol. A default `server.json` config looks like this:

```
{
  "port": "$PORT:8080",
  "host": "0.0.0.0",
  "securityLayer": "none"
}
```

One thing to note is that you can fall back to the environment variable in this configuration by specifying the environment variable, prefixed with a `$` sign. For example, in `server.json`, you will notice that the port is set to `$PORT:8080`.

This implies that the port in our config file will be set to the value of the environment variable `PORT`, and if it does not exist, then it will default to 8080. This is really powerful, as you can have environment specific variables to change the configuration on a production environment, but have a default value for development to make it easier for someone to get started with your Vapor application.

Trying to access the Vapor configuration in your application is easy, as well. All you need to do is specify the path in your config file, and the type of value, and it will return that value. In this line of code, we are extracting the config stored inside of `app.json` inside of the `Config` folder. We are extracting the value called `name`, stored inside of the `shopping-list` property, and want to get it as a string type. We fall back to using `Groceries` as the default value if the `name` or `shopping-list` properties are not defined inside of the `app.json` config file:

```
let shoppingListName = drop.config["app", "shopping-list", "name"]?.string ?? "Groceries"
```

## Vapor droplet

A droplet is a service container that gives you access to many features provided by Vapor. It makes it easy to do the following tasks:

- Access configurations specified in the config files in the `Config` folder
- Make network requests using Vapor's engine client

- Register routes for your application so that you can specify which URL path gets served by what file in your application
- Add middleware to your application
- Use providers in your application, which are other Swift packages that follow certain provider protocols, making it easy to add functionality to your application
- Start the application

One droplet is created inside of a Vapor application, and a `Config` is passed to it when constructing a new instance of the `Droplet` class. In our project, you will find a file called `Config+Setup.swift`, which contains an extension of that `Config` class; and, as the name implies, the `Config` class contains configurations that will be used by the `Droplet` object to configure the application according to the configs specified. One such configuration in this object is related to providers, which, as mentioned, are other Swift packages that implement certain protocols needed by Vapor to extend the functionality of the application. For example, in our project, we add a `LeafProvider` to be able to render HTML views by calling `addProviders` inside of `setupProviders` in the `Config` class:

```
extension Config {
  public func setup() throws {
    Node.fuzzy = [JSON.self, Node.self]
    try setupProviders()
  }

  private func setupProviders() throws {
    try addProvider(LeafProvider.Provider.self)
  }
}
```

In our project, you will also find `Droplet+Setup.swift`, which is another class extension for the `Droplet` class, to add a new setup method. This is where the routes are configured by creating an instance of the `Routes` class, inside which the routes for our application are created:

```
extension Droplet {
  public func setup() throws {
    let routes = Routes(view)
    try collection(routes)
  }
}
```

Finally, in `main.swift`, which is the entry point of our application, `config.setup()` is called before it is passed into the `Droplet` initializer. This setup adds the `LeadProvider` to the config object before it is consumed by the `Droplet`. Then, `setup` is called on `Droplet` to configure the routes for the application before it is told to `run`, which boots up our server, and our Vapor application is ready to serve requests:

```
import App
let config = try Config()
try config.setup()
let drop = try Droplet(config)
try drop.setup()
try drop.run()
```

## Views

In Vapor, **Views** return HTML content. They can return pure HTML pages, or you can use renderers like Leaf to dynamically generate HTML that is returned as part of a request. All of the views reside in the `Resources/Views` folder, and, in our project, you will find three such files:

- `base.leaf`
- `hello.leaf`
- `welcome.leaf`

We will go into more detail about Leaf and HTML rendering in later chapters, but, in short, Leaf files are template files that are used by `LeafProvider` to generate HTML, and the HTML is generated by calling the `view` method on `droplet`, as such:

```
drop.get { req in
  return try self.view.make("welcome")
}

drop.get("hello") { req in
  return try view.make("hello", [
    "name": "World"
  ], for: req)
}
```

[ 98 ]

Resources such as Javascript, CSS, and image assets need to be placed in the `Public` folder. Any content in this folder will be accessible by just pointing to the path of the public resources. For example, going to `http://localhost:8080/styles/app.css` will load the CSS file from the `Public/styles` folder.

## Controllers

In Vapor, **Controllers** are similar to the Controllers in an iOS app, organizing the functionality and controlling the flow of each request from the user. They are responsible for getting the request and performing certain actions, such as getting data from the database, massaging it (if needed), and then rendering in HTML view or plain text before sending it back to the client. These controllers can be used to create RESTful resources.

> **TIP**: **Representational State Transfer (REST)** is a popular architectural style commonly used when building websites and APIs. It has five constraints: the web service needs to provide uniform interfaces, be stateless, be cacheable, be portable with the client-server model, and have a layered architecture.

In our project, we have one controller, `HelloController`, which is a RESTful controller that responds to two REST methods. We will cover REST in more detail in a later chapter, but think of REST as a limited set of actions that you can perform on a resource, such as getting all of the resources, getting one specific resource, updating one specific resource, or deleting a resource. In our `Hello` controller, we implemented two such actions. One was the `index` action, which returns a plain HTML page with **Hello World**, and another was the `show` action, which returns a dynamic page with the name appended, following `Hello`, based on the name passed in the URL route. The following is the code for these two actions, and, as you can see, we are calling `droplet.view`, which is passed into the initializer of the `HelloController` object and available as an instance variable:

```
/// GET /hello
func index(_ req: Request) throws -> ResponseRepresentable {
  return try view.make("hello", [
    "name": "World"
  ], for: req)
}

/// GET /hello/:string
func show(_ req: Request, _ string: String) throws -> ResponseRepresentable
{
  return try view.make("hello", [
    "name": string
```

# Getting Started with Vapor

```
    ], for: req)
  }
```

Controllers at the end of each action need to return an object that conforms to the type `ResponseRepresentable`. This protocol makes the consumer of the API more flexible, as they can return any object that conforms to the protocol of `ResponseRepresentable`. Vapor extends `String` and a few other classes, like `JSON`, to extend the protocol so that you can return them directly to the controller; `drop.view.make` itself returns an object of type `View`, which conforms to `ResponseRepresentable` by implementing the `makeResponse` method:

```
extension View: ResponseRepresentable {
  public func makeResponse() -> Response {
    return Response(status: .ok, headers: [
      "Content-Type": "text/html; charset=utf-8"
    ], body: .data(data))
  }
}
```

## Summary

In this chapter, we covered a lot of topics related to Vapor, and we hope that by now you have a better understanding of what Vapor is and how it is more than just a web server. We also learned about some of the packages that Vapor depends on, such as the Vapor Engine, and how we can build a lightweight server without having to use Vapor if our use case is not to build a large scale web application. We also learned how easy it is to support web sockets using the Engine. Then, we dove into building a Vapor application from scratch to understand that a Vapor application is nothing but a Swift executable package. We then learned about the Vapor toolbox, and how it makes it easy to bootstrap a Vapor project using a command-line tool. Lastly, we examined a Vapor project in detail to understand how it all works and how it is structured so that we have a better understanding of how to write code for our application using Vapor's conventions.

In the next chapter, we will start building our Shopping List API application using Vapor, with the help of the toolbox. We will cover providers in more detail and look into one of the providers created by the Vapor team, called **Fluent**, which makes it easy to fetch and save data in the database.

# 4
# Configuring Providers, Fluent, and Databases

In the previous chapter, we learned about Vapor and its packages, as well as how to build a basic web server using those packages. We learned about the Vapor toolbox and how to use the toolbox to Bootstrap a new Vapor application. We also learned about the general structure of a Vapor application. In this chapter, we will look into Providers, which are packages that can be imported into your Vapor application and provide it with additional functionality. In particular, we will examine the Fluent provider and learn about what Fluent is and its purpose in Vapor applications. We will also touch upon databases, and one database, in particular, called MongoDB in this chapter. This chapter will lay the foundation of our server-side API for the Shopping List app we built in `Chapter 2`, *Creating the Native App* and will connect all of the concepts mentioned in the chapter with our application. More specifically, in this chapter, we will learn the following:

- How to Bootstrap an API based Vapor application?
- What is a Vapor Provider, and how to use it in our application?
- How to build a Provider of our own?
- What is Fluent, and how to use the Fluent provider?
- Databases and MongoDB, and how to get started with them
- How to connect your application to MongoDB to fetch and save data in the database?

# Shopping List API Vapor app

We will start with a new Vapor application, which will act as an API server for our iOS application. We will keep building on top of this application in the next few chapters to learn about different aspects of Vapor; towards the end, we will have a fully functional server that will serve as both an API and a web server, showing our Shopping List on the iOS app and also on the web.

To get started, we will begin with an official API template provided by Vapor. We will follow the following steps to Bootstrap our project and start coding it using Xcode:

1. Open the Terminal and create a new API based Vapor application using the toolbox:

    ```
    $ vapor new ShoppingListServer --template=ankurp/api-template
    ```

2. This will create the new application based on the API template. Go into this folder in the Terminal and create an Xcode project file using the following command:

    ```
    $ vapor xcode -y
    ```

3. The preceding command will create an Xcode project file for the Vapor application and open up the Xcode project. We can now write our code in the Xcode IDE, instead of using a plain text editor to write code for our Vapor application. To run our Vapor application, we need to switch the **Scheme** to **Run**, and make sure that **My Mac** is selected before clicking the play button to start our server:

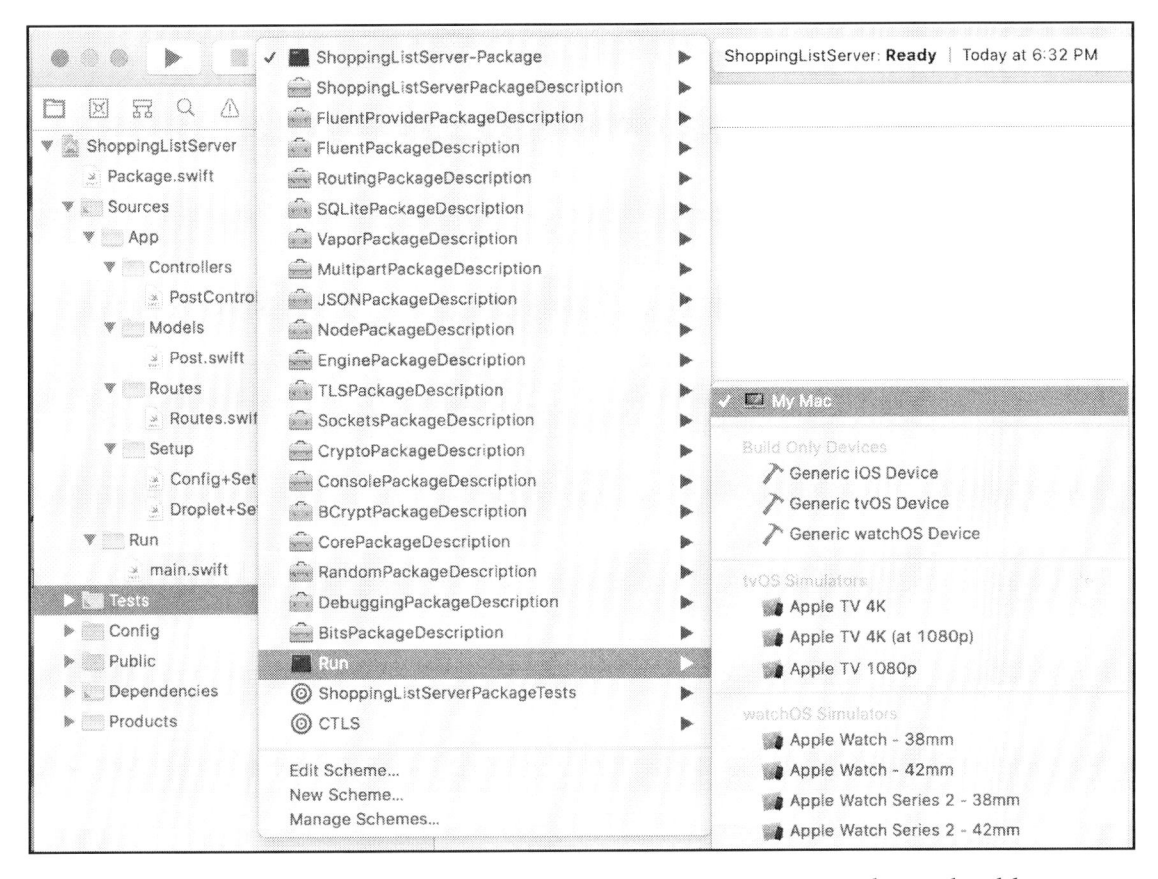

4. Open the browser to `http://localhost:8080/hello` and you should see a JSON object in the browser:

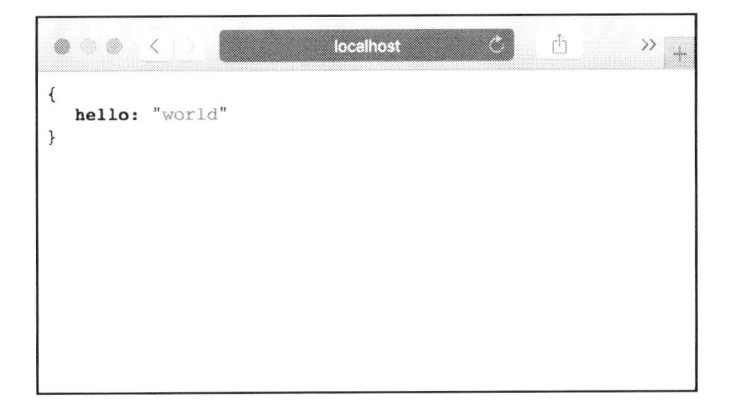

*Configuring Providers, Fluent, and Databases*

We now have a base API server project running and it returns a JSON response. We will use this template to build our shopping list server, but before we modify the existing files in the project, let's see how the sample code in the project works.

# What are Providers?

**Providers** are Swift packages that extend the functionality of a Vapor application. This is done by implementing the Provider protocol, which Vapor expects all Providers to have. The protocol is simple and is shown in the following code snippet:

```
public protocol Provider {
    static var repositoryName: String { get }
    static var publicDir: String { get }
    static var viewsDir: String { get }

    init(config: Config) throws
    func boot(_ config: Config) throws
    func boot(_ droplet: Droplet) throws
    func beforeRun(_ droplet: Droplet) throws
}
```

If you have a class that implements this Provider protocol, then you can use that class as a Provider in your Vapor application. Since you have `config` and `droplet` being passed into your Provider, you have an entry point to extend the Vapor application by adding additional routes and you also have a life cycle method that gets invoked before `droplet.run()` is called, in case you need to perform an action before the server starts. There are abundant Provider packages on GitHub; the convention is to suffix the repo name with `-provider` and suffix the package name with `Provider`. For example, the Leaf provider that was used in the template web project in the previous chapter is installed using the URL `https://github.com/vapor/leaf-provider` and it has the package name `LeafProvider`.

# Building your first Provider

To understand how Providers work in practice, we will go through the exercise of building a simple Provider of our own and adding it to our application. The Provider that we build will be a `HealthcheckProvider` that provides a health check route for our application and returns a success 200 status code with a JSON response, indicating that the server is running and is healthy.

To get started on building the Provider, we will create a new Swift package, publish it, and then import it into our Shopping List Vapor application. So, let's start building out first Provider by following these steps:

1. Create a folder, call it `HealthcheckProvider`, and open the folder in the Terminal.
2. Once you are in the `HealthcheckProvider` folder, run the following command in the Terminal to initialize a Swift package:

    ```
    $ swift package init
    ```

3. Inside `Package.swift`, add Vapor to the dependencies section:

    ```
    dependencies: [
      .package(url: "https://github.com/vapor/vapor.git",
    .upToNextMajor(from: "2.4.4")),
    ],
    ```

4. Also, add `"Vapor"` as the dependency for the `HealthcheckProvider` target under the targets section:

    ```
    .target(
        name: "HealthcheckProvider",
        dependencies: ["Vapor"]),
    ```

5. Now, go to the `Sources/HealthcheckProvider` folder and rename the `HealthcheckProvider.swift` file to `Provider.swift`.

6. Once the file is renamed, we can start adding code to our provider. To make a Provider, we need to follow the Provider protocol defined by Vapor. This is easy to do; we implement the `Vapor.Provider` protocol in our `Provider` class as follows:

    ```
    import Vapor
    public final class Provider: Vapor.Provider {
    ```

7. Then, we need to add the `repositoryName` static variable in our class, as required by the Provider protocol; this will be the name of our Provider. We will also define a variable called `healthcheckUrl` that will hold the route for our `healthcheck` endpoint:

    ```
    public static let repositoryName: String = "healthcheck-provider"
    public var healthCheckUrl: String?
    ```

[ 105 ]

*Configuring Providers, Fluent, and Databases*

8. Next, we will add an initializer for our class, which will take a `Config` object and set the `healthcheckUrl` based on the health check URL defined in the `healthcheck.json` files under the `Config` folder:

    ```
    public init(config: Config) throws {
      if let healthCheckUrl = config["healthcheck", "url"]?.string {
        self.healthCheckUrl = healthCheckUrl
      }
    }
    ```

9. Next, we need to define the `boot` method, as defined in the protocol. Since we do not do anything in this method, we can leave the body of the method empty. This method is called after the Provider has been initialized:

    ```
    public func boot(_ config: Config) throws {}
    ```

10. There is another `boot` method that needs to be defined and this is called by the droplet when it is initialized. The `Droplet` object is passed into this `boot` method and it is a good place to define our `healthcheck` route:

    ```
    public func boot(_ drop: Droplet) {
      guard let healthCheckUrl = self.healthCheckUrl else {
        return drop.console.warning("MISSING: healthcheck.json config in Config folder. Healthcheck URL not addded.")
      }
      drop.get(healthCheckUrl) { req in
        return try Response(status: .ok, json: JSON(["status": "up"]))
      }
    }
    ```

    In this method, we check if `healthcheckUrl` was initialized, as it can be undefined due to missing `healthcheck.json` file, which contains the URL for the `healthcheck` endpoint. If we have a value for `healthcheckUrl`, then we define a GET route in our application at that URL path which responds with a JSON response.

11. The last protocol method we need to define is the `beforeRun` method, which is called before the droplet starts running. Since we do not have anything to do, we define an empty function:

    ```
    public func beforeRun(_ drop: Droplet) {}
    ```

12. Now, let's compile our library. We should be able to build our Provider without any error using the `swift build` command in the Terminal.

Great! We just built our first Provider. Before we publish this to the GitHub repository, let's add a test to make sure out library works as it should. This is easy to do, as our package comes with a `Test` folder, where we write our tests. To start writing a test for our Provider, we need to follow the following steps:

1. Add `Vapor` and `Testing` modules to your `HealthcheckProviderTests` target in the `Package.swift` file. We will be using Vapor and `Testing` modules in our test:

    ```
    .testTarget(
      name: "HealthcheckProviderTests",
      dependencies: ["HealthcheckProvider", "Vapor", "Testing"]),
    ```

2. Then, in your test Swift file in the `Tests/HealthcheckProviderTests` folder, import Vapor and `Testing` modules by adding the import statements to the top of the file:

    ```
    @testable import Vapor
    import Testing
    ```

3. Then, we override the `setUp` method in the test class so that we can have the `Testing` module trigger a failure when Vapor's testing module detects a failure in any of the assertions for the tests we write:

    ```
    override func setUp() {
      Testing.onFail = XCTFail
    }
    ```

4. Then, remove the sample `testExample` method in the file, as we will add our own `testHealthcheck` method that will create a new Vapor app using our health check Provider and verify that the health check returns a success status response with a JSON object. In the following code, we first create a config object and set a `healthcheck.url` value in that config. Then, we add our `healthcheck` Provider to our `config` and create a new Vapor app by initializing a `droplet` with this `config`. To test that everything is working correctly, we make a request and test that the response is good and has the required JSON property and value we are looking for:

    ```
    func testHealthcheck() {
      var config = try! Config(arguments: ["vapor", "--env=test"])
      try! config.set("healthcheck.url", "healthcheck")
    ```

[ 107 ]

*Configuring Providers, Fluent, and Databases*

```
        try! config.addProvider(HealthcheckProvider.Provider.self)
        let drop = try! Droplet(config)
        background {
          try! drop.run()
        }

        try! drop
          .testResponse(to: .get, at: "healthcheck")
          .assertStatus(is: .ok)
          .assertJSON("status", equals: "up")
    }
```

5. Finally, we need to update `allTests` to point to the `testHealtcheck` method we added and remove the sample `testExample`:

```
static var allTests = [
  ("testHealthcheck", testHealthcheck),
]
```

6. Now, let's run the test using the `swift test` command in the Terminal. You should see the following output and see the test pass:

```
$ swift test
Compile Swift Module 'HealthcheckProviderTests' (1 sources)
Linking ./.build/x86_64-apple-
macosx10.10/debug/HealthcheckProviderPackageTests.xctest/Contents/M
acOS/HealthcheckProviderPackageTests
Test Suite 'All tests' started at 2017-11-13 19:39:47.230
Test Suite 'HealthcheckProviderPackageTests.xctest' started at
2017-11-13 19:39:47.230
Test Suite 'ProviderTests' started at 2017-11-13 19:39:47.230
Test Case '-[HealthcheckProviderTests.ProviderTests
testHealthcheck]' started.
Could not load config files from:
/Users/apatel/Downloads/HealthcheckProvider/Config/
Try using the configDir flag
ex: .build/debug/Run --configDir=/absolute/path/to/configs
The default hash should be replaced before using in production.
The default cipher should be replaced before using in production.
No command supplied, defaulting to serve...
GET /healthcheck
Starting server on 0.0.0.0:8080
Test Case '-[HealthcheckProviderTests.ProviderTests
testHealthcheck]' passed (0.098 seconds).
Test Suite 'ProviderTests' passed at 2017-11-13 19:39:47.328.
    Executed 1 test, with 0 failures (0 unexpected) in 0.098 (0.098)
seconds
```

```
Test Suite 'HealthcheckProviderPackageTests.xctest' passed at
2017-11-13 19:39:47.328.
    Executed 1 test, with 0 failures (0 unexpected) in 0.098 (0.098)
seconds
Test Suite 'All tests' passed at 2017-11-13 19:39:47.328.
    Executed 1 test, with 0 failures (0 unexpected) in 0.098 (0.099)
seconds
```

You have done a great job making your first Provider and writing tests to verify that it works. Now, you can publish this to GitHub, or any git repository if you want to, as we will be using this Provider in our Shopping List Vapor application later. To publish, all you need to do is complete the following steps:

1. Initialize the git repo using the `git init` command
2. Create a repo on GitHub and call it `healthcheck-provider` to follow the naming convention of Vapor Providers and to make it easy to install Providers from the command line using Vapor's toolbox
3. Add the URL to the remote repo using the following command; replace `username` with your GitHub username:

   ```
   git remote add origin git@github.com:username/healthcheck-
   provider.git
   ```

4. Commit and tag the code using the following two commands:

   ```
   $ git add ./
   $ git commit -m "Initial Commit"
   $ git tag 1.0.0
   ```

5. Finally, push and publish the package using the `git push origin master --tags;`command.

## Exercise time

You have done a great job writing your first tests for your Swift package. Now it's time for a small exercise. We just added a test to verify that our Provider docs what it is supposed to do when we have configured everything correctly. However, we have not tested the cases where the `healthcheck.json` config file is missing, or where the config for the `healthcheck.url` is not specified. For this exercise, write another test that verifies that the server starts up when the `healthcheck` config is not specified and that it returns a **404 Not Found** when making a `GET` request to the `/healthcheck` route.

# Adding a Provider

Let's switch over to the `ShoppingListServer` project now. Adding a Provider is simple and is done in a few steps. For that, we need to first update our `Package.swift`, add our Provider in our `Config` setup file and add any config files that are needed in the `Config` folder. The following are the specific steps that you need to take to add a Provider to your Vapor application:

1. Open up the `Package.swift` file and add the `Provider` package to the `dependencies` section. Replace username with the github username that you used to publish your Swift package:

    ```
    .package(url: "https://github.com/username/healthcheck-
       provider.git", .upToNextMajor(from: "1.0.0")),
    ```

2. Under `App` target, add `HealthcheckProvider` as a dependency, along with other dependencies:

    ```
    .target(name: "App", dependencies: ["Vapor", "FluentProvider",
    "HealthcheckProvider"],
    ```

3. Open the Terminal and go to the root level of your project folder where you just edited the `Package.swift` file and run the following command to pull the new dependency we added and also to update our Xcode project file. Running this command is required every time you make changes to our `Package.swift` file to update the dependencies and our Xcode project so we can import the dependency without any errors in our code.

    3. `$ vapor xcode -y`

4. Now, open the `Config+Setup.swift` file under the `Sources/App/Setup` folder and import the `HealthcheckProvider` module by adding it to the top:

    ```
    import HealthcheckProvider
    ```

5. Now we need to tell the config object to add our Provider by adding this line inside of the `setupProviders` method:

    ```
    try addProvider(HealthcheckProvider.Provider.self)
    ```

6. Lastly, we need to add a new file called `healthcheck.json` under the `Config` folder in your project. Add the following JSON, which will tell our Provider to use the `url` specified in the JSON file as the URL for the `healthcheck` route:

   ```
   {
     "url": "/healthcheck.html"
   }
   ```

7. Now, we need to update our Xcode project by running the `vapor xcode -y` command in the Terminal, inside of our project folder.
8. We can confirm that everything is working by building and running the project in Xcode and going to `http://localhost:8080/healthcheck.html`; here, we have extended our application to add a new `healthcheck` route using the `HealthcheckProvider` we just created:

```
{"status":"up"}
```

Great job if you were able to get this far. You not only have an understanding of a Provider, but have also just created a Provider and published it on GitHub, and also consumed it in your Vapor application. Now, we will move on to understanding one of the Providers that will be very useful for our application and that is the `FluentProvider` that is already included in our application.

# Getting started with databases

Any large scale web application needs some kind of storage to maintain its state. Saving the state as a raw text file or in binary file format, like we did in the Shopping List iOS app with the help of `UserDefaults`, is not ideal and does not scale or perform well. To solve this problem, databases were created, which are collections of tables that can save data in a structured format, with the ability to retrieve and save data at very high speeds. Also, databases decouple data from our application and data can be transferred or consumed by another application, making the data portable. You can create relationships between tables inside of a database, just like you would create relationships in between objects in object-oriented programming languages. Such databases are known as **relational databases**. This helps us organize data just like we would in object-oriented programming languages and makes it easy for us to map the database tables to the relations we have in our application, such as a Shopping List that has multiple items.

To manage these databases, you require an application called a **database management system**, which handles retrieving, inserting, updating, and deleting data from the database tables. They also handle the creation and deletion of tables and provide the functionality to enforce data types for the columns. There are several database management systems; these are the names of some of them:

- MySQL
- PostgreSQL
- MongoDB
- SQLite

Databases are collections of structured tables and have schemas which define the column types and the constraints on those columns, such as a column being left empty or needing to default to a certain value if left blank. Recently, there has been a rise in NoSQL based databases, which are less rigid and allow the insertion of data that can be structured or unstructured. This makes developing more flexible when the structure of our data may change or when we are not aware of what information we need to store yet. MongoDB is one of those NoSQL databases and it can be queried to fetch and store data on a large scale.

# What is MongoDB?

**MongoDB** is a document-oriented database that stores documents in collections, just like how a traditional database stores rows in a table. The stored documents are in a JSON-like format, and a schema can be defined on a collection to restrict the documents to having certain attributes or properties present or to be of a certain data type. It has its own query language, which is different from SQL, but it is easy to understand and pick up. Because MongoDB is a NoSQL database, it has few benefits. One such benefit is that it is easy to get started, as it is schema-less by default; looking at the data returned from the query, it is easy to understand, as it is structured as a JSON object with key-value pairs. MongoDB is also scalable, with support for splitting the database using a technique called **sharding**, which is hard to do with traditional SQL databases.

# How to install and run MongoDB

In our Vapor application, we will use MongoDB to store our Shopping List and items data. To get started with MongoDB, we first need to install it on our system, which is easy to do by taking the following steps:

1. Install `mongodb` using the `homebrew` package installed on macOS, or, if you are on Debian based Linux, install it using the `apt-get` package:

   ```
   $ brew install mongodb
   Updating Homebrew...
   ==> Downloading
   https://homebrew.bintray.com/bottles/mongodb-3.4.10.sierra.bottl
   ######################################################################
   ##### 100.0%
   ==> Pouring mongodb-3.4.10.sierra.bottle.tar.gz
   ==> Caveats
   To have launchd start mongodb now and restart at login:
     brew services start mongodb
   Or, if you don't want/need a background service you can just run:
     mongod --config /usr/local/etc/mongod.conf
   ==> Summary
     /usr/local/Cellar/mongodb/3.4.10: 19 files, 287.8MB
   ```

2. You have the option to always start `mongodb` and have it run in the background using the following code:

   ```
   $ brew services start mongodb
   ```

Alternatively, you have the option to not run it as a background service by using this command, but you need to make sure to start it up every time you need to connect to mongodb:

```
$ mongod --config /usr/local/etc/mongod.conf
```

3. To verify that mongodb is running correctly on your machine, you can run the following command in the Terminal; it connects to the mongodb instance running locally on your machine:

```
$ mongo
MongoDB shell version v3.4.10
connecting to: mongodb://127.0.0.1:27017
MongoDB server version: 3.4.10
Server has startup warnings:
2017-11-14T15:08:44.634-0500 I CONTROL  [initandlisten]
2017-11-14T15:08:44.634-0500 I CONTROL  [initandlisten] ** WARNING: Access control is not enabled for the database.
2017-11-14T15:08:44.634-0500 I CONTROL  [initandlisten] ** Read and write access to data and configuration is unrestricted.
2017-11-14T15:08:44.634-0500 I CONTROL  [initandlisten]
2017-11-14T15:08:44.634-0500 I CONTROL  [initandlisten]
2017-11-14T15:08:44.634-0500 I CONTROL  [initandlisten] ** WARNING: soft rlimits too low. Number of files is 256, should be at least 1000
```

Great! We now have mongodb running locally. Now, we can go ahead and start using it in our Vapor application, but before we do so, let's understand a few more buzzwords.

# What are ORM and Fluent?

**ORM** stands for **object-relational mapping** and is a very important technique in application development, especially for those applications that interact with databases. Traditionally, to store or retrieve data from the database, you need to write SQL, which stands for the **structured query language**. After executing an SQL query, you get back a table full of data that needs to be mapped to objects of a certain class, to make it easy to interact with the raw data that is returned from the database.

For example, if we have a table full of Shopping Lists, then it would be good if we got back an array of objects of the type `ShoppingList`, instead of an array of dictionary objects containing column names and column value key pairs. Using a mapping technique, we can convert this raw data stored in the database into an object of a certain type, and vice versa. This allows us to write more concise and elegant code, without having to worry about how to convert a row of data into an object of a certain type. This mapping technique is called ORM and Vapor's team has done a great job of creating an ORM for Swift called **Fluent**.

Fluent is Swift's ORM, which works with both SQL and NoSQL databases. It provides an easy to use API for working with databases and supports simple operations like creating, reading, updating, and deleting, and more advanced operations like joins. Fluent is also decoupled from Vapor, so it can be used by other Swift applications, as it is its own Swift package, just like Vapor's Engine. To use Fluent in our Vapor application, we need to use `FluentProvider`, which is installed by default in our API template project.

## Fluent in action

To understand how ORM and Fluent work, let's see how we can build models for our Shopping List app by creating our first model called `Item`. Using `FluentProvider`, we will be able to create, fetch, save, update, and delete an item object in any database we want, as long as there is a database driver available for the database we plan on using. In this exercise, we will learn to build a small Swift package, to learn how Fluent works and to understand how to save and retrieve items from the SQLite database, which is easy to get started with. To get started, follow these steps:

1. Create a new folder called `FluentDemo` and open the folder in the Terminal.
2. Initialize a Swift package using the `swift package init --type executable`.
3. Once the package is initialized, add the Fluent package by adding it to `Package.swift`:

    ```
    .package(url: "https://github.com/vapor/fluent.git", from: "2.4.2"),
    ```

4. Also, add `Fluent` to the dependencies section of the `FluentDemo` target.

*Configuring Providers, Fluent, and Databases*

5. Now, open `main.swift` inside of `Sources/FluentDemo`, and remove the sample code, and add the following to the top of the file. This will import the `Fluent` module:

   ```
   import Fluent
   ```

6. Then, we will create a driver, which is the way Fluent communicates with the database. Fluent comes with `SQLiteDriver` by default, which lets you work with an SQLite database. We then create a database object by initializing it with the driver:

   ```
   let driver = try SQLiteDriver(path: "main.sqlite")
   let database = Database(driver)
   ```

7. Now, we need to create our model class. We will start by creating the `Item` class first, and it will implement the Entity protocol, which is defined in `Fluent` modules. Fluent can only persist objects that implement this protocol, which lets us map the values from the database into an item object and map an item object into a database row object:

   ```
   final class Item: Entity {
   ```

8. We will add three instance variables. The first two should be familiar, but the third one is unique to Fluent and is required to store additional attributes that are only present in the database, such as ID:

   ```
   var name: String
   var isChecked: Bool
   let storage = Storage()
   ```

9. We create an initializer for our class, which takes in two parameters:

   ```
   init(name: String, isChecked: Bool = false) {
     self.name = name
     self.isChecked = isChecked
   }
   ```

[ 116 ]

10. We now implement the Entity protocol methods to let Fluent perform the mapping:

    ```
    init(row: Row) throws {
      name = try row.get("name")
      isChecked = try row.get("isChecked")
    }

    func makeRow() throws -> Row {
      var row = Row()
      try row.set("name", name)
      try row.set("isChecked", isChecked)
      return row
    }
    ```

11. We also need to make our `Item` implement `Preparation` protocol, which is defined in Fluent. Preparations let you perform certain actions in the database, such as creating a database table (if it is not created already) or deleting the table if we need to delete the class in the future. This is easy to do; we have our `Item` implement the two protocol methods prepare and revert as follows:

    ```
    extension Item: Preparation {
      static func prepare(_ database: Database) throws {
        try database.create(self) { items in
          items.id()
          items.string("name")
          items.bool("isChecked")
        }
      }

      static func revert(_ database: Database) throws {
        try database.delete(self)
      }
    }
    ```

12. As you can see, we created the table in `prepare` and defined the column names and types. We also specified deletion of the table on revert.

13. Now, we need to hook everything up so that the `prepare` is called every time the code is run, to ensure the table is present. Don't worry the `prepare` is smart enough to make sure that it does not create an item's table if it already exists. We also need to tell `Item` what database to use to query. Both of these are done as follows:

    ```
    try database.prepare([Item.self])
    Item.database = database
    ```

## Creating an item

Now that we have all of the code written out, we can see how Fluent makes it easy to create a new item in the database using its high-level API. We will test that everything works by first creating an item and saving it to the database:

1. We need to add the following code towards the end of `main.swift`:

    ```
    let item = Item(name: "Apple")
    try item.save()
    ```

2. Now, let's run this code using the `swift run` command, and you will see the database file called `main.sqlite` created inside of your `FluentDemo` folder. This is the database file where the item's tables, along with its data, is stored.

3. We can check that it saved the data in the database by opening the `sqlite` file in the Terminal using the `sqlite3` command as such `sqlite3 main.sqlite`:

    ```
    $ sqlite3 main.sqlite
    SQLite version 3.19.3 2017-06-27 16:48:08Enter ".help" for usage hints.
    sqlite> .tables
    fluent items
    sqlite> select * from items;
    1|Apple|0
    ```

The previous command lets us explore data stored in the `main.sqlite` database file. We first run the `.tables` command to list all of the tables and then execute a SQL query to print all of the rows in the `items` table. As you can see, the data stored in the database contains an `id` in the first column, which is numeric. This `id` is used to find a specific item quickly. In the second column, we have the name. The third column contains the boolean value for `isChecked` that is represented as `0` for false and `1` for true.

## Updating an item

To perform an update operation, it is as simple as modifying the object and calling the `save` method on it again, to update that item in the database with its new values:

```
item.name = "Orange"
try item.save() // This will update the name to Orange in database
```

## Getting all items

Fluent provides convenient methods on the `Item` class so that we can perform a query on the `Item` collection or table as a whole. To fetch all of the records from the database from a specific table, all we need to do is invoke `all` of its class, as seen here:

```
try print(Item.all())
```

The preceding code will fetch all of the rows from the item's table, convert the table into an array of item type objects and print it in the console.

## Finding an item

The quickest way to get a specific item from the database is to find it by ID. We can find an item by passing the ID into the static `find` method on our item class. Try this out by adding the following to the end of the `main.swift` file and running it. This code will print **Apple** in the console:

```
try print(Item.find(item.id)!.name)
```

## Finding items using filter

Fluent makes it easy to find multiple items using the `filter` method, which is similar to performing a WHERE clause in SQL. To see how this works, add the following line to the bottom of the `main.swift` file and it will print the names of all items that are unchecked:

```
let uncheckedItems = try Item.makeQuery().filter("isChecked", .equals, false).all()
uncheckedItems.forEach { print($0.name) }
```

You can also chain the filter methods so that you can filter based on two or more columns:

```
let uncheckedItems = try Item.makeQuery().filter("isChecked", .equals,
false).filter("name", .equals, "Apple").all()
uncheckedItems.forEach { print($0.name) }
```

## Deleting an item

To delete, it is as simple as finding an object and invoking the `delete` method on it:

```
let item = Item.find(1)
try item.delete()
```

## Counting items

To get the count of items in the table, just invoke the `count` method on the `Item` class, as follows:

```
let count = try Item.count()
print(count)
```

We hope this helps you to understand how powerful Fluent is and how it uses the ORM technique to map objects into rows in the database to map data from the database into objects used in our program or app. Using Fluent, we can write at a high level and do not need to learn SQL or how to construct queries to perform basic **Create**, **Read**, **Update**, and **Delete** (**CRUD**) actions.

# Relations in Fluent

Relations are a way to connect two different models. In object-oriented programming, relations help us architect a software solution by relating it to the real world. Similarly, we need to create relations in the database to model the way we write code in object-oriented programming languages. Luckily, most of the databases support relations and are often referred to as relational databases.

For example, we already have two models, one called `ShoppingList` and one called `Item`, that have a relation between each other in our iOS app. Each `ShoppingList` has many items and each `Item` belongs to a `ShoppingList`. These relations are represented in our code in the form of an array of `Item` objects, or as a reference variable pointing to the `ShoppingList`. In databases, we cannot save data in such a format, as we have different tables for different models. So, let's see how we can represent this in the database tables and what types of relations we can create.

There are three kinds of relationships between models; they are as follows:

- One to one
- One to many
- Many to many

Let's look into these relationships in detail.

## One to one (parent-child relation)

A one to one relation is when a model relates to one, and only one, other models. An example of such a relation would be that a Person model has one Government ID, and a Government ID can belong to one, and only one, Person. In this relation, both models have only one reference to each other, and no more. In Vapor, this type of relation is known as a Parent/Child relation. The database table for such a relation would look like this:

`Persons`:

| Column Name | Column Type |
| --- | --- |
| id | Identifier |
| name | String |

`government_ids`:

| Column Name | Column Type |
| --- | --- |
| id | Identifier |
| number | Int |
| person_id | Identifier (Foreign Key) |

The following is how we would express this relation in our two model classes:

```
extension GovernmentId {
  let personId: Identifier
  var person: Parent<GovernmentId, Person> {
    return parent(id: personId)
  }
}

extension Person {
  var governmentId: GovernmentId? {
    return (children() as Children<Person, GovernmentId>).first()
  }
}
```

Here, we are using the `Parent` and `Children` classes that are defined in the Fluent module. These classes are wrappers to help Vapor query the database correctly and get related model from the database correctly. There are also two helper methods, provided by the Entity class and called **parent** and **children**, that perform those database queries to fetch the related model.

## One to many

A one to many relation is a type of relation where one model object has many objects of another model type. This is easy to relate to, as our Shopping List app has this kind of relation. In the app, we have one shopping list, which has many items; but an item belongs in only one Shopping List. The table would look similar to a one to one relation, and, for our Shopping List example, it would contain the following two tables:

`shopping_lists`:

| Column Name | Column Type |
| --- | --- |
| id | Identifier |
| name | String |

items:

| Column Name | Column Type |
|---|---|
| id | Identifier |
| name | String |
| is_checked | Boolean |
| shopping_list_id | Identifier (Foreign Key) |

This kind of relation can be represented in the code as follows:

```
extension Item {
  let shoppingListId: Identifier
  var shoppingList: Parent<Item, ShoppingList> {
    return parent(id: shoppingListId)
  }
}

extension ShoppingList {
  var items: Children<ShoppingList, Item> {
    return children()
  }
}
```

This type of relation is known as a Parent/Children relation in Vapor, and, looking at the code, we can see why. Just like a Parent/Child relation, the item has one parent; but unlike the previous example, a shopping list has many children, which are items of the `Item` type, and we get them by simply calling the `children` method on the `ShoppingList` entity.

Another example of this relation is an employee/manager relationship, where an employee has only one manager, but a manager has many employees to manage.

## Many to many

Many to many is the last type of relation that can exist, where one model object can relate to many other objects of another model type and vice versa. An example of this would be an employee working on many projects and a project having many employees. This kind of relation is known as the Sibling relation in Vapor.

A pivot table is needed; this is a table that stores the mapping of one model to many models of other types, and vice versa. The database tables for this relation would look like this:

employees:

| Column Name | Column Type |
|---|---|
| id | Identifier |
| name | String |

projects:

| Column Name | Column Type |
|---|---|
| id | Identifier |
| name | String |

employee_project:

| Column Name | Column Type |
|---|---|
| employee_id | Identifier (Foreign Key) |
| project_id | Identifier (Foreign Key) |

This relation is represented in code as follows:

```
extension Employee {
  var projects: Siblings<Employee, Project, Pivot<Employee, Project>> {
    return siblings()
  }
}
extension Project {
  var employees: Siblings<Project, Employee, Pivot<Project, Employee>> {
    return siblings()
  }
}
```

Here, we use the `siblings` method provided by Fluent as part of Entity. This method looks at the pivot table, which is the `employee_projects` table, finds all of the models that map to the projects for employees and employees for projects, constructs model objects, and returns those.

*Chapter 4*

This was a basic dive into the types of relations that we can have in Vapor using Fluent, and how easy it makes it to create relationships between models, allowing us to fetch data from the database. We will learn more about relations in the next chapter, as we make a concrete implementation of the one to many relation for our Shopping List and Item model.

# Connecting with MongoDB

Connecting with MongoDB is as simple as adding a MongoDB database provider to our Vapor application and telling Fluent to use `mongodb` as the database driver. A database driver allows an application to connect to the database and act as an adapter, which lets Fluent use a standard API to connect with different types of databases. The Fluent module also includes a memory and SQLite database driver and the API template defaults to using the in-memory database driver. We need to update this to start using the `mongodb` driver, so that we can connect with the `mongodb` server running locally on our machine.

The following is a table listing some of the popular databases that are supported, along with the config value for the driver to be used by Fluent:

| Type | Fluent Config Value | Package | Class |
|---|---|---|---|
| Memory | memory | `FluentProvider` | `Fluent.MemoryDriver` |
| SQlite | sqlite | `FluentProvider` | `Fluent.SQLiteDriver` |
| MySQL | mysql | `MySQLProvider` | `MySQLDriver.Driver` |
| PostgreSQL | postgresql | `PostgreSQLProvider` | `PostgreSQLDriver.Driver` |
| MongoDB | mongo | `MongoProvider` | `MongoDriver` |

## Configuring Fluent config

The Fluent config file is where we need to specify which driver to use, in order for our Vapor application to start communicating with it. The config file is located in the `Config` folder, named `fluent.json`. The config file has comments for configuration, which can be modified. Let's look at some of them:

- `driver`: By default, this is set to memory, but we will need to modify this to **mongo** so that it can use the mongo driver to communicate without MongoDB database.

- keyNamingConvention: This config is used to translate properties that are in camel case (that is, isChecked) into snake case (that is, is_checked), with the use of an underscore as the separator for words.
- migrationEntityName: This is the name of the table that will hold the list of preparations that have been performed. As we noted in the FluentDemo exercise, we had to pass a class that implements the Preparation protocol so that it can prepare the database and also provides a method for reverting, in case it needs to be removed. By default, the table that stores the list of preparations performed is called fluent, which you can see by opening the main.sqlite file in the FluentDemo and selecting the values in the fluent table by entering the SELECT * FROM fluent; query.
- log: This is set to false, but if you are curious as to what query is run, set it to true to see the SQL that is run for each of the API calls we make.

There are other configs, as well, but these should help you figure out how Fluent does all of its magic and how we can configure it inside of the fluent.json config file.

## Mongo config - mongo.json

Just like in the HealthcheckProvider, there is a convention to have a unique config file for each of the Providers. As such, we need to add a new mongo.json file inside of the Config folder of our project, which will contain the url of the mongodb instance we want to connect to. In our case, the JSON file will look like this:

```
{
  "url": "mongodb://<db-user>:<db-password>@<host>:<port>/<database>"
}
```

We will get rid of <db-user> and <db-password>, since we do not have those set for our local instance, to quickly get started; however, for production databases, you will have credentials to access the database for security. For host, we will replace it with localhost, since we have mongodb running locally; for port, we will use 27017, which is the default port mongodb uses if it is not modified in the /usr/local/etc/mongod.conf file. Finally, for database, we will use shopping-list as the name for our database, which it will create if it does not exist on the first run. So, our final mongo.json config would look like this:

```
{
  "url": "mongodb://localhost:27017/shopping-list"
}
```

# Adding MongoProvider

Now, we need to add `MongoProvider` to our project by adding it to the package's dependencies and we also need to specify the module as a dependency in the `Target` section of `App`:

```
// swift-tools-version:4.0
import PackageDescription
let package = Package(
    name: "ShoppingListServer",
    products: [
        .library(name: "App", targets: ["App"]),
        .executable(name: "Run", targets: ["Run"])
    ],
    dependencies: [
        .package(url: "https://github.com/vapor/vapor.git",
                 .upToNextMajor(from: "2.4.4")),
        .package(url: "https://github.com/vapor/fluent-provider.git",
                 .upToNextMajor(from: "1.2.0")),
        .package(url: "https://github.com/ankurp/healthcheck-provider.git",
.upToNextMajor(from: "1.0.0")),
        .package(url:
"https://github.com/vapor-community/mongo-provider.git",
                 .upToNextMajor(from: "2.0.0")),
    ],
    targets: [
        .target(name: "App", dependencies: ["Vapor", "FluentProvider",
                    "HealthcheckProvider", "MongoProvider"],
                exclude: [
                    "Config",
                    "Public",
                    "Resources",
                ]),
        .target(name: "Run", dependencies: ["App"]),
        .testTarget(name: "AppTests", dependencies: ["App", "Testing"])
    ]
)
```

*Configuring Providers, Fluent, and Databases*

Now, let's run `vapor xcode -y` in the Terminal inside of our project which will regenerate the Xcode project, and download the `MongoProvider` dependencies. Once that is done and Xcode launches again, we will add `MongoProvider` to our config object, just like we did for `HealthcheckProvider` earlier:

1. First, open the `Config+Setup.swift` file in Xcode and add `import MongoProvider` to the top of the file to import the module.
2. Next, add the following line to the `setupProvider` method to add `MongoProvider` to the list of our Providers in our `Config` object:

   ```
   try addProvider(MongoProvider.Provider.self)
   ```

3. To start using `mongodb` we need to do one more thing and that is to specify it in the `fluent.json` config file. Open this file and change **driver** to **mongo** as such:

   ```
   "driver": "mongo",
   ```

4. Now, build and run, and make sure `mongodb` is running in the Terminal in another window. You should have this running, but if it is closed or shut down, then you can start it up using the following command in a new Terminal window:

   ```
   $ mongod --config /usr/local/etc/mongod.conf
   ```

Now, run the application, and if everything is configured correctly, the application will start up, and you should see the following printed in the console inside of Xcode:

```
The current hash key "0000000000000000" is not secure.
Update hash.key in Config/crypto.json before using in production.
Use `openssl rand -base64 <length>` to generate a random string.
The current cipher key "AAAAAAAAAAAAAAAAAAAAAAAAAAAAAAAAAAAAAAAAAAA=" is not secure.
Update cipher.key in Config/crypto.json before using in production.
Use `openssl rand -base64 32` to generate a random string.
Query logging is unsupported
Database prepared
No command supplied, defaulting to serve...
Starting server on 0.0.0.0:8080
```

*Chapter 4*

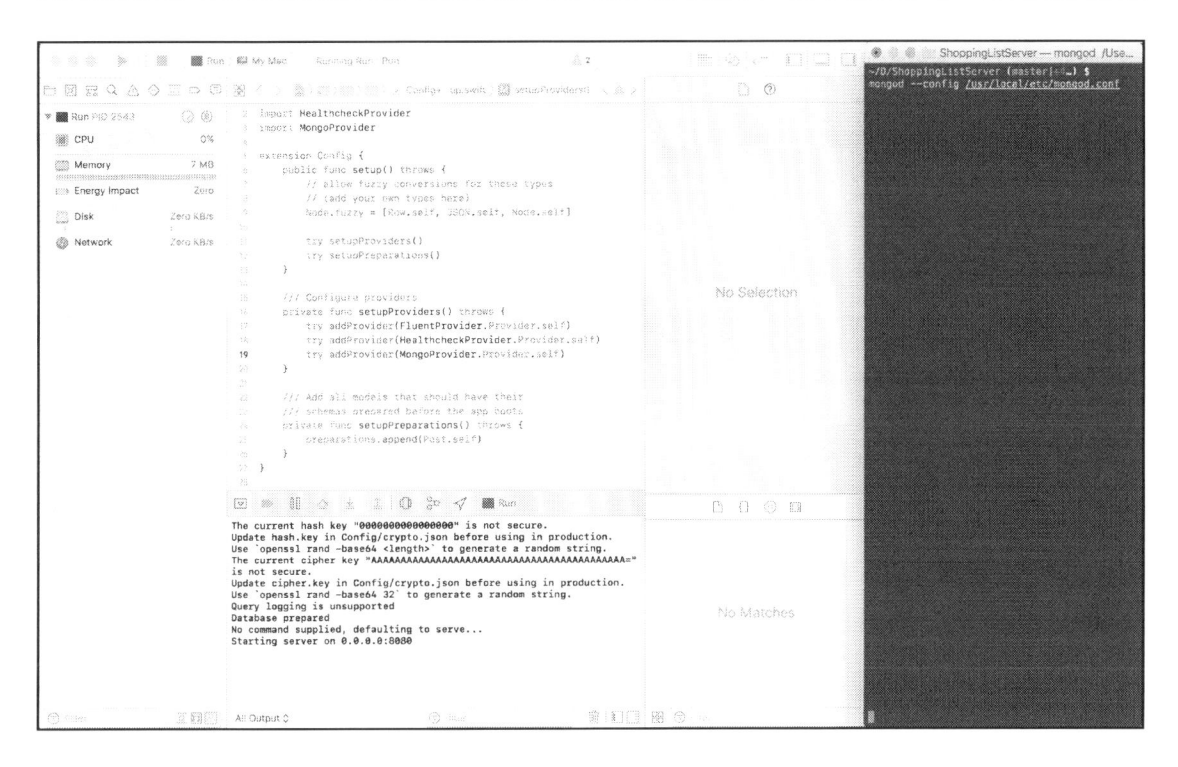

![Screenshot of Xcode showing Swift code with MongoProvider setup and console output with server startup messages, alongside a Terminal window running mongod]

Once we have the server started up, we can confirm that the database is created. Since we are using Vapor's API template project, which comes with sample code for a model called `Post`, we can confirm that it created the database in `mongodb`, ran the database preparations, and noted the preparations that are performed in the fluent table. To verify in `mongodb`, first open a new Terminal window and type `mongo`. This will connect to the `mongodb` server instance running locally on your machine by default. If the host and port are different, you can specify them as options to the `mongodb` command:

```
$ mongo
MongoDB shell version v3.4.10
connecting to: mongodb://127.0.0.1:27017
MongoDB server version: 3.4.10
Server has startup warnings:
2017-11-19T13:06:21.875-0500 I CONTROL  [initandlisten]
2017-11-19T13:06:21.875-0500 I CONTROL  [initandlisten] ** WARNING: Access control is not enabled for the database.
2017-11-19T13:06:21.875-0500 I CONTROL  [initandlisten] ** Read and write access to data and configuration is unrestricted.
2017-11-19T13:06:21.875-0500 I CONTROL  [initandlisten]
2017-11-19T13:06:21.875-0500 I CONTROL  [initandlisten]
2017-11-19T13:06:21.875-0500 I CONTROL  [initandlisten] ** WARNING: soft
```

[ 129 ]

```
rlimits too low. Number of files is 256, should be at least 1000
```

Once you see the prompt, type in `show dbs`, and it will print all of the databases that exist in your local `mongodb`. We should expect to see `shopping-list` as one of the databases in our local `mongodb`:

```
> show dbs
shopping-list 0.000GB
```

To query our `shopping-list` database, we need to switch to it, and we can do so using the `use` command in the `mongodb` prompt:

```
> use shopping-list
switched to db shopping-list
```

To view all of the tables in `mongodb`, which are known as collections, we need to enter the following command:

```
> show collections
fluent
```

Now, let's confirm that Fluent has run the database preparation for the `Post` model by querying `mongodb` using the following command:

```
> db.fluent.find()
{ "_id" : ObjectId("5a11df6e46268e1b69ecbc89"), "name" : "Post",
"updated_at" : ISODate("2017-11-19T19:45:50.399Z"), "batch" :
NumberLong(1), "created_at" : ISODate("2017-11-19T19:45:50.399Z") }
```

To confirm that our Vapor application is truly serving data from our `mongodb` databases, let's create one entry in our **posts** collection inside of `mongodb`. Then, we can confirm that we get back this post in our JSON response from our Vapor application by going to `http://localhost:8080/posts`. To create a new post, enter the following in the `mongodb` prompt:

```
> db.posts.insertOne({
... content: "First Post"
... })
{
  "acknowledged" : true,
  "insertedId" : ObjectId("5a11e3310b800caf2edc91db")
}
```

[ 130 ]

Once inserted, you will get back an acknowledgment that is was successful with an ID for the post that was inserted into the database. You can use this ID to find the same post in the database again. We will now confirm that our Vapor application gives us back the `Post` that we just inserted by going to `http://localhost:8080/posts`, which is a route that returns all posts that are saved in the post-collection:

```
[
    {
        id: "oid:5a11e3310b800caf2edc91db",
        content: "First Post"
    }
]
```

To see how this `/posts` route works, and how it is able to give us back the data fetched from the Mongo database, let's open up the sample controller file that came with this project, called `PostController.swift`. We will cover controllers and routes in more detail in the next chapter, but when you make a request to `/posts`, the route invokes code in the index method of this file, which contains the following code:

```
func index(_ req: Request) throws -> ResponseRepresentable {
    return try Post.all().makeJSON()
}
```

In this method, we do not make use of the request object that is passed in, since we want to return all of the posts found in the database. We also cover the posts to JSON objects using the `makeJSON` method, which is defined in the `Post` model class. This is how the controller returns us all of the posts by invoking the Fluent provided `all()` method on our Post model and converting it to JSON, before sending it back to the browser for us to see.

## Summary

Well done! If you have made it this far. By now, you should have a good understanding of how to persist data in Vapor applications. You should now know what Providers are and how they work because you just made one. Also, you should know how to use a provider and be familiar with the steps we need to take when adding any kind of Provider. You should also know how Fluent works and how Vapor uses Fluent's awesome APIs to make it easy to write code to create, read, update, and delete (CRUD) items from the database. You should have an understanding of databases and MongoDB and how to get started with it, and also how to log in to the database to query and modify data directly in the database.

In the next chapter, we will go over controllers in more detail. Towards the end of this chapter, we did touch upon `PostController` to look at how the `/posts` route is able to give us back data for all of the posts that are saved in the database. In the next chapter, we will learn about a RESTful resource pattern that, used with controllers, makes it easy to implement routes that follow an architectural pattern that is often used on the web, especially for building APIs.

# Building a REST API using Vapor

5

In the previous chapter, we covered several topics related to Vapor applications, such as how to extend the functionality of a Vapor application using Providers, and we dove into the Fluent provider as it is the most-used Provider in any Vapor application. It is also Vapor's and Swift's ORM to create, read, update, and delete data in the database using a high-level API. In this chapter, we will cover another important topic in building web applications that are related to routing, especially when building an API server.

Giving structure to our routes makes our applications easier to manage and easier for others to consume. There are several popular patterns in the industry when it comes to creating routes for your application, especially when building API routes to perform actions, such as create, read, update, and delete, on a specific type of item. If we look at our Shopping List iOS application, we have a Shopping List and an Item Model. We can perform CRUD actions on those two Models. Such Models are classified as resources and we can follow a REST architectural pattern that has a specified pattern for generating routes for resources and HTTP methods that can be invoked on those routes. In this chapter, we will get hands-on experience with creating RESTful routes for two of our Models and will cover the following topics along the way:

- What is routing? How does it work? How can we set up different kinds of routes?
- What are controllers and how do they work in Vapor?
- What is REST? What are resources?

# Routing in Vapor

Routing is a very important feature of any web application. It is the interface through which you can access the application and perform certain actions on it. HTTP is the protocol used in routing. We went through the basics of HTTP in Chapter 1, *Getting Started with Server Swift*, and as you might be aware, HTTP protocol requires a method, a path, a set of headers, and an optional body to make a request to the server. The server then responds back with a message that contains a status code, a set of Response headers, and a message body.

## HTTP methods

For most of the web, there are five commonly used HTTP methods, which are as follows:

- GET
- POST
- PATCH
- PUT
- DELETE
- OPTIONS

There are also other methods that are less used and can be passed in the request to a web application. If it is able to handle it, the routing rules will determine who should be handling the request.

Vapor's droplets give us easy-to-use APIs to construct routes for these commonly used HTTP methods. All we need to do is call the droplet instance with its appropriate HTTP method. When a request comes to Vapor on the matching path with the same HTTP method, the handler Response for it will be called with the request object. Here you can see how easy it is to set up a route to under /app to accept different HTTP methods, such as GET, POST, PATCH, PUT, and DELETE:

```
drop.get("app") { req in
  return "GET /app"
}

drop.post("app") { req in
  return "POST /app"
}

drop.patch("app") { req in
```

```
    return "PATCH /app"
}

drop.put("app") { req in
    return "PUT /app"
}

drop.delete("app") { req in
    return "DELETE /app"
}
```

If you want to add a custom HTTP method route to your application, you can do so using the `add` method on a droplet:

```
drop.add(.other(method: "CONNECT"), "app") { (_ req: Request) throws ->
ResponseRepresentable in
    return "CONNECT /app"
}
```

# Routers

Routing can be simple or complex. When you are dealing with large web applications, you need a structure and a certain set of rules that help organize all of these rules for routing, otherwise, it becomes a nightmare to figure out who is handling which request. This is where routers come into the picture.

Routers are used in web applications as a way to encapsulate the rules for handling an incoming request from the user. There can be one or multiple handlers for the entire application, or you can even make the handlers modular with the use of controllers, which we will cover in the next section. To understand this concept of routing, let's get started by creating some routing rules and see how it all works. To start with, we will create a new Swift package and create a small Vapor application where we will experiment with different routing rules:

1. Create a new folder called `Router` and open the folder in the Terminal
2. Create a Swift executable package using the following command:

```
$ swift package init --type executable
```

# Building a REST API using Vapor

3. Add Vapor as the dependency in `Package.swift` in both the dependencies and target sections:

   ```
   import PackageDescription

   let package = Package(
     name: "Router",
     dependencies: [
        .package(url: "https://github.com/vapor/vapor.git",
   .upToNextMajor(from: "2.4.4")),
     ],
     targets: [
       .target(
         name: "Router",
         dependencies: ["Vapor"]),
     ]
   )
   ```

4. Let's edit our `main.swift` inside of `Sources/Router` by replacing it with the following code:

   ```
   import Vapor

   let drop = try Droplet()

   drop.get("hello") { (_ req: Request) throws ->
   ResponseRepresentable in return "Hello, world."
   }

   try drop.run()
   ```

5. Run the Vapor application by running `swift run` in the Terminal and go to `http://localhost:8080/hello`

It's not that exciting as we have done this before. One difference in this example is that we have explicitly typed out the parameters and return type for the closure. There are three ways you can return a Response to a request:

- Returning a Response object
- Returning an object that conforms to the `ResponseRepresentable`
- Throwing an error

[ 136 ]

In our example, we are returning a `Hello, World` string literal. Since it is not a Response object and it does not throw any errors, that means it must implement the `ResponseRepresentable` protocol in the form of an extension to the built-in Swift String type. The following is the definition of this protocol:

```
public protocol ResponseRepresentable {
   func makeResponse() throws -> Response
}
```

As you can see and might have seen in previous exercises or sample code, we have defined the `makeResponse` method in the Model classes. This is the method that lets Vapor convert objects of any type into a Response object that can be used by Vapor to send back to the user as an HTTP Response. If we look at the extension defined on the built-in String class in Swift, we can see how the Response object, is generated as part of its `makeResponse` method:

```
extension Swift.String: ResponseRepresentable {
   public func makeResponse() -> Response {
       return Response(
           status: .ok,
           headers: ["Content-Type": "text/plain; charset=utf-8"],
           body: self.makeBytes()
       )
   }
}
```

Vapor has extended the String and Foundation data classes as a convention so that we can return objects of both of those types and Vapor will convert them to Response objects that are sent back to the user. As a result, there is a convention to make your Models implement the `ResponseRepresentable` protocol so that you can return a Model directly in the request handler and leave the logic to convert it to a Response object for the Model so that it can be reused in other handlers. We can update our `hello` route example and change it to return a Response object instead and it would behave the same although this seems a bit more verbose and unnecessary:

```
drop.get("hello") { (_ req: Request) throws -> ResponseRepresentable in
   return Response(
     status: .ok,
     headers: ["Content-Type": "text/plain; charset=utf-8"],
     body: "Hello, world.".makeBytes()
   )
}
```

## Nested routing

You can create a route with nested paths, such as /welcome/hello, by simply adding a route with the following nested path:

```
drop.get("welcome/hello/world") { req in
  return "GET request for /welcome/hello/world"
}
```

Additionally, you can split up the paths and pass them as additional parameters to the method, as follows:

```
drop.get("welcome", "hello", "world") { req in
  return "GET request for /welcome/hello/world"
}
```

This has the benefit of extracting values from the path into parameters that get passed into the req object.

## Dynamic routing

So far, we looked at routes that were static and did not change, but modern applications can have dynamic or user-generated content and need to handle URL paths that change. We can handle those using parameters that we can specify in our routes. Let's see how we can create these routes. To do so, we need to follow these steps:

1. In our main.swift file, add the following new handler, which will get called with a request object that will contain a parameter:

    ```
    drop.get("hello", String.parameter) { (_ req: Request) throws -> ResponseRepresentable in
      let name = try req.parameters.next(String.self)
      return "Hello \(name)"
    }
    ```

2. Build and run the application again using the swift run command and go to http://localhost:8080/hello/John

Here you can see we can pass an additional path after /hello/ and it is passed as a dynamic parameter in our request object. We get the parameter and convert it to a String type object using the following line:

```
let name = try req.parameters.next(String.self)
```

[ 138 ]

This is one of the ways we can dynamically pass an ID or some argument via our request so that we can generate a different Response for different requests. There is another way we can specify the parameter and the route and expect it to be passed into our request object. We can do so by adding another method to our example as follows:

1. In our `main.swift` file, add a route with a new path by adding the following code:

   ```
   drop.get("item",":id") { (_ req: Request) throws -> ResponseRepresentable in
     let id = req.parameters["id"]?.int
     return "Requesting Item with id \(id!)"
   }
   ```

2. Build and run using `swift run` and go to `http://localhost:8080/item/100`

Here you can see we get back a text Response saying **Requesting Item with id 100**. In our GET route, we specified `:id` as the second argument, which tells Vapor to do its magic to extract the text followed by the `/item` path and save it under the `id` subscript inside of the `req.parameters` object. We get the parameter value by subscripting the parameters object with the `id` key:

```
req.parameters["id"]
```

Parameters are returned as Node objects, which is another Vapor package to handle the ability to convert a value to different types. Using computed property, a feature available in Swift, the Node class object converts the wrapped value into the `Int` type and returns it. It also supports converting to other types, such as String or Boolean. In our case, to convert to `int`, we just needed to call `.int` on the returned optional Node object:

```
req.parameters["id"]?.int
```

As we learned before, there are three ways you can return out of a request handler; the third way is by throwing an error. Vapor catches any thrown errors and shows a **400 Bad Request**, **404 Not Found** or **500 Server Error** page based on what type of error is raised. For example, the following route will throw a **400 Bad Request** error when the name parameter cannot be converted to an `Int` type. This helps get rid of the forceful unwrapping of the optional and also guarantees the ID is of the `Int` type by the time we use it:

```
drop.get("item", ":id") { (_ req: Request) throws -> ResponseRepresentable in
  guard let id = req.parameters["id"]?.int else {
    throw Abort.badRequest
  }
```

```
    return "Requesting Item with id \(id)"
}
```

## Wildcard routing

Let's say you want to catch all paths that end under `hello`. This is easy to do with the wildcard character in your path. For example, the following route will get called any time someone requests it:

- /welcome
- /welcome/to/vapor/
- /welcome/to/vapor/and/swift

```
        drop.get("welcome", "*") { req in
          return "Welcome"
        }
```

## Routing parameters

Vapor has made it easy to pass a custom parameter type in the route and it will convert the text path name into the parameter we are requesting, as long as the class of the type we are requesting has implemented the `Parameterizable` protocol. The protocol consists of one property and one method:

```
    public protocol Parameterizable {
      static var uniqueSlug: String { get }
      static func make(for parameter: String) throws -> Self
    }
```

Let's say we want to get an `Item` object from the database using an `id` that is passed as a parameter in the URL. We can get a specific item two ways. One is by extracting the `id` from the parameter and converting it to the `Identifier` type, and then finding the `Item` in the database where the identifier matches and returning it as the Response. Another is by having our Model implement the `Parameterizable` protocol in the `make` method, return an `Item` object by finding the `Item` in the database where the `Identifier` matches with the ID passed in the `make` method as a parameter. The code for our Item Model will look like this:

```
    class Item: Parameterizable {
      static var uniqueSlug = "item"
      static func make(for parameter: String) throws -> Item {
```

```
      let id = Identifier(parameter)
      if let item = try Item.find(id) {
        return item
      } else {
        throw Abort.notFound
      }
    }
  }

  drop.get("items", Item.parameter) { req in
    let item = try req.parameters.next(Item.self)
    return item
  }
```

In the preceding code, we extended our `Item` class to implement the `Parameterizable` protocol and added the `make` method, which returns the item and lets us extract the `Item` from the request object if the item ID is passed in the URL as `/items/123`, using just this line:

```
  let item = try req.parameters.next(Item.self)
```

This makes our controller's handler as small as possible and also moves the the responsibility of converting an item ID into an `Item` object to the `Item` class. This makes the code more reusable and also makes our route handler slim, making it easier to figure out the intent of each route.

# Vapor Models

Before we move on to the topic of controllers, we will go back to our `ShoppingList` Vapor application and create two Vapor Models that will be saved in the database using Fluent. These two Models are the `ShoppingList` Model and the Item Model. Vapor's **Model** is an extension on top of Fluent's **Entity** protocol that conveniently implements certain methods in the protocol so we do not have to write the implementation of these methods for every Model we write. Let's see how we can create these two Models using Vapor's Model protocol.

# The Shopping List Model

To create a Shopping List Model, all we need to do is inherit our class from the Model protocol, add a few methods that will be used to create an instance of that type using data from the database, and save the state of an instance into the database. Let's perform the following steps to create our first Shopping List Model in Vapor:

1. Delete the `Post.swift` Model file included as part of our template project inside the `Models` folder. Also delete the `PostController.swift` inside the `Controllers` folder.

2. Next open the `Routes.swift` file and remove all of the code inside of the `setupRoutes()` method as we will not be using the PostController in our app and any sample routes that are defined. Also open the `Config+Setup.swift` file and remove the following line as we will no longer be saving Post model in our database.

   ```
   preparations.append(Post.self)
   ```

3. In that same `Models` folder, create a new empty file and call it `ShoppingList.swift`. Check `App` inside of targets.

4. In that, we will first import the modules that we need:

   ```
   import Vapor
   import FluentProvider
   import HTTP
   ```

5. Let's define our class and make it inherit from Model, which is provided to us by the Vapor module. Model is a protocol extension that extends the `Entity` protocol that we used in the chapter 4, *Configuring Providers, Fluent, and Databases*, from the `FluentProvider` module. Model adds additional functionality to `Entity` by implementing the Parameterizable protocol so that we do not need to write the code again:

   ```
   final class ShoppingList: Model {
   ```

6. Let's declare the instance variables for our `ShoppingList` class. Our Shopping List will have a name and some items. We also need to add storage, which is used to store additional attributes, such as `id`, that we may not have in our `ShoppingList` class. Since a `ShoppingList` has a one-to-many relationship with the Item Model, we will return an object of the `Children` type, which will invoke the query to fetch items from the **items** table in the database:

   ```
   let storage = Storage()
   var name: String
   var items: Children<ShoppingList, Item> {
     return children()
   }
   ```

7. Specify the name of the column or property in the database row or document for each of those instance variables. In our case, we need to specify the keys for ID and name since those are the two columns or properties that will be stored in the database for every Shopping List object we create. Since Shopping List has many items, we will store them in a separate table using a separate Item Model:

   ```
   struct Keys {
     static let id = "id"
     static let name = "name"
   }
   ```

8. Define the initializers for our Model instance. These initializers will help us create a new `ShoppingList` object given a name or a `ShoppingList` object from row information passed to us from the database:

   ```
   init(name: String) {
     self.name = name
   }

   init(row: Row) throws {
     name = try row.get(ShoppingList.Keys.name)
   }
   ```

9. Add a method to do the opposite, which is to convert a `ShoppingList` object into a database row by implementing a `makeRow` method and then close the class block by adding a closing curly brace } at the end of the file:

```
func makeRow() throws -> Row {
  var row = Row()
  try row.set(ShoppingList.Keys.name, name)
  return row
}
```

## Preparation protocol

Now we have a Shopping List Model that can create, read, update, and delete the Shopping List from the database. But there are a few things missing. Our Model does not know which table or collection to save or read from, and we have not specified the rules on how to create the table or collection for the first time. We need to do so by implementing the preparations protocol, which consists of two methods. One is called `prepare`, which runs once and is a good place for us to create our table or collection and specify the columns and any restriction on those columns. The other method is called `revert`, which is used to revert the changes done in prepare, which will be to delete the database table. To add preparation, we need to follow these steps:

1. Inside of the `ShoppingList.swift` file inside of the `Models` folder, add an extension on the `ShoppingList` class to implement the `Preparation` protocol:

   ```
   extension ShoppingList: Preparation {
   ```

2. Add the `prepare` method inside this extension. In here, we create a table or collection by passing self inside of `database.create`. This will create a table based on the class name. So in the case of `ShoppingList`, it will create a table or collection called `shopping_list` since it uses lowercase characters for the name and also uses snake case, where it appends an underscore (_) before any capital letter but not before the first letter in the class name. Also inside of this, we specify the builder to create an `id` column and a `name` column that is of the String type:

   ```
   static func prepare(_ database: Database) throws {
     try database.create(self) { builder in
       builder.id()
       builder.string(ShoppingList.Keys.name)
     }
   }
   ```

3. Add the `revert` method, which will revert the creation of the table or collection. Also add a closing curly brace } at the end of the file to close the extension block:

   ```
   static func revert(_ database: Database) throws {
     try database.delete(self)
   }
   ```

## JSONConvertible protocol

Now we have the `ShoppingList` Model ready, but we still need to extend it to support converting it to a JSON object and converting a JSON object into a `ShoppingList` Model, which is similar to converting it to a row for the database. This will help us return the instance of this class as a JSON representation, which is the universal format and is similar to XML in exchanging data across applications. We will also be using this JSON Response in our iOS app. To convert `ShoppingList` to JSON and vice versa, we need to extend the class with two methods. One will be an initializer that will take in a JSON object and create a new `ShoppingList` instance, and another will be a `makeJSON` method that will convert the `ShoppingList` to a JSON object. To get started, we will need to follow these steps:

1. In the `ShoppingList.swift` file, add the following extension to implement the `JSONConvertible` protocol:

   ```
   extension ShoppingList: JSONConvertible {
   ```

2. Add a `convenience` initializer that will call the `ShoppingList` initializer with the name argument after extracting the name from the JSON object:

   ```
   convenience init(json: JSON) throws {
     self.init(name: try json.get(ShoppingList.Keys.name))
   }
   ```

3. Add a `makeJSON` method that will return a JSON object that contains properties of our `ShoppingList` Model. Also add a closing curly brace } at the end of the file to close the extension block:

   ```
   func makeJSON() throws -> JSON {
     var json = JSON()
     try json.set(ShoppingList.Keys.id, id)
     try json.set(ShoppingList.Keys.name, name)
     try json.set("items", items.all())
     return json
   }
   ```

That is it, with just these two methods, our `ShoppingList` can convert JSON into a `ShoppingList` and convert a `ShoppingList` object into the JSON format.

## ResponseRepresentable protocol

The final thing we need to do is make our Model `ResourceRepresentable`. As mentioned earlier in this chapter, the route handler needs to return a `ResourceRepresentable` object in order for Vapor to generate a Response object that gets sent back to the client who made the request. Luckily, the Vapor module has made it very easy for us to add this method simply by adding an extension on our Model, as follows:

```
extension ShoppingList: ResponseRepresentable { }
```

This line of code extends our `ShoppingList` Model to inherit all methods implemented by `ResponseRepresentable`. By default, the protocol requires the implementation of the `makeResponse` method that Vapor implements for us in the `Model.swift` class of the Vapor package. In that file, the `ResponseRepresentable` protocol has a concrete implementation of `makeResponse` for any class that implements `JSONRepresentable`, and since we have made our Model able to implement `JSONConvertible`, it gets this `makeResponse` method for free. This is what the extension on `ResponseRepresentable` protocol looks like, as implemented by Vapor:

```
extension ResponseRepresentable where Self: JSONRepresentable {
  public func makeResponse() throws -> Response {
    return try makeJSON().makeResponse()
  }
}
```

## Updateable protocol

There is one more protocol that comes in handy when we want to update a Model in the database table, and that is the `Updateable` protocol. This protocol simply needs the Model class to define a static computed property that should return an array of `UpdateableKeys`. `UpdateableKey` is nothing but a wrapper class that needs the name of the property that can be updated and the type.

It will extract that value from the request object and pass it into the callback, where you can use it to update the property of your existing object. Implementing this is very easy and requires extending your Model class and adding the following computed property:

```
extension ShoppingList: Updateable {
  public static var updateableKeys: [UpdateableKey<ShoppingList>] {
    return [
      UpdateableKey(ShoppingList.Keys.name, String.self) { shoppingList, name in
        shoppingList.name = name
      }
    ]
  }
}
```

In the preceding example, you can see we are returning an array of `UpdateableKey` objects. One of the keys we update is the `name` property in the Shopping List object. We pass the name of the `name` property along with the type for the name, which is String. It then calls the closure function with the Shopping List object that needs to be updated and the new property value, which we simply assign to the Shopping List object. This will come in handy when we want to update our Shopping List object given a Request object in the route handler, as we will learn later on in this chapter.

## Item Model

Great, now we have a working `ShoppingList` Model, but it won't compile yet since it depends on the `Item` Model as our `ShoppingList` has many items. To fix this, we need to create an `Item` Model similar to the `ShoppingList` Model. To do so, we need to follow these steps:

1. Just like `ShoppingList.swift`, create a new file called `Item.swift` inside of the `Models` folder and make sure `App` target is checked otherwise you might get a compile error.
2. Copy the following code for the `Item.swift` class:

   ```
   import Vapor
   import FluentProvider
   import HTTP

   final class Item: Model {
     let storage = Storage()
     var name: String
     var isChecked: Bool = false
   ```

```swift
      var shoppingListId: Identifier
      var list: Parent<Item, ShoppingList> {
        return parent(id: shoppingListId)
      }
      struct Keys {
        static let id = "id"
        static let name = "name"
        static let isChecked = "is_checked"
        static let shoppingListId = "shopping_list__id"
      }

      init(name: String, isChecked: Bool, shoppingListId: Identifier) {
        self.name = name
        self.isChecked = isChecked
        self.shoppingListId = shoppingListId
      }

      init(row: Row) throws {
        name = try row.get(Item.Keys.name)
        isChecked = try row.get(Item.Keys.isChecked)
        shoppingListId = try row.get(Item.Keys.shoppingListId)
      }

      func makeRow() throws -> Row {
        var row = Row()
        try row.set(Item.Keys.name, name)
        try row.set(Item.Keys.isChecked, isChecked)
        try row.set(Item.Keys.shoppingListId, shoppingListId)
        return row
      }
    }

    extension Item: Preparation {
      static func prepare(_ database: Database) throws {
        try database.create(self) { builder in
          builder.id()
          builder.string(Item.Keys.name)
          builder.bool(Item.Keys.isChecked)
          builder.parent(ShoppingList.self)
        }
      }

      static func revert(_ database: Database) throws {
        try database.delete(self)
      }
    }

    extension Item: JSONConvertible {
```

```
        convenience init(json: JSON) throws {
          self.init(
            name: try json.get(Item.Keys.name),
            isChecked: try json.get(Item.Keys.isChecked),
            shoppingListId: try json.get(Item.Keys.shoppingListId)
          )
        }
        func makeJSON() throws -> JSON {
          var json = JSON()
          try json.set(Item.Keys.id, id)
          try json.set(Item.Keys.name, name)
          try json.set(Item.Keys.isChecked, isChecked)
          try json.set(Item.Keys.shoppingListId, shoppingListId)
          return json
        }
      }

      extension Item: Updateable {
        public static var updateableKeys: [UpdateableKey<Item>] {
          return [
            UpdateableKey(Item.Keys.name, String.self) { item, name in
              item.name = name
            },
            UpdateableKey(Item.Keys.isChecked, Bool.self) { item,
isChecked in
              item.isChecked = isChecked
            },
            UpdateableKey(Item.Keys.shoppingListId, Identifier.self) {
item, shoppingListId in
              item.shoppingListId = shoppingListId
            }
          ]
        }
      }

      extension Item: ResponseRepresentable { }
```

Now if you try to build the project in Xcode, it will compile without any errors or warnings. We have our Models set up to work with Vapor, so all we need to do now is set up our controllers so that they can handle requests to create, read, update, and delete Shopping Lists and Items.

*Building a REST API using Vapor*

# Controllers in Vapor

**Controllers** in Vapor, like in iOS applications, control the flow of the applications from a user request to the Response. Web applications typically follow a Model View Controller pattern where the request from the user goes to the router, and the router determines which controller and the function inside that controller to trigger to generate a Response. This is similar to user inputs, such as touch events in iOS apps, which trigger the `ViewController` to perform actions such as transitioning to another view controller or rendering a new view in the same View Controller.

At the beginning of this chapter, we explored different kinds of routes and how they are handled by a closure function. Now we will learn how to pass a controller class to the route so that the controller can handle one or multiple routes.

# RESTful Controller

In most cases, we will be creating controllers that will be responsible for handling requests to create, read, update, or delete a resource. These kind of CRUD operations performed on a resource make the controller resourceful. Vapor has made it easy to create such controllers by simply inheriting from their resources controller class, making it easy and straightforward to implement. Let's implement these RESTful controllers for our `ShoppingList` and `Item` Model so we can create, read, update, and delete them in the database using the API request. To get started, we need to follow these steps:

1. Create a new file in the `Controllers` folder. Add a new empty file called `ItemController.swift` and make sure `App` target is checked.
2. Import the modules we need:

   ```
   import Vapor
   import HTTP
   ```

3. Define the `ItemController` class that implements the `ResourceRepresentable` protocol. This protocol requires the controller to implement the `makeResource` method, which returns a resource object that contains the mapping of the controller methods to the RESTful actions:

   ```
   final class ItemController: ResourceRepresentable {
   ```

4. Add the `index` method, which in REST returns all of the items from our database. Using the Fluent Model, the implementation is very simple. This method is called when a GET request is made to /items:

   ```
   func index(_ req: Request) throws -> ResponseRepresentable {
     return try Item.all().makeJSON()
   }
   ```

5. Implement the create action, which is called `store`. This methods is called when a POST request is made to the /items route. The POST request body also contains a JSON representation of item. item is extracted from the request by implementing an extension method on the Request class called item(), which we will implement later in this file:

   ```
   func store(_ req: Request) throws -> ResponseRepresentable {
     let item = try req.item()
     try item.save()
     return item
   }
   ```

6. Implement the read action, which is called `show`. This method is called when a GET request is made to the items routes along with the ID as such /items/123:

   ```
   func show(_ req: Request, item: Item) throws -> ResponseRepresentable {
     return item
   }
   ```

7. Implement the delete method, which will delete a specific item when a DELETE HTTP request is made to the items routes along with the item ID. For example, a DELETE request to /items/123, where 123 is the ID of the item in the items table in the database:

   ```
   func delete(_ req: Request, item: Item) throws -> ResponseRepresentable {
     try item.delete()
     return Response(status: .ok)
   }
   ```

8. Implement the `clear` method, which clears all of the entries in the database tables by deleting all of them. This method is invoked when you make a DELETE HTTP request to the `/items` route without any ID, which tells our controller that we want to delete all the items in the database:

   ```
   func clear(_ req: Request) throws -> ResponseRepresentable {
     try Item.makeQuery().delete()
     return Response(status: .ok)
   }
   ```

9. Implement two `update` methods. The first one will partially update the Model with values passed in the request. If an attribute is not passed in the request, then it will skip over it and keep the existing value. This request is called a PATCH request, it is made to the specific item routes that also contains the ID:

   ```
   func update(_ req: Request, item: Item) throws -> ResponseRepresentable {
     try item.update(for: req)
     try item.save()
     return item
   }
   ```

10. The other update method we need to implement will try to update all of the attributes of the object even if the attributes are not passed and will replace attributes that are not passed with null or nil values:

    ```
    func replace(_ req: Request, item: Item) throws -> ResponseRepresentable {
      let new = try req.item()
      item.name = new.name
      item.isChecked = new.isChecked
      try item.save()
      return item
    }
    ```

11. Implement the `makeResource` method, which will make our controller resourceful as it implements the `ResourceRepresentable` protocol. The `Resource` object returned from `makeResource` will be used to route requests to the appropriate method in our controller so that the CRUD operation can be performed on our `Item` Model. Also add a closing curly brace `}` at the end of the file to close the class block:

    ```
    func makeResource() -> Resource<Item> {
      return Resource(
        index: index,
    ```

```
                store: store,
                show: show,
                update: update,
                replace: replace,
                destroy: delete,
                clear: clear
            )
        }
```

The project should not compile just yet. We need to implement the `item()` method in the `Request` class so that we can call `req.item()` and generate an `Item` object from a user's request:

```
    extension Request {
      func item() throws -> Item {
        guard let json = json else { throw Abort.badRequest }
        return try Item(json: json)
      }
    }
```

Our controller is set up correctly now, but we will not be able to route requests to this controller until we specify it in our `Routes.swift` file. In this file, we need to add the following line inside the `setupRoutes()` method towards the end of the method:

```
    resource("items", ItemController())
```

This tells the Vapor application to route all requests beginning with `/items` to `ItemController`. The following is the table summarizing the HTTP request and the controller method it triggers for our `ItemController`:

| HTTP Method | Route | Controller method |
| --- | --- | --- |
| GET | /items | ItemController.index |
| POST | /items | ItemController.store |
| GET | /items/:id | ItemController.show |
| DELETE | /items/:id | ItemController.delete |
| DELETE | /items | ItemController.clear |
| PATCH | /items/:id | ItemController.update |
| PUT | /items/:id | ItemController.replace |

# Shopping List controller

We now have a working API route for the `Items` Model. To complete our API server, we need to create a controller for `ShoppingList`, which will be resourceful, just like `ItemController`. To create a controller for `ShoppingList`, we need to perform the following steps:

1. Create a new Swift file in the `Controllers` folder and name it `ShoppingListController.swift`
2. Add the following code to the empty file:

```
import Vapor
import HTTP

final class ShoppingListController: ResourceRepresentable {
  func index(_ req: Request) throws -> ResponseRepresentable {
    return try ShoppingList.all().makeJSON()
  }
  func store(_ req: Request) throws -> ResponseRepresentable {
    let shoppingList = try req.shoppingList()
    try shoppingList.save()
    return shoppingList
  }
  func show(_ req: Request, shoppingList: ShoppingList) throws -> ResponseRepresentable {
    return shoppingList
  }
  func delete(_ req: Request, shoppingList: ShoppingList) throws -> ResponseRepresentable {
    try shoppingList.delete()
    return Response(status: .ok)
  }
  func clear(_ req: Request) throws -> ResponseRepresentable {
    try ShoppingList.makeQuery().delete()
    return Response(status: .ok)
  }
  func update(_ req: Request, shoppingList: ShoppingList) throws -> ResponseRepresentable {
    try shoppingList.update(for: req)
    try shoppingList.save()
    return shoppingList
  }
  func replace(_ req: Request, shoppingList: ShoppingList) throws -> ResponseRepresentable {
    let new = try req.shoppingList()
    shoppingList.name = new.name
```

*Chapter 5*

```
        try shoppingList.save()
        return shoppingList
    }
    func makeResource() -> Resource<ShoppingList> {
        return Resource(
            index: index,
            store: store,
            show: show,
            update: update,
            replace: replace,
            destroy: delete,
            clear: clear
        )
    }
}

extension Request {
    func shoppingList() throws -> ShoppingList {
        guard let json = json else { throw Abort.badRequest }
        return try ShoppingList(json: json)
    }
}
```

3. Add the Shopping Lists route by adding the following line in the `Routes.swift` inside of the `setupRoutes()` method towards the end:

   ```
   resource("shopping_lists", ShoppingListController())
   ```

4. Update the `setupPreparations()` method inside of the `Config+Setup.swift` file to the following:

   ```
   private func setupPreparations() throws {
       preparations.append(ShoppingList.self)
       preparations.append(Item.self)
   }
   ```

Good job! If you have made it this far, you now have a working API server that can create, read, update, and delete items and Shopping Lists objects from the database. Let's start up the server and test out our API.

[ 155 ]

# REST API in action

Let's try out our API by making a simple HTTP request. We will start with creating API requests and then confirm that the resources are created correctly by fetching the newly created resource. We will also test, update, delete, and clear the database to make sure it works as expected. Let's see it in action.

## Creating the Shopping List

Creating a `ShoppingList` using the API is simple: make a `POST` HTTP request with the JSON representation of our Shopping List object so that it can create a new instance of it and save it in the database. The following is a screenshot of the `POST` HTTP request made to my local API server using an app called **Postman**:

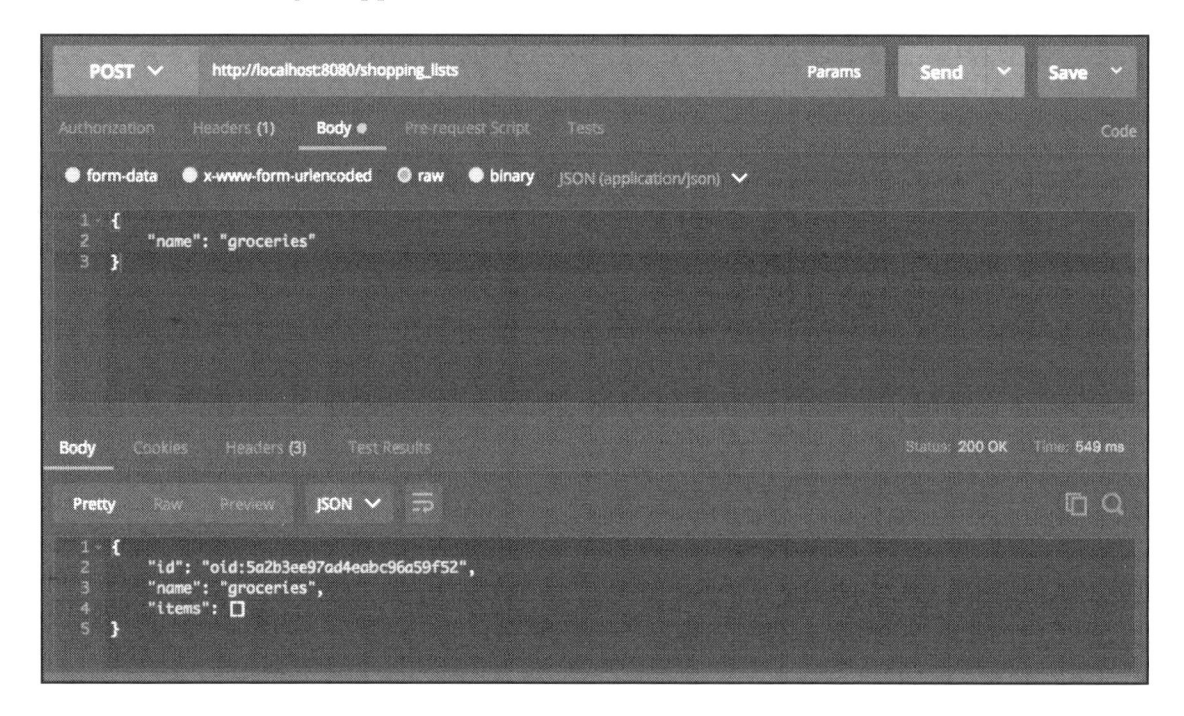

You should see the server respond back with a JSON object that contains the ID of the newly created Shopping List. We specified the name of the Shopping List in our `POST` request and we can see it created it correctly by looking at the name passed in the Response. Also, since this is a new Shopping List, it does not have items so the items array is empty.

## Getting the Shopping List

We can get the Shopping List that we just created by making a `GET` request to the items with the ID of the item, and we should get back the JSON representation of the Shopping List. The following is a screenshot of the `GET` request; you can see the same JSON object being returned as part of the Response:

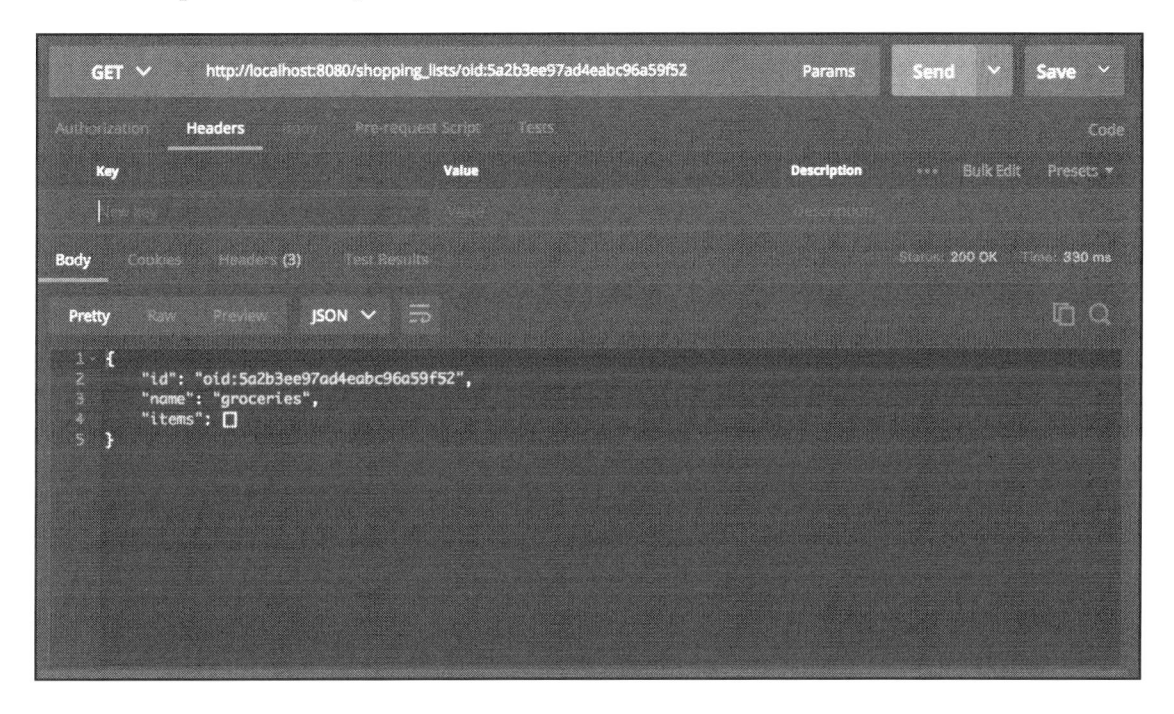

We can also make a `GET` request to `/shopping_list` to get all of the Shopping Lists. Instead of getting one object in the Response, we will get back an array of objects:

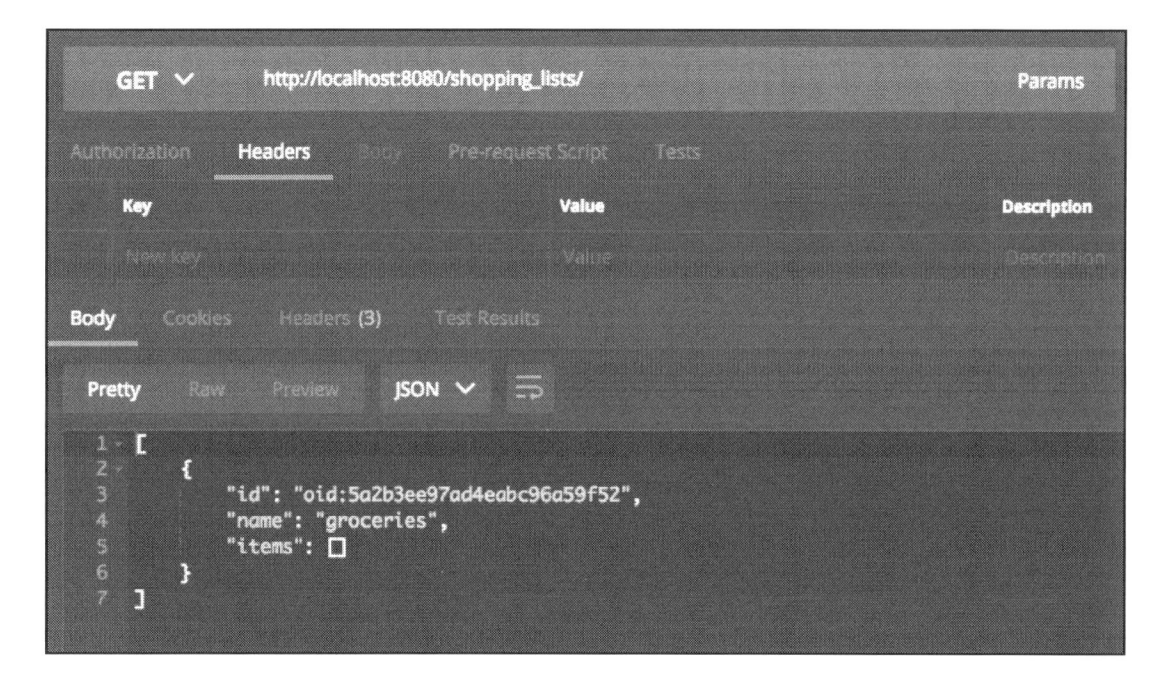

```
[
    {
        "id": "oid:5a2b3ee97ad4eabc96a59f52",
        "name": "groceries",
        "items": []
    }
]
```

# Updating the Shopping List

To update the Shopping List, we need to make a PATCH request to the `/shopping_lists` endpoint followed by the ID of the Shopping List in the URL. It will return the updated Shopping List object represented in JSON format:

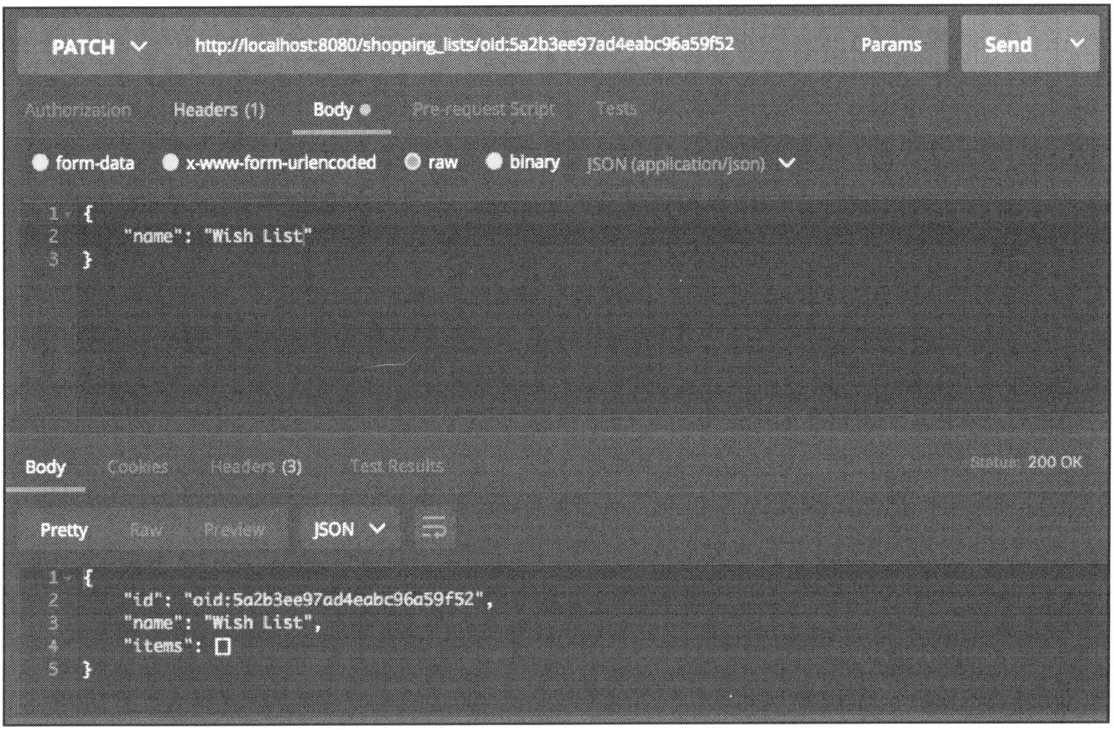
PATCH
http://localhost:8080/shopping_lists/oid:5a2b3ee97ad4eabc96a59f52
Params
Send
Authorization
Headers (1)
Body
Pre-request Script
Tests
form-data
x-www-form-urlencoded
raw
binary
JSON (application/json)
{
"name": "Wish List"
}
Body
Cookies
Headers (3)
Test Results
Status: 200 OK
Pretty
Raw
Preview
JSON
{
"id": "oid:5a2b3ee97ad4eabc96a59f52",
"name": "Wish List",
"items": []
}

*Building a REST API using Vapor*

## Deleting the Shopping List

To delete the Shopping List, we need to make the `DELETE` request to the `/shopping_lists` endpoint followed by the ID of the shopping list in the URL that we want to delete. It will just respond with an OK status without any Response if the Shopping List is deleted correctly:

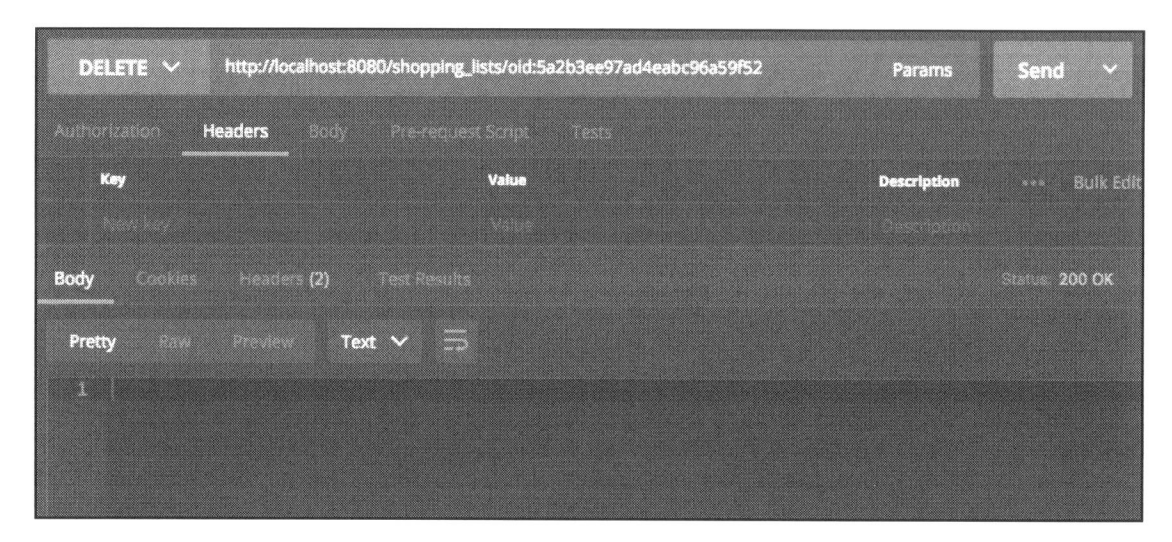

## Creating items

We can create an item by making a `POST` request to `/items`, but before we do so, make sure to create a Shopping List as we just deleted it using the `DELETE` request. Once you have the Shopping List created, make sure to copy the ID as we will need it to make an item object. When making an item, we need to specify the name, whether it is checked or not, and the Shopping List ID it belongs to. The following is a sample request to create an item and the Response we get back on successful creation:

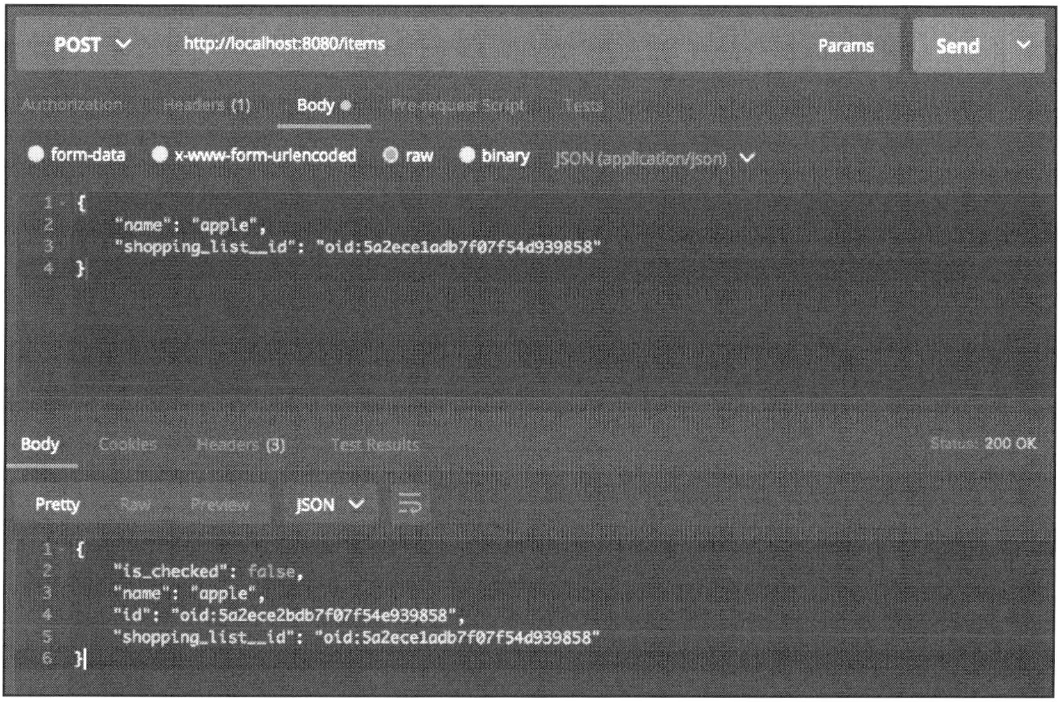
POST
http://localhost:8080/items
Params
Send
Body
form-data
x-www-form-urlencoded
raw
binary
{
"name": "apple",
"shopping_list__id": "oid:5a2ece1adb7f07f54d939858"
}
Body
Status: 200 OK
Pretty
JSON
{
"is_checked": false,
"name": "apple",
"id": "oid:5a2ece2bdb7f07f54e939858",
"shopping_list__id": "oid:5a2ece1adb7f07f54d939858"
}

Great! We just created an item and associated it with a Shopping List. One thing to note is that even though we did not pass the `is_checked` property in the `POST` request, it defaulted the `isChecked` property to `false`, as configured in our `Item` class.

# Building a REST API using Vapor

Now if we make a `GET` request to the `shopping_list` endpoint with the shopping list ID passed in the URL, you will see the details of the shopping list, such as its name and all its items. You will also see the item we just created in the `shopping_list` show Response as well:

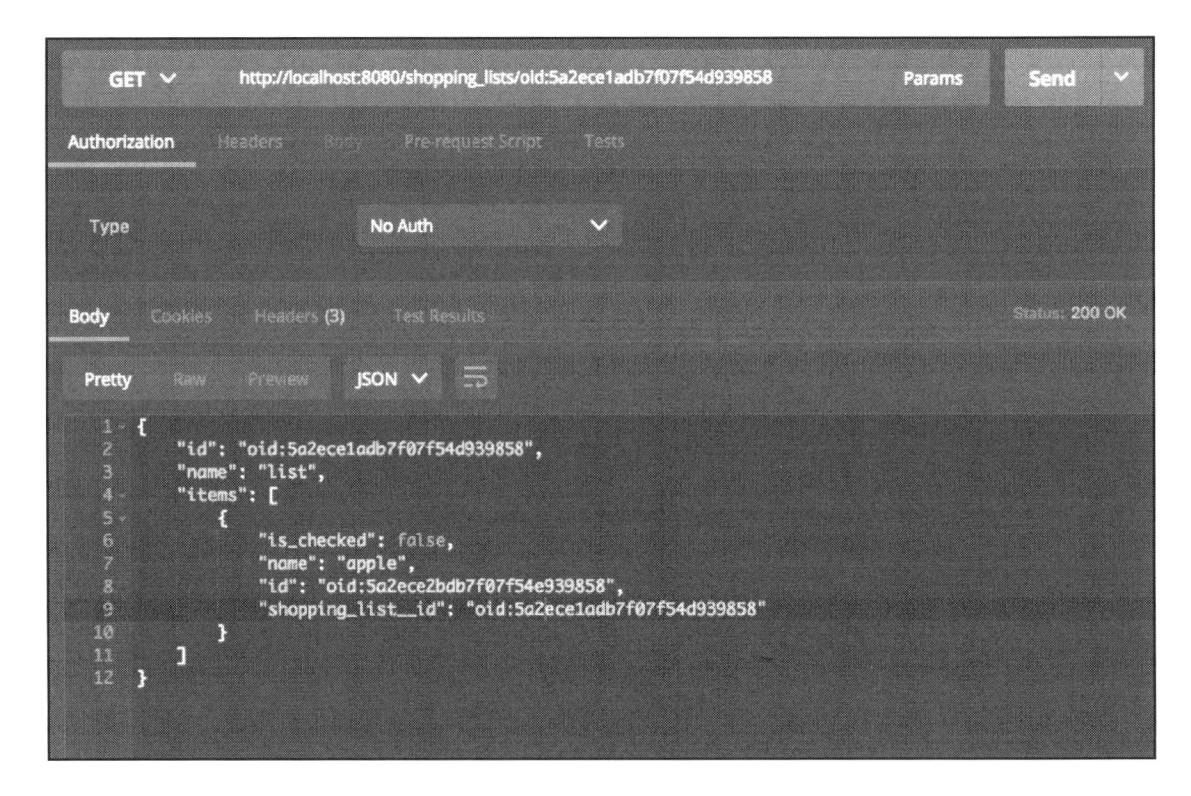

```
GET  http://localhost:8080/shopping_lists/oid:5a2ece1adb7f07f54d939858

Status: 200 OK

{
    "id": "oid:5a2ece1adb7f07f54d939858",
    "name": "list",
    "items": [
        {
            "is_checked": false,
            "name": "apple",
            "id": "oid:5a2ece2bdb7f07f54e939858",
            "shopping_list__id": "oid:5a2ece1adb7f07f54d939858"
        }
    ]
}
```

# Exercise

Try deleting the item you just created using the API endpoint. Verify it is deleted by going to the show action of that item and also the show action of the shopping list to confirm that the item has been deleted correctly.

Also, create a new item in a shopping list and update the `is_checked` status of that item to `true` (if it is false already), using the PATCH HTTP request. Confirm it is updated by invoking the show action on the Shopping List and confirm that the `is_checked` status of that item is marked as `true`.

# Summary

In this chapter, we learned about several topics ranging from routing to Vapor Models to RESTful controllers. By now you should have a good understanding of how to create routes in Vapor applications and how to handle the requests to those routes. You should also be comfortable with the three different ways you can respond to a request, which are by returning a Response object, an object that implements `ResponseRepresentable` protocol, and by throwing different kinds of errors. You should also be comfortable creating Vapor Models, which are like Fluent Entity but with extra functionality. You should also understand REST in more detail and know the basic commands in REST. Finally, you should be able to create a controller that is RESTful and responds to the REST actions.

In the next chapter, we will go back to the iOS app and learn how to consume the API we just created. We can fetch and save data over the network rather than just persisting the Shopping List data natively on the iOS app. We will also learn how easy it is to convert the JSON data into objects in iOS.

# 6
# Consuming API in App

In the previous chapter, we learned how to route requests, how to use controllers, and how to make RESTful routes for our models that will persist data into the MongoDB database. In this chapter, we will consume the API routes we just created in our Shopping List iOS app. Most modern iOS applications need to communicate with a server to fetch data to show on the app. They also update data on the server so that you can start where you left off in case the app is closed or you try to view the app on a different device or platform, such as the web. To make such seamless integration work, we need to ask the server for the data and have all of the data persisted remotely.

In this chapter, we will switch back to working on our iOS app written in Swift. We will focus on how we can refactor our project so that we can run both the Vapor server and the iOS in one Xcode Workspace. Then, we will integrate the API into our app by refactoring the existing iOS app so that it can fetch data from our API rather than reading and saving to disk using `UserDefaults`. We will also use other RESTful endpoints provided by our Vapor API server to create a Shopping List, delete a Shopping List, create an item in the Shopping List, and delete an item. We will also update a Shopping List item by checking it and unchecking it, and all of this will be saved remotely in the database thanks to our Vapor server. By the end of this chapter, you will have a better understanding of the following topics:

- Viewing and starting both server and iOS apps using a single Xcode Workspace window to edit and debug code
- Making network requests from the iOS app
- Converting JSON data into models and converting models into JSON data to send to the API server
- Adding and deleting Shopping Lists and items as well as checking and unchecking items in the server

# Xcode Workspace

One of the benefits of using Swift as a language to build both server-side components and frontend native apps is the ability to use one integrated development environment (IDE) to work on both server and frontend apps. Xcode, which is a powerful IDE for iOS development, can also be used for building server-side applications using Swift and the Swift Package manager. In `Chapter 4`, *Configuring Providers, Fluent, and Databases*, we started working on our Vapor application, and we used Xcode to run and debug our application instead of a plain text editor. We can use the same Xcode IDE to combine both the iOS project and the Vapor project into one Workspace so that we can run both the iOS app and the Vapor app using the same Xcode window, instead of having to toggle between two separate Xcode windows.

We can do this using a feature in Xcode called Workspace. Workspace allows you to combine multiple Xcode projects together into one Xcode window. The benefit of using Xcode's Workspace is the ability to edit code for both our iOS and server app without having to switch between windows. We can also build, run, and debug both of our iOS and server apps, which are run on different platforms, using this same Xcode Workspace, making development easy and fun. Let's see how we can combine the two projects into a single Workspace. To do so, we need to follow these steps:

1. Create a new folder called `ShoppingList` where we will store both of our iOS and Vapor projects.
2. Open the Xcode app and create a new Workspace by going to **File** | **New** | **Workspace**...:

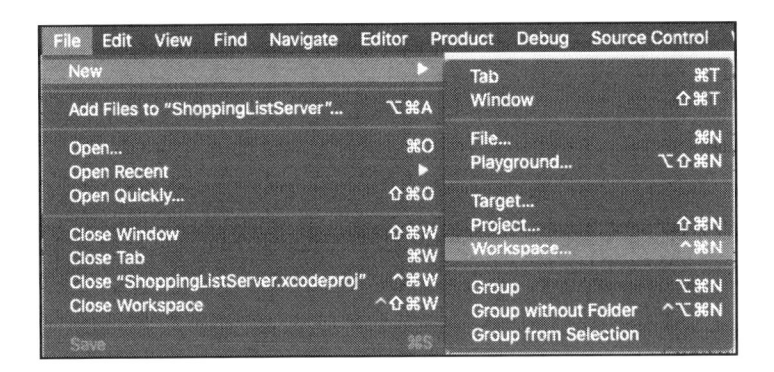

3. In the new Workspace prompt, go to the `ShoppingList` folder we just created, give your Workspace a name, such as `ShoppingList`, and click **Save**:

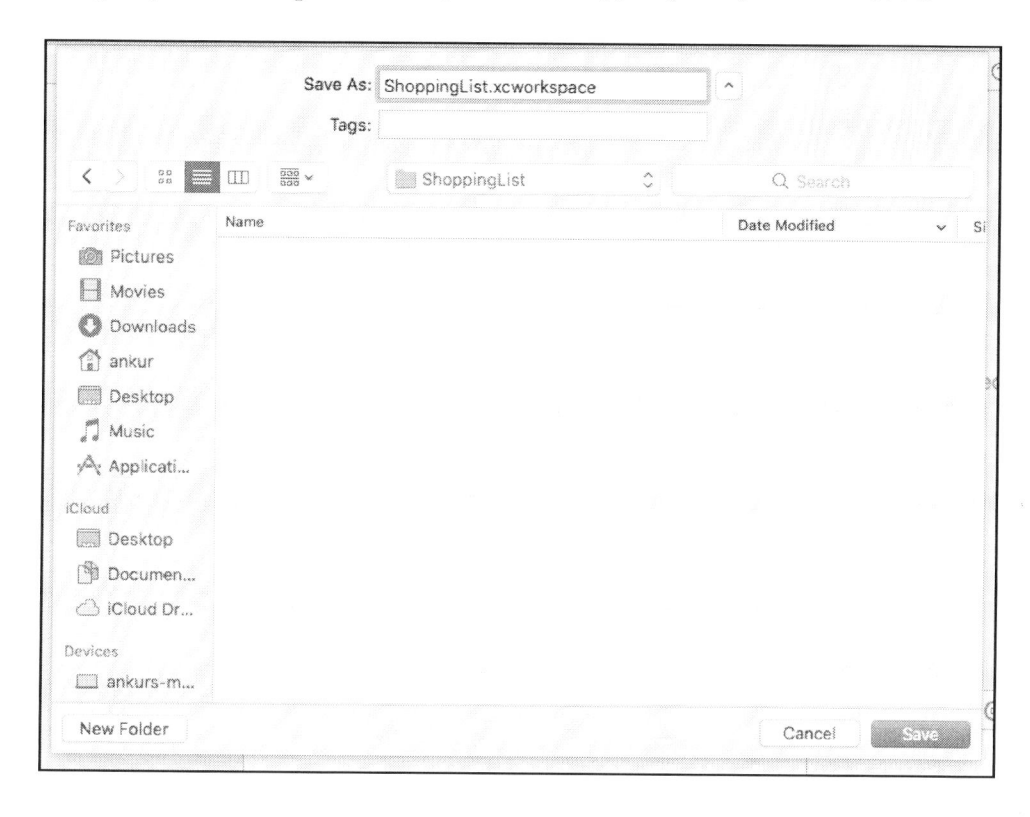

*Consuming API in App*

4. In the `ShoppingList` folder where you have the Workspace file, create two new folders, one called `App` and the other called `Server`, as follows:

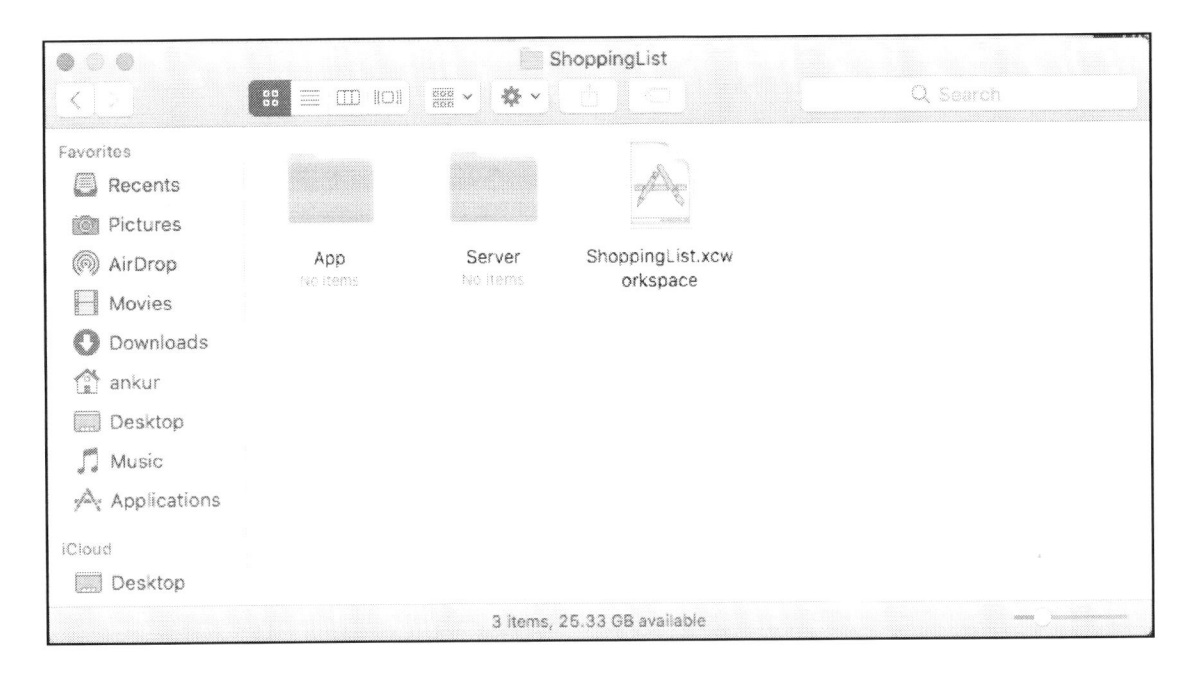

5. Copy or move the files for your `ShoppingList` iOS project into the `App` folder and the Vapor application into the `Server` folder. After all of the files have been copied, the folder for `App` should look like the following image:

*Consuming API in App*

6. The `Server` folder should look like the following:

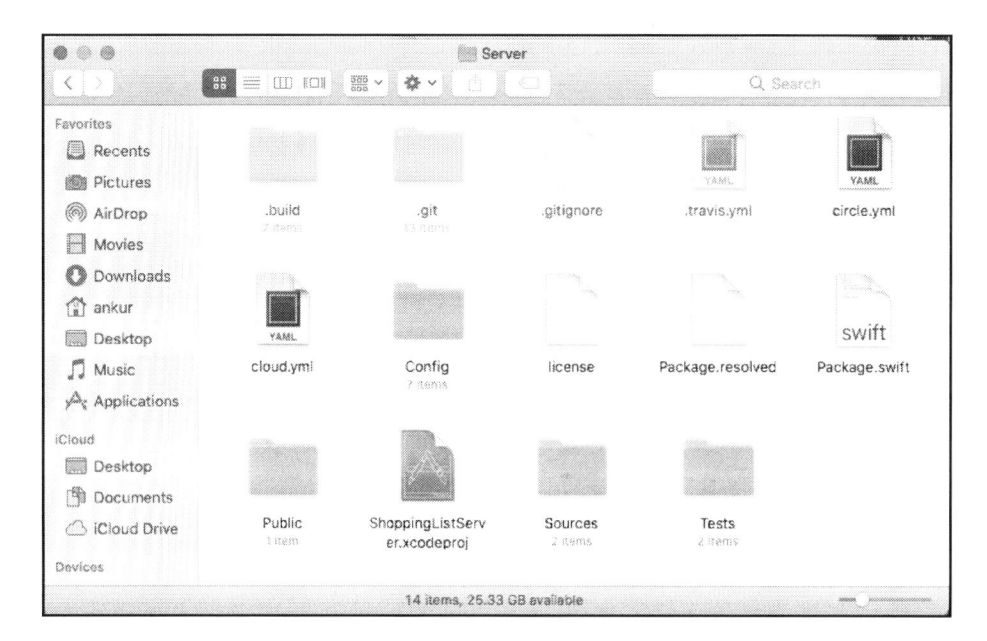

7. Make sure to close all Xcode windows and projects. Open the Xcode Workspace file called `ShoppingList.xcworkspace`. Drag the `ShoppingListServer.xcodeproj` file from the `Server` folder into the Workspace, as follows:

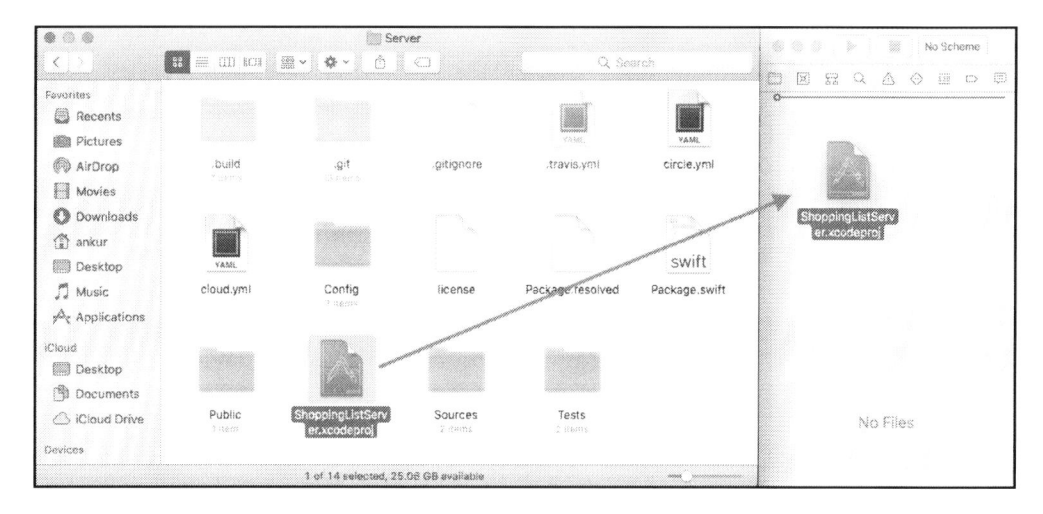

8. Once the `ShoppingListServer` project is added, we can now add the iOS project by going into the `App` folder and dragging the `ShoppingList.xcodeproj` folder as shown in the following figure. Make sure to have it at the top level and not have it nested inside the `ShoppingListServer` project:

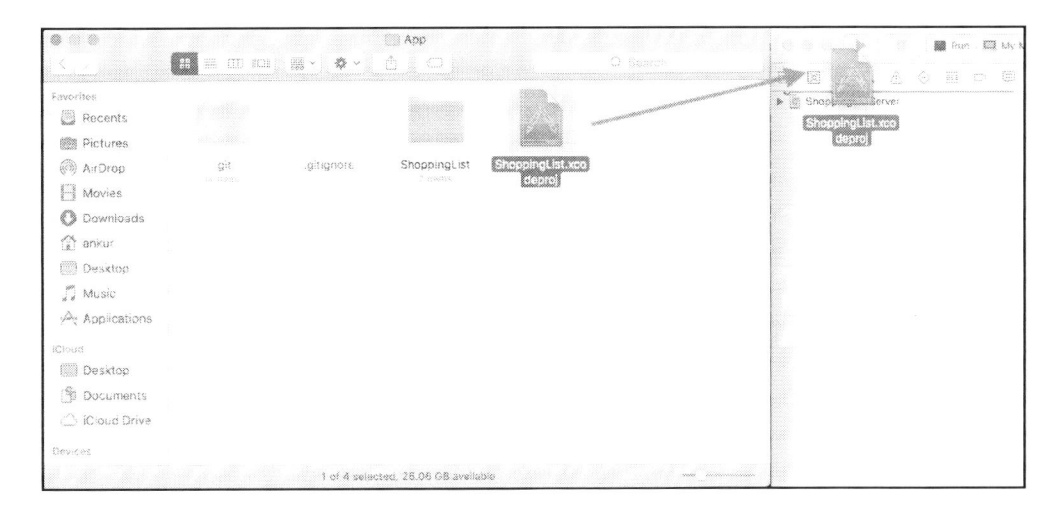

9. We are almost done. We have both the projects in our Workspace. To make it easier to find the **Run** configuration for just the iOS app and the Vapor app, we need to get rid of some of the schemes by clicking on the **Active schema** and selecting **Manage Schemes...**:

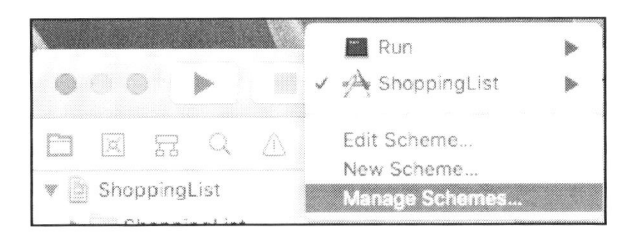

[ 171 ]

*Consuming API in App*

10. In the **Manage Schemes...** window, uncheck all schemes except for **Run** and **ShoppingList** as the **Run** scheme will build and run the Vapor app and the `ShoppingList` will run the iOS app:

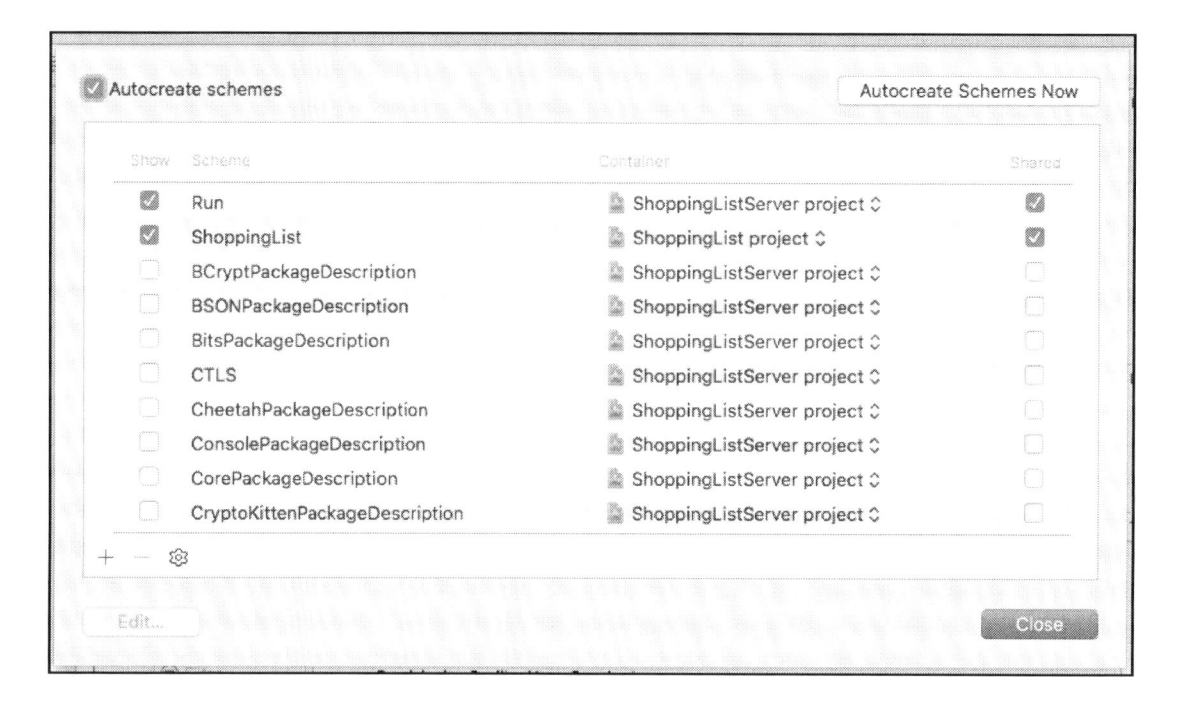

| Show | Scheme | Container | Shared |
|---|---|---|---|
| ☑ | Run | ShoppingListServer project ◊ | ☑ |
| ☑ | ShoppingList | ShoppingList project ◊ | ☑ |
| ☐ | BCryptPackageDescription | ShoppingListServer project ◊ | ☐ |
| ☐ | BSONPackageDescription | ShoppingListServer project ◊ | ☐ |
| ☐ | BitsPackageDescription | ShoppingListServer project ◊ | ☐ |
| ☐ | CTLS | ShoppingListServer project ◊ | ☐ |
| ☐ | CheetahPackageDescription | ShoppingListServer project ◊ | ☐ |
| ☐ | ConsolePackageDescription | ShoppingListServer project ◊ | ☐ |
| ☐ | CorePackageDescription | ShoppingListServer project ◊ | ☐ |
| ☐ | CryptoKittenPackageDescription | ShoppingListServer project ◊ | ☐ |

Great! Now you should have both apps in a single Xcode Workspace so that we can edit and run both the server and client apps via one window while having the ability to put breakpoints on both the Vapor and iOS apps from the Xcode editor:

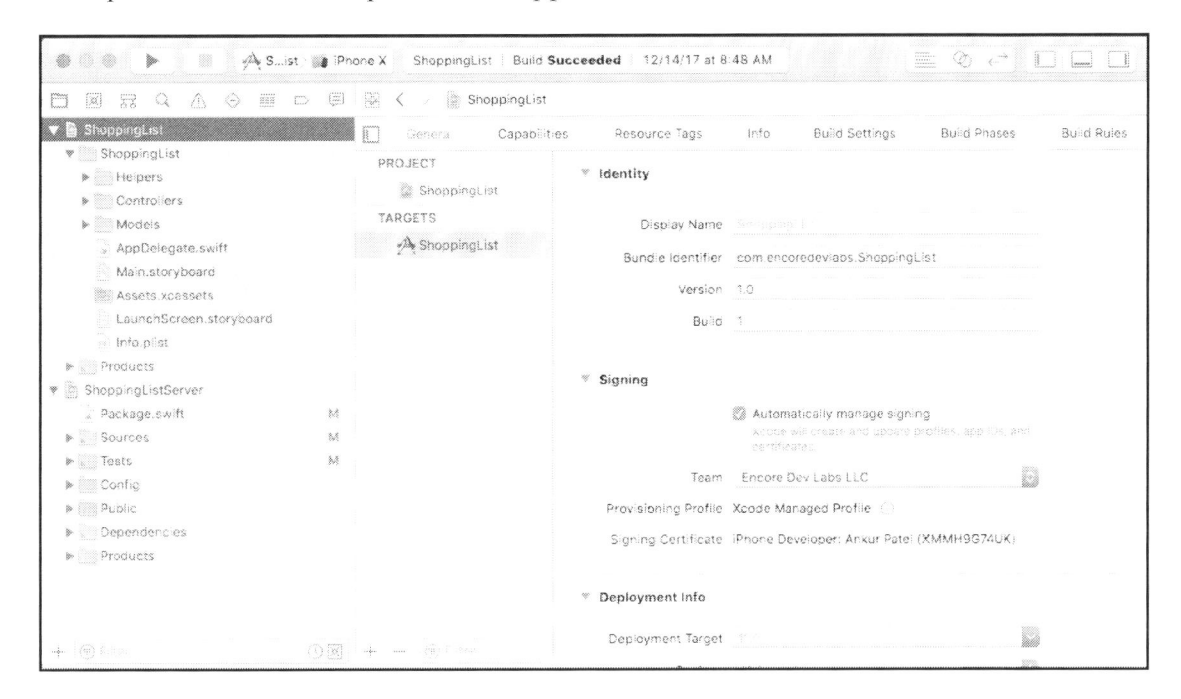

## Making network requests

To get our app to communicate with the internet, we need to make a few changes. By default, in the newer version of the iOS, HTTP network requests that are not secure as HTTPs are blocked unless we explicitly tell them to allow it. Since we will be making network requests to our Vapor app, which is running locally as HTTP and not HTTPs, we need to set this in the `Info.plist` file of the iOS project. We will also add one more configuration to store the base URL of our Vapor server in this `Info.plist`, so we can reference it from one place.

## Network configuration

To add the previously mentioned two configurations, we need to follow these steps:

1. Open the `Info.plist` file and click on the small + icon that appears when you hover over the **Information Property List** toward the top of this file:

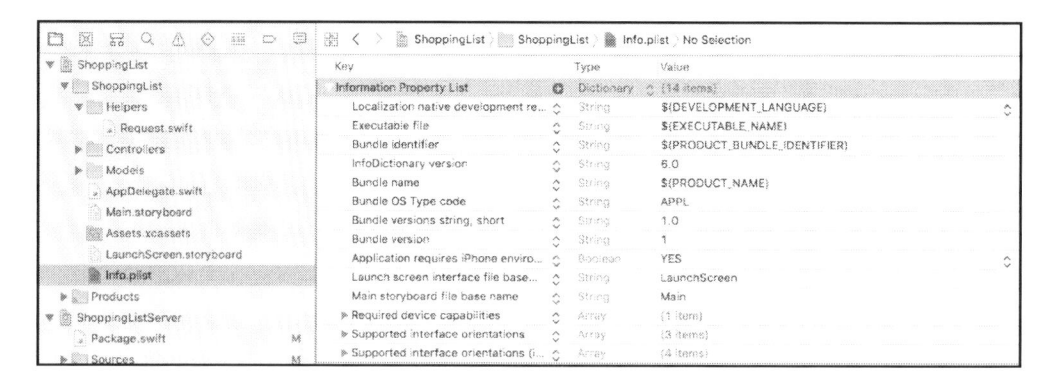

2. This will create a new entry in this property list file.
   Type `NSAppTransportSecurity` and press *Enter*. This will change the text to **App Transport Security Settings**:

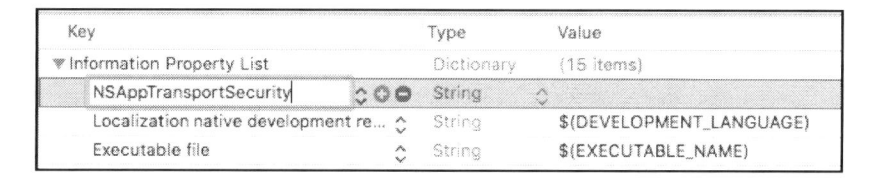

3. Hover over the **App Transport Security Settings** and click on the + icon again and select **Allow Arbitrary Loads**:

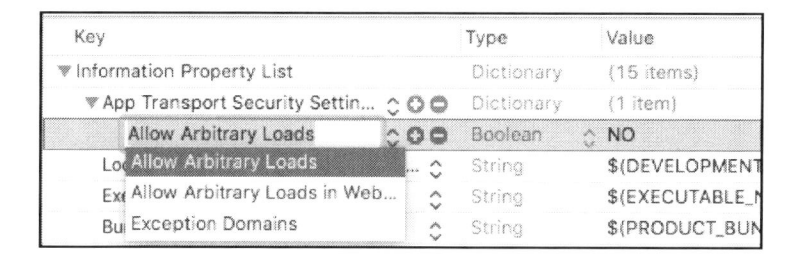

Then change the Boolean Value to YES. We are done with our first network configuration:

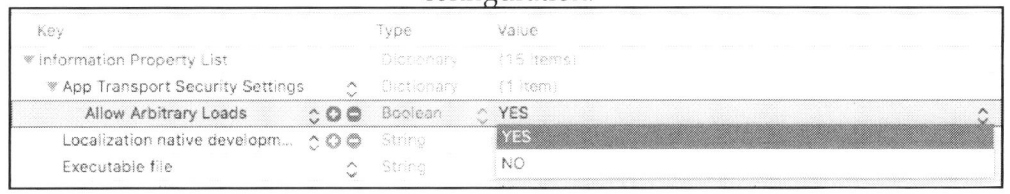

4. Add the base URL to our `Info.plist`. To do so, we need to click on the + icon again next to the **Information Property List** and enter **BaseURL**:

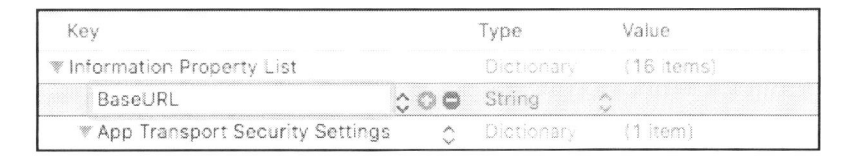

5. In the String Value field enter `http://localhost:8080`, which is the base URL where we will have our Vapor server running on the default 8080 port:

We now have our app configured to communicate with the network. Next, we will look into how we can create a small helper file to make these network requests.

# Request helper

Making a network request is easy to do in Swift using the Foundation framework by Apple. But having to type it out every time we need to make a network request can be verbose and tedious. So, for that purpose, it is best to create a helper function that we can call to make the network request. We will create a small helper function in our iOS project that will take a URL path and make a request to the host specified in the base URL of our `Info.plist` configuration file.

In this helper function, we can also pass the HTTP method we want to make and it will default to a `GET` request if it is not passed. We can also pass data to our helper method, which will be sent in the HTTP body of the request for the `POST` and `PATCH` requests. Finally, this helper function will take a closure function that will invoke the callback in the main thread so that we can take the response from the server and update the UI as appropriate. To add this helper method, we need to follow these steps:

1. Create a new Group inside the `ShoppingList` folder in our iOS project and call it `Helpers`:

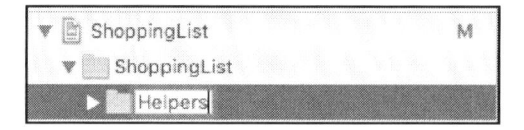

2. Create a new Swift file inside the `Helpers` folder and call it `Request.swift`
3. Copy the following code into the `Request.swift`:

```
import Foundation

let baseUrl = Bundle.main.infoDictionary!["BaseURL"]!

func request(url: String, httpMethod: String = "GET", httpBody:
Data? = .none, completionHandler: @escaping (Data?, URLResponse?,
Error?) throws -> Void) {
  var request = URLRequest(url: URL(string: "\(baseUrl)\(url)")!)
  request.httpMethod = httpMethod
  if let data = httpBody {
    request.httpBody = data
    request.allHTTPHeaderFields = [
      "content-type": "application/json"
    ]
  }
  URLSession.shared.dataTask(with: request, completionHandler: {
data, response, error in
    DispatchQueue.main.async {
      do {
        try completionHandler(data, response, error)
      } catch {}
    }
  }).resume()
}
```

Build the iOS app project and it should compile without any errors. If you look in this file, we get the base URL from our `Info.plist` using the following line and set it globally since it won't be changing throughout the running state of the application:

```
let baseUrl = Bundle.main.infoDictionary!["BaseURL"]!
```

The helper function body is simple as well. It will add data into the `httpBody` of the request if it is passed in the function and will also set the header to specify the content type to be JSON format since we will be using JSON format for sending data over to our Vapor server.

One other thing to note is that UI updates can only happen on the main thread in iOS. When we make a network request, it creates a new thread and the completion handler is called on that thread when the network request is completed. So as a convenience, we invoke the callback function passed in the handler inside the main thread as we will make UI updates once the request to our Vapor API server is completed.

# Fetching data from the server

Now that we have set our helper file to make network requests and configurations, we can begin making the requests to our API server. We will make a network request to our API server hitting the `/shopping_lists` route, which will return all of the Shopping Lists along with all of its items represented in JSON format. Swift 4 makes converting JSON into models a lot easier, thanks to the codable protocol that our models inherit from. Using a `JSONDecoder`, we will convert the JSON returned by our API into our models and render those on the iOS table view instead of the Shopping List that we persisted to disk using `UserDefaults` in Chapter 2, *Creating the Native App*.

To get started with loading data from our API server, we need to make changes to our `ShoppingList` model to implement a load method to make the network request to our API server. We also need to modify the Item model slightly and get rid of the old code to load and save data to disk using `UserDefaults`. Finally, we need to update our `ShoppingListTableViewController` so that it calls the updated methods on `ShoppingList` to load data from our Vapor server. To get started, we need to follow these steps:

1. Open the `Item.swift` file inside the iOS project and add an additional attribute on top called `id` so that it can store the `id` of the item that is stored in the database. Make it an optional `String` type for now:

    ```
    var id: String?
    ```

*Consuming API in App*

2. Specify the `CodingKeys` in the class so that the `JSONDecoder`, which we will use later, is able to map the value from the JSON to our model's instance variables correctly. We also need to type out which field value in the JSON gets mapped to the `isChecked` variable of our model since it is using snake case instead of camel case:

   ```
   private enum CodingKeys: String, CodingKey {
     case id
     case name
     case isChecked = "is_checked"
   }
   ```

3. Remove the `Array` extension that contains the `save` and static `load` function as we will no longer be using that to load and save our data. Instead, we will be saving the data to the database by making network calls via our Vapor API server.

Now that we have updated our Item model, let's update our `ShoppingList` model. To do so, we need to make the following changes:

1. Open the `ShoppingList.swift` file inside our iOS project and add an `id` instance variable of an optional String type. This will be used to store the `id` of our `ShoppingList` model that is fetched from the server:

   ```
   var id: String?
   ```

2. Get rid of the `didSet` on our items instance variable as we will not be saving them to disk:

   ```
   var items: [Item]
   ```

3. Remove the `onUpdate` instance variable as we will not be triggering the `onUpdate` now. Also, remove the convenience `init` method that took an `onUpdate` parameter as we will no longer be using that.

4. Add a static load method that will make the network request to load the `ShoppingList`. This will make the `GET` request to /shopping_lists and invoke a callback function that is passed as a parameter to the load function. This callback will be passed an array of the `ShoppingList` models that we have converted from JSON format to the `ShoppingList` type:

   ```
   static func load(onCompletion: @escaping ([ShoppingList]) -> Void)
   {
     request(url: "/shopping_lists") { data, response, error in
       let shoppingLists = try
   ```

```
          JSONDecoder().decode([ShoppingList].self, from: data!)
          onCompletion(shoppingLists)
        }
      }
```

5. In this file, we will add `case id` to the `enum CodingKeys` so that it can map the `id` field in the JSON to the `id` instance variable of our `ShoppingList` model.

Great! Now we have both models updated. The last thing to do is update our `ShoppingListController` so that it can use these new methods to load Shopping Lists from our server. To do so, we need to make the following changes:

1. Open the `ShoppingListTableViewController.swift` file and modify the instance variable lists to be an empty array for now. We will load this asynchronously in the background as we do not want to block the app from loading because the network request can take some time or may fail:

   ```
   var lists: [ShoppingList] = []
   ```

2. In our `viewDidLoad`, we need to add a refresh control so that we can refresh our data. The convention in iOS is to have a pulldown to update the UI control, which is very easy to add using a few lines of code. Add the following lines inside the `viewDidLoad` method towards the end:

   ```
   refreshControl = UIRefreshControl()
   refreshControl?.addTarget(self, action: #selector(loadData), for:
   .valueChanged)
   loadData()
   ```

3. We need to define one new method, called `loadData`, which will get called when our table view loads and when the user pulls down to refresh data from the server again. In this snippet of code, we add a special `@objc` keyword before the function so that it is accessible to the selector passed to the `refreshControl`:

   ```
   @objc func loadData() {
     ShoppingList.load() { lists in
       self.lists = lists
       self.tableView.reloadData()
       self.refreshControl?.endRefreshing()
     }
   }
   ```

*Consuming API in App*

4. The last line we need to update is the line where we create a new `ShoppingList` inside of `didSelectAdd`. We need to update the initializer by not passing the `onUpdate` parameter as we have removed that initializer and variable from our `ShoppingList` class.

Great! We are done now with our changes. We can now start both our Vapor application and our iOS app, and have our iOS load the Shopping List with all of the items from the database. To see all of this work together, follow these steps:

1. Build and run the **Run** Scheme on the **My Mac** platform. This should build and run without any errors. Make sure you have the MongoDB database running in the background. If MongoDB is not running, you will get an error. To start MongoDB, you can run the following command on your macOS:

    ```
    ~ $ mongod --config /usr/local/etc/mongod.conf
    ```

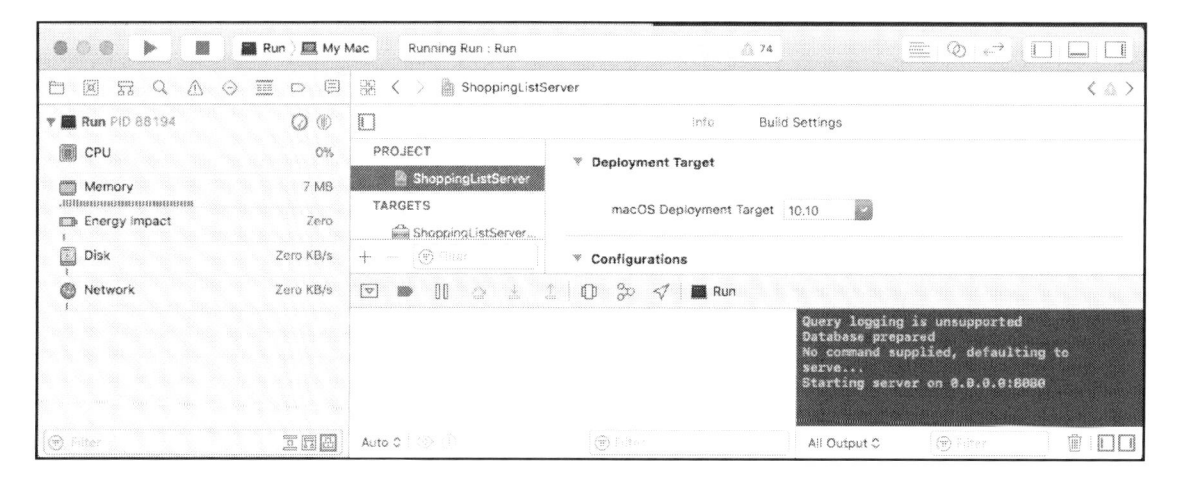

2. Once the Vapor application is started, switch the **Scheme** to `ShoppingList` and select any iOS simulator you like, then build and run. The build should succeed and you should see the simulator run the app with the `ShoppingList` being fetched from the API server:

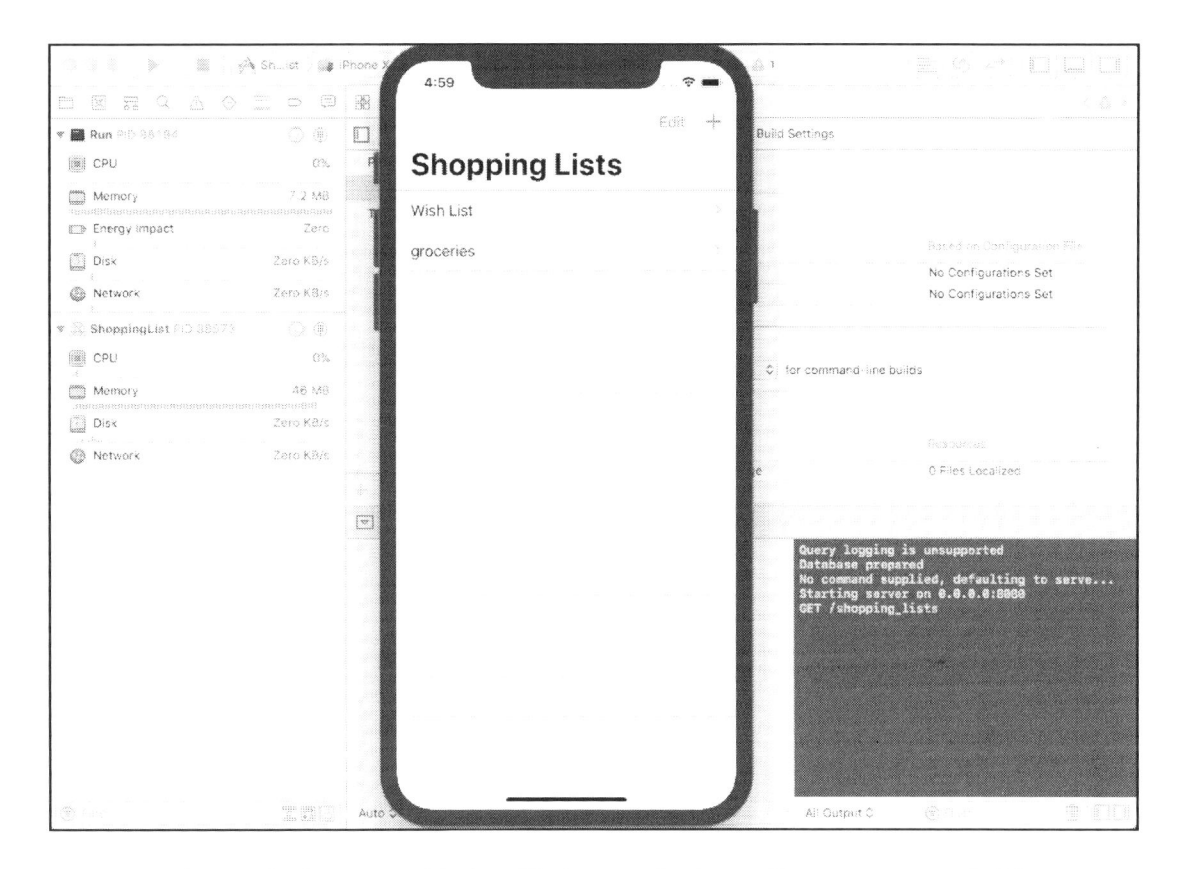

Awesome! Great job if you got this far. We just ran both our Vapor server and iOS app inside the same Xcode window. Not only that, we can see that, app load and fetch the data from our API server. We can verify this by looking at the logs from our Vapor server inside of Xcode and looking for `GET /shopping_lists`.

# Debugging the app and server side by side

One of the benefits of using Xcode and Swift for both frontend and backend development is the ability to develop and debug both iOS and Vapor apps at the same time. To see this in action we need to do the following:

1. Open `ShoppingListController.swift` in the server project and put a breakpoint by clicking on the line number that is inside the index method, as follows:

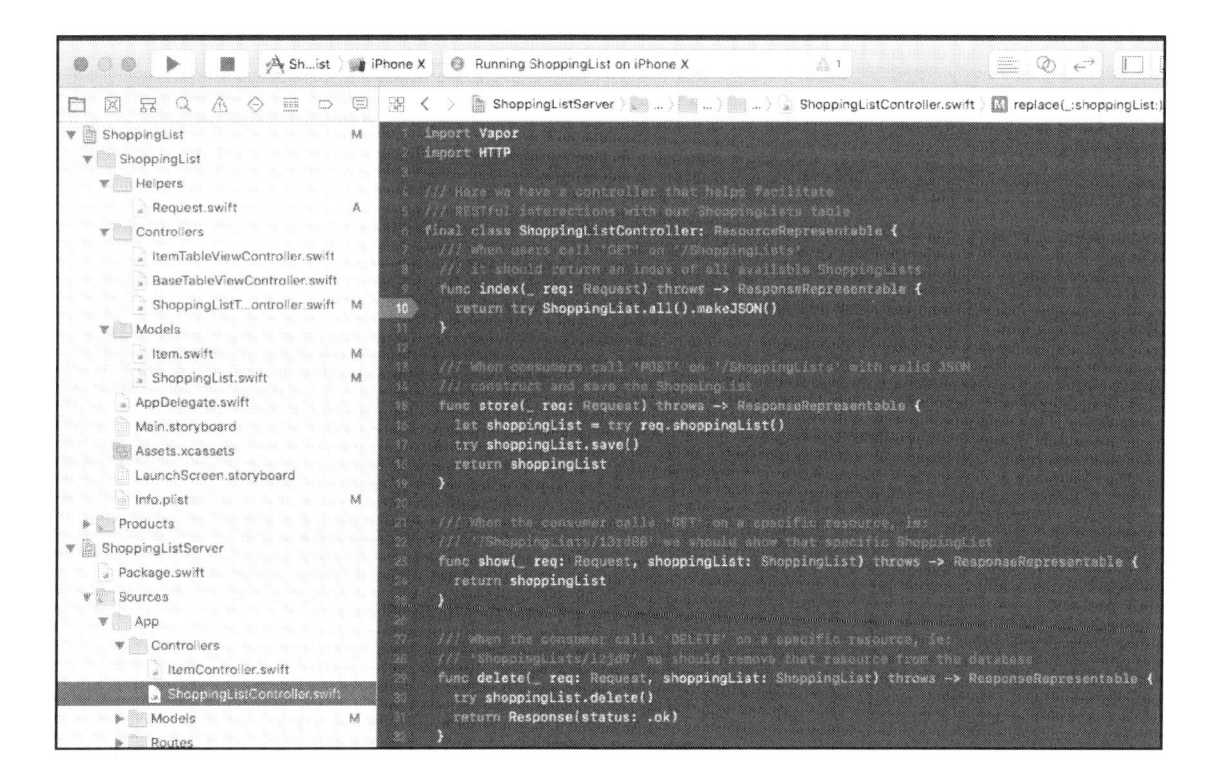

2. Go to the `ShoppingList.swift` model in our iOS project and click on the line inside the completion handler of the request so we can inspect the response we get back from the server, as follows:

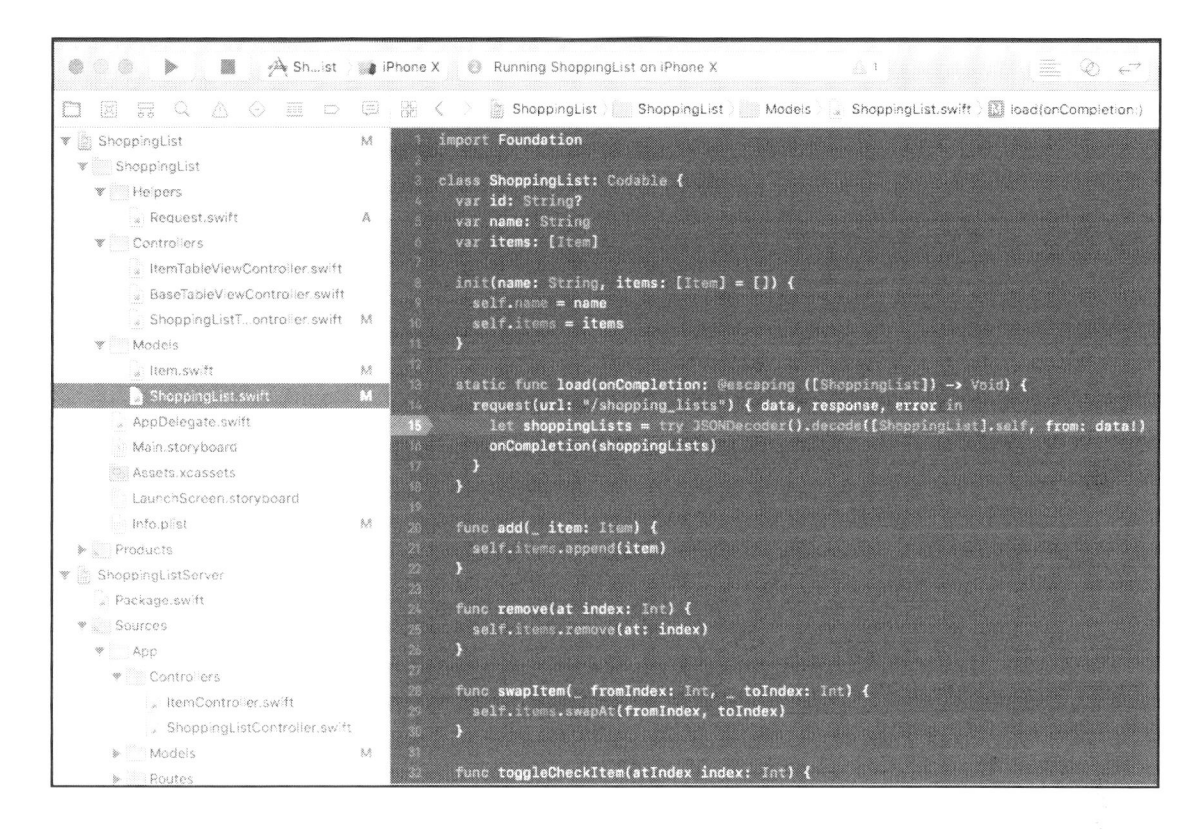

```swift
import Foundation

class ShoppingList: Codable {
    var id: String?
    var name: String
    var items: [Item]

    init(name: String, items: [Item] = []) {
        self.name = name
        self.items = items
    }

    static func load(onCompletion: @escaping ([ShoppingList]) -> Void) {
        request(url: "/shopping_lists") { data, response, error in
            let shoppingLists = try JSONDecoder().decode([ShoppingList].self, from: data!)
            onCompletion(shoppingLists)
        }
    }

    func add(_ item: Item) {
        self.items.append(item)
    }

    func remove(at index: Int) {
        self.items.remove(at: index)
    }

    func swapItem(_ fromIndex: Int, _ toIndex: Int) {
        self.items.swapAt(fromIndex, toIndex)
    }

    func toggleCheckItem(atIndex index: Int) {
```

*Consuming API in App*

3. Trigger a request to fetch the data again from the app by pulling down on the table view:

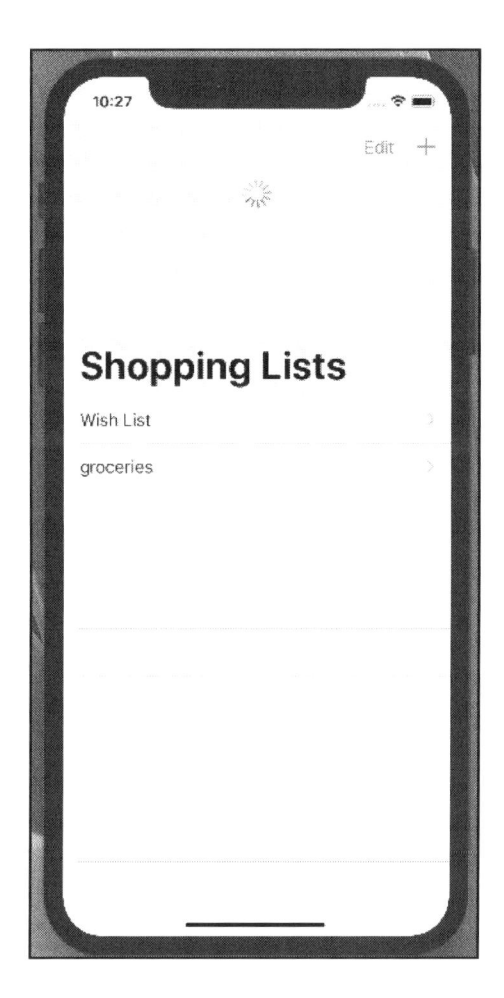

*Chapter 6*

Once you have triggered a refresh by pulling down on the table view, you would have seen the Xcode pause execution at the line where we put the breakpoint in the index method of the Shopping List controller. Here we can inspect the `req` and print objects in the console, if needed, to help us debug an issue and figure out whether the issue is originating from the server side or on the client side:

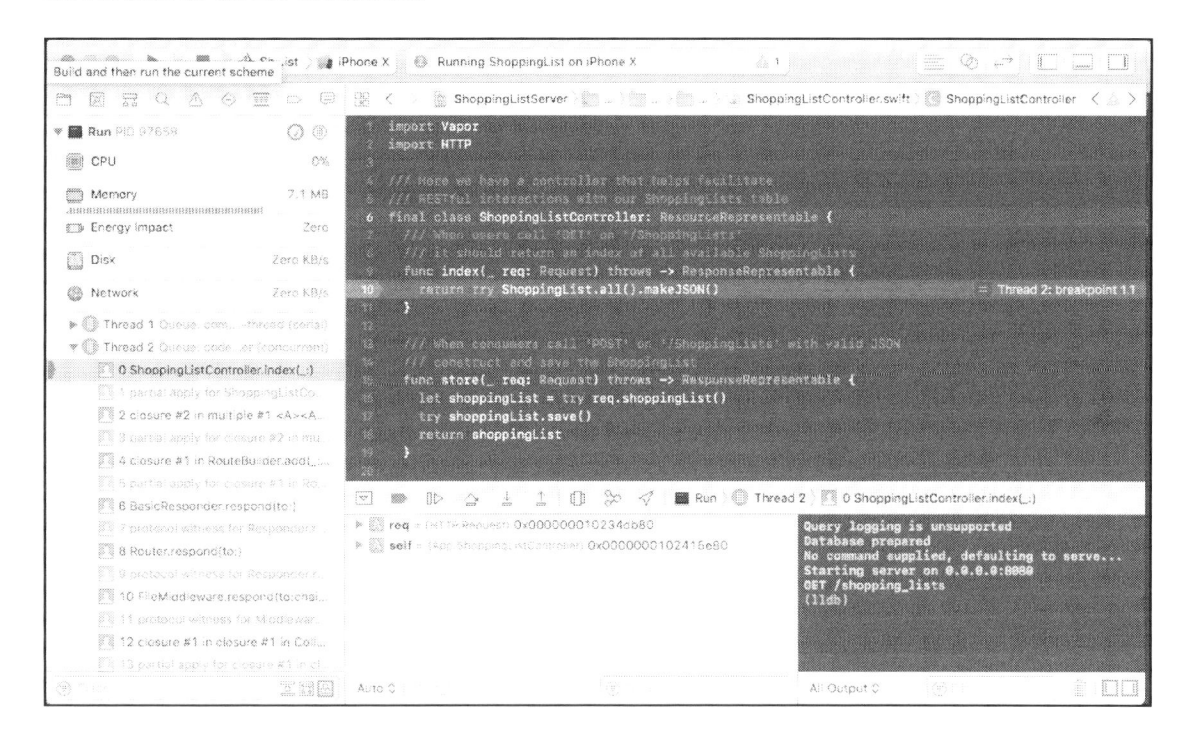

*Consuming API in App*

Now we can let the code resume by pressing the **Continue program execution** or, if we wanted step over or step into a function. Once we let the code continue, we will pause the code execution again in the same Xcode window but on the iOS side of the `ShoppingList.swift` file. Here Xcode will pause the code just like we did for the server, but on iOS, and we can inspect variables, step over, and let the code execution continue:

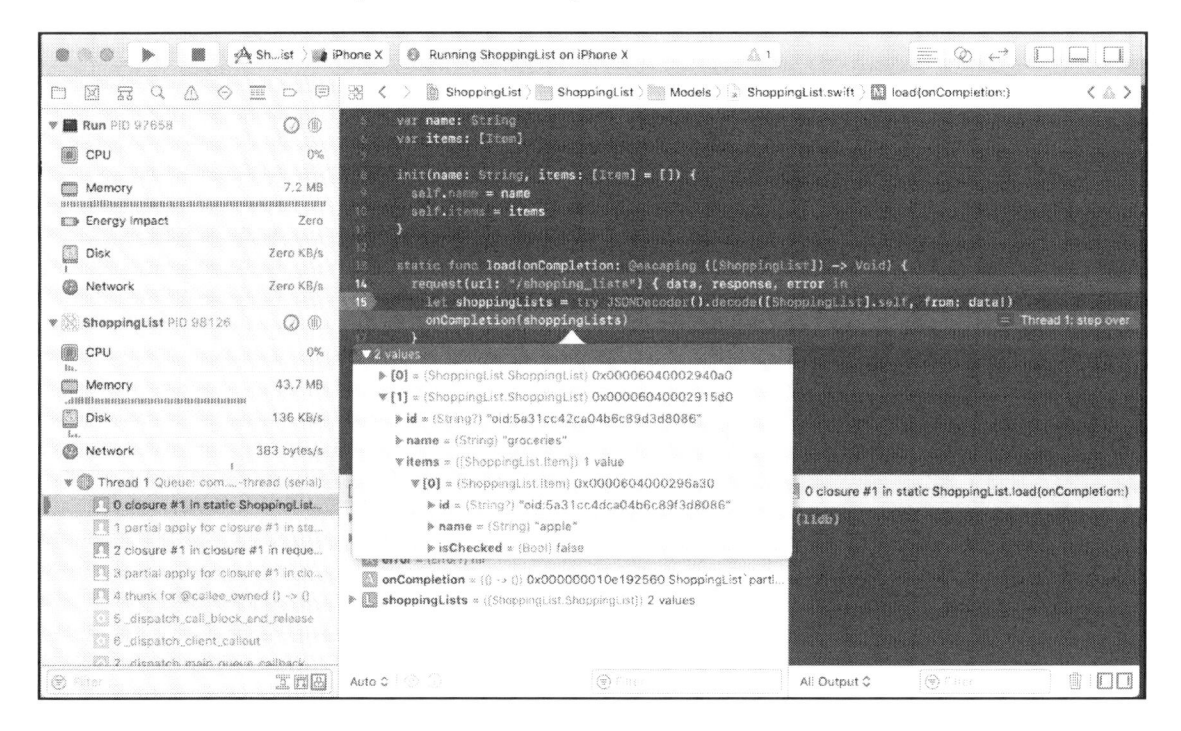

## Adding a Shopping List

To add a Shopping List to our app is as simple making a `POST` request to the `/shopping_lists` endpoint with the JSON representation of our Shopping List Model that we want to create. We need to make this request to our Vapor API server and wait for a success response that contains the newly created shopping list object in JSON format. We will then convert it to a `ShoppingList` model and call the `onCompletion` handler function that is passed so that the `ShoppingListTableViewController` can add this new shopping list in its array of lists and tell the Table View to reload with this new Shopping List that is saved on the server.

*Chapter 6*

To implement the add functionality that persists the new Shopping List in the database via our API, we need to follow these steps:

1. Open the `ShoppingList.swift` file in the iOS project and add a new computed property called `data`. This property will return an optional data type and it will return data in JSON format. We will use `JSONSerializer` to convert a dictionary representation of our Shopping List object to a data type that is sent over in the HTTP body request:

   ```
   var data: Data? {
     get {
       let parameters = ["name": name] as [String : Any]
       do {
         return try JSONSerialization.data(withJSONObject: parameters, options: [])
       } catch {
         return .none
       }
     }
   }
   ```

2. Create a save method that will make the network request using the request helper function. In this request function, we will specify the HTTP method to be `POST` and also pass data to be sent in `httpBody` by passing the computed property we just created. In this function, we will take an `onCompletion` function that will be called when the request is completed and the list object is created from the JSON payload:

   ```
   func save(onCompletion: @escaping (ShoppingList) -> Void) {
     request(url: "/shopping_lists", httpMethod: "POST", httpBody: data) { data, _, _ in
       let decoder = JSONDecoder()
       let list = try decoder.decode(ShoppingList.self, from: data!)
       onCompletion(list)
     }
   }
   ```

[ 187 ]

*Consuming API in App*

3. Go to our `ShoppingListTableViewController.swift` file and update one line inside the `didSelectAdd` method. We need to update the line where we create a new Shopping List object after getting input from the user. We will instead call the save method, which takes a closure function. This closure function is called after the network request successfully saves the Shopping List to the database via the API endpoint. We will update the Table View only when this success closure function is called. The entire `didSelectAdd` function needs to look like this:

```swift
@IBAction func didSelectAdd(_ sender: UIBarButtonItem) {
    requestInput(title: "Shopping list name",
      message: "Enter name for the new shopping list:",
      handler: { listName in
        let listCount = self.lists.count
        ShoppingList(name: listName).save() { list in
          self.lists.append(list)
          self.tableView.insertRows(at: [IndexPath(row: listCount, section: 0)], with: .top)
        }
    })
}
```

Build and run just the iOS app scheme on the iPhone simulator. Before adding a new Shopping List, add a breakpoint inside the `store` method of the `ShoppingListController.swift` file on the line where we return the `shoppingList` object so that we can inspect the newly created Shopping List model on the server side before it is sent to our iOS app. After adding the breakpoint, add a new Shopping List by tapping on the plus icon in the top-right corner, give it a new name, and tap **Add**:

*Chapter 6*

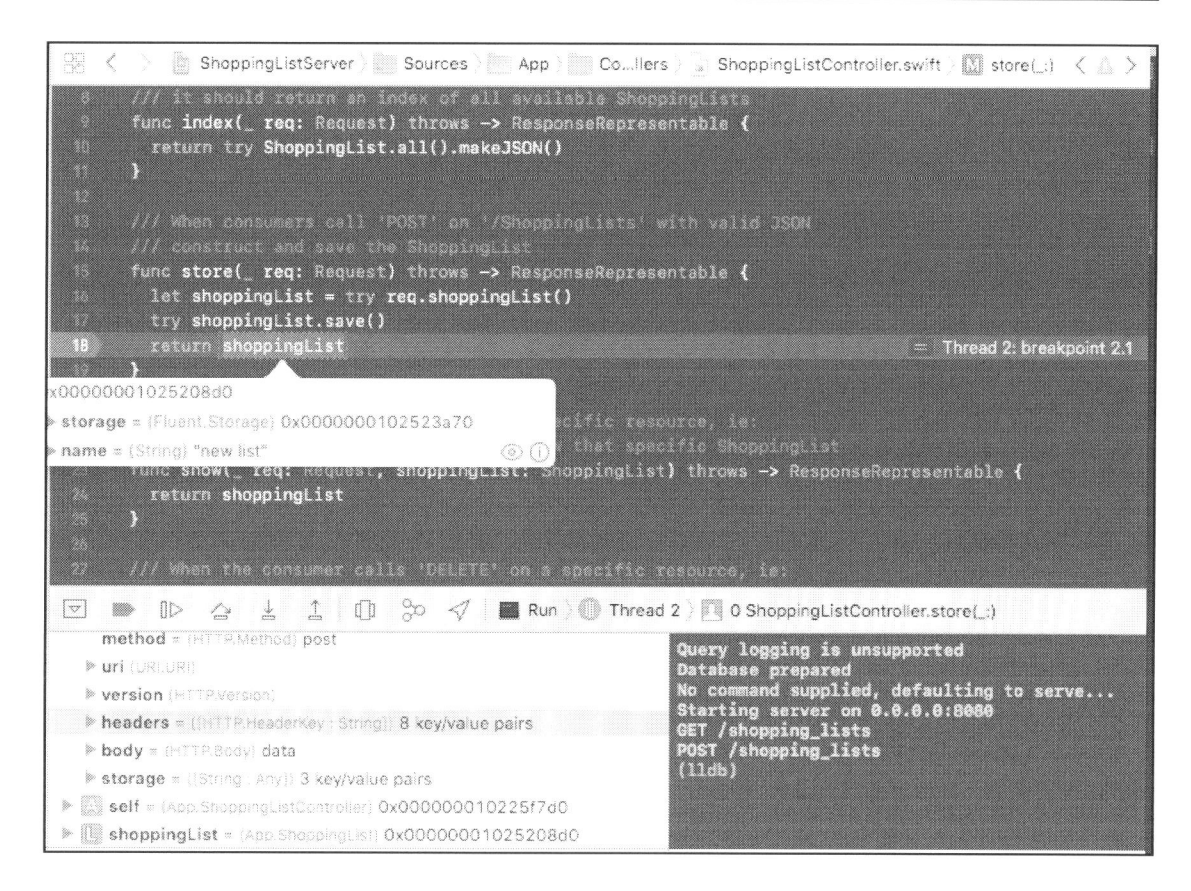

```
func index(_ req: Request) throws -> ResponseRepresentable {
    return try ShoppingList.all().makeJSON()
}

/// When consumers call 'POST' on '/ShoppingLists' with valid JSON
/// construct and save the ShoppingList
func store(_ req: Request) throws -> ResponseRepresentable {
    let shoppingList = try req.shoppingList()
    try shoppingList.save()
    return shoppingList
}
```

You should see Xcode pause at our breakpoint inside the `store` method. Here you can confirm that we created a new Shopping List object with the same name that you entered in the app, which confirms that the save happened successfully and our app is sending the correct data in the POST request to generate this Shopping List object on the server side.

[ 189 ]

You can now let this run by pressing the **Continue** button and you should see it show up in the iOS app as well:

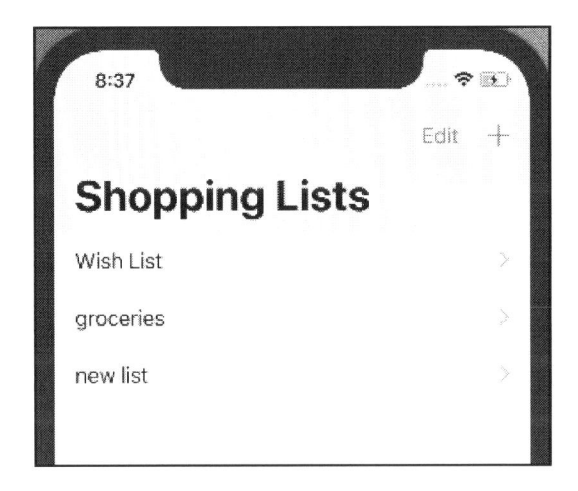

## Deleting a Shopping List

To delete a Shopping List is similar to adding. We need to define a new `delete` method on the Shopping List class. In that method, make a `DELETE` request to the `/shopping_lists/:id` endpoint where `:id` is the ID of our Shopping List model. We already have to delete implemented in our Table View Controller but we need to invoke this new `delete` method from our Table View Controller, and, on a successful `DELETE` request to our API server, we need to update the Table View by reloading it. To add the delete functionality, we need to follow these steps:

1. Open the `ShoppingList.swift` file from our iOS project and add the following `delete` method to the class. In this method, we make the request by specifying the `DELETE` HTTP method and also pass the `id` of the Shopping List we want to delete in the URL. On completion, we call the `onCompletion` closure function passed as part of the `delete` method invocation:

    ```
    func delete(onCompletion: @escaping () -> Void) {
      request(url: "/shopping_lists/\(id!)", httpMethod: "DELETE") {
    data, _, _ in
        onCompletion()
      }
    }
    ```

2. Go to the `ShoppingListTableViewController.swift` file. Inside of the `tableView(_:commit:forRowAt:)` method, we will update the method body to the following lines of code. Instead of removing right away, we will make the network request. On success, we will remove it and update the `tableView`:

```
override func tableView(_ tableView: UITableView, commit
editingStyle: UITableViewCellEditingStyle, forRowAt indexPath:
IndexPath) {
  if editingStyle == .delete {
    let list = lists[indexPath.row]
    list.delete() {
      self.lists.remove(at: indexPath.row)
      tableView.deleteRows(at: [indexPath], with: .fade)
    }
  }
}
```

Now build and run the iOS app. Now if you swipe to delete a Shopping List or tap on **Edit** and **Delete** a Shopping List, it will make a network request to our API and delete it from the database:

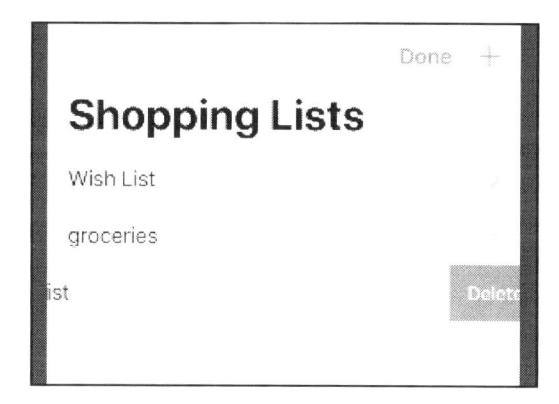

**Shopping Lists**

Wish List

groceries

ist                                          Delete

Consuming API in App

To confirm this, you can pull down on the table view to refresh the data from the server. You will also see the `DELETE` request recorded in the console of the Vapor app in Xcode:

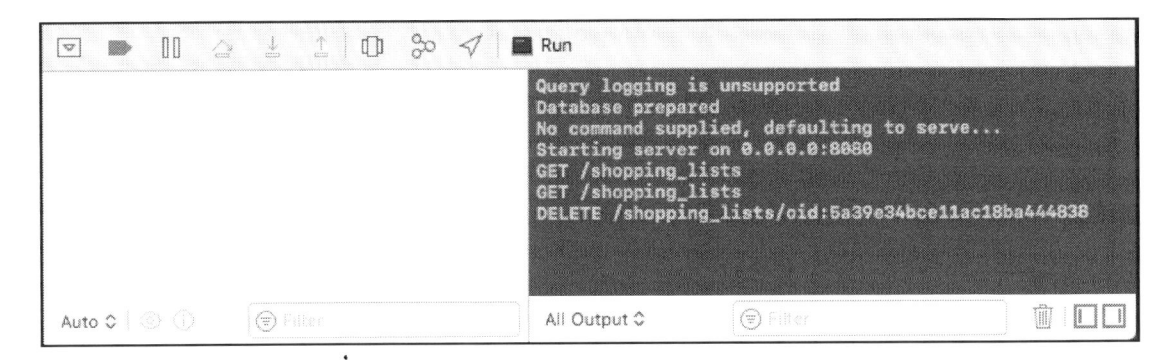

```
Query logging is unsupported
Database prepared
No command supplied, defaulting to serve...
Starting server on 0.0.0.0:8080
GET /shopping_lists
GET /shopping_lists
DELETE /shopping_lists/oid:5a39e34bce11ac18ba444838
```

## Exercise

Great! So by now, you should know how to make network requests to fetch a Shopping List with its items, create a new Shopping List, and delete a Shopping List. Now it's time for a short exercise to implement the ability to add or delete an item in a Shopping List. Currently, we can add and delete items from the Shopping List via our app, but it does not make any network requests. Implement the add and delete functionality, similar to the Shopping List, so that it persists the changes in the database via our API server.

## Adding a Shopping List Item

If you have successfully implemented the create and delete functionality for an item in the Shopping List, then good job! If not, we will walk through how you can do so. It is very similar to how we implemented it on the Shopping List. To implement the functionality for adding items to a Shopping List, we need to follow these steps:

1. Open the `Item.swift` file inside the iOS project and add a new instance variable to store the `shoppingListId`. This variable will be passed to the API server along with the `name` and the `isChecked` state of the item when creating it so that it can associate this item with the shopping list it is being added to:

   ```
   var shoppingListId: String?
   ```

2. Add the data commuted property, similar to the one we added in the `ShoppingList` class, which will convert our object into JSON data that will be passed to our API server. In this case, we will use `JSONEncoder` instead of `JSONSerializer`. The reason why we did not convert `ShoppingList` to JSON data using this method was that it would encode the items inside the Shopping List. Also, items are specified as a property that needs to be encoded and decoded as part of the `CodingKeys`:

   ```
   private let encoder = JSONEncoder()
   var data: Data? {
     get {
       return try! encoder.encode(self)
     }
   }
   ```

3. Add a new coding key for the `shoppingListId`, as follows:

   ```
   case shoppingListId = "shopping_list__id"
   ```

We are done making changes to `Item.swift` but we are not done yet. We need to update the `ShoppingList` class again so that it can make the network request to our API server upon adding an item. On completion of the network request, reload the table view to show the newly added item. To do so, we need to make the following changes:

1. Open the `ShoppingList.swift` file from the iOS project and update the `add` method so that it takes a `onCompletion` handler, which will get called when the item is created on the server and a confirmation is received and after it is added to the Shopping List's items array:

   ```
   func add(_ item: Item, onCompletion: @escaping () -> Void) {
   ```

2. Inside this method, set the passed item's `shoppingListId` attribute to the `id` attribute of the shopping list object:

   ```
   item.shoppingListId = id
   ```

3. Make the network request and, when it completes, create an item object from the JSON response using the `JSONDecoder`. Then add this item to the items array and call the `onCompletion` callback. The entire `add` method would look like this after the change:

   ```
   func add(_ item: Item, onCompletion: @escaping () -> Void) {
     item.shoppingListId = id
     request(url: "/items/", httpMethod: "POST", httpBody: item.data)
   ```

# Consuming API in App

```
        { data, response, error in
            let decoder = JSONDecoder()
            let item = try decoder.decode(Item.self, from: data!)
            self.items.append(item)
            onCompletion()
        }
    }
}
```

Now that we have the `add` method created, the last thing to do is update our `ItemTableViewController` so that it can call this updated method and update the Table View after the item is successfully created on the server. To do so, we need to make a small change in the `ItemTableViewController.swift` file and update the `didSelectAdd` method. We need to pass a closure function in the `self.list.add` method and invoke the `tableView.insertRow` method. So, the updated method would look like the following:

```
@IBAction func didSelectAdd(_ sender: UIBarButtonItem) {
    requestInput(title: "New shopping list item",
      message: "Enter item to add to the shopping list:",
      handler: { itemName in
        let itemCount = self.items.count;
        self.list.add(Item(name: itemName)) {
            self.tableView.insertRows(at: [IndexPath(row: itemCount, section: 0)], with: .top)
        }
    })
}
```

Now go ahead and build and run the iOS app on the simulator. Add an item by first going into a Shopping List and tapping on the plus icon on the top-right corner and giving it a name. You should see the item show up and if you go back and reload the Shopping List data by pulling down to refresh, you should see the item you just added in the Shopping List you previously selected. We can also confirm that it successfully made the network request by checking the logs for our Vapor application and looking for a POST request being made to `/items`, as follows:

```
Starting server on 0.0.0.0:8080
GET /shopping_lists
POST /items/
```

[ 194 ]

# Deleting an item

Deleting an Item is very similar to deleting a Shopping List where we need to make a `DELETE` request to the `/items` endpoint instead, with the ID of the item passed in the URL. Just like addition, we need to update the `remove` method inside the `ShoppingList` class so that it can make a network request to delete and invoke an `onCompletion` handler that we can use to update the `tableView`. For this, we need to make two changes. They are as follows:

1. Inside of the `ShoppingList.swift` file of the iOS project, update the method signature of the `remove` method to take an extra parameter called the `onCompletion` closure function. Inside this function, make the network request to delete the item from the server. On success, remove the item from the Shopping List's items array and call the `onCompletion` handler. The updated `remove` method looks like the following:

    ```
    func remove(at index: Int, onCompletion: @escaping () -> Void) {
      let itemId = self.items[index].id!
      request(url: "/items/\(itemId)", httpMethod: "DELETE") { _, _, _ in
         self.items.remove(at: index)
         onCompletion()
      }
    }
    ```

2. Inside the `ItemTableViewController` class, we need to update the `tableView(_:commit:forRowAt:)` method where we need to pass a closure function when calling `list.remove`. Inside of that closure, delete the row from Table View. The entire function after the update would look like this:

    ```
    override func tableView(_ tableView: UITableView, commit editingStyle: UITableViewCellEditingStyle, forRowAt indexPath: IndexPath) {
      if editingStyle == .delete {
        list.remove(at: indexPath.row) {
          tableView.deleteRows(at: [indexPath], with: .fade)
        }
      }
    }
    ```

Now build and run. Go to any Shopping List that has any items and delete an item by swiping to the left. This will make the network request to our API, which we can confirm by looking at the server logs. We should see the item removed from our table view:

```
Starting server on 0.0.0.0:8080
GET /shopping_lists
POST /items/
GET /shopping_lists
GET /shopping_lists
DELETE /items/oid:5a3ed6c395d5b82d2c315840
```

## Checking and unchecking an item

To check and uncheck an item is simple. For this, we would need to make a PATCH or PUT HTTP request. If we were just sending a single attribute to update, we would make a PATCH request. If we are passing all of the attributes then we would make a PUT request. The difference is that in the PUT request, any attributes that are not passed are saved as NULL in the database. In PATCH requests, only the attributes that are passed are updated, and the ones that are not passed remain unchanged. In our case, since we already have a computed property called data, which contains all of the attributes of an item object in JSON format, we can make either a PUT or PATCH request. To make checking and unchecking work, we would need to first invert the value of isChecked and then make a PUT request to the server by passing the JSON representation of the item object in the body of the request. Then we would need to parse the response and convert the JSON back to an item and pass the item in the completion handler so that it can be updated in the table view by the Table View Controller. To makes these changes, follow these steps:

1. Update the toggleCheck method inside the Item class to take an extra parameter called the onCompletion handler:

    ```
    func toggleCheck(onCompletion: @escaping (Item) -> Void) {
    ```

2. Inside of this method, invert the value of the isChecked attribute for the item:

    ```
    self.isChecked = !self.isChecked
    ```

3. Make the network call to the item-specific endpoint that contains the item ID in the URL. On completion, decode the JSON response into an item object and pass that in the `onCompletion` handler that is passed. The updated `toggleCheck` method will look like the following:

   ```
   func toggleCheck(onCompletion: @escaping (Item) -> Void) {
     self.isChecked = !self.isChecked
     request(url: "/items/\(id!)", httpMethod: "PUT", httpBody: data)
   { data, _, _ in
       let decoder = JSONDecoder()
       let item = try decoder.decode(Item.self, from: data!)
       onCompletion(item)
     }
   }
   ```

4. Update the `toggleCheckItem` method inside of the `ShoppingList` class to the following, where it takes an `onCompletion` handler and passes that to the item being toggled:

   ```
   func toggleCheckItem(atIndex index: Int, onCompletion: @escaping
   (Item) -> Void) {
     self.items[index].toggleCheck(onCompletion: onCompletion)
   }
   ```

5. Update the `tableView(_:didSelectRowAt:)` method of the `ItemTableViewController` class by passing a closure function along with the `list.toggleCheckItem` method call. Inside of the closure, update the table view for the row that the item is on:

   ```
   override func tableView(_ tableView: UITableView, didSelectRowAt
   indexPath: IndexPath) {
     list.toggleCheckItem(atIndex: indexPath.row) { _ in
       tableView.reloadRows(at: [indexPath], with: .middle)
     }
   }
   ```

Great! Now we are feature complete. Let's build and run. You should now be able to go into a Shopping List and tap on an item to see the item toggle from the checked to unchecked state and vice versa. To confirm this is indeed working, we can look at the network request being made to our server and see the `PUT` requests being recorded in the console for every time a selection is made to an item:

```
Starting server on 0.0.0.0:8080
GET /shopping_lists
POST /items/
```

```
GET     /shopping_lists
GET     /shopping_lists
DELETE  /items/oid:5a3ed6c395d5b82d2c315840
GET     /shopping_lists
PUT     /items/oid:5a31cc4dca04b6c89f3d8086
PUT     /items/oid:5a31cc4dca04b6c89f3d8086
```

# Summary

If you have made it this far, then great job! You have not only created an API server using Swift but also built a network-based iOS application that uses the API you built to load and save data. There are a few things we can improve in the app, such as having better error handling, as we have not taken care of a situation where there is no network connection or there is a bad network taking the network request a long time to return. Nevertheless, you should have a good understanding of how to make a network request from your iOS application and make different kinds of HTTP requests, such as GET, POST, PUT, and DELETE. You should also have a better grasp on how to convert Swift class objects to JSON data to send to our API server, and convert JSON data from the API response into Swift class objects to be used in our iOS code. This has become a lot easier, starting with Swift 4, due to the codable protocol and CodingKeys, which helped map out keys from the JSON object to attributes in our class. We also covered the best practice of handling network requests asynchronously by passing a closure function so that it can be called later on when the network request has returned and make UI changes only in the main thread.

Now that our iOS app is complete, in the next chapter we will make a web version of our ShoppingList and learn how to use LeafProvider to render HTML templates in the browser. We will add some Javascript and CSS to spice up the web application and create, update, and delete Shopping Lists from the browser.

# 7
# Creating Web Views and Middleware

In the preceding chapter, we jumped back to iOS and refactored our app so that we can use our Vapor API server to load, create, update, and delete Shopping Lists and items. Now, in this chapter, we will discuss how to make our Vapor application into a web application that can also serve HTML pages. As we have seen before in `Chapter 3`, *Getting Started with Vapor*, building web servers using Vapor is easy, and we can dynamically generate HTML based on the request we receive. We used Vapor only to serve API requests, but, in this chapter, we will extend our Vapor application so that it can server web content that can be rendered on the browser. Just like native mobile applications, the web is another platform where we can use server-side Swift and Vapor to be able to serve our Shopping List application for users to consume.

In this chapter, we will do just that and create a web interface using HTML, CSS, and JavaScript. Through this web application, we will be able to add and delete a shopping list and also be able to add, edit, and delete items within a shopping list. The HTML templates will all be rendered on server side using Vapor's Leaf view rendering engine. We will add some CSS to spice up our page and sprinkle in JavaScript so that we can make the network request to our existing API endpoints to perform the CRUD operations similar to the native iOS app. By the end of this chapter, we will cover the following topics:

- How to add view rendering to a Vapor app
- What is Leaf and how to use it to generate HTML
- How to create and use middleware in Vapor so that we can generate both HTML and JSON responses for our routes

- How to make network requests from the browser
- How to perform CRUD operations on our web app so that we have the same feature parity as our native iOS app

So let's get started.

# View rendering in Vapor app

In `Chapter 3`, *Getting Started with Vapor*, we created a web application using Vapor that simply printed Hello World. We also got a little flavor of dynamic HTML generation using Leaf where we passed a name in the URL route that got rendered in the HTML. In that example application, we got everything out of box configured and working. In our current `ShoppingListServer` Vapor application, we do not have a view renderer and instead render data in the JSON format only. To add HTML rendering, we will need to add a template rendering engine. Currently, there is one rendering engine that is officially supported by Vapor team, and that is Leaf.

## What is Leaf?

**Leaf** is a pure Swift templating engine that lets you generate text output, given a template file and a bunch of variables. Leaf can be used by other server-side Swift frameworks and is not specific to HTML rendering. It can be used to generate code or any textual configuration file. In Vapor, it is used to render HTML, and to use Leaf in a Vapor application, we will need to use the Leaf Provider, which, as we learned in previous chapters, implements certain protocols methods needed by Vapor to make a Swift package compatible in order to be consumed.

To understand how Leaf works, let's make a basic Vapor application that uses Leaf to render some text dynamically. The following are the steps to get started with a basic Vapor app with the Leaf rendering engine:

1. Create a new folder and call it `LeafExperiment`. Now, open the folder in the Terminal, and create a Swift executable package using the following command:

    ```
    swift package init --type executable
    ```

2. Now, inside your `Package.swift` file, add Vapor and Leaf as dependencies and specify them in the target section also:

```
dependencies: [
  .package(url: "https://github.com/vapor/vapor.git", from:
"2.4.0"),
  .package(url: "https://github.com/vapor/leaf.git", from:
"2.0.2"),
],
targets: [
  .target(
    name: "LeafExperiment",
    dependencies: ["Vapor", "Leaf"]),
]
```

3. Now, open up the `main.swift` file and copy the following code:

```
import Vapor
import Leaf

let stem = Stem(DataFile(workDir: "./"))
let drop = try Droplet()

drop.get("hello", ":name") { req in
  guard let name = req.parameters["name"]?.string else {
    throw Abort.badRequest
  }
  let leaf = try stem.spawnLeaf(at: "hello")
  let context = Context(["name": Node(name)])
  let rendered = try stem.render(leaf, with: context)
  let response = Response(status: .ok, body: rendered)
  response.headers["content-type"] = "text/html"
  return response
}

try drop.run()
```

4. Create a new file called `hello.leaf` and save it at the root level of this Swift package and copy the following contents into the file. This is the file that will be rendered to HTML by the Leaf engine:

```
<h1>Hello #(name)!</h1>
```

*Creating Web Views and Middleware*

5. Now, run the `swift run` command, which will download the dependencies, build the executable, and run our simple Vapor app and go to `http://localhost:8080/hello/world` in the browser:

![Hello world! browser screenshot at localhost:8080/hello/world]

Awesome! We just rendered HTML dynamically using text passed in the URL. To understand how this works, let's go over the code line by line:

1. The first thing we do is import our dependencies, which are Vapor and Leaf:

   ```
   import Vapor
   import Leaf
   ```

2. Next, we will need to initialize an instance of Stem, which is Swift's rendering engine. In the initializer, we will pass the project folder so that it can search for template files from there. In our demo, we set the path to be the root level of the package. We also create an instance of Droplet to create our Vapor app:

   ```
   let stem = Stem(DataFile(workDir: "./"))
   let drop = try Droplet()
   ```

3. Next, we will create a `hello` route and expect a parameter to be passed after the `/hello/` route. We extract the parameter, and, if it is not found and is not of the string type, we throw a Bad Request error to show the 400 Bad Request page. This Bad Request page is rendered by Vapor by catching the thrown `Abort.badRequest`:

   ```
   drop.get("hello", ":name") { req in
     guard let name = req.parameters["name"]?.string else {
       throw Abort.badRequest
     }
   ```

4. Next, we will create a Leaf instance from the stem. The `spawnLeaf` takes the name of the template file, which, in our case, is called `hello`, and it adds the `.leaf` extension to it by default. We also have the `hello.leaf` file at the root level of our page, so it will search for the `hello.leaf` file relative to that folder. We then create a context object, which contains the variables that will be passed to the `stem.render` method along with the Leaf and get back the rendered template as raw bytes. These variables passed in the context object are the same variables that we can reference inside our Leaf template as follows `#(name)`:

   ```
   let leaf = try stem.spawnLeaf(at: "hello")
   let context = Context(["name": Node(name)])
   let rendered = try stem.render(leaf, with: context)
   ```

5. We finally create a response object and set the content type to HTML before returning it in the closure function:

   ```
   let response = Response(status: .ok, body: rendered)
   response.headers["content-type"] = "text/html"
   return response
   }
   ```

6. Lastly, we start up the Vapor app by calling `drop.run()`:

   ```
   try drop.run()
   ```

[ 203 ]

*Creating Web Views and Middleware*

I hope this simple Swift executable package demonstrates how Leaf works and how Vapor uses it under the hood to generate HTML from Leaf template files. You might have also noticed that in our web template example in Chapter 3, *Getting Started with Vapor*, it was able to find the `hello.leaf` file from inside the `Resources/Views` folder because Vapor sets the `DataFile` to that folder when creating a new stem instance:

```
let stem = Stem(DataFile(workDir: "./Resources/Views"))
```

Now, let's dive back into our `ShoppingListServer` application and add Leaf to it, and take a look at how easy it is to start rendering HTML in our Vapor application.

# Adding Leaf Provider

To add Leaf-rendering support to our Vapor application, we will need to use Leaf Provider. It uses the same Leaf package under the hood, but implements Vapor's Provider protocol so that it can be used without writing much code and specifying it as our view renderer in the `droplet.json` config. To add Leaf Provider to our Vapor app, we will need to perform the following steps:

1. Open up our `ShoppingListServer` Xcode project and add `leaf-provider` as a dependency inside our `Package.swift`:

    ```
    .package(url: "https://github.com/vapor/leaf-provider.git",
    .upToNextMajor(from: "1.1.0")),
    ```

2. Next, specify it as a dependency for our `App` target:

    ```
    .target(name: "App", dependencies: ["Vapor", "FluentProvider",
    "HealthcheckProvider", "MongoProvider", "LeafProvider"],
    ```

3. Now, open up the `Config+Setup.swift` file and import the `LeafProvider` by specifying it on the top of the file:

    ```
    import LeafProvider
    ```

4. Now, we will need to add the `LeafProvider` to our app. We can do this by adding the following line in our `setupProviders` method in the `Config+Setup.swift` file:

    ```
    try addProvider(LeafProvider.Provider.self)
    ```

[ 204 ]

5. Lastly, open the `droplet.json` file inside the `Config` folder, and add the following `"view": "leaf"` config property toward the end. This will tell the Vapor app to start using `LeafProvider` for view rendering:

```
{
  "server": "engine",
  "client": "engine",
  "console": "terminal",
  "log": "console",
  "hash": "crypto",
  "cipher": "crypto",
  "middleware": ["error", "date", "file"],
  "commands": ["prepare"],
  "view": "leaf"
}
```

That is it. We have configured and installed all of the dependencies to start using Leaf, but we are not done yet. To test it out, we will need to create some template files. We will first start by creating a `Resources/Views` folder and then create a `base.leaf`, which contains HTML. You can create these folders and files directly from Xcode or create them from the command line and rerun `vapor xcode -y` so that the `Views` folder is visible in Xcode along with the `base.leaf` file. We will also create two folders in the `Public` folder called `js` and `css` and store our JavaScript and CSS files there, which are served as static files by Vapor. To set this all up, we will need to follow these steps:

1. First, create a `Resources` folder at the root level of the project. Then, create a `Views` folder inside it. In there, create an empty file and call it `base.leaf`, as follows:

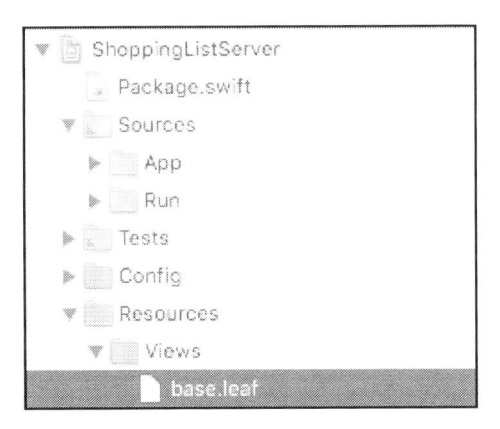

2. Next, open up the `base.leaf` file and copy the following contents into the file:

```html
<!DOCTYPE html>
<html>
<head>
  <title>#import("title")</title>
  <link rel="stylesheet" href="/css/app.css">
</head>
<body>
  <div class="row column container-padded">
    <h1>Shopping List App</h1>
    #import("content")
  </div>
  <script src="https://code.jquery.com/jquery-3.2.1.min.js"></script>
  <script src="/js/app.js"></script>
</body>
</html>
```

3. Next, create two folders inside the `Public` folder, called `js` and `css`. Inside of the `Public/js` folder, create an empty file called `app.js` and create an empty file called `app.css` inside the `Public/css` folder, as follows:

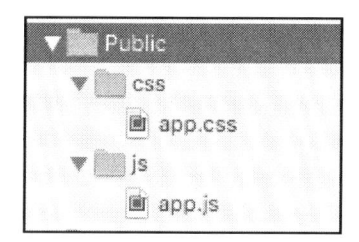

```
▼ Public
  ▼ css
      app.css
  ▼ js
      app.js
```

4. Copy the following contents to the `app.css` file to make our web app look nice:

```css
@import 'https://cdnjs.cloudflare.com/ajax/libs/foundation/6.4.3/css/foundation.min.css';
body { background: #efefef; }
.row.column.container-padded {
  display: flex;
  flex-wrap: wrap;
  justify-content: center;
}
.row.column.container-padded h1 {
  flex: 1 1 100%;
  text-align: center;
}
```

```css
.add-shopping-list {
  align-self: center;
  flex: 1 1 100%;
  text-align: center;
  margin: 30px;
}
.shopping-list-card {
  flex: 1 0 320px;
  margin: 10px;
  background-color: #fefefe;
  border-radius: 0;
  max-width: 320px;
}
.shopping-list-card .delete-list,
.shopping-list-card .delete-item {
  font-family: sans-serif;
  font-size: 1.4rem;
  padding: 10px;
  color: red;
  cursor: pointer;
}
.shopping-list-card .card-divider {
  border-bottom: 2px solid #cacaca;
  background: inherit;
  display: flex;
  justify-content: space-between;
}
.shopping-list-card .card-divider h3 {
  margin-bottom: 0;
}
.shopping-list-card ul {
  list-style-type: none;
  margin: 0;
}
.shopping-list-card ul li {
  background-color: #efefef;
  margin: 10px 0;
  padding: 10px;
  display: flex;
  align-items: center;
}
.shopping-list-card ul input[type="checkbox"] {
  margin: 0;
}
```

# Creating Web Views and Middleware

```
.shopping-list-card ul label {
  position: relative;
  font-size: 1rem;
  flex: 1;
}
```

5. Now, open the `Routes.swift` file and add a `get` request handler inside the `setupRoutes` method, which will render the `base.leaf` template on going to root page:

```
get() { req in
   return try self.view.make("base")
}
```

6. Now, build and run the server in Xcode and then navigate to `http://localhost:8080`.

If everything is set up correctly, then you should see **Shopping List App** in the browser:

Great job! Now, we have our Vapor application serving as an API server and also a web server.

# Serving JSON and HTML formats

Currently, if you take a look at the routes of our application, we have a root route that rendered `base.leaf`. We also have two resourceful routes, `/shopping_lists` and `/items`, which serve JSON data. It would be great if we could respond with the HTML response when users request `/shopping_lists` from the browser and serve JSON representation of our Shopping Lists when they go to the same `/shopping_lists` endpoint, but now the request is made from the iOS app. Luckily, we can do this thanks to a powerful feature in Swift called **Generics**. To make this work, we would need to refactor our resourceful controllers. We also need to use a middleware, which will help us respond with the HTML and JSON responses based on who is making the request. For example, it will respond with an HTML response when a request is made from a browser; otherwise, it will respond with JSON. So, let's begin our refactoring by first creating a middleware.

## Creating a middleware

You might be wondering what is a middleware? Middleware is very similar to a route handler as it gets passed a request and needs to return a response object. You can layer multiple middleware on a single or multiple routes and these middleware are invoked before our controller code is executed. So, you can do some preprocessing on the request before forwarding the same request forward to the controller. The response we get from the controller can also be modified inside of a middleware function before sending it back to the user. This is exactly what we want to do, and that is to let our middleware forward the request to the `ShoppingListController` and the `ItemController` so that it can generate a response first. Then, we take the response and generate HTML using our Leaf view renderer or simply as JSON, depending on whether the request is coming from the browser or not. To get started with creating our first Vapor middleware, we will need to follow these steps:

1. First, create a new folder called `Middlewares` inside the `App` folder. In this folder, create a new file called `ResponseFormatterMiddleware.swift`.
2. Inside this file, import `FluentProvider`, which will import the module so that we can reference Model protocol in this file:

   ```
   import FluentProvider
   ```

*Creating Web Views and Middleware*

3. Next, we will extend the response object so that it contains two computed properties, one called `resource` and another called `resources`. Both of these will store our Model object or array of models so that we can extract it from the response object and generate a new response. This new response will either be a HTML view or JSON view, depending on who is making the request:

   ```
   extension Response {
     var resource: (Model & JSONConvertible)? {
       get {
         return storage["resource"] as? (Model & JSONConvertible)
       }
       set(resource) {
         storage["resource"] = resource
       }
     }
     var resources: [(Model & JSONRepresentable)]? {
       get {
         return storage["resources"] as? [(Model & JSONRepresentable)]
       }
       set(resources) {
         storage["resources"] = resources
       }
     }
   }
   ```

4. Next, we define our middleware class, which implements the middleware protocol. We also create a instance variable to store the view renderer, which gets passed in the initializer of the middleware:

   ```
   public class ResponseFormatterMiddleware: Middleware {
     let viewRenderer: ViewRenderer
     public init(config: Config) throws {
       self.viewRenderer = try config.resolveView()
     }
   ```

5. We then define the required middleware protocol method called `respond`, as follows:

   ```
   public func respond(to request: Request, chainingTo next:
   Responder) throws -> Response {
     let response = try next.respond(to: request)
     if let resource = response.resource {
       if request.accept.prefers("html") {
         let resourceName = type(of: resource).name
         return try viewRenderer.make(resourceName, [
           "\(resourceName)": resource.makeJSON()
   ```

[ 210 ]

```
            ]).makeResponse()
        } else {
            return try resource.makeJSON().makeResponse()
        }
    } else if let resources = response.resources {
        if request.accept.prefers("html") {
            let resourcesName = request.uri.lastPathComponent!
            return try viewRenderer.make(resourcesName, [
                "\(resourcesName)": resources.map({ try $0.makeJSON() })
            ]).makeResponse()
        } else {
            return try JSON(resources.map({ try $0.makeJSON().wrapped })).makeResponse()
        }
    }
    return response
}
```

There is a lot of code here but we are basically calling the next route responder, which calls the next middleware in the chain. If there is no more middleware, then it will call the controller method associated with that route. In our case, the next method will either call the corresponding method inside our `ItemController` if the request is made to the `/items` route or the corresponding method inside of our `ShoppingListController` if the request is made to the `/shopping_lists` route. Then, it will extract the resource object and check whether the user request has set the accepts HTML only response header. If it does, then it replies with HTML response by rendering a Leaf template, otherwise, it will convert the resources to JSON and return that as a response. It does the same thing for multiple resources.

6. To start using this middleware in our Vapor app, we will need to specify it in our `Config+Setup.swift` file by adding the following line inside of the setup method:

    ```
    addConfigurable(middleware: ResponseFormatterMiddleware.init, name: "response-formatter")
    ```

7. The last thing to do is to tell Vapor to start using it by adding the name of our middleware `"response-formatter"` to the `droplet.json` config's middleware section, as follows:

    ```
    {
        "server": "engine",
        "client": "engine",
        "console": "terminal",
    ```

```
            "log": "console",
            "hash": "crypto",
            "cipher": "crypto",
            "middleware": [
              "error",
              "date",
              "file",
              "response-formatter"
            ],
            "commands": ["prepare"],
            "view": "leaf"
         }
```

Now, we can build and run our application, and it should function the same. If we navigate to `http://localhost:8080/`, it should give us back the same HTML page, but, this time, it first calls our middleware and then the `get handler` we added inside our `Routes.swift` file. You can confirm this by putting breakpoints in Xcode:

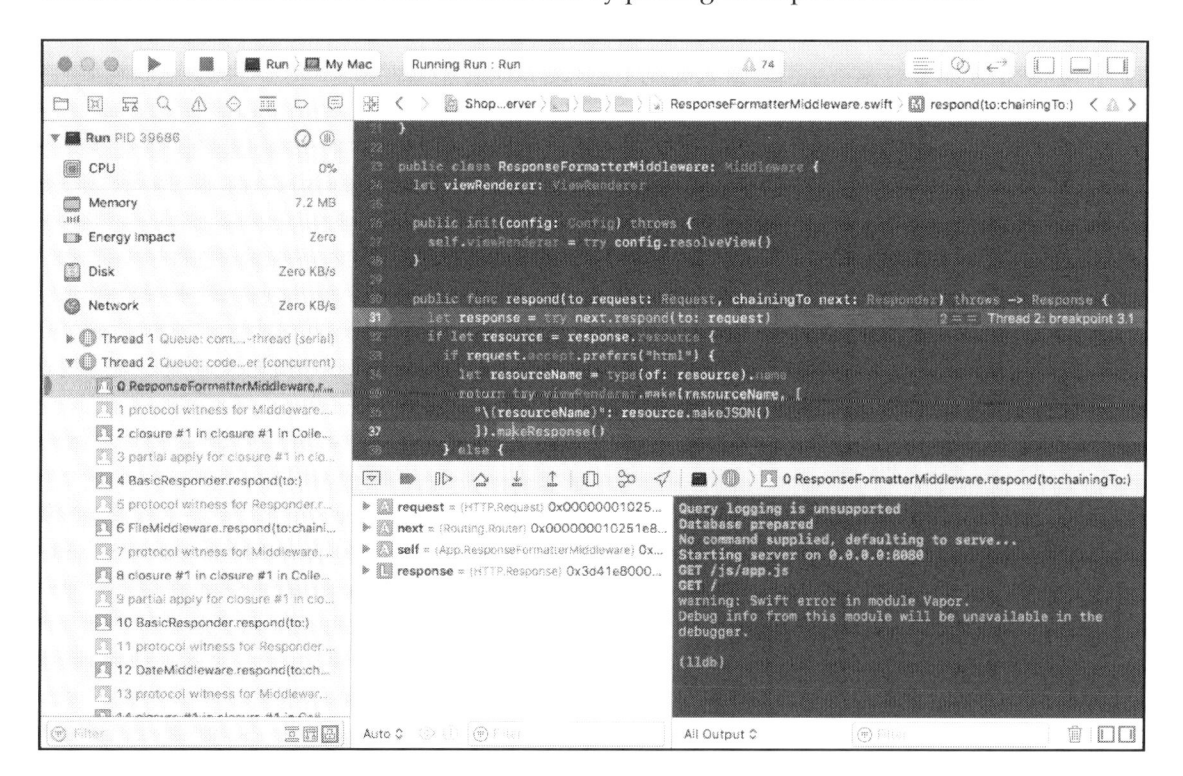

*Chapter 7*

The preceding and the following screenshots show how the request first funnels through the middleware before actually running the home page handler by placing breakpoint inside the middleware and the home page handler code:

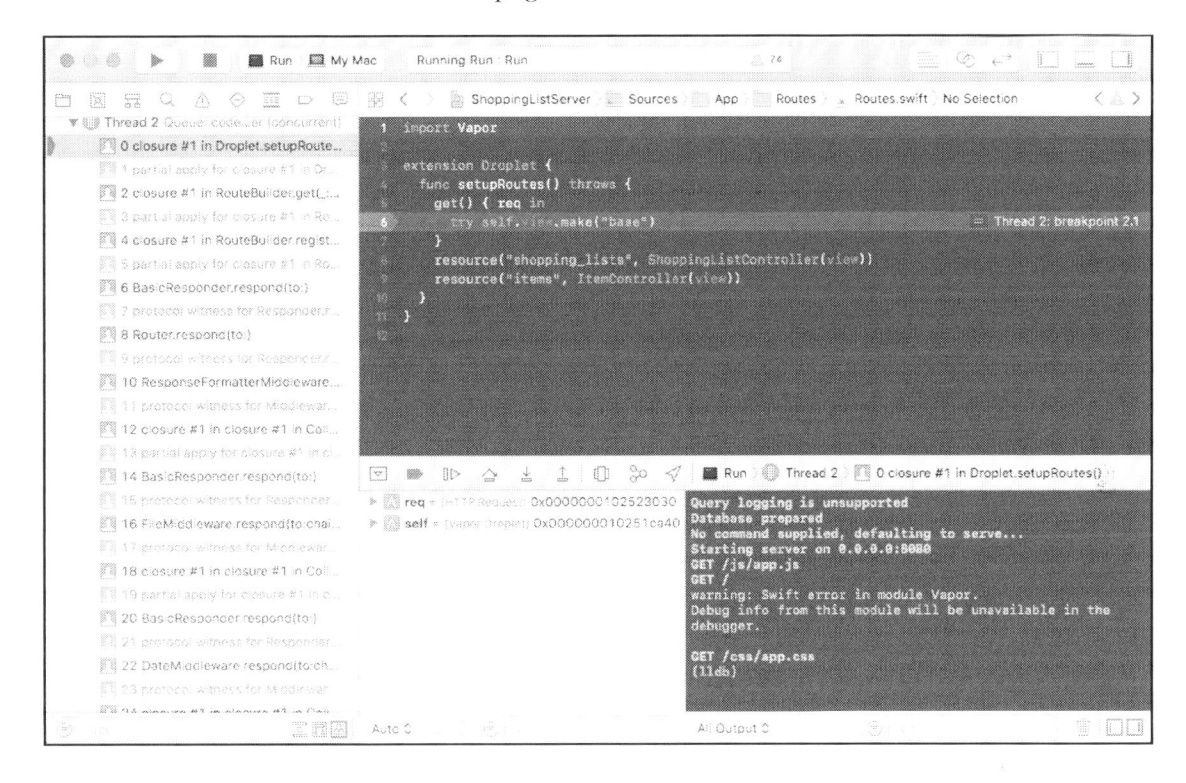

## Creating a BaseResourceController

If you look at the code for our `ShoppingListController` and our `ItemController`, you will see a lot of similarities between the two. The only difference is the type of class that is expected in the request. For example, in the show method of `ItemController`, it is expecting Item to be passed as a second argument and in `ShoppingListController` it is expecting an object of `ShoppingList` type. Using generics in Swift, we can create a `BaseResourceController` so that we can share the code between the two controllers. The following are the steps to do this refactoring:

1. Create an empty new file called `BaseResourceController.swift` inside the `Controllers` folder.

[ 213 ]

2. In there, import `FluentProvider`, as we will be referencing Model protocol in this file:

   ```
   import FluentProvider
   ```

3. Next, we will define a new protocol called `Replaceable`, which, just like `Updateable`, needs to be implemented in our Vapor model classes. The purpose of this protocol is to define this method so that it can copy all attributes of the object passed to itself:

   ```
   protocol Replaceable {
      func replaceAttributes(from: Self) -> Void
   }
   ```

4. Next, we will need to define and implement the methods of our `BaseResourceController`:

   ```
   class BaseResourceController<T: Model & JSONConvertible &
   Updateable & Replaceable>: ResourceRepresentable {
     func index(_ req: Request) throws -> ResponseRepresentable {
        let response = Response(status: .ok)
        let resources = try T.all()
        response.resources = resources
        return response
     }
     func store(_ req: Request) throws -> ResponseRepresentable {
        let response = Response(status: .ok)
        guard let json = req.json else { throw Abort.badRequest }
        let resource = try T(json: json)
        try resource.save()
        response.resource = resource
        return response
     }
     func show(_ req: Request, resource: T) throws ->
   ResponseRepresentable {
        let response = Response(status: .ok)
        response.resource = resource
        return response
     }
     func delete(_ req: Request, resource: T) throws ->
   ResponseRepresentable {
        try resource.delete()
        return Response(status: .ok)
     }
     func clear(_ req: Request) throws -> ResponseRepresentable {
        try T.makeQuery().delete()
        return Response(status: .ok)
   ```

```
    }
    func update(_ req: Request, resource: T) throws ->
ResponseRepresentable {
        let response = Response(status: .ok)
        try resource.update(for: req)
        try resource.save()
        response.resource = resource
        return response
    }
    func replace(_ req: Request, resource: T) throws ->
ResponseRepresentable {
        let response = Response(status: .ok)
        guard let json = req.json else { throw Abort.badRequest }
        let new = try T(json: json)
        resource.replaceAttributes(from: new)
        try resource.save()
        response.resource = resource
        return response
    }
    func makeResource() -> Resource<T> {
        return Resource(
            index: index,
            store: store,
            show: show,
            update: update,
            replace: replace,
            destroy: delete,
            clear: clear
        )
    }
}
```

5. Inside all of the RESTful methods in our `BaseResourceController`, the resource or resources are set on the response object that is returned, and this is the same resource or resources object that will be used by the middleware we have just created to generate the HTML or JSON response.

6. Now is the best part, which is removing a lot of code. We need to update the `ShoppingListController.swift` file to contain only the following line:

```
final class ShoppingListController:
BaseResourceController<ShoppingList> {}
```

7. We also need to update the `ItemController.swift` file to the following by removing all of the code and replacing it with the following line:

```
final class ItemController: BaseResourceController<Item> {}
```

8. Now, we will need to implement the `Replaceable` protocol in both of our Models first by adding the following extension in our `ShoppingList.swift` file:

```
extension ShoppingList: Replaceable {
  func replaceAttributes(from list: ShoppingList) {
    self.name = list.name
  }
}
```

9. Then, add the following extension to our `Item.swift` file:

```
extension Item: Replaceable {
  func replaceAttributes(from item: Item) {
    self.name = item.name
    self.isChecked = item.isChecked
    self.shoppingListId = item.shoppingListId
  }
}
```

The last thing to do is to set up our Leaf templates files for both Shopping List and Item. To set up these files, create four empty files inside the `Resources/Views` folder called `item.leaf`, `items.leaf`, `shopping_list.leaf`, and `shopping_lists.leaf`.

Copy the following into `shopping_lists.leaf` to render all of the Shopping Lists into HTML:

```
#extend("base")
#export("title") { Shopping List }
#export("content") {
  #loop(shopping_lists, "shopping_list") {
    #extend("shopping_list")
  }
  <a class="add-shopping-list">+ Create New Shopping List</a>
}
```

Copy the following into `shopping_list.leaf` to render a single Shopping List into HTML:

```
<div id="#(shopping_list.id)" class="shopping-list-card card">
  <div class="card-divider">
    <h3>#(shopping_list.name)</h3>
    <button class="delete-list">X</button>
  </div>
  <div class="card-section">
    <ul>
      #loop(shopping_list.items, "item") {
        #extend("item")
      }
    </ul>
    <a id="#(id)" class="add-item">+ Add an Item</a>
  </div>
</div>
```

Copy the following into `items.leaf` to render all of the items into HTML:

```
<ul>
  #loop(items, "item") {
    #extend("item")
  }
</ul>
```

Copy the following into `item.leaf` to render an item into HTML:

```
<li>
  <input
    id="#(item.id)"
    type="checkbox"
    #if(item.is_checked) { checked=true }
  />
  <label for="#(item.id)">#(item.name)</label>
  <button class="delete-item">X</button>
</li>
```

*Creating Web Views and Middleware*

We are done! Now, build and run the server, and navigate to `http://localhost:8080/shopping_lists` in the browser. You should see your Shopping Lists on the web:

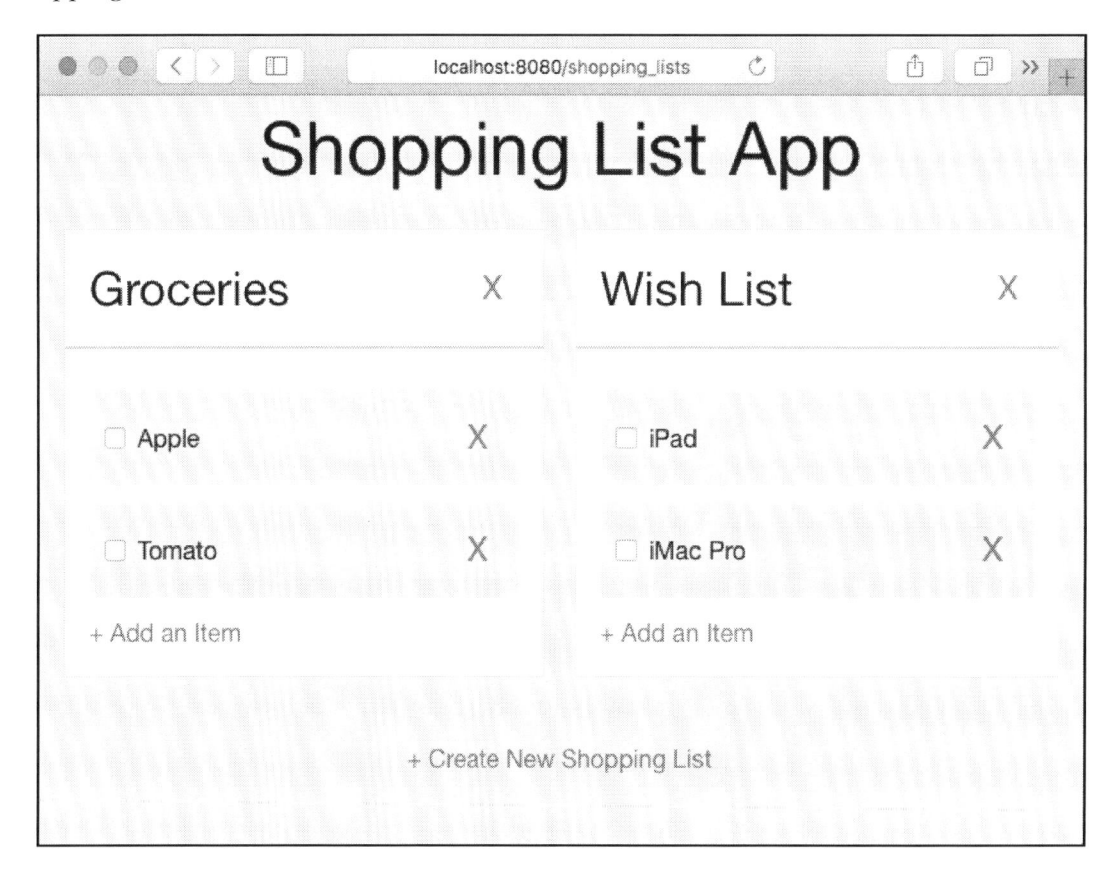

However, if you make the request from the console using the `curl` command without setting the accept HTTP header, then you will get the response back in JSON format:

```
[~ $ curl http://localhost:8080/shopping_lists/
[{"id":"oid:5a459c163fb3fc5026c6f4aa","name":"Groceries","items":[{"is_checked":false,"name":"Apple","id":"oid:5a459c193fb3fc5027c6f4aa","shopping_list__id":"oid:5a459c163fb3fc5026c6f4aa"},{"is_checked":false,"name":"Tomato","id":"oid:5a459c1c3fb3fc5028c6f4aa","shopping_list__id":"oid:5a459c163fb3fc5026c6f4aa"}]},{"id":"oid:5a459c213fb3fc5029c6f4aa","name":"Wish List","items":[{"is_checked":false,"name":"iPad","id":"oid:5a459c243fb3fc502ac6f4aa","shopping_list__id":"oid:5a459c213fb3fc5029c6f4aa"},{"is_checked":false,"name":"iMac Pro","id":"oid:5a459c323fb3fc502bc6f4aa","shopping_list__id":"oid:5a459c213fb3fc5029c6f4aa"}]}]
~ $
```

# Adding JavaScript

Our Vapor server now looks great and renders a beautiful web page, but, at the present, is not very functional. It has an add link and a cross button to delete a Shopping List and an item, but none of these work. The reason is because we have not written code to do anything when a user clicks on the link or on the delete button. To add this functionality, we will need to write some JavaScript. We have created an `app.js` file, but it is currently empty. So let's see how we can add the same functionality as our native iOS app to add, edit, and delete a Shopping List and its items. We will use jQuery, which is a popular JavaScript library that we have included in our `base.leaf` template to help us achieve dynamic behavior in our web app. In the following section, we will look at the code snippets that we need to add to our `app.js` file to add a similar functionality as our iOS app to our web app.

## Creating a new Shopping List

To add the functionality to create a Shopping List on the web app, we will use jQuery's `on` method, which takes an event such as click and invokes a callback function that is passed. In this callback, we will prompt the user for a name to give to their new Shopping List and make a POST request to our `/shopping_lists` endpoint to create a new Shopping List on the server. We will get back the HTML fragment of our new Shopping List and add that to the HTML, otherwise show an error message as an alert dialog. The following is the entire code to do all of that:

```
$('.add-shopping-list').on('click', function(event) {
  var $link = $(event.target);
  var name = window.prompt('What is the name of your new Shopping List?', '');
  if (!name) return;
  $.ajax({
    url: '/shopping_lists',
    type: 'POST',
    headers: {
      accept: 'text/html',
      'content-type': 'application/json; charset=UTF-8'
    },
    processData: false,
    data: JSON.stringify({
      name: name
    }),
    success: function(response) {
      $(response).insertBefore($link);
    },
    error: function(result) {
      alert('Error Adding new Shopping List');
    }
  });
});
```

# Deleting a Shopping List

To delete a Shopping List, we will similarly set up a click event listener on the button with the `delete-list` class name. Upon clicking, we will get the ID of the Shopping List, which is set on the Shopping List card and make a DELETE request to our API. Upon success, we will remove this card from the HTML, otherwise show an error message in the form of an alert dialog. The following is the code to do this:

```
$('body').on('click', '.delete-list', function(event) {
   var $button = $(event.target);
   var $shoppingList = $button.parents('.shopping-list-card');
   $.ajax({
     url: '/shopping_lists/' + $shoppingList.attr('id'),
     type: 'DELETE',
     success: function() {
       $shoppingList.remove();
     },
     error: function(result) {
       alert('Error deleting shopping list');
     }
   });
});
```

# Adding an Item

Adding an Item is similar to adding a Shopping List. We will first prompt the user for the name of the item to add to their Shopping List and then make a POST request to the `/items` endpoint. Upon success, we will get back the HTML fragment of the item that just got created and add it to the Shopping List card. If there is an error, we will show it as an alert dialog to the user. The following is the code to do just that:

```
$('body').on('click', '.add-item', function(event) {
   var $shoppingList = $(event.target).parents('.shopping-list-card');
   var itemName = window.prompt('What item do you want to add to your shopping list?', '');
   if (!itemName) return;
   $.ajax({
     url: '/items',
     type: 'POST',
     headers: {
       accept: 'text/html',
       'content-type': 'application/json; charset=UTF-8'
     },
     processData: false,
```

```
      data: JSON.stringify({
        name: itemName,
        shopping_list__id: $shoppingList.attr('id')
      }),
      success: function(response) {
        $shoppingList.find('ul').append(response);
      },
      error: function(result) {
        alert('Error Adding item');
      }
    });
  });
```

## Deleting an Item

Deleting an item is as simple as setting up a click listener on the button with the `delete-item` class name. Upon clicking, we will make a DELETE request to our API, and on success, we remove the item from the HTML, otherwise show an error message in the form of an alert dialog. The code for this is as follows:

```
  $('body').on('click', '.delete-item', function(event) {
    var $button = $(event.target);
    var $checkbox = $button.siblings('input');
    $.ajax({
      url: '/items/' + $checkbox.attr('id'),
      type: 'DELETE',
      success: function() {
        $checkbox.parent().remove();
      },
      error: function(result) {
        alert('Error deleting item');
      }
    });
  });
```

## Checking and unchecking an Item

The last feature missing from the web app is the ability to check and uncheck an item such that its state is saved on the server. This is easily achieved by setting up a change event listener on the input checkbox, and upon check and unchecking, it will trigger the callback function. We extract the checkbox from the event and get the checked state and make a PATCH request to our API on the item's endpoint. Upon success, we will need to do nothing, but if there is an error, we show the error message in the form of an alert dialog and revert the checkbox state so that the user can try again. The following is the code for adding this:

```
$('body').on('change', 'input[type=checkbox]', function(event) {
  var checkbox = event.target;
  $.ajax({
    url: '/items/' + checkbox.getAttribute('id'),
    type: 'PATCH',
    data: {
      is_checked: checkbox.checked
    },
    error: function(result) {
      alert('Error saving changes to item');
      checkbox.checked = !checkbox.checked;
    }
  });
});
```

Once all of the JavaScript code snippets have been added to `app.js`, you can reload the page and try it out, and everything should work as expected.

One last thing is to have the root route redirect the user to `/shopping_lists` so that users see their Shopping Lists instead of a blank page when navigating to `http://localhost:8080`. To do so, we will need to replace the `get()` handler inside the `setupRoutes` method in the `Routes.swift` file to the following:

```
get() { _ in Response(redirect: "/shopping_lists") }
```

[ 223 ]

# Summary

In this chapter, you created a web page using Vapor. By now, you should have a good understanding of how Leaf works and how you can use it in any of the server-side Swift packages along with your Vapor app. You also learned the best practice of refactoring your code so that you can share code between both of your controllers using the powerful feature of generics available in Swift. You also created a Vapor middleware to dynamically generate HTML or JSON output for your request so that you can use the same routes for both your iOS app and the web app you just created.

Hopefully, this chapter gave you background on server-side rendering of HTML templates and how you can add CSS and JavaScript. Using some CSS, you were able to make your page look nice, and adding some JavaScript, you were able to make your web page link a single page app without having to write a lot of code or having to set up a build pipeline for your assets.

In the next chapter, you will learn the best practices for testing our Vapor application. You will also learn the best practices for setting up a project for open source development and how to create a Continuous Integration pipeline so that you can build and test your code automatically every time you make any changes. This will help you detect any issue sooner rather than later and prevent bad code from being merged into the repository.

# Testing and CI

In the preceding chapter, we covered how to render HTML views with the help of Leaf, Swift's templating engine. We also made a middleware and used it to show HTML response for requests coming from the browser and JSON response for everything else, including our mobile app. By now, you should have a good understanding of how Vapor can be used to make both an API server and a web server.

In this chapter, we will focus on how to test our Vapor application server. We will also discuss how to write tests that run on both macOS and Linux. Also, we will discuss how to add **Continuous Integration** (**CI**) pipeline for our server app. This will trigger tests every time we have an event, from a submission of a Pull Request to our code on GitHub, or a merge to master branch of our repository. Using free services, such as Travis CI on open source projects, we will set up a CI pipeline for our Vapor server on GitHub.

By the end of this chapter, you should have a good understanding on the following topics:

- Testing Vapor app
- Setting up a test environment for your Vapor app
- Testing the RESTful endpoint
- Configuring an automated test pipeline
- Best practices for running tests on projects managed via GitHub

So, let's get started by first setting up tests for our Vapor application.

## Testing the Vapor application

Testing a Vapor application is same as testing a Swift package. In `Chapter 1`, *Getting Started with Server Swift*, you got a primer on Swift packages, and you wrote your first test for that package. Writing test is very similar, and our Vapor application comes with some dummy tests. If we look at the `Test/AppTests` folder, we will see the following two files:

- `RouteTests.swift`
- `Utilities.swift`

`RouteTests.swift` contains two tests that test the routes of our Vapor application and ensure that the output we are getting from our Vapor app is what we expect to get. For Swift to run our test, we will need to start up the server, and, for that, we will need to define some helper extension methods on the `Droplet` class, and those are defined in the `Utilities.swift` file, where it creates a Droplet configured with the test environment, as follows:

```
static func testable() throws -> Droplet {
    let config = try Config(arguments: ["vapor", "--env=test"])
    try config.setup()
    let drop = try Droplet(config)
    try drop.setup()
    return drop
}
```

## Setting up the test environment

The preceding code defines a static method on the `Droplet` class so that we can create a server instance without having to write all of this code to configure it and can set the environment to test. We can set up a different database for test environment so that we can use that instead of our local development database, as we would need to reset or clear it every time after all tests finish running.

To set up environment-specific config file for using a different database for test environment, we will need to perform the following steps:

1. In Xcode, inside the `Config` folder, create a new folder called `development`. Inside this folder, we can put any config files, and the configuration values from these files will be used in development environment.
2. Now, move the `mongo.json` file inside the `Config` folder into the newly created `development` folder.
3. Next, create a `test` folder inside the `Config` folder, and, as you can now see, it will contain JSON config files that will be loaded only in a test environment.
4. Then, create a new file called `mongo.json` inside the `Test` folder, and copy the following JSON config into it:

   ```
   {
      "url": "mongodb://localhost:27017/shopping-list-test"
   }
   ```

Thats it! We have just created an environment-specific database configuration, where Vapor will use the `shopping-list` mongo database in development environment and the `shopping-list-test` in test environment. This will help us create Shopping Lists and items independent of development and clear them at the end of the test run.

# Running tests

Vapor tests can be run directly from the command line or from Xcode. You can also run a specific test directly from Xcode if you want to debug and fix a specific issue instead of running an entire test suite, which could take a long time for large projects.

*Testing and CI*

Before we get started with running our tests inside Xcode, we will need to delete the `PostControllerTests.swift` file inside `Tests/AppTests`. Running tests in Xcode is a two-step process, and there are multiple ways to run the tests. The first way involves a two-step process:

1. First, switch the scheme to `ShoppingListServer-Package` and select **My Mac**:

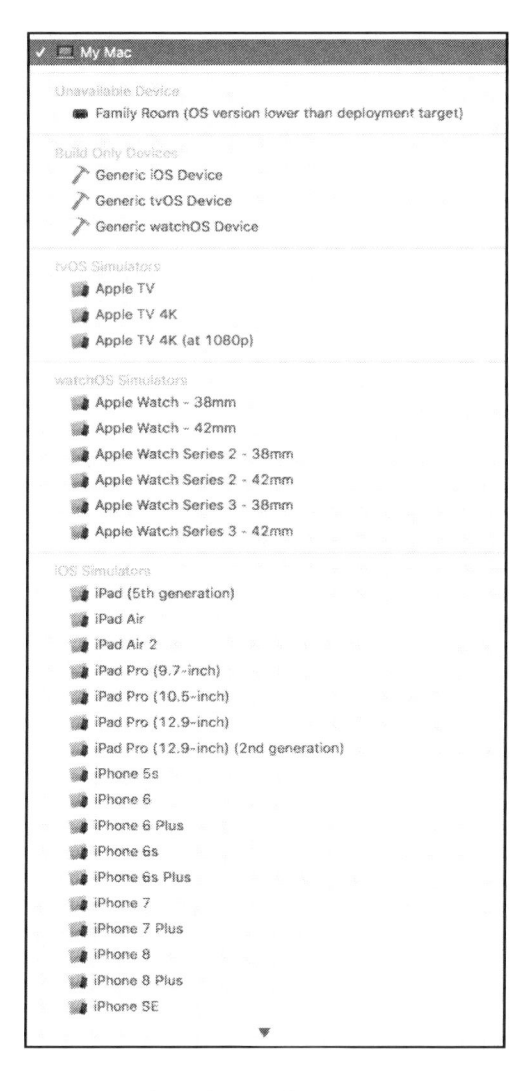

2. Then, press *Command + U*, which will run the entire test suite that consists of tests in the `RouteTests.swift`.

*Chapter 8*

The test should compile and run, but will fail since the dummy tests work with the default template project that we cloned. Since then, we have modified the code a lot so that the defaults tests are no longer valid and needed. Let's make the test suite pass by removing old tests and add tests that actually test our Vapor application by following these steps:

1. Delete all of the code inside the `RouteTests.swift` file.
2. Next, import the dependencies to test and import our application code to test it:

   ```
   import XCTest
   import Foundation
   import Testing
   import HTTP
   @testable import Vapor
   @testable import App
   ```

3. Next, let's define the test class and call it `RouteTests` and make it inherit from the `TestCase` class that is defined in `Utilities.swift file`. `TestCase` is a subclass of `XCTestCase` so that it can some setup that is Vapor specific:

   ```
   class RouteTests: TestCase {
   }
   ```

4. Inside this class, we will need to create a Vapor server instance in this class using the testable static method that is defined in the `Utilities.swift` file:

   ```
   let drop = try! Droplet.testable()
   ```

5. Next, we will add few tests as methods inside this class that will make request to the Vapor server and assert that the response is as it is expected. Some basic tests are as follows:

   ```
   func testHealthcheck() throws {
     try drop
       .testResponse(to: .get, at: "healthcheck.html")
       .assertStatus(is: .ok)
       .assertJSON("status", equals: "up")
   }
   func testRootRoute() throws {
     try drop
       .testResponse(to: .get, at: "/")
       .assertStatus(is: .seeOther)
       .assertHeader("Location", contains: "/shopping_lists")
   }
   ```

[ 229 ]

6. Finally, to make the test work in Linux, we will need to add the following static variable, which lists all of the tests:

```
static let allTests = [
   ("testHealthcheck", testHealthcheck),
   ("testRootRoute", testRootRoute),
]
```

7. Now, run the tests using the *Command + U* to run all of the tests.

The tests should all pass now, and everything should be checked green. Awesome!

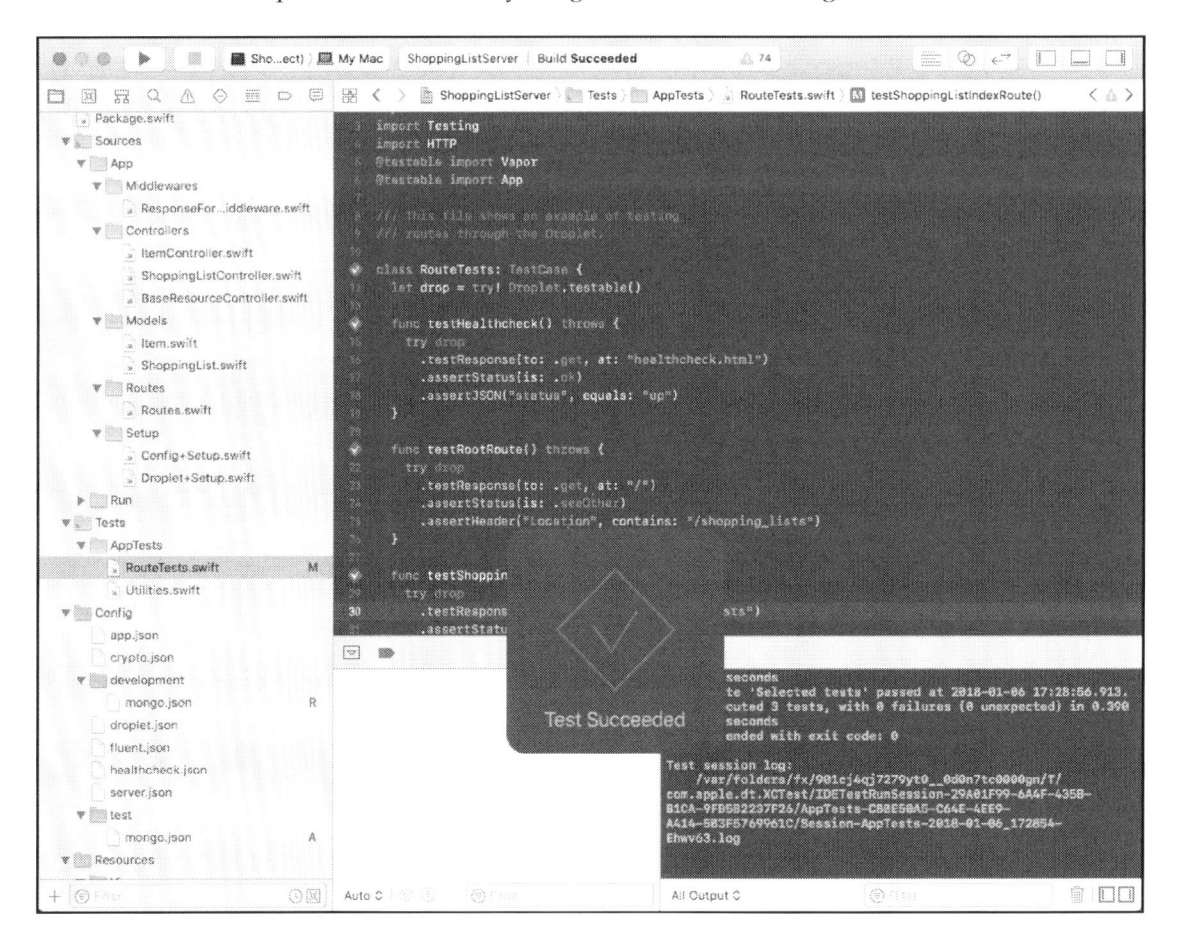

Another way to run all of the tests from a specific test file or to run a specific test inside a test file is by clicking on the diamond icon at the top of the left sidebar to open the Test Navigator. From here, you can press the Play button next to the entire file or a specific test:

## Testing RESTful routes

So far, we have added tests for routes. Now, let's take a look at how we can test our `ShoppingListController`. To test our controller, we would need to write test for each of the RESTful actions and assert that the result at the end of the action is as expected. To make our code modular, it would be good to create a separate test file for these tests. So, to get started writing tests for our Shopping List Controller, follow these steps:

1. Create a new empty file called `ShoppingListControllerTests.swift` inside the `Tests/AppTests` folder and make sure that you add it to the `AppTests` target.

2. Inside this file, add the following lines of code; this will import the required modules for testing, and we will define our test class:

    ```
    import XCTest
    import Foundation
    import Testing
    import HTTP
    @testable import Vapor
    @testable import App

    class ShoppingListControllerTests: TestCase {
      let drop = try! Droplet.testable()
    ```

```
        override func tearDown() {
          super.tearDown()
          try! ShoppingList.makeQuery().delete()
        }
    }
```

That is it, and we are now ready to write our tests for Shopping List Controller. One thing you might have noticed is the `tearDown` method that is different from the `RouteTests` class. We have added this to ensure that the database is reset after every test run so that we do not have any Shopping Lists in the database that could interfere with the test run. Now let's go ahead and write our first test.

## Fetching all Shopping Lists

The first method we will test is the index action in Shopping List Controller. This test will make a GET request to `/shopping_lists`, which will invoke the index action. The index action should return all of the Shopping Lists in the database, and, since we do not have any entries when we run the test, we should get back an empty array as the response. To add this test, perform the following steps:

1. First, create a new method called `testShoppingListIndex`:

    ```
    func testShoppingListIndex() throws {
    }
    ```

2. Next, add the following code inside this newly created method that will make a GET request to `/shopping_lists`. It will then assert that the response body is an empty array:

    ```
    try drop
        .testResponse(to: .get, at: "/shopping_lists")
        .assertStatus(is: .ok)
        .assertBody(equals: "[]")
    ```

That is it, and, with this, we have just created our first controller-specific test. Run the test using *Command + U* or clicking on Play inside the Test Navigator for this file.

# Creating a Shopping List

Now, we are ready to write tests. To test creation of the Shopping List, we will need to first make a POST request to /shopping_lists and verify that we get back a JSON response. Using the ID from the response, we will verify that the Shopping List has been created by making a GET request to that specific Shopping List. We will also make a request to the /shopping_lists endpoint to verify that we get back all of the Shopping Lists from the database and confirm that the only element in the array is the one Shopping List that we just created. Let's take a look at how we can write this test:

1. First, create a new method called testShoppingListCreate:

   ```
   func testShoppingListCreate() throws {
   }
   ```

2. Inside this method, we will make a POST request to the /shopping_lists endpoint:

   ```
   let shoppingListName = "Shopping List Test Name"
   var reqBody = JSON()
   try reqBody.set("name", shoppingListName)
   
   let list = try drop
     .testResponse(to: .post,
                   at: "/shopping_lists",
                   headers: ["content-type": "application/json"],
                   body: reqBody)
   try list
     .assertStatus(is: .ok)
     .assertJSON("name", equals: shoppingListName)
     .assertJSON("items", equals: JSON([]))
   ```

3. We will extract the id from the response and assign it to the listId variable. If the response is not correctly formatted, then we will fail the test:

   ```
   guard let listJSON = list.json else {
     XCTFail("Response should contain JSON")
     return
   }
   guard let listId = listJSON["id"]?.string else {
     XCTFail("JSON should contain id")
     return
   }
   ```

[ 233 ]

*Testing and CI*

4. Next, we will make a request to the Shopping List-specific endpoint to confirm that the Shopping List was created successfully and check whether the response has the correct name, `id`, and items in the JSON:

```
try drop
    .testResponse(to: .get, at: "/shopping_lists/\(listId)")
    .assertStatus(is: .ok)
    .assertJSON("id", equals: listId)
    .assertJSON("name", equals: shoppingListName)
    .assertJSON("items", equals: JSON([]))
```

5. Lastly, we will make a request to the Shopping Lists endpoint and confirm that the response contains one element in the array and that the element has the same `id`, name, and items property:

```
let lists = try drop
    .testResponse(to: .get, at: "/shopping_lists")

guard let listsJSON = lists.json?.array else {
  XCTFail("Response should contain array of shopping lists as JSON")
    return
}

XCTAssertEqual(listsJSON.count, 1, "Shopping List should have 1 item in array")
XCTAssertEqual(listsJSON[0]["id"]?.string, listId, "Shopping List id is the same as the one created")
XCTAssertEqual(listsJSON[0]["name"]?.string, shoppingListName, "Shopping List name is the same as the one created")
```

Now you can build and run the tests, and all of the test should pass. Next, we will look at how we can test deletion.

## Deleting the Shopping List

Testing the delete endpoint is similar to testing the creation endpoint. We will first need to create a Shopping List and then extract the `id` from the response and make a DELETE request to the Shopping List endpoint. We can then verify that it deleted the Shopping List by checking the `/shopping_lists` endpoint and confirming that there are no Shopping Lists saved in the database:

```
func testShoppingListDelete() throws {
    let shoppingListName = "Shopping List Test Name"
```

```
      var reqBody = JSON()
      try reqBody.set("name", shoppingListName)
      let list = try drop
        .testResponse(to: .post,
                      at: "/shopping_lists",
                      headers: ["content-type": "application/json"],
                      body: reqBody)
      try list
        .assertStatus(is: .ok)
        .assertJSON("name", equals: shoppingListName)
      guard let listJSON = list.json else {
        XCTFail("Response should contain JSON")
        return
      }
      guard let listId = listJSON["id"]?.string else {
        XCTFail("JSON should contain id")
        return
      }
      try drop
        .testResponse(to: .delete, at: "/shopping_lists/\(listId)")
        .assertStatus(is: .ok)
      let lists = try drop
        .testResponse(to: .get, at: "/shopping_lists")
      guard let listsJSON = lists.json?.array else {
        XCTFail("Response should contain array of shopping lists as JSON")
        return
      }
      XCTAssertEqual(listsJSON.count, 0, "Shopping List should have 0 item in array")
    }
```

## Updating the Shopping List

Testing the update endpoint of our Shopping List is similar to the previous two tests. We will first need to create a new Shopping List and then make a PATCH request with updated values for the Shopping List. The code for this would look like this:

```
    func testShoppingListUpdate() throws {
      var shoppingListName = "Shopping List Test Name"
      var reqBody = JSON()
      try reqBody.set("name", shoppingListName)
      let list = try drop
        .testResponse(to: .post,
                      at: "/shopping_lists",
                      headers: ["content-type": "application/json"],
                      body: reqBody)
```

```
    try list
      .assertStatus(is: .ok)
      .assertJSON("name", equals: shoppingListName)
    guard let listJSON = list.json else {
      XCTFail("Response should contain JSON")
      return
    }
    guard let listId = listJSON["id"]?.string else {
      XCTFail("JSON should contain id")
      return
    }
    shoppingListName = "Another Name"
    try reqBody.set("name", shoppingListName)
    try drop
      .testResponse(to: .put,
                    at: "/shopping_lists/\(listId)",
                    headers: ["content-type": "application/json"],
                    body: reqBody)
      .assertStatus(is: .ok)
    let lists = try drop
      .testResponse(to: .get, at: "/shopping_lists")
    guard let listsJSON = lists.json?.array else {
      XCTFail("Response should contain array of shopping lists as JSON")
      return
    }

    XCTAssertEqual(listsJSON.count, 1, "Shopping List should have 1 item in array")
    XCTAssertEqual(listsJSON[0]["id"]?.string, listId, "Shopping List id is the same as the one created")
    XCTAssertEqual(listsJSON[0]["name"]?.string, shoppingListName, "Shopping List name is the same as the one created")
  }
```

# Exercise

Now that we have our test written for the Shopping List to test out the CRUD operations inside our `ShoppingListController`, it's time for a short exercise. Similar to how we tested Shopping List API endpoints, write tests to verify the `ItemController` and its API endpoints. This includes testing Item creation and verifying that it is added to the Shopping List by clicking on the show action of the Shopping List it was added to.

# Automated testing pipeline

Usually, when working on larger projects with multiple people, you would want to ensure that the code quality does not degrade over time. There are several ways to do this; one way is by reviewing code before merging it. You can also require tests to be added for a new feature or require existing tests to be updated to ensure that you have enough code coverage for the feature or a bug fix is being introduced. We can create a checklist for the contributors to add test, but having a way to run the tests for every code change request sent along with running tests every time any changes are merged into the repository is the best way to detect issues early and fix them before they go to production. This practice of running tests on your project on a regular basis is known as **Continuous Integration** and ensures that there are no issues in production.

Having a CI pipeline helps developers find issues earlier by running the tests automatically and can act as a gatekeeper before deploying code to production. It helps find issues where code changes added in one place can break the app's functionality elsewhere that the developer is not aware of by running in a clean environment that mimics production along with all of the latest changes from other developers. Considering these benefits, we will take a look at how to add such an automated pipeline to our Vapor project. To set up a CI pipeline for our Vapor app, we will use **Travis CI**, which is a service provided for free for open source projects that allows you to build, run, and test your app and give a status update on whether it succeeded or failed so that you can fix the problem before merging the code. Also, if the code was recently merged, it will alert you to the error so that you can fix it right away instead of having the issue go unnoticed until someone discovers it.

Adding Travis CI to your project requires publishing your project on GitHub. Once the project is published and has a `.travis.yml` config setup, you will need to give Travis CI the permission to read from the repository and run the command every time a PR is created and every time code is merged to the master branch. Once everything is set up in Travis CI, you can stay assured that Travis will ensure that breaking code does not make it into production. To get started with Travis CI, follow these steps:

1. Inside the project directory for your Vapor application, delete the `circle.yml` file if it exists, since we will not be using Circle CI service.

2. Now open the `Tests/AppTests/ShoppingListControllerTests.swift` file and add the following static variable inside the `ShoppingListControllerTests` class to make the tests run on Linux:

   ```
   static let allTests = [
     ("testShoppingListIndex", testShoppingListIndex),
     ("testShoppingListCreate", testShoppingListCreate),
     ("testShoppingListDelete", testShoppingListDelete),
     ("testShoppingListUpdate", testShoppingListUpdate)
   ]
   ```

3. Next, update the `Tests/LinuxMain.swift` file by changing the line containing `PostControllerTests` to `ShoppingListControllerTests` in the following line. You may not see the `LinuxMain.swift` file in Xcode, so edit it using a plain text editor:

   ```
   testCase(ShoppingListControllerTests.allTests),
   ```

4. You should already have a `.travis.yml` file in your folder as we got it for free when we cloned our project from the API Vapor template. Add the **mongodb** services line toward the end of the config and remove the `after_success` config. Also, update the `osx_image` to `xcode9.2` and install mongodb using brew on macOS. The final config file looks as follows; this config tells Travis to run on both Mac and Linux platform and to run the build before running the tests:

   ```
   os:
       - linux
       - osx
   language: generic
   sudo: required
   dist: trusty

   osx_image: xcode9.2
   before_install:
       - if [ $TRAVIS_OS_NAME == "osx" ]; then
             brew tap vapor/tap;
             brew update;
             brew install vapor;
             brew install mongodb;
             sudo mkdir -p /data/db;
             brew services start mongodb;
         else
             eval "$(curl -sL https://apt.vapor.sh)";
             sudo apt-get install vapor;
   ```

```
                sudo chmod -R a+rx /usr/;
        fi

script:
    - swift build -c release
    - swift test

services:
   - mongodb
```

5. Now commit all code and push it up to a GitHub repository, if you have not done so already, using the following command in the terminal; make sure that all of your changes are merged into master before pushing:

   ```
   $ git add .
   $ git commit -m "Adding Test"
   $ git push origin master
   ```

6. Now navigate to https://travis-ci.org and sign in with your GitHub Account. If you are logging in to Travis CI for the first time, you will need to provide GitHub Permission to Travis to view your repositories:

*Testing and CI*

7. Once you have signed in, go to Accounts from your Profile and search for your repository, which contains the Vapor application code. Enable the switch for your repository. Once it is enabled, click on the repository name that will take you to the build page for this repo:

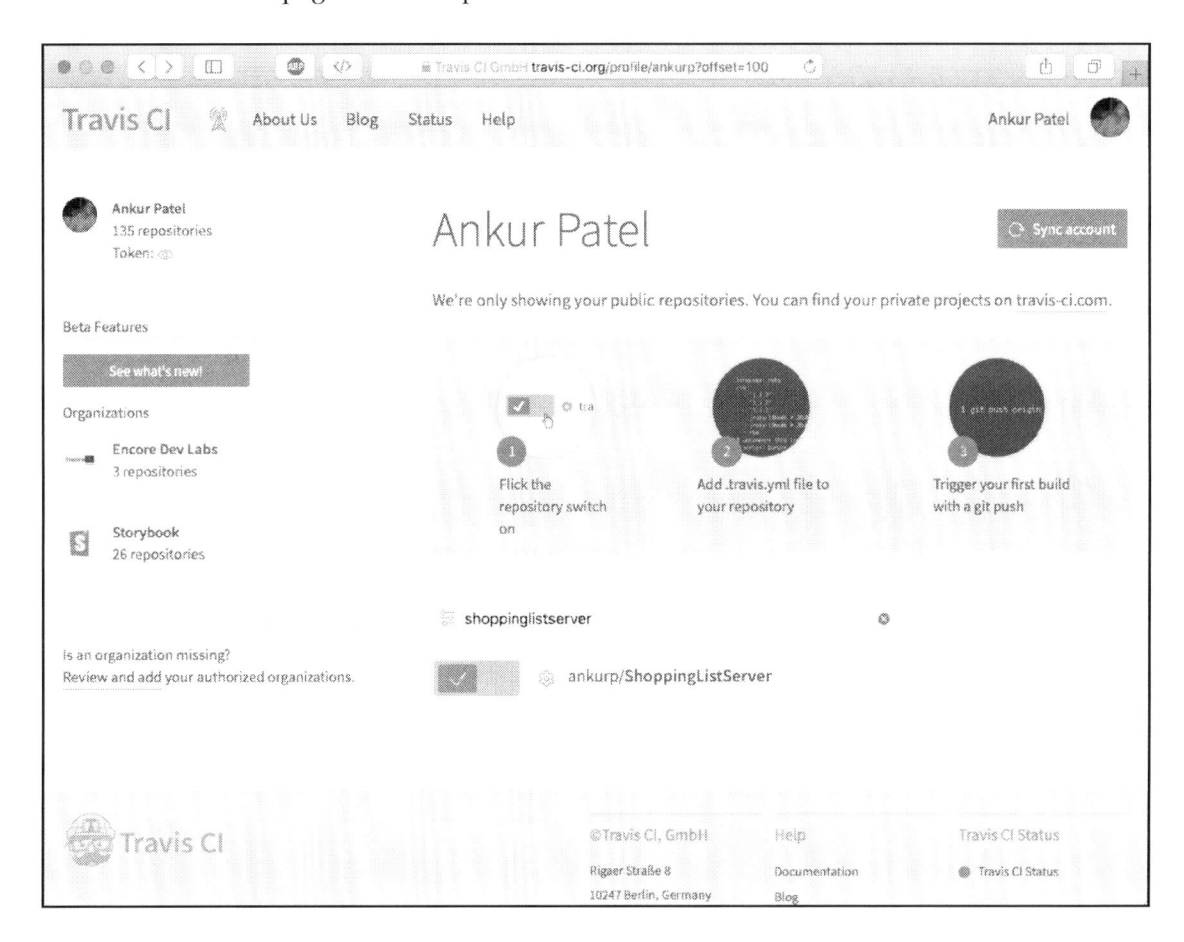

8. From here, you can view previous builds and view logs for them and even trigger new builds. Since we do not have any build, we will trigger them by hovering over the **More Options** icon and clicking on **Trigger build**:

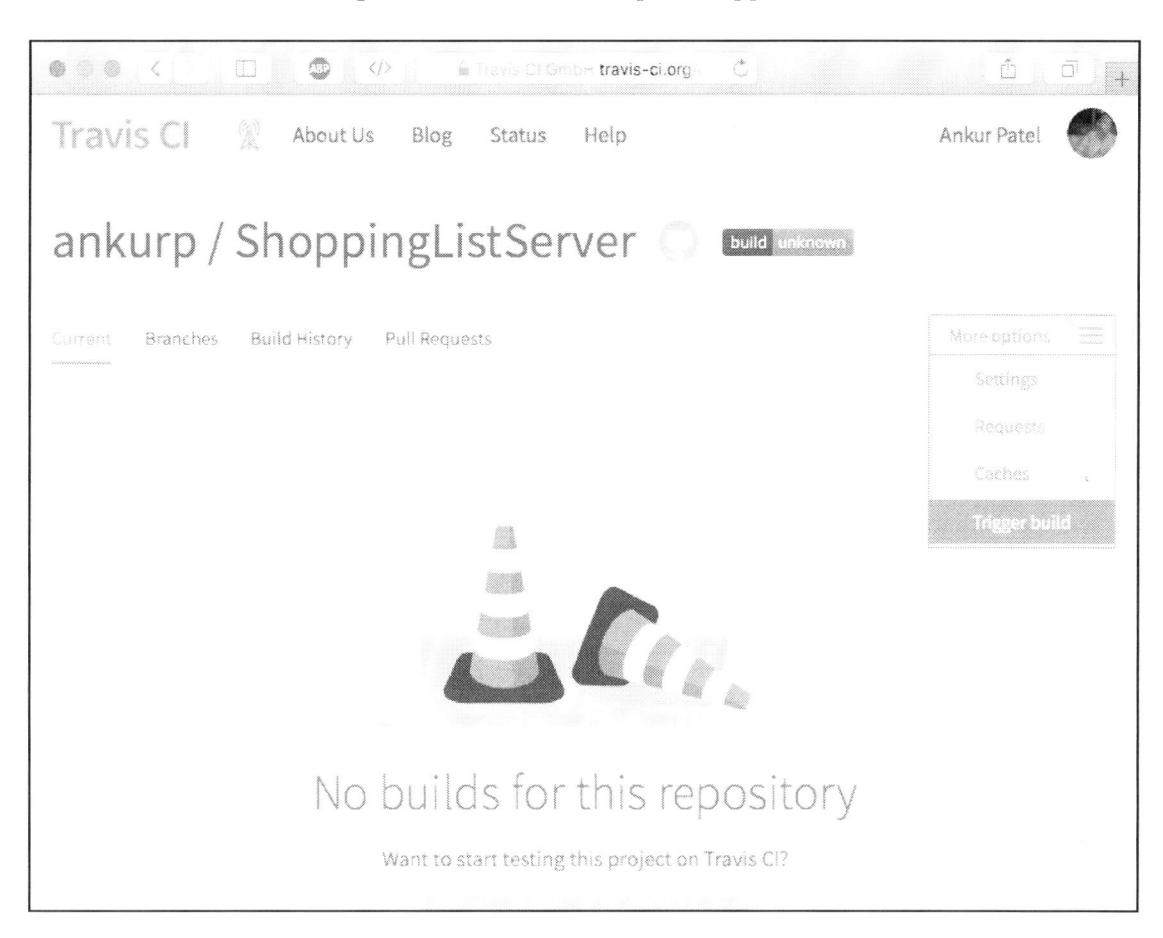

9. Once the build is started, you should see it run on both Mac and Linux platforms:

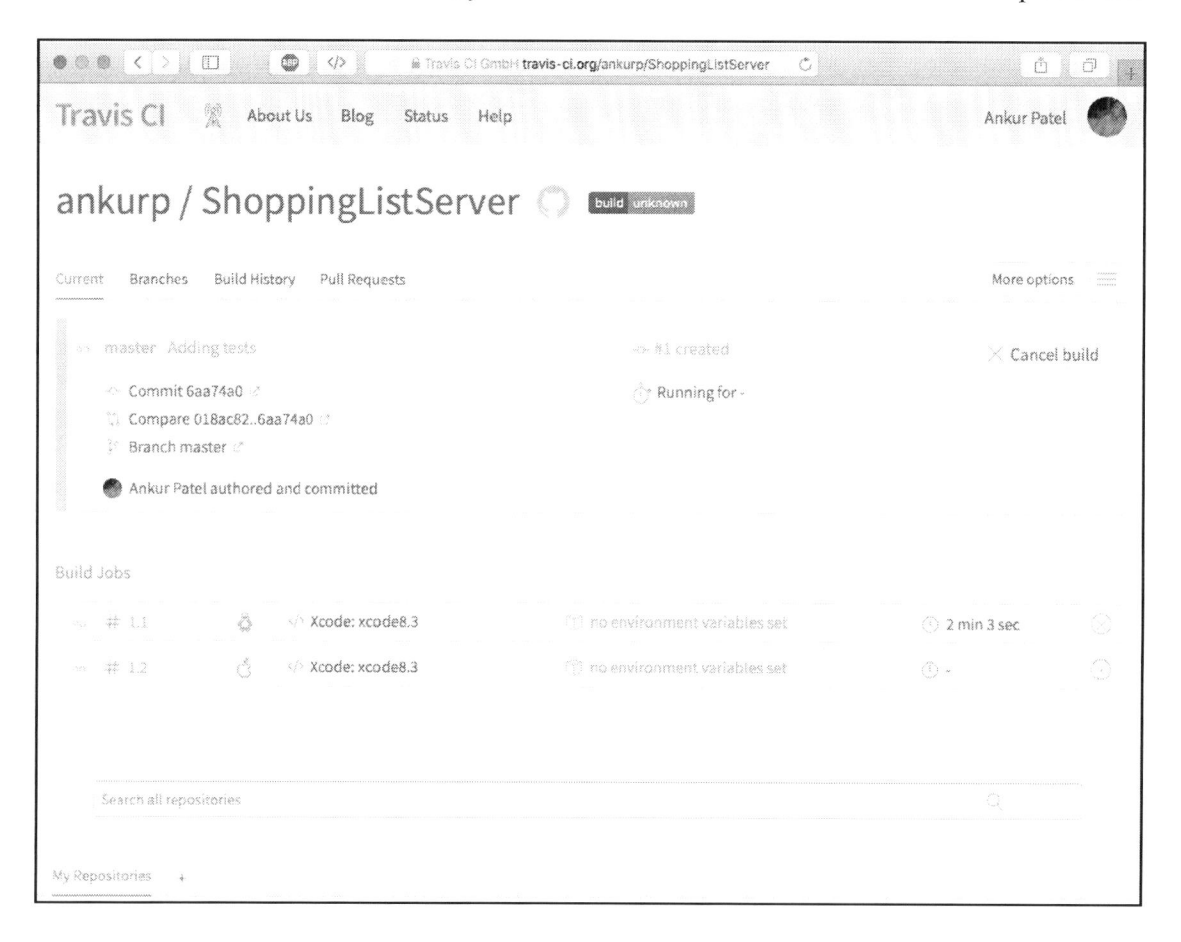

Great! You have just set up a build and test pipeline for your project on GitHub. Now everything you push to master or merge a pull request into master branch will automatically trigger a new build in Travis.

Travis will email you when the build has finished, and it will let you know whether it failed or succeeded. Travis also lets you embed a badge containing the status of the last build to let everyone know how the project is doing. We will do just that by adding it to our README.md file. Let's take a look at how we can do so:

1. Create a README.md file inside your Vapor application at the root level if it does not exist. You will need to edit this file in a plain text editor, as it may not be available inside your Xcode project.
2. Inside this file, add the following text and replace <github-user> with your GitHub username, and replace <github-repo> with the name of your repo:

   ```
   # Shopping List Server

   [![Build Status](https://travis-ci.org/<github-user>/<github-repo>.svg?branch=master)](https://travis-ci.org/<github-user>/<github-repo>)
   ```

3. Save the file and commit the changes. Push it up to GitHub, and you should see the Travis CI badge on your GitHub repo page:

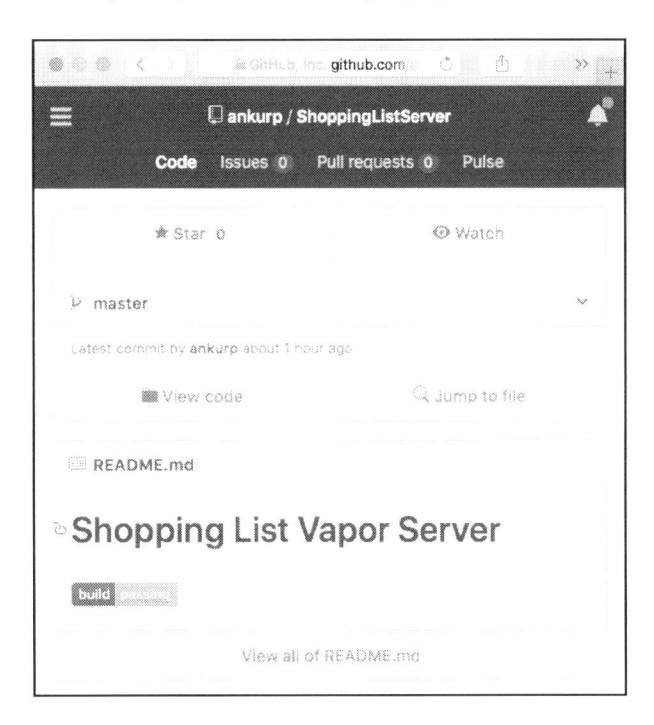

[ 243 ]

# Enabling Travis build check on Pull request

We have Travis configured to run every time any changes are merged into master branch. We can also use Travis to build and test Pull requests. We can even prevent Pull requests that have failed tests from being merged using GitHub's status check feature. Using Travis will help prevent bad code from being merged into master and ensure that failing builds do not get merged into master. To enable this, we need to update few settings on GitHub. Perform the following steps to enable Travis on every Pull request:

1. Go to the **Settings** page of your repo on GitHub and click on **Branches**.
2. Under the **Protected branches** section, click on **Choose a branch...** and select **master**:

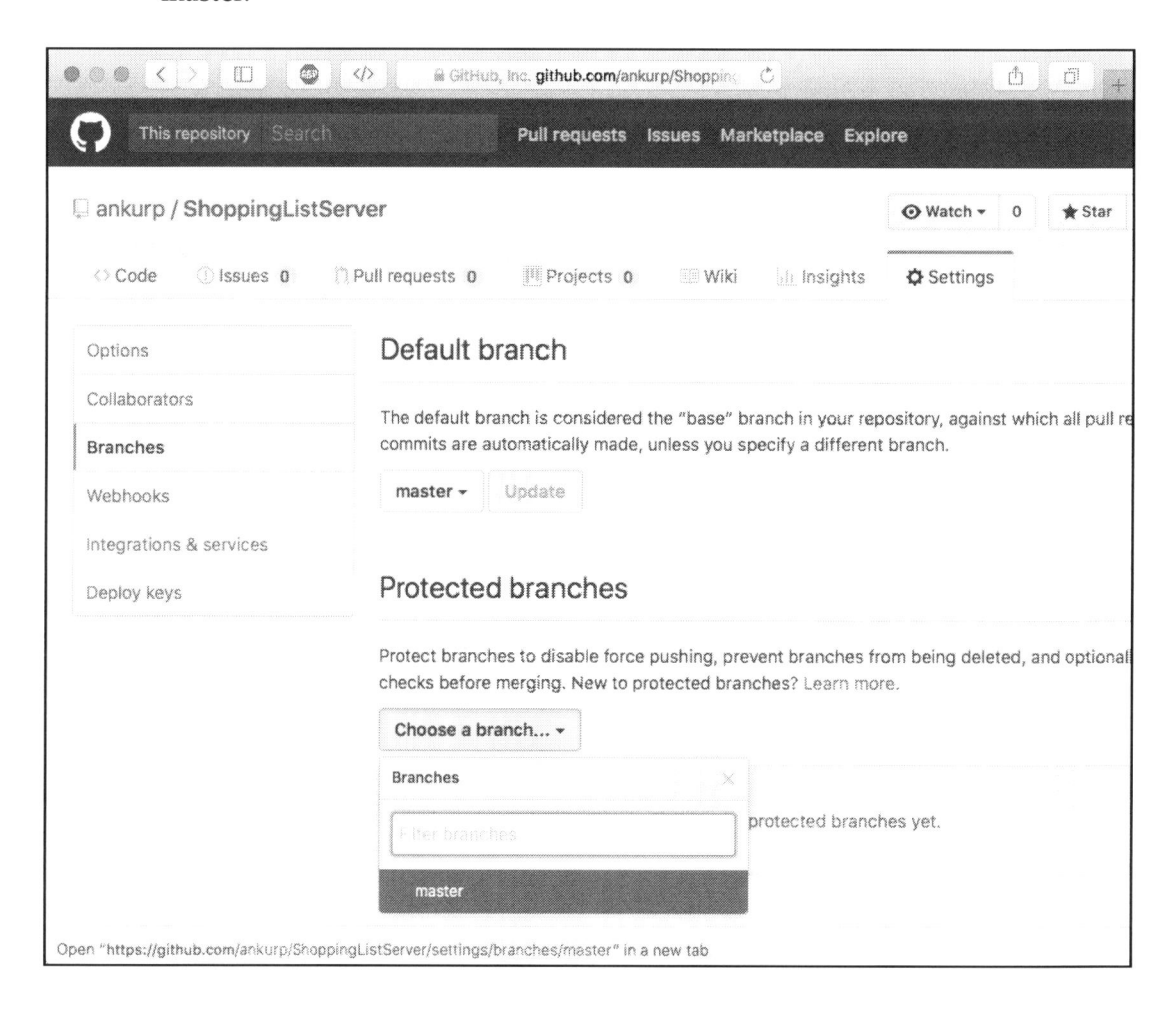

3. Check **Protect this branch**. This should reveal more options, and now check **Require status checks to pass before merging**. Then, check **Require branches to be up to date before merging**, and finally check `continuous-integration/travis-ci`:

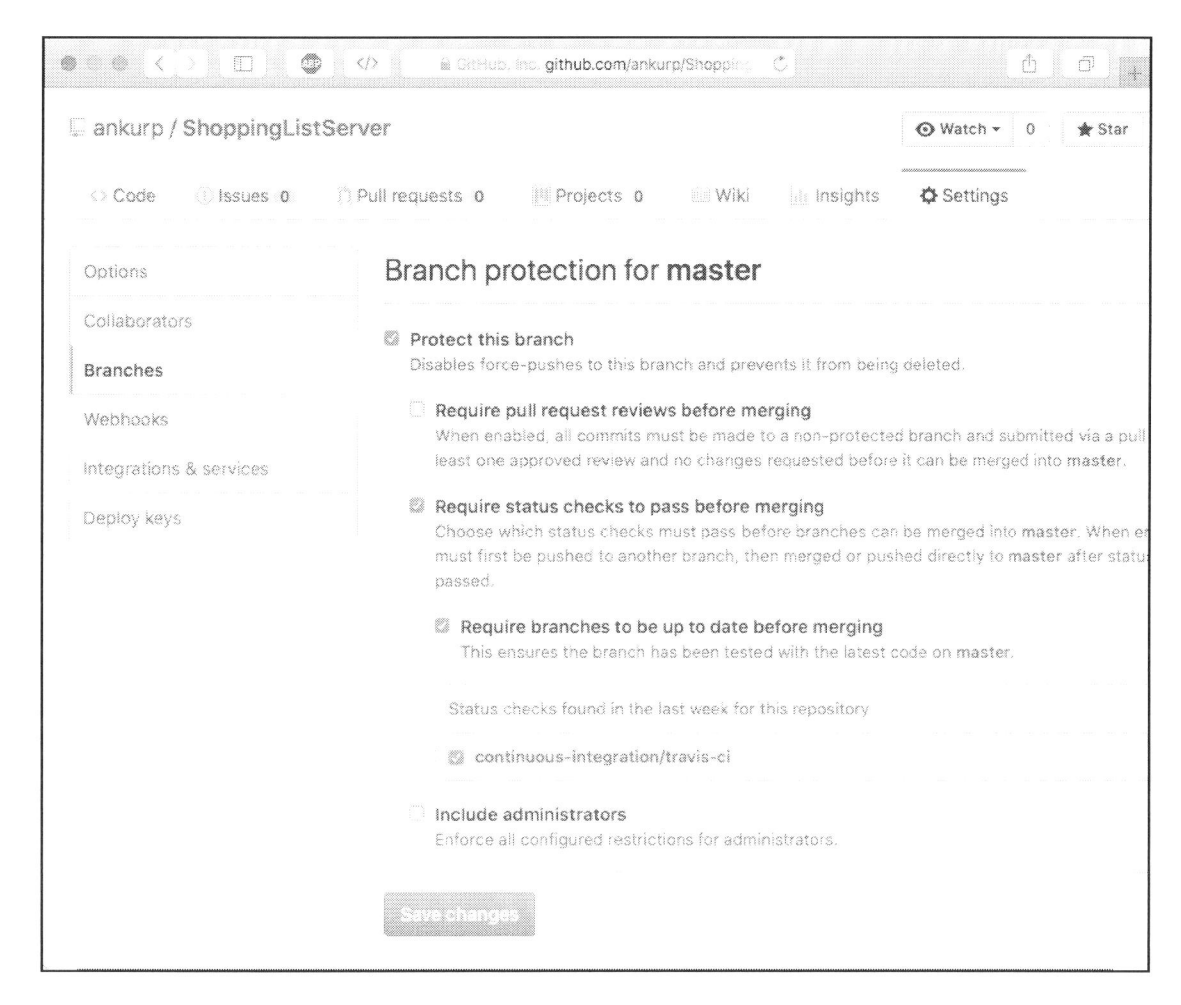

4. Now, click on **Save changes**:

That is it, and now if you or someone else creates a Pull Request, then it will prevent the Pull Request from being merged until the Travis CI status check passes:

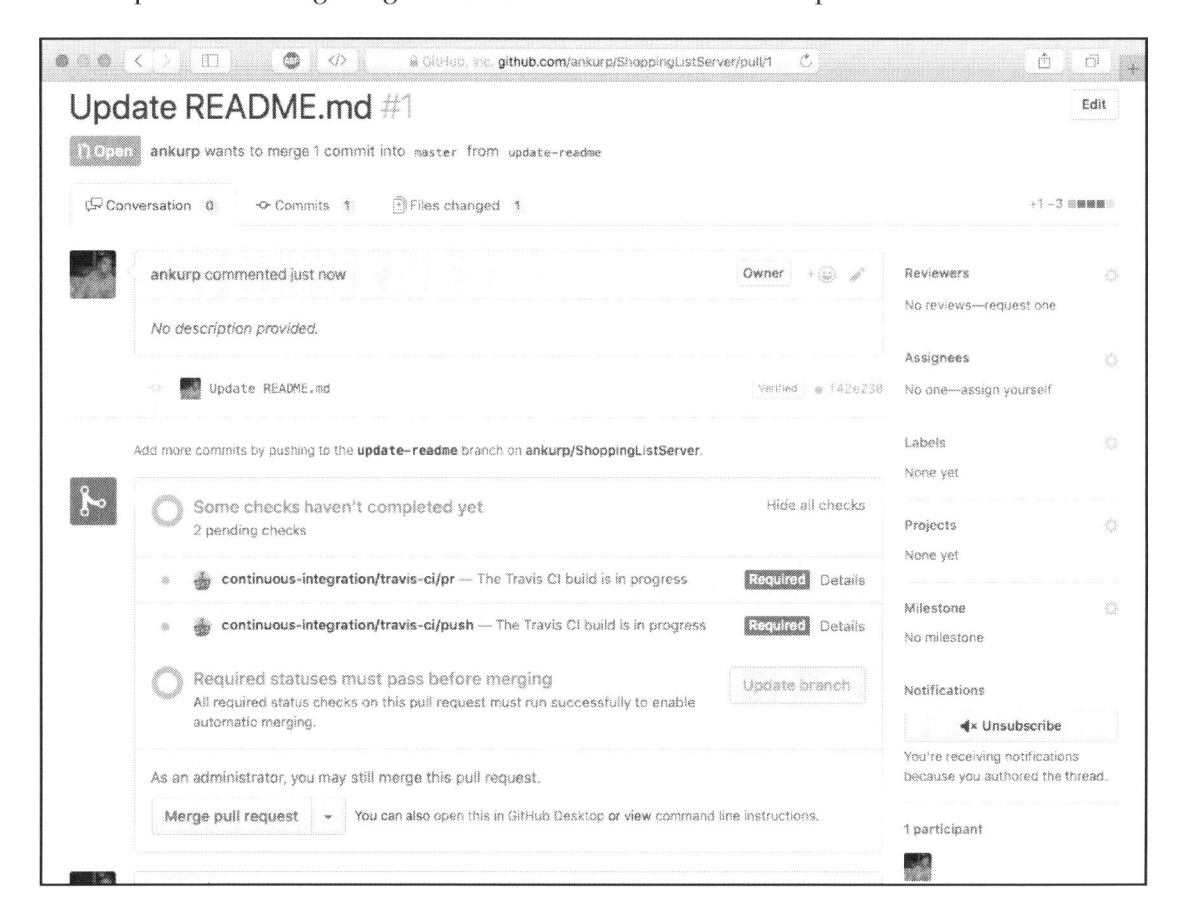

## Summary

Great job if you made it this far in the book. You have not only written an app but also a web and an API server in Swift. In this chapter, you expanded on the Shopping List app idea and wrote tests for the server application. You configured a CI pipeline to run those tests automatically. By now, you should have a good understanding of how to write tests for your Vapor application. You also should have a good background in setting up a CI Pipeline for your future projects using Travis or other CI services.
In the next chapter, you will learn how to deploy your Shopping List app to Vapor's cloud service and also take a look at other cloud services.

# 9
# Deploying the App

In the previous chapter, we learned how to write tests for our server-side Shopping List application. We also learned how to create an automated pipeline to run tests for our code so that we can maintain code quality and fix problems early on rather than discovering them later in production. In this chapter, we will look at how we can deploy our app to the cloud so that we can have it running 24/7 and access it via the internet from anywhere. We will also set up an automated pipeline such that our code will deploy automatically when the tests in Travis pass for our master branch. With this, our project not only has **Continuous Integration** (**CI**) but also **Continuous Deployment** (**CD**) setup, making it a lot easier for a team of developers to maintain a server-side Swift application along with a client-side iOS app without needing a dedicated Dev Ops team to ensure that code is deployed to production. In this chapter, we will specifically cover the following topics:

- What cloud services can we deploy to?
- How to deploy vapor app to one of such cloud services called Heroku?
- How to set up a Continuous Deployment pipeline?

So, let's get started with deploying our app and see it live in Production so that we can share it with others.

## Where can we deploy a Vapor App?

Vapor applications can be deployed anywhere we can run Swift. Currently, Swift only runs on macOS and Ubuntu distribution of Linux. There are multiple options when it comes to where to deploy your Vapor App. You can deploy your Vapor app on a dedicated physical machine or a virtual machine, but the hassle of setting it up and maintaining the server machine yourself can be cumbersome.

You can also deploy your Vapor app to a cloud service provider, such as AWS, Google Cloud Platform, Heroku, or Vapor Cloud. These companies provide Platform as a Service (PaaS), where you do not need to configure the OS to install the required dependencies and instead, just specify the version of Swift and other services you need, such as MongoDB, and it will provide you with those so that your Vapor app can run without a lot of configuration. This also allows you to not have to worry about figuring out what hardware you need upfront, as you can scale the hardware easily with such services by launching replicas of your server, which is known as **Horizontal scaling**. The reason we can do this is because we do not store the state in the Vapor app but in the database.

To deploy our Vapor app, we will look at one such service provided by Heroku, since it is easy to get started with and support deployment of server-side Swift apps. Let's look at how we can deploy our Shopping List Server app to Heroku.

# Deploying to Heroku

Heroku is a Platform as a Service provider that lets you deploy apps of multiple platforms on their servers. Basically, Heroku hosts server apps in such a way that you can scale them horizontally by launching multiple replicas of your app or vertically, by scaling the hardware spec such as increasing memory, CPU, or disk space. This allows you to start out small and help you run your app elegantly without having to worry about all the infrastructure that you need to configure, set up, and maintain a MongoDB server or load balancer.

Deploying is easy as well. It is as simple as pushing code using git. The magic of how it builds and runs the app is in the build packs, which are written by the Heroku team and sometimes by the community; they let you build and run the app on the server without having to write your own deployment scripts. This build pack needs to be added for our Vapor app and Vapor toolbox has a handle script to automate all of this for us, making it a lot more pleasant to deploy to Heroku.

To get started with Heroku deployment, we first need to install the Heroku CLI, which can be installed by following these steps:

1. Open the Terminal app on your macOS and run the following brew command to install the CLI:

    ```
    brew install heroku/brew/heroku
    ```

2. Once Heroku is installed, you can type `heroku help` in the Terminal and it will print all the available commands for Heroku CLI:

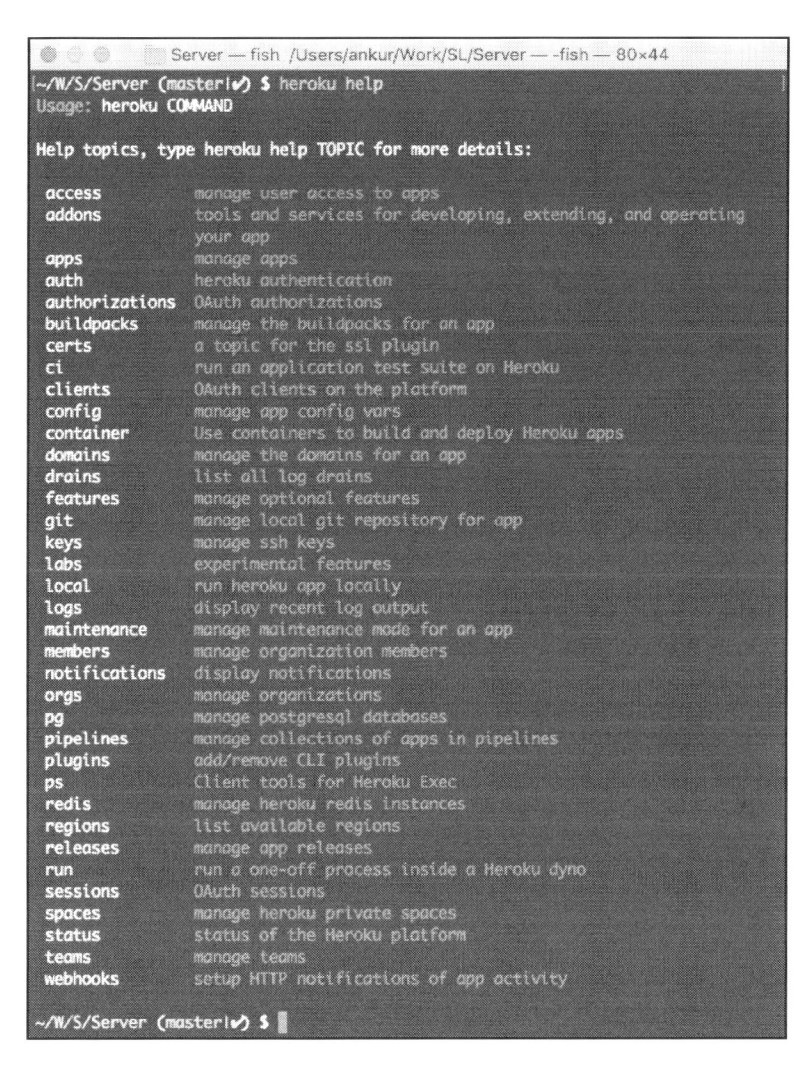

```
~/W/S/Server (master|✔) $ heroku help
Usage: heroku COMMAND

Help topics, type heroku help TOPIC for more details:

 access          manage user access to apps
 addons          tools and services for developing, extending, and operating
                 your app
 apps            manage apps
 auth            heroku authentication
 authorizations  OAuth authorizations
 buildpacks      manage the buildpacks for an app
 certs           a topic for the ssl plugin
 ci              run an application test suite on Heroku
 clients         OAuth clients on the platform
 config          manage app config vars
 container       Use containers to build and deploy Heroku apps
 domains         manage the domains for an app
 drains          list all log drains
 features        manage optional features
 git             manage local git repository for app
 keys            manage ssh keys
 labs            experimental features
 local           run heroku app locally
 logs            display recent log output
 maintenance     manage maintenance mode for an app
 members         manage organization members
 notifications   display notifications
 orgs            manage organizations
 pg              manage postgresql databases
 pipelines       manage collections of apps in pipelines
 plugins         add/remove CLI plugins
 ps              Client tools for Heroku Exec
 redis           manage heroku redis instances
 regions         list available regions
 releases        manage app releases
 run             run a one-off process inside a Heroku dyno
 sessions        OAuth sessions
 spaces          manage heroku private spaces
 status          status of the Heroku platform
 teams           manage teams
 webhooks        setup HTTP notifications of app activity

~/W/S/Server (master|✔) $
```

*Deploying the App*

Before we can proceed, we need to create a free account on Heroku. To do so, go to `https://signup.heroku.com` and, once the account is created, you will be able to run one web process for free every month:

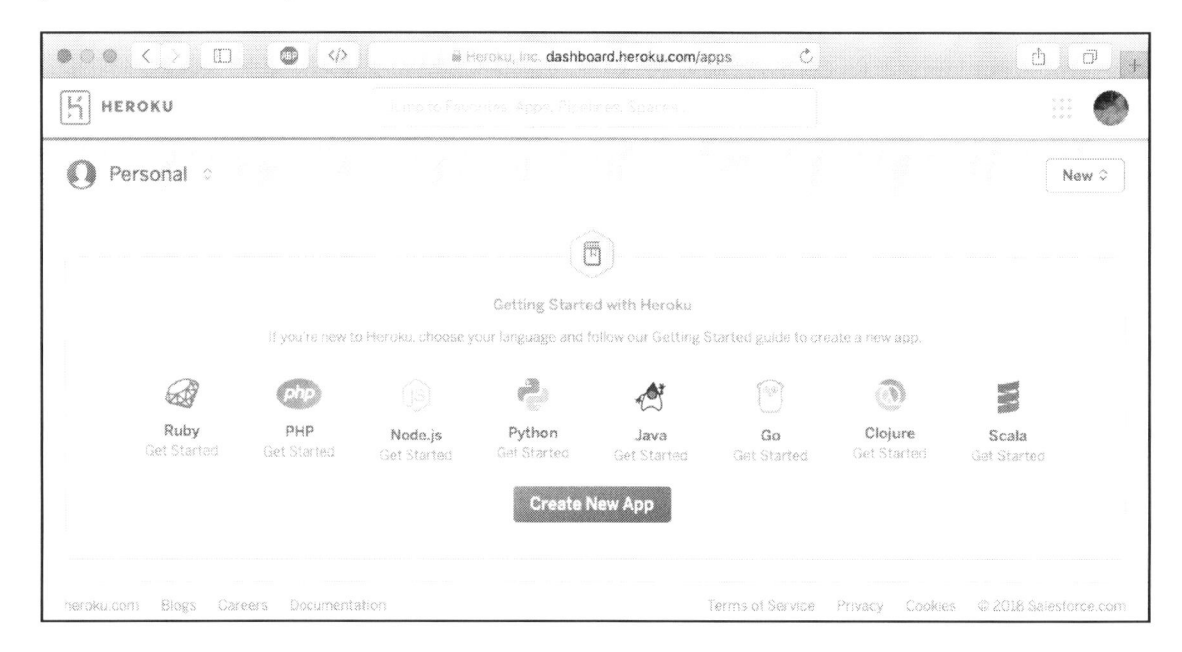

Using your Heroku credentials, you will log in to your account using the Heroku CLI. To log in, run the following command:

```
$ heroku login
```

You will be promoted to enter the email you signed up with and the password for your Heroku account and, once successful, you will get a confirmation:

# Priming the app for deployment

Before we can deploy our app, we need to set up a production config for our database. For our database, we will be using MongoDB as an add on service provided in Heroku for free. Enabling this service will pass the location of the MongoDB service as an environment variable to our app and we can use this to connect our app to the database. We will need to tell our app the location of this MongoDB server. Specifying it is as easy as creating a new folder called `production` under the `Config` folder and adding a `mongo.json` file inside of the `production` folder. To create this config, follow these steps:

1. Open the Terminal and, inside the root level of your Vapor project, create a new folder called production inside of `Config`:

    ```
    $ mkdir Config/production/
    ```

2. Next, create an empty file called `mongo.json` inside of the `production` folder and copy the following config:

    ```
    {
      "url": "$MONGODB_URI"
    }
    ```

That's it, and, if you noted, we specified the URL of our MongoDB to be the value that is set in the environment variable called `MONGODB_URI`. This variable will be set when we enable the free MongoDB service via the Heroku CLI later on.

# Configuring and deploying Vapor to Heroku

The Vapor team has done a great job of integrating Heroku into the Vapor toolbox. We can initialize a Procfile, add the Vapor build pack, and set up a git remote for Heroku to push to, all using one command. A **Procfile** is basically a file where we can specify all the processes we want to run; for our Vapor app, we will be creating one web process only that will run our Vapor app. Heroku uses build packs, which are a list of scripts, to build and run the app on the server. Vapor build pack is basically what we need to get our app to deploy to Heroku. Finally, a new Heroku git remote needs to be configured, so that we can push to that remote with our master branch to start the deployment. Basically, it will push all the code that we have locally, in our master branch, to the Heroku server to be built and run using the Vapor build pack.

*Deploying the App*

To initialize Heroku in our Vapor project, we need to run the following commands:

1. Ensure that you commit all of your changes made so far in git before proceeding to the next step:

   ```
   $ git add .
   $ git commit -m "Saving change"
   ```

2. In the Terminal, go to the root level of your Vapor project and run the following command:

   ```
   $ vapor heroku init
   ```

3. You will be promoted with a question to enter a custom name for your app. Press *Y* and then *Enter* if you want to give a custom name to your app. Ensure that the name is in lowercase characters and only contains letters, hyphens, and numbers. You will then be prompted for the app name; enter a name that is not already taken in Heroku:

   > **TIP**: Do not use the example app name specified as follows, as it is in use already:

   ```
   Would you like to provide a custom Heroku app name?
   y/n> y
   Custom app name:
   > vapor-shopping-list
   ```

4. Next, you will be asked whether you want to deploy to regions other than the US:

   ```
   Would you like to deploy to a region other than the US?
   y/n> n
   https://vapor-shopping-list.herokuapp.com/ |
   https://git.heroku.com/vapor-shopping-list.git
   ```

5. Then, you will be asked if you want to use a custom Heroku buildpack other than the one supported by Vapor. Press *N* and then *Enter* as as we are not doing anything custom:

   ```
   Would you like to provide a custom Heroku buildpack?
   y/n> n
   Setting buildpack...
   ```

6. Now, you will be asked whether you have a custom Executable name. For our app, we do not. After you answer this question, a Procfile will be created, which will contain the command to start the Vapor app on the Heroku server, and it will add and commit the changes to the git repository:

   ```
   Are you using a custom Executable name?
   y/n> n
   Setting procfile...
   Committing procfile...
   ```

7. Finally, it will ask whether you want to deploy your app now. Press *Y* and then *Enter*, and the deployment will start. It will take some time, but once done, it will print the URL to your app in the end:

   ```
   Would you like to push to Heroku now?
   y/n> y
   This may take a while...
   Building on Heroku ... ~5-10 minutes [Done]
   Spinning up dynos [Done]
   Visit https://dashboard.heroku.com/apps/
   App is live on Heroku, visit
   https://vapor-shopping-list.herokuapp.com/ |
   https://git.heroku.com/vapor-shopping-list.git
   ```

## Deploying the App

Cool! We just configured our app to deploy to Heroku, and it deployed it as well:

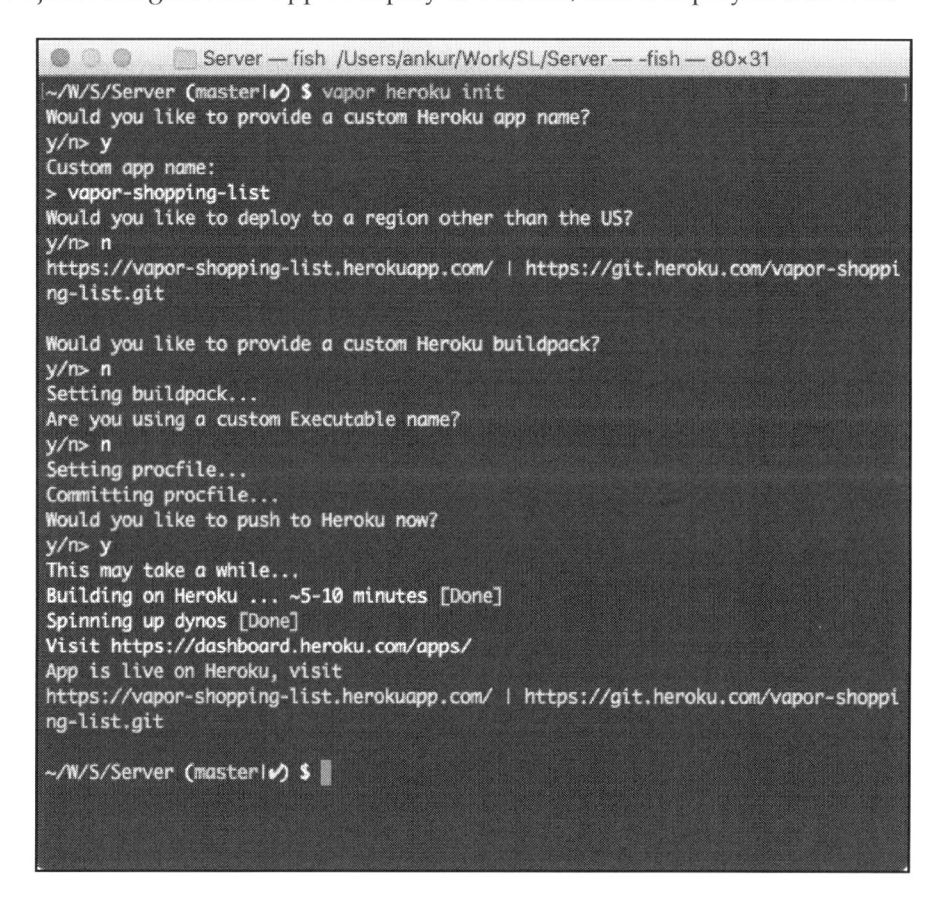

```
~/W/S/Server (master|✓) $ vapor heroku init
Would you like to provide a custom Heroku app name?
y/n> y
Custom app name:
> vapor-shopping-list
Would you like to deploy to a region other than the US?
y/n> n
https://vapor-shopping-list.herokuapp.com/ | https://git.heroku.com/vapor-shoppi
ng-list.git

Would you like to provide a custom Heroku buildpack?
y/n> n
Setting buildpack...
Are you using a custom Executable name?
y/n> n
Setting procfile...
Committing procfile...
Would you like to push to Heroku now?
y/n> y
This may take a while...
Building on Heroku ... ~5-10 minutes [Done]
Spinning up dynos [Done]
Visit https://dashboard.heroku.com/apps/
App is live on Heroku, visit
https://vapor-shopping-list.herokuapp.com/ | https://git.heroku.com/vapor-shoppi
ng-list.git

~/W/S/Server (master|✓) $
```

# Adding the MongoDB Heroku addon

We are not done yet. If you go to the URL printed in the console where your app is hosted on Heroku, you will note that it is broken and shows an **Application error** page, as follows:

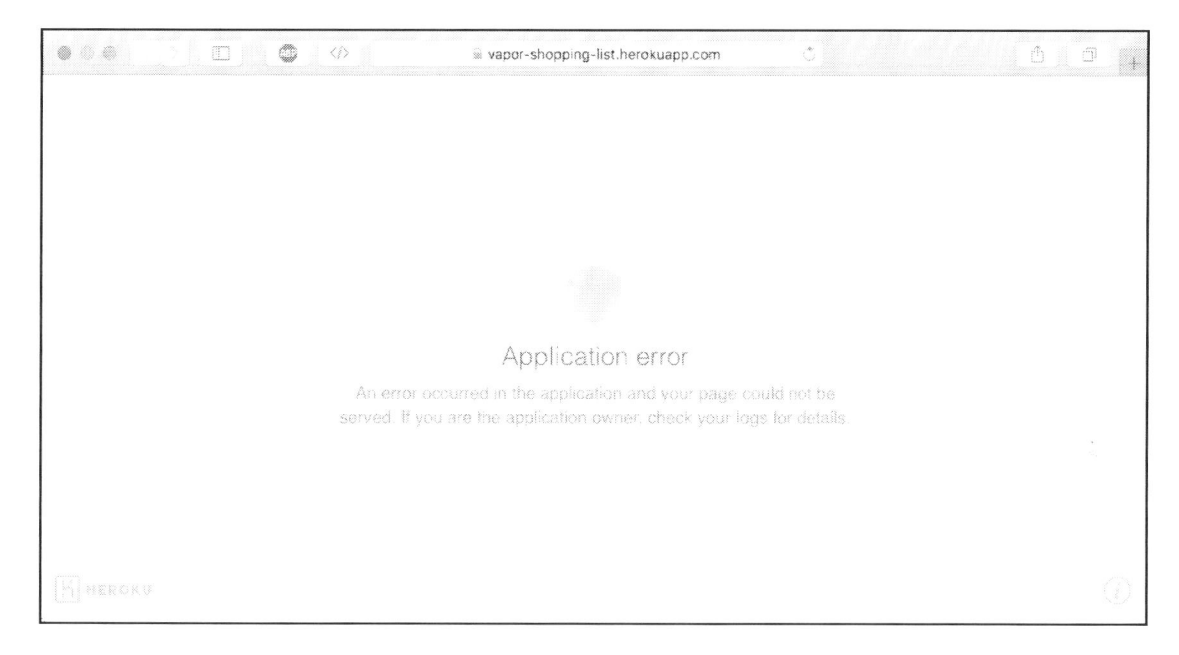

The reason this is happening is because we have not created a MongoDB service and passed the URL to the service to our app so that our Vapor app can connect to it. This can be easily resolved by running the following command in the Terminal, which will create a free MongoDB server instance for our app and restart our app:

```
$ heroku addons:create mongolab:sandbox
```

## Deploying the App

Ensure that you verify your Heroku account by adding a Credit Card, if you have not done so already. Even though it is a free service, a Credit Card is required on file for verification to avoid abuse of Heroku's free service.

```
~/W/S/Server (master|✓) $ heroku addons:create mongolab:sandbox
Creating mongolab:sandbox on ⬢ vapor-shopping-list... free
Welcome to mLab.  Your new subscription is being created and will be available s
hortly.  Please consult the mLab Add-on Admin UI to check on its progress.
Created mongolab-cubic-73099 as MONGODB_URI
Use heroku addons:docs mongolab to view documentation
~/W/S/Server (master|✓) $
```

Once you have added the mongolab add-on, the app should restart. Now, if you visit your Shopping List app again by visiting the URL provided by Heroku in the browser, you should see your Vapor app render the Shopping List on the web, as illustrated:

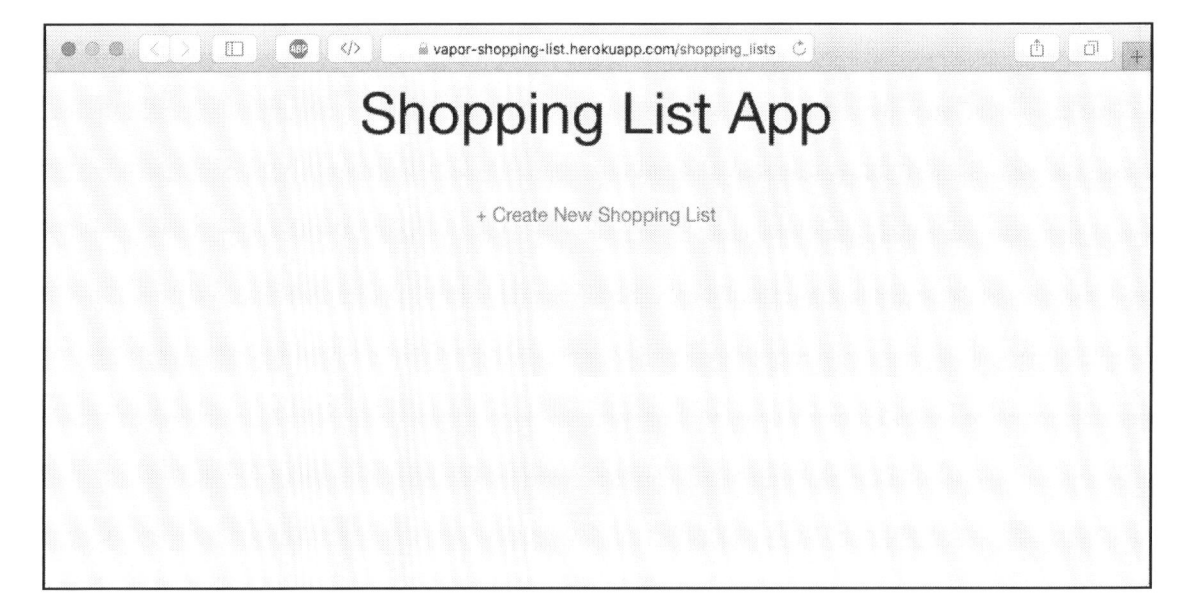

# Shopping List App

+ Create New Shopping List

# Setting up Continuous Deployment

We have configured an automated pipeline for testing our repository every time there is a merge into the master branch. It would be great if we could automatically deploy our app after the code is merged into master and when all the tests pass with the recently merged changes. We can do just that with Heroku by configuring it in their web portal. To get started with Continuous Deployment, follow these steps:

1. First, log in to the Heroku website and go to the Dashboard.
2. Select your app from the list and go to the project details page.
3. On this page, click on the **Deploy** tab.
4. In the **Deployment method** section, click on **GitHub**.
5. In the **Connect to GitHub** section, search for your `Shopping List` repository under your account and press the **Connect** button next to the repository, as demonstrated here:

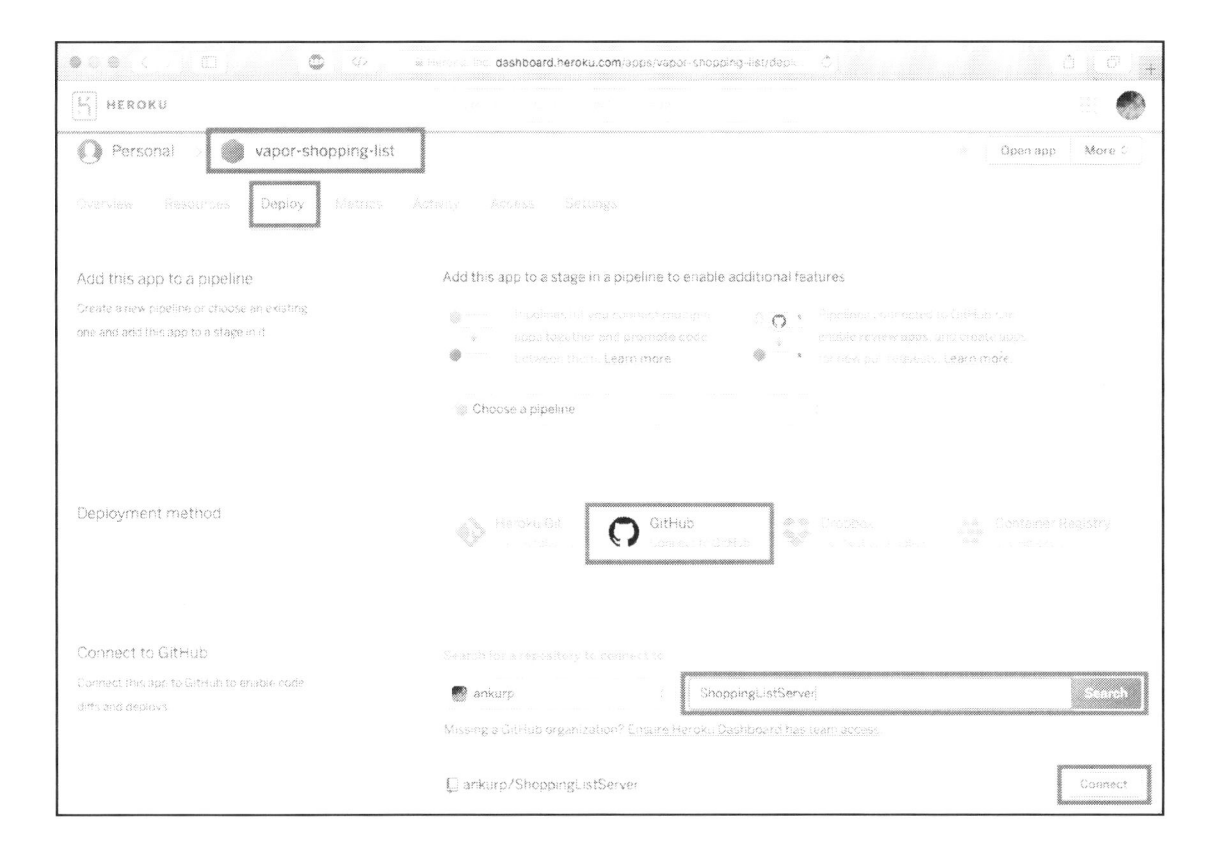

*Deploying the App*

6. Once the GitHub repository is connected, go to the **Automatic deploys** section and ensure that the **master** branch is selected. Also, check **Wait for CI to pass before deploy** before pressing on the **Enable Automatic Deploys** button:

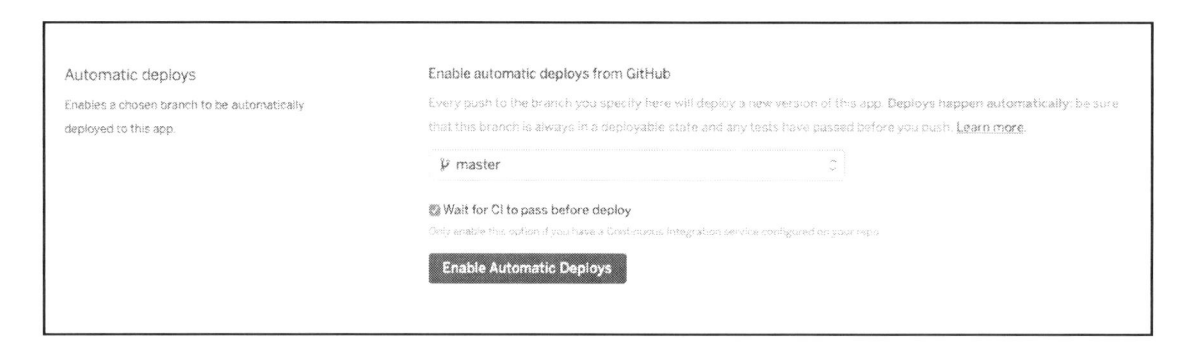

Good job if you made it this far. We have just set up a Continuous Deployment pipeline. Next time you merge code into the master branch and when the tests pass in Travis CI for the master branch, the code from your GitHub repository that you just connected will automatically deploy to Heroku:

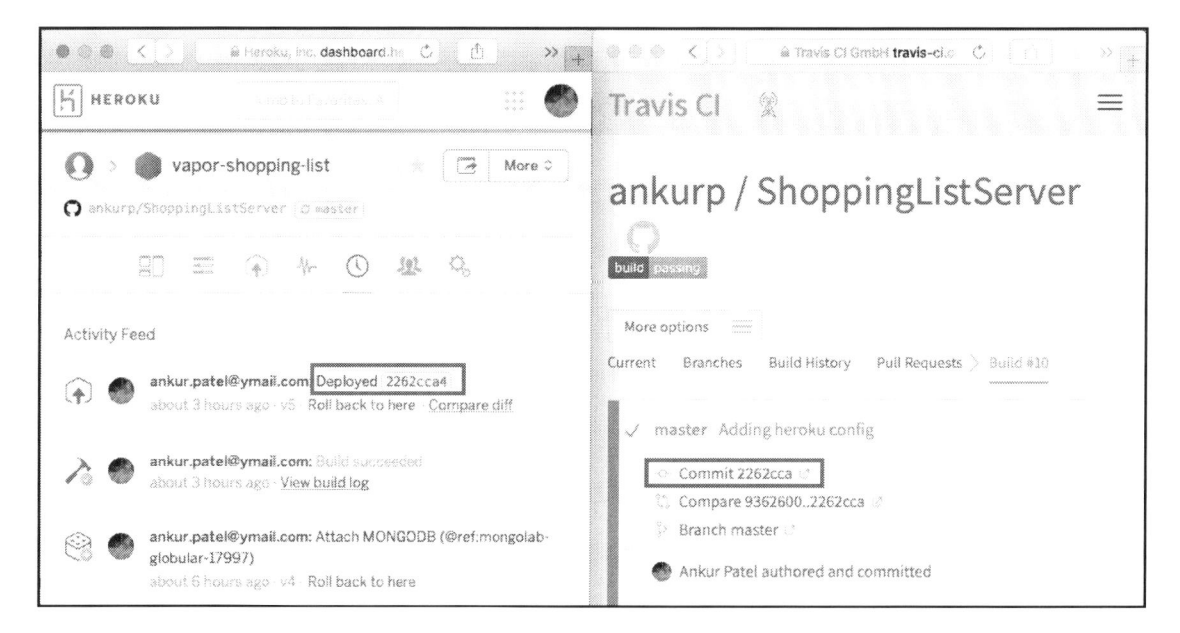

# Exercise

There are a lot of cloud service providers. A few big players include AWS, Google Cloud Platform, and Microsoft Azure. Vapor has its own cloud service as well, which is easy to deploy. Vapor Toolbox supports deploying to their own cloud service out of box by specifying the deploy configuration in the `cloud.yml` file. As part of a short exercise, try to deploy the shopping list app to Vapor's cloud similar to how we did it for Heroku.

# Summary

In this chapter, we finally got to publish our work for others to see through the cloud so that we can access it over the internet. By now, you have a good understanding of how to publish a Vapor app to Heroku, a cloud service provider. Lastly, we set up a Continuous Deployment pipeline to automatically deploy the latest code when it passes the CI check.

In the next chapter, we will learn how to add authentication to our Vapor app so that we can have a Shopping List associated with a user and only that user can make changes to their own Shopping List.

# 10
# Adding Authentication

Good job if you have made it this far. You used Swift not only to build an iOS app, but also a full stack web application, and you also set up tests and an automated deployment pipeline for your app, so that you can develop and deploy code with ease. Now, in this chapter, you will finish off your Shopping List app by adding the concept of users to your app and associating Shopping Lists with a specific user.

Currently, our app does not support multiple user accounts. We show all of the Shopping Lists to anyone who opens the app or goes to the web app. There is no concept of users creating their own Shopping List and being able to get only their Shopping List. We will be changing that in this chapter, and to do so, we will need to add a User model. We will also need to create a way for users to register and authenticate themselves to log in. Then, every time a user creates a Shopping List, it will be associated with the user who created it. This is similar to how items are associated with a Shopping List. We will cover several topics in this chapter, ranging from user creation to sessions to token creation for API requests for our app. More specifically, in this chapter, we will discuss the following topics:

- Creating a User model and merging associated Shopping Lists with a user account
- Configuring and generating registration/login routes
- Password protecting certain routes
- Keeping a user authenticated in the browser using Session
- Generating web forms to register and to log in
- Creating a Token model and associating with a user to make API requests from an iOS app
- Updating the index action to return Shopping Lists belonging to a user
- Updating the iOS app to support authentication and token-based API requests

There are a lot of topics to cover, so let's get started by first creating a User model.

## Creating a User model

To support the concept of registering for an app, we will need to first create a User model. A user, similar to a Shopping List or an Item model in our Vapor app, will be a class that contains certain properties, such as name, email, and password. When a user tries to register for our app, they will provide us with their name, email, and password, and we will take those and create a new user record if it does not already exist. In our app, we will use email as the ID by which a user can log in along with their password. Some websites or apps may even have a concept of username, which can be added as a property to the User model; however, for our app, email will suffice to serve as a unique identifier by which we can find a user account.

The user will need to provide a password when registering, and using that password, they will be able to log in. We cannot simply store the password in its original text form in the database, as there are a lot of security concerns since your database can be hacked into in rare cases, and someone can steal the passwords easily. Luckily, there are industry standard ways of storing password using hashing functions. Hashing makes it impossible for someone to steal anyone's password even if our database was hacked.

## Best practices for storing password

Hashing, which we touched upon in `Chapter 3`, *Getting Started with Vapor*, when creating our Vapor app, is very useful for a lot of things, including password encryption. Certain hashing algorithms such as **BCrypt** and **SHA-256** can be thought of as functions that can take in some text and generate unintelligible text that is long and hard to memorize. The beauty of these hashing functions is that they will generate a new random string that cannot be reversed to its original form. Even a slight change in one character can generate output that is completely different, making it a lot harder to figure out the original text that was hashed. Knowing this quality of the hashing function, we can generate a hash of the user's password and store it in the database when the user registers.

Next time when they try to log in, we will find the user record in the database with the email ID provided in the login form. We then hash the password provided in the login form with the same hash function and check whether it matches with the password that is stored in the database. If it does, we can mark the user as logged in and create a session for that user, so that they can be logged in until they decide to log out.

A lot of the concepts mentioned, such as hashing functions, sessions, and authentication, have been thought through by the Vapor team. They are provided in the Vapor package itself and some in the `AuthProvider` package, which makes implementing authentication relatively easy. To get started, let's import `AuthProvider` first into our Vapor project by following these steps:

1. First, add `AuthProvider` to your `Package.swift` file:

    ```
    .package(url: "https://github.com/vapor/auth-provider.git",
    .upToNextMajor(from: "1.2.0")),
    ```

2. Specify `AuthProvider` as a dependency in the `target` section of the app:

    ```
    .target(name: "App", dependencies: ["Vapor", "FluentProvider",
    "HealthcheckProvider", "MongoProvider", "LeafProvider",
    "AuthProvider"],
    ```

3. Next, regenerate the Xcode project file by running the following command in the Terminal:

    ```
    vapor xcode -y
    ```

*Adding Authentication*

# Getting started with the User model

Great! Now that we have AuthProvider added to the project, we can build and run our app to confirm we have imported it correctly. Now, let's go ahead and define our User model next:

1. Create a new file called `User.swift` inside the `Models` folder in your Vapor app and make sure that you check **App** under **Targets**:

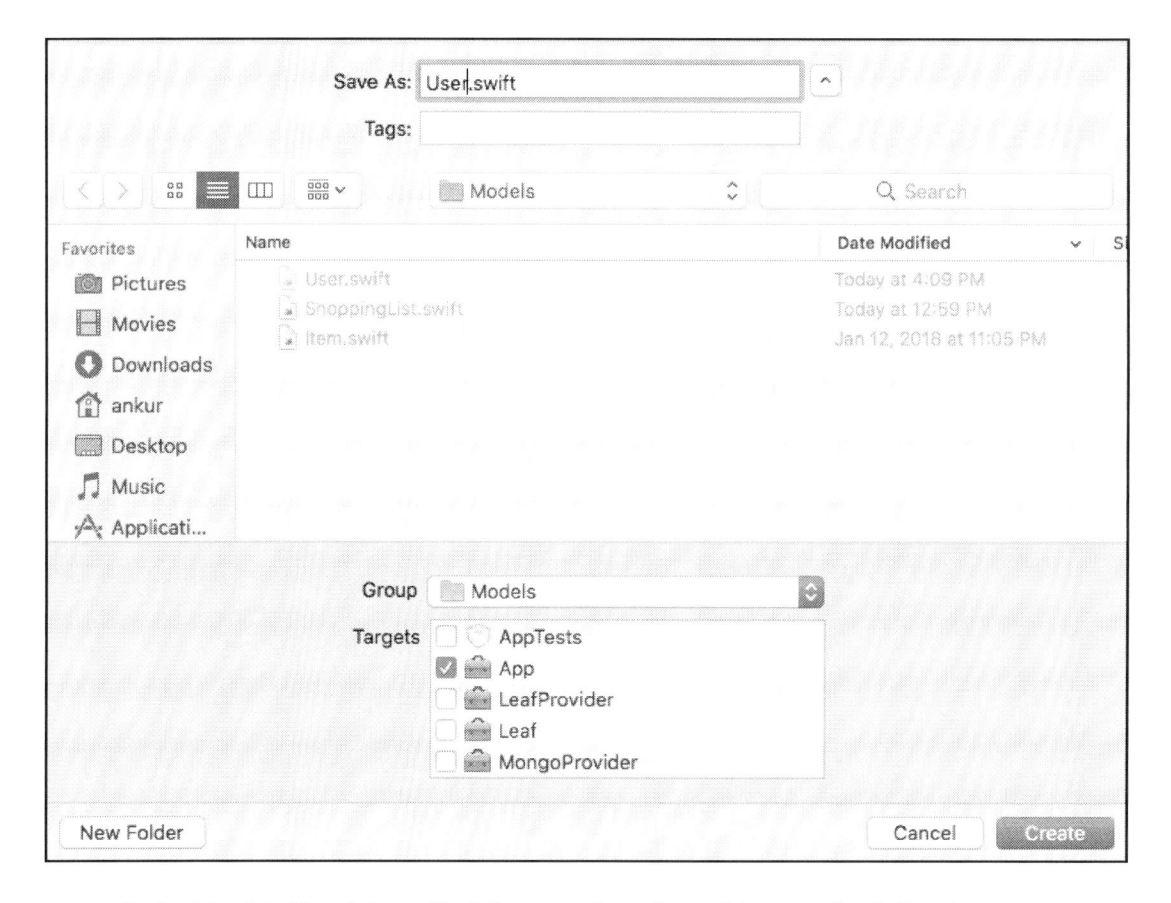

2. Inside this file, delete all of the sample code and import the following dependencies:

   ```
   import FluentProvider
   import HTTP
   import Fluent
   import AuthProvider
   ```

3. Next, define the class, and we will make it implement both the `Model` and `SessionPersistable` protocols:

   ```
   final class User: Model, SessionPersistable {
   ```

4. Next, we will define the following attributes in the class, similar to the `ShoppingList` or `Item` model that we implemented in Chapter 5, *Building a REST API using Vapor*:

   ```
   let storage = Storage()
   struct Keys {
     static let id = "id"
     static let name = "name"
     static let email = "email"
     static let password = "password"
   }
   var name: String
   var email: String
   var password: String
   ```

5. Next, define the initializers and `makeRow` method as part of the Model protocol:

   ```
   init(name: String, email: String, password: String) {
     self.name = name
     self.email = email
     self.password = password
   }
   init(row: Row) throws {
     name = try row.get(Keys.name)
     email = try row.get(Keys.email)
     password = try row.get(Keys.password)
   }
   func makeRow() throws -> Row {
     var row = Row()
     try row.set(Keys.name, name)
     try row.set(Keys.email, email)
     try row.set(Keys.password, password)
     return row
   }
   ```

*Adding Authentication*

6. Next, we will implement the `hashPassword` and `passwordVerifier` computed properties in the `User` class as part of the `PasswordAuthenticatable` protocol. As previously mentioned, we will not be storing the raw password in the database, but, instead, a hash of the password and these two computed properties help with that. Since we cannot set the property as it is read only, we need to reference a `private` variable, as follows:

   ```
   private var _userPasswordVerifier: PasswordVerifier? = nil
   extension User: PasswordAuthenticatable {
     var hashedPassword: String? {
       return password
     }
     public static var passwordVerifier: PasswordVerifier? {
       get { return _userPasswordVerifier }
       set { _userPasswordVerifier = newValue }
     }
   }
   ```

7. Next, we will define the `prepare` method for the database preparation to create our User table where we will store the user record:

   ```
   extension User: Preparation {
     static func prepare(_ database: Database) throws {
       try database.create(self) { builder in
         builder.id()
         builder.string(Keys.name)
         builder.string(Keys.email)
         builder.string(Keys.password)
       }
     }
     static func revert(_ database: Database) throws {
       try database.delete(self)
     }
   }
   ```

8. Finally, we will make an extension on the `Request` class so that it can return, us the `User` object, making the request `AuthProvider` helper defined by the `AuthProvider` itself on the `Request` class via extension:

   ```
   extension Request {
     func user() throws -> User {
       return try auth.assertAuthenticated()
     }
   }
   ```

[ 266 ]

9. Now, let's switch files and open `Config+Setup.swift` and add our User model in the list of preparation to run inside of the `setupPreparation` method:

    ```
    preparations.append(User.self)
    ```

10. Next, we will configure the `PasswordVerifier` by switching to the `Droplet+Setup.swift` file and add the following method. This will use the hash method provided by Vapor and set it as the default password verified for the User. As previously mentioned, we will not store the raw password in the database so that when a user submits a login form with their email as a user ID and password, Vapor will first hash the password using the password verifier function and then check with the hashPassword for that user, which is the password retrieved from the database:

    ```
    private func setupPasswordVerifier() throws {
      guard let verifier = hash as? PasswordVerifier else {
        throw Abort(.internalServerError, reason: "\(type(of:
        hash)) must conform to PasswordVerifier.")
      }
      User.passwordVerifier = verifier
    }
    ```

11. Now, call this method inside of the `setup` method in the same `Droplet+Setup.swift` file:

    ```
    public func setup() throws {
      try setupRoutes()
      try setupPasswordVerifier()
    }
    ```

12. Also, add the `AuthProvider` as the dependency in this `Droplet+Setup.swift` file by adding the following line to the top:

    ```
    import AuthProvider
    ```

13. Lastly, we will change the `hash` function that Vapor uses by default to use `bcrypt` so that it cannot be reversed to the original password. This can easily be done by changing the `hash` config inside the `Config/droplet.json` file:

    ```
    "hash": "bcrypt",
    ```

14. You will also need to make a config file called `bcrypt.json` inside the `Config` folder, which will contain options that get passed to the `bcrypt` function. Inside this new file, add the following config. The higher the cost, the harder it is to find the password that matches the hash, but it is slower, which might have a performance implication for high traffic website:

```
{
  "cost": 4
}
```

This is a nice place to pause and build and run our application to make sure that everything is configured correctly. You should be able to run the application at this point without any errors. Next, we will take a look at how we can associate Shopping Lists with a user, so that a User can have multiple Shopping Lists and a Shopping List belongs to one user.

# User has many Shopping Lists

A User has many Shopping Lists, to create a **has-many** relation between User and Shopping List model, we will need to do a similar exercise like we did for Shopping List and Item model. Each `ShoppingList` object would need to keep an ID to the user it belongs to so that we can query for all Shopping Lists for that user. To add this, we will need to follow these steps:

1. Open the `ShoppingList.swift` file in your Vapor app and add the following new property as an instance variable inside the `ShoppingList` class to store `userId`:

    ```
    var userId: Identifier
    ```

2. Next, create a user-computed property, which will allow us to get the user to a Shopping List:

    ```
    var user: Parent<ShoppingList, User> {
      return parent(id: userId)
    }
    ```

3. Now, add the `userId` column name that will be used by MongoDB to store the user ID inside of the database collection:

    ```
    static let userId = "user__id"
    ```

4. Now, we will need to update our initializer so that it can take the `userId` as a parameter and assign it to its `userId` property. We will also need to update the `makeRow` method so it can set the `userId` correctly in the row that will be inserted into the database:

```
init(name: String, userId: Identifier) {
  self.name = name
  self.userId = userId
}
init(row: Row) throws {
  name = try row.get(ShoppingList.Keys.name)
  userId = try row.get(ShoppingList.Keys.userId)
}
func makeRow() throws -> Row {
  var row = Row()
  try row.set(ShoppingList.Keys.name, name)
  try row.set(ShoppingList.Keys.userId, userId)
  return row
}
```

5. Now, update the database preparation so that it generates a foreign key column, which will store the user ID in the Shopping List record so that we can create the belongs to the relationship between Shopping List and User model:

```
static func prepare(_ database: Database) throws {
  try database.create(self) { builder in
    builder.id()
    builder.string(ShoppingList.Keys.name)
    builder.parent(User.self)
  }
}
```

6. Now update the `JSONConvertible` extension by adding references to `userId` in the initializer and `makeJSON` method:

```
extension ShoppingList: JSONConvertible {
  convenience init(json: JSON) throws {
    self.init(
      name: try json.get(ShoppingList.Keys.name),
      userId: try json.get(ShoppingList.Keys.userId)
    )
  }
  func makeJSON() throws -> JSON {
    var json = JSON()
    try json.set(ShoppingList.Keys.id, id)
    try json.set(ShoppingList.Keys.name, name)
```

```
            try json.set(ShoppingList.Keys.userId, userId)
            try json.set("items", items.all())
            return json
        }
    }
```

7. Lastly, add the `userId` reference to the `Replaceable` extension:

```
extension ShoppingList: Replaceable {
  func replaceAttributes(from list: ShoppingList) {
    self.name = list.name
    self.userId = list.userId
  }
}
```

This is a good point to take a break. You should be able to build and run your Vapor server without any errors which will confirm that you have configured everything correctly so far in the Shopping List model. Next, we will look at how we can add registration and login pages to our Vapor app so that we authenticate a user before showing them the Shopping Lists in the browser instead of showing all of the Shopping Lists that we currently do.

# Adding Registration and Login

To add Registration and Login web pages is as simple as setting up a route in our `Routes.swift` and creating a Leaf template file that will render the HTML forms. For our Leaf template, we will need to create a signup form for the new user and a login form for users that have registered already. To get started with adding these forms to our Vapor app, we need to follow these steps:

1. First, open the `Routes.swift` file and remove everything inside the `setupRoutes` method as we will be setting up two kinds of routes, one for authenticated users and another for unauthenticated.
2. Next, import the `AuthProvider` and `Sessions` dependencies that we will need later by adding the following two lines to the top of the file:

```
import AuthProvider
import Sessions
```

3. Next, inside the `setupRoutes` method, add the following two methods that we will define soon:

   ```
   func setupRoutes() throws {
     self.setupUnauthenticatedRoutes()
     self.setupAuthenticatedRoutes()
   }
   ```

4. Now, let's define the `setupUnauthenticatedRoutes` method. This will be the method where we will define a `/register` route, which will accept a POST request only. This POST request will be sent by the Registration form in the browser to our Vapor server and we will extract values from the form and create a user record if it does not exists. The implementation looks like this:

   ```
   func setupUnauthenticatedRoutes() {
     post("register") { req in
       guard let form = req.formURLEncoded,
         let name = form["name"]?.string,
         !name.isEmpty,
         let email = form["email"]?.string,
         !email.isEmpty,
         let password = form["password"]?.string,
         !password.isEmpty else {
         throw Abort(.badRequest)
       }

       guard try User.makeQuery().filter("email", email).first() == nil else {
         throw Abort(.badRequest, reason: "A user with that email already exists.")
       }

       let encryptedPassword = try self.hash.make(password.makeBytes()).makeString()
       let user = User(name: name, email: email, password: encryptedPassword)

       try user.save()
       return "User Account Created Successfully"
     }
   }
   ```

[ 271 ]

*Adding Authentication*

5. Next, we will define the authenticated routes that will protect the Shopping List and items routes so that no one can view them unless the user is logged in. Thanks to Vapor's `AuthProvider` and Sessions, a lot of the heavy lifting related to authenticating and creating sessions after authentication has been taking care of. All we need to do is initialize the Auth and Session middleware and add them to our Vapor routes:

```
func setupAuthenticatedRoutes() {
  let passwordMiddleware =
PasswordAuthenticationMiddleware(User.self)
  let memory = MemorySessions()
  let persistMiddleware = PersistMiddleware(User.self)
  let sessionsMiddleware = SessionsMiddleware(memory)
  let redirect = RedirectMiddleware.login(path: "/")
  let shoppingListController = ShoppingListController()
  let itemController = ItemController()
  let loginRoutes = grouped([sessionsMiddleware,
persistMiddleware])
  loginRoutes.get() { req in
    if req.auth.isAuthenticated(User.self) {
      return Response(redirect: "/shopping_lists")
    }
    return try self.view.make("welcome")
  }
  loginRoutes.post("login") { req in
    guard let email = req.formURLEncoded?["email"]?.string,
      let password = req.formURLEncoded?["password"]?.string
  else {
        throw Abort(.badRequest)
    }
    let credentials = Password(username: email, password:
password)
    let user = try User.authenticate(credentials)
    req.auth.authenticate(user)
    return Response(redirect: "/shopping_lists")
  }
  let authRoutes = grouped([redirect, sessionsMiddleware,
persistMiddleware, passwordMiddleware])
  authRoutes.resource("shopping_lists", shoppingListController)
  authRoutes.resource("items", itemController)
  authRoutes.get("logout") { req in
    try req.auth.unauthenticate()
    return Response(redirect: "/")
  }
}
```

6. Now, all we need to do is add our Leaf template, which will render the HTML forms. For this, create a new file under `Resources/Views` called `welcome.leaf` and paste the following HTML code:

```html
<!DOCTYPE html>
<html>
<head>
  <title>Welcome to Shopping List App</title>
  <link rel="stylesheet" href="/css/app.css">
</head>
<body>
  <div class="row grid-x">
    <form class="medium-6 columns" action="/register" method="post">
      <h1 class="text-center">Sign Up</h1>
      <input type="hidden" name="type" value="registerUser" />
      <input type="email" name="email" placeholder="Email" id="linkInput">
      <input type="text" name="name" placeholder="Name" id="linkInput">
      <input type="password" name="password" placeholder="Password" id="linkInput">
      <input class="button" type="submit" value="Sign Up">
    </form>
    <div class="columns">OR</div>
    <form class="medium-6 columns" action="/login" method="post">
      <h1 class="text-center">Login</h1>
      <input type="hidden" name="type" value="loginUser" />
      <input type="email" name="email" placeholder="Email" id="linkInput">
      <input type="password" name="password" placeholder="Password" id="linkInput">
      <input class="button" type="submit" value="Login">
    </form>
  </div>
  <script src="https://code.jquery.com/jquery-3.2.1.min.js"></script>
  <script src="/js/app.js"></script>
</body>
</html>
```

*Adding Authentication*

7. Now, add the following CSS to the `app.css` file under the `Public/css` folder so that it styles the form correctly:

```
.grid-x {
  justify-content: center;
}

div.columns {
  align-self: center;
}

form.columns {
  padding: 20px;
  max-width: 300px;
}

form input[type=submit] {
  width: 100%;
}
```

8. Build and run the app now and go to `http://localhost:8080/`, and you should see that the `welcome.leaf` template is rendered with both the Login and Sign up forms:

Awesome! We now have Registration and Login forms created. Go ahead and try it out. You should be able to create a new user by typing in your email, name, and password. Once the account is created, you can go back and log in and try to log in with the email and password you have just entered, and you will be redirected automatically to the Shopping Lists routes listing all of the Shopping Lists.

There is still one issue, and that is, we are displaying all Shopping Lists instead of displaying the Shopping List belonging to the user who is logged in. That can easily be solved by updating our `ShoppingListController`.

## Showing user specific Shopping Lists

To show a user-specific Shopping List, we need to scope our database query. Currently, the database query fetches all resources of the type being requested. We need to search for resources in the database that contain user ID that equals the user ID of the requesting user. This can be done by overriding two methods in our `ShoppingListController`, which inherits from `BaseResourceController`. The two methods we need to override are the `index` and the `store` method.

In the `index` method, we need to query for all Shopping Lists which contains the user ID of the user making the request, and in the `store` method, we need to set the `userId` property to the user ID of the user making the request before saving the user record in the database. To make this work the way we want, we need to follow these steps:

1. Open the `ShoppingListController.swift` file, and inside the class, override the `index` method with this implementation. In this method, we added one line to get the user from the request and then filter the database query by receiving only Shopping Lists belonging to that user:

```
override func index(_ req: Request) throws -> ResponseRepresentable
{
  let response = Response(status: .ok)
  let user = try req.user()
  let resources = try ShoppingList.makeQuery().filter(ShoppingList.Keys.userId, user.id).all()
  response.resources = resources
  return response
}
```

2. Next, override the `store` method to set the `userId` property before saving it as follow:

```
override func store(_ req: Request) throws -> ResponseRepresentable
{
    let response = Response(status: .ok)
    guard let json = req.json else { throw Abort.badRequest }
    let user = try req.user()
    let list = try ShoppingList(json: json)
    list.userId = user.id!
    try list.save()
    response.resource = list
    return response
}
```

3. Now, build and run and let's test it out.

After going to `http://localhost:8080/` and logging in using the user you just created, you should not see any Shopping Lists. This means that our query is working as expected. Try creating a new Shopping List, and it should create it without any errors, and reloading the page should show you your newly creating shopping list also. You can also test whether other users do not see your Shopping List by signing out of the session by going to `http://localhost:8080/logout` and creating a new user.

# Adding token-based authentication for app

Great job if you have made it this far, as you have not only added authentication and registration to your app but also created a web app that can be used by multiple users to create Shopping Lists and items that only they can view and edit. The way users stay authenticated on the web is due to sessions, and they do not need to enter their password for every request they make. This is possible due to browsers storing the session token in the cookie of the browser, which gets sent to the server every time a request is made. Using the token in the cookie, it is able to decipher the user making the request by looking it up in the in-memory sessions dictionary. So this works seamlessly in the browser, but, for mobile apps making the request, there is no cookie or way to store the cookie.

For such apps, we need a different type of authentication system, which is called **token-based authentication** where we will send a token similar to the token stored in the cookie. This token will be sent in the header of the request, and our Vapor app will use this token to look up the user making the request. The token will also be issued when the app tries to authenticate the user using the username and password. Our server will then reply with a token that the app will store in memory or in the disk on the app so that when it makes any request it keeps passing this token to the server for every request. To map the token to the user ID, we will need to store the token in the database with the user ID.

Implementing this would require us to create a Token model, associate the token with a user model, add the Token model to the list of preparations, and set up routes and middleware for token-based authentication for our mobile app. The following are the steps for implementing it:

1. Create a new file called `Token.swift` inside of the `Models` folder similar to User and check the App target when creating the file.
2. Erase the sample code in this new file and import the following dependencies first. `Crypto` is a new dependency, which is needed to generate a random unique token that will be saved to the database along with the `user ID`:

    ```
    import Vapor
    import FluentProvider
    import Crypto
    ```

3. Next, we will define our `Token` class and add a static `generate` method, which will generate a random token to be used for authentication for a specific user:

    ```
    final class Token: Model {
      let storage = Storage()
      var token: String
      var userId: Identifier
      var user: Parent<Token, User> {
        return parent(id: userId)
      }
      struct Keys {
        static let id = "id"
        static let token = "token"
        static let userId = "user_id"
      }
      init(string: String, user: User) throws {
        token = string
        userId = try user.assertExists()
      }
      init(row: Row) throws {
        token = try row.get(Keys.token)
    ```

## Adding Authentication

```
      userId = try row.get(Keys.userId)
    }
    func makeRow() throws -> Row {
      var row = Row()
      try row.set(Keys.token, token)
      try row.set(Keys.userId, userId)
      return row
    }
    static func generate(for user: User) throws -> Token {
      let random = try Crypto.Random.bytes(count: 16)
      return try Token(string: random.base64Encoded.makeString(),
      user: user)
    }
  }
```

4. Next, we will define the database preparation methods on our `Token` class:

```
  extension Token: Preparation {
    static func prepare(_ database: Database) throws {
      try database.create(self) { builder in
        builder.id()
        builder.string(Keys.token)
        builder.parent(User.self)
      }
    }
    static func revert(_ database: Database) throws {
      try database.delete(self)
    }
  }
```

5. Finally, we will implement the `JSONConvertible` protocol and make our Token `ResponseRepresentable` so that it can be returned directly from the controller instead of having to wrap it with a `Response` object:

```
  extension Token: JSONRepresentable {
    func makeJSON() throws -> JSON {
      var json = JSON()
      try json.set("token", token)
      return json
    }
  }
  extension Token: ResponseRepresentable { }
```

6. Now, go to the `Config+Setup.swift` file and add Token to the list of preparations inside the `setupPreparations` method as such:

   ```
   private func setupPreparations() throws {
     preparations.append(ShoppingList.self)
     preparations.append(Item.self)
     preparations.append(User.self)
     preparations.append(Token.self)
   }
   ```

7. Now, we need to switch to the `User.swift` file and make the User class implement the `TokenAuthenticatable` protocol extension so that it can authenticate using the Token:

   ```
   final class User: Model, SessionPersistable, TokenAuthenticatable {
   ```

8. As part of the `TokenAuthenticatable` protocol, we need to specify the type of our Token model, which we need to do by adding the following line inside our User class again:

   ```
   public typealias TokenType = Token
   ```

9. Now, the last thing we need to do is initialize the `TokenAuthenticationMiddleware` and specify the routes under which the token should be used to authenticate. For this, we need to switch to the `Routes.swift` file and add the following lines of code toward the end of the `setupAuthenticatedRoutes` method:

   ```
   let tokenMiddleware = TokenAuthenticationMiddleware(User.self)
   let tokenAuthRoutes = grouped(tokenMiddleware)
   tokenAuthRoutes.resource("api/shopping_lists",
   shoppingListController)
   tokenAuthRoutes.resource("api/items", itemController)
   grouped(passwordMiddleware)
     .post("api/tokens") { req in
       let user = try req.user()
       let existingToken = try
   Token.makeQuery().filter(Token.Keys.userId, user.id).first()
       let token = try Token.generate(for: user)
       try token.save()
       try existingToken?.delete()
       return token
   }
   ```

[ 279 ]

Adding Authentication

Great! Now we can build and run the server without any issues. In the preceding code, we informed the router to run the token authentication middleware only when requests are for /api/shopping_lists or /api/items endpoints, both of which forward requests to the same Shopping List and item controller. The reason for having a different route is because the existing /shopping_lists and /items routes are being authenticated using PasswordAuthenticationMiddleware and SessionsMiddleware, which require either email/password to be passed or the session token to be passed in the cookie to consider the user as authenticated.

We also defined a new /tokens route, which requires password-based authentication, and once the user has passed the email and password in the POST request to /tokens, it will generate a new token, associate it with the user, save it in the database, and reply with that token. Now, any future request to /api/shopping_lists or /api/items will not require email and password to be passed in order to authenticate the user. Only passing the token in the header is sufficient, and the request will go through to our controllers and reply with the resources we requested:

```
Last login: Wed Jan 31 12:32:24 on ttys016
Welcome to fish, the friendly interactive shell
~ $ echo -n 'ankur@email.com:password' | openssl base64
YW5rdXJAZW1haWwuY29tOnBhc3N3b3Jk
~ $ curl -XPOST 'http://localhost:8080/api/tokens' -H 'Authorization: Basic YW5r
dXJAZW1haWwuY29tOnBhc3N3b3Jk'
{"token":"qPfKDnD7nYvz7nvw7srPoA=="}
~ $ curl 'http://localhost:8080/api/shopping_lists' -H 'Authorization: Bearer qP
fKDnD7nYvz7nvw7srPoA=='
[{"items":[{"is_checked":false,"name":"Apple","id":"oid:5a71f8936f58a73ba24fc83b
","shopping_list__id":"oid:5a71f8916f58a73ba14fc83b"},{"is_checked":true,"name":
"Tomatoes","id":"oid:5a71f8a26f58a73ba34fc83b","shopping_list__id":"oid:5a71f891
6f58a73ba14fc83b"}],"name":"Groceries","user__id":"oid:5a71f8836f58a73ba04fc83b"
,"id":"oid:5a71f8916f58a73ba14fc83b"}]
~ $
```

## Testing the token-based authentication

We can test this out using curl commands in the Terminal. To test the token-based authentication flow, follow these steps:

1. Open the Terminal and generate first a base64-encoded string of email and password of the user we will need to authenticate as. You can do so using the following command in the Terminal. Replace the email with the email of the user you created previously from the browser and password with the user's password:

   ```
   $ echo -n 'ankur@email.com:password' | openssl base64
   ```

2. Running the preceding command will generate a base64-encoded version of the username and password, and now we will use this to get the token from our Vapor server by making a POST request to /tokens and pass the username and email in the header using the following command:

   ```
   $ curl -XPOST 'http://localhost:8080/api/tokens' -H 'Authorization: Basic YW5rdXJAZW1haWwuY29tOnBhc3N3b3Jk'
   ```

3. Our server will respond back with the token, which we can be now used to make request to our /api/ endpoints. We can store this token in a secure manner and can make request using this token without having to specify user email and password:

   ```
   $ curl "http://localhost:8080/api/shopping_lists" -H 'Authorization: Bearer 8vNF7BVjIJ6fLeX3fSbUVw=='
   ```

## Adding authentication flow to iOS app

Currently, our iOS will be broken as we have added password and token-based authentication to our Vapor server. We will need to update the iOS such that we ask the user for their email and password on launching of the app and use that to generate a token. Then, we save the token in the `UserDefaults` of the app and send this token to any request our API make from our app.

*Adding Authentication*

Since `UserDefaults` can only be accessed by the app itself, it is safe enough for our Shopping List app, but for a production-ready app, you might want to consider Keychain API to securely store the token. So let's dive into the app and see how we can update it to support token-based authentication and get it working again:

1. First, open the iOS ShoppingList project in Xcode and open the `Request.swift` file. We will be updating the request method so that we can pass headers in the HTTP request as well. We will do this by updating the function signature to the following:

    ```swift
    func request(url: String, httpMethod: String = "GET", httpBody:
    Data? = .none, httpHeaders: [String: String] = [String: String](),
    completionHandler: @escaping (Data?, URLResponse?, Error?) throws
    -> Void) {
    ```

2. Then, inside of the `request` function, we update the function body so that we can set the Authorization header to be set to the token if the token is available inside of UserDefault. The entire `request` function would look like this:

    ```swift
    var request = URLRequest(url: URL(string: "\(baseUrl)\(url)")!)
    var headers = httpHeaders
    if let data = UserDefaults.standard.value(forKey:
    String(describing: Token.self)) as? Data,
      let token = try? PropertyListDecoder().decode(Token.self, from:
    data) {
       headers["Authorization"] = "Bearer \(token.token)"
    }
    request.httpMethod = httpMethod
    if let data = httpBody {
      request.httpBody = data
      headers["content-type"] = "application/json"
    }
    request.allHTTPHeaderFields = headers
    URLSession.shared.dataTask(with: request, completionHandler: {
    data, response, error in
      DispatchQueue.main.async {
        do {
          try completionHandler(data, response, error)
        } catch {}
      }
    }).resume()
    ```

[ 282 ]

3. This will cause the build to break since we have not defined the `Token` class yet. Let's do that by creating a new empty Swift file inside of the `Models` folder in our iOS project. Copy the following code to define our `Token` class and make it inherit from the `Codable` protocol so that it is able to convert the JSON response from the server to a `token` object that we can use in our code:

```
class Token: Codable {
  var token: String
  init(_ token: String) {
    self.token = token
  }
}
```

4. Now, we should be able to build our project successfully without any errors. Next, we will add a new view controller where the users will enter their credentials and the view controller will make a request to our **/tokens** endpoint to generate a token, and if it is successful, then it will take the user to the `ShoppingListTableViewController`, where it will make the network request with the token. To add this new view controller, add a new `Cocoa` class to the `Controllers` directory and call it `LoginViewController` and inherit from `UIViewController` as such:

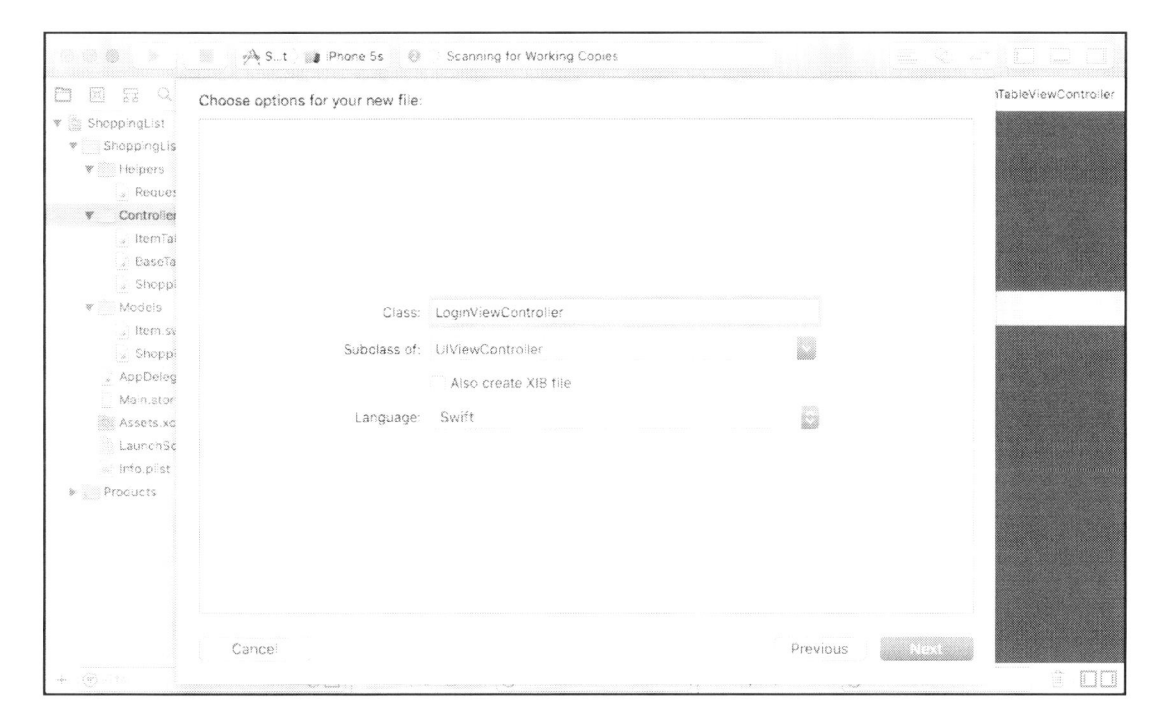

[ 283 ]

## Adding Authentication

5. Then, copy the following code into the view controller:

```swift
import UIKit
class LoginViewController: UIViewController {
@IBOutlet weak var emailField: UITextField!
 @IBOutlet weak var passwordField: UITextField!

 override func viewDidLoad() {
 super.viewDidLoad()
 if let data = UserDefaults.standard.value(forKey:
 String(describing: Token.self)) as? Data,
 let _ = try? PropertyListDecoder().decode(Token.self,
 from: data) {
     self.performSegue(withIdentifier: "showShoppingList",
     sender: self)
     }
 }
@IBAction func didSelectLoginButton(_ sender: UIButton) {
 let emailPassword = "\(emailField.text!):\
 (passwordField.text!)"
 let base64EncodedEmailPassword =
 Data(emailPassword.utf8).base64EncodedString()
 request(url: "/tokens",
 httpMethod: "POST",
 httpHeaders: ["Authorization": "Basic \
 (base64EncodedEmailPassword)"]) {
 data, _, _ in
 do {
     let decoder = JSONDecoder()
     let token = try decoder.decode(Token.self, from: data!)
     let encoder = try? PropertyListEncoder().encode(token)
     UserDefaults.standard.set(encoder, forKey:
     String(describing: Token.self))
     UserDefaults.standard.synchronize()
     self.passwordField.text = ""
     self.performSegue(withIdentifier: "showShoppingList",
     sender: self)
     } catch {
         let alertController = UIAlertController(title: "Error
         Logging In", message:
         "Email or password is wrong. Please check your
         credentials and try again.", preferredStyle: .alert)
         alertController.addAction(UIAlertAction(title:
         "Dismiss", style: .default))
         self.present(alertController, animated: true)
         }
     }
 }
```

}
       }

6. Next, we need to update our BaseURL and prefix it with /api since we updated the token-based routes to live under /api so that the token middleware can authenticate instead. To do so, open the Info.plist file and change the BaseURL to point to the following URL:

    http://localhost:8080/api

7. Lastly, we will add the following method to the ShoppingListTableViewController as we will add a Logout button on the top-left corner of the navigation bar so that the user can log out of their session. This is as simple as adding the following method to the ShoppingListTableViewController class; this method removes the token from UserDefaults and dismisses the Shopping List view and takes us back to the Login view:

```
@IBAction func didSelectLogoutButton(_ sender: UIBarButtonItem) {
    UserDefaults.standard.removeObject(forKey: String(describing: Token.self))
    UserDefaults.standard.synchronize()
    self.dismiss(animated: true)
}
```

That is it in terms of updating our code. The app should build successfully, but it will not work just yet. We still need to update our Main Storyboard so that we can show the LoginViewController as the initial view controller and have it transition to the ShoppingListViewController if the token is set in the UserDefaults. Let's take a look at how we can do that.

## Bringing it all together in the Storyboard

To get our app working again with our Vapor API using token-based authentication, we need to add a new View Controller to our storyboard, which is the entry point of our app. This view controller will be the LoginViewController, and it will show the ShoppingListView controller if there is a token in the UserDefaults already. This transition will take place using **segues**. If you are not familiar with segues, then they are a way in Xcode to create a transition between two view controllers, and you can specify the type of animation or transition you want between the two view controllers.

# Adding Authentication

Segues can be invoked programmatically like we will do in `LoginViewController` or can be invoked due to a touch event, such as a user selection of a Shopping List inside of the table view causing the `ShoppingListViewController` to transition to the `ItemTableViewController`. We will also configure the UI in the storyboard by adding two text fields, which will store the user's email and password, and add a button to submit the credentials to our API server to generate a token. So let's dive into the storyboard and make the following changes:

1. Open the `Main.storyboard` file and drag a new Navigation Controller into the Storyboard and delete the Table View Controller that the Navigation Controller came with by default:

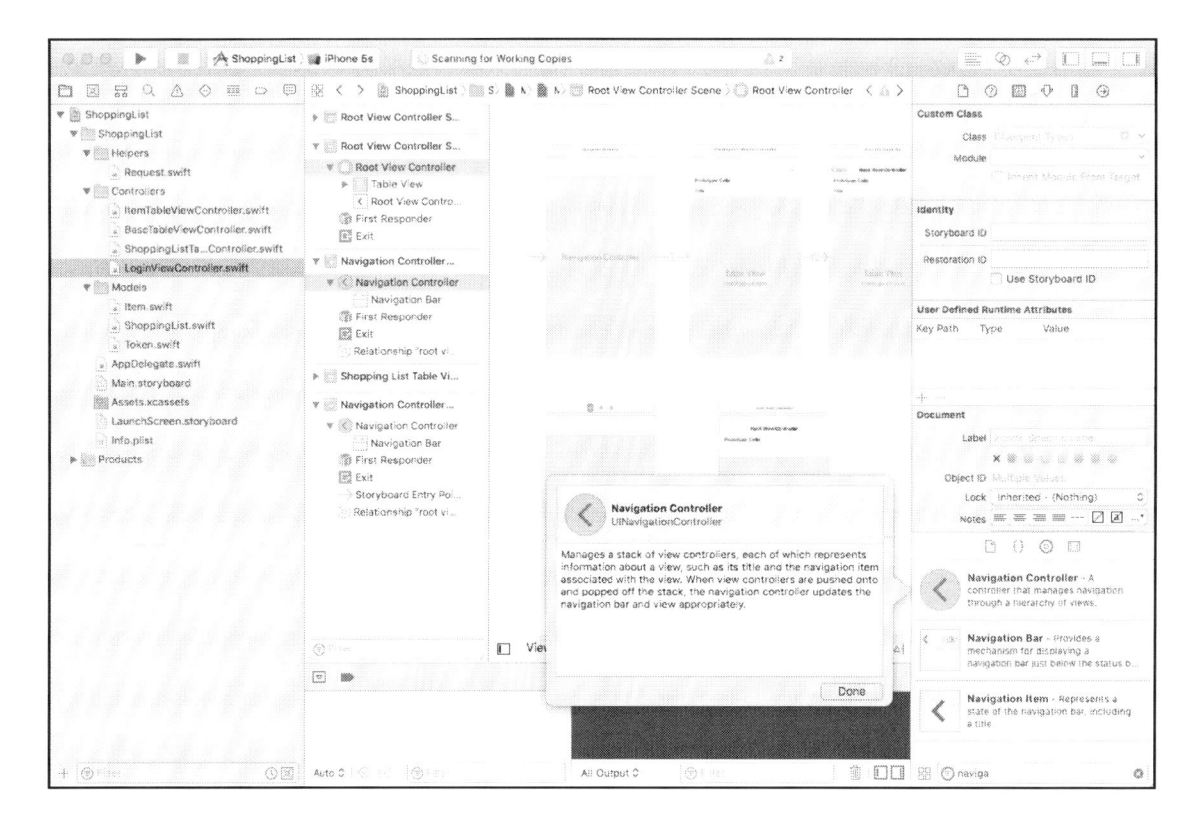

![Screenshot of Xcode storyboard with Navigation Controller]

*Chapter 10*

2. After deleting it, drag a simple View Controller into the Storyboard:

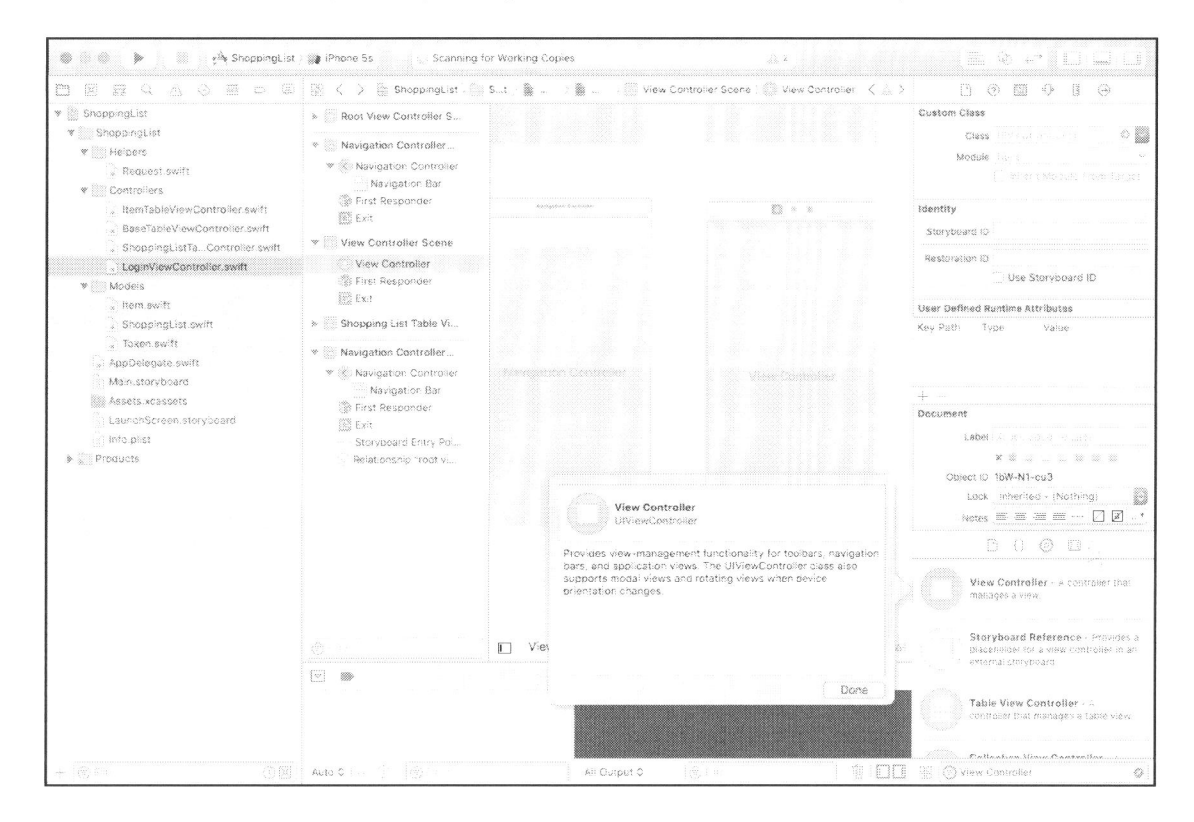

3. Make the new View Controller the root view controller of the Navigation Controller by pressing the *Control* key and dragging from the Navigation Controller to the View Controller and selecting the root view controller menu item:

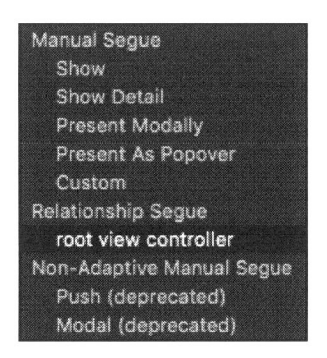

*Adding Authentication*

4. Now, set the Custom Class of the new View Controller to **LoginViewController**:

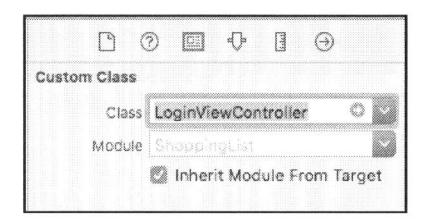

5. Now, drag a View into the **LoginViewController** object as we do not have a View inside of our LoginViewController in our Storyboard.
6. Then, drag two Text Fields into the **LoginViewController**. One will be for email and another for password. Add them, one below the other, toward the top of the view and align them to the center as such.

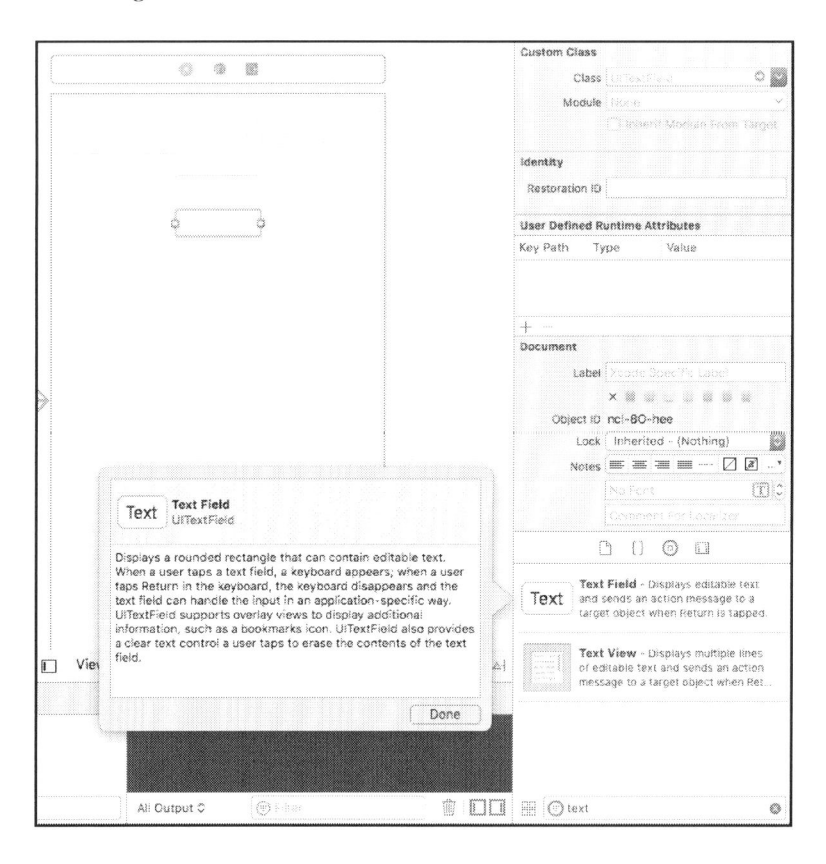

*Chapter 10*

7. Now, drag a button that will submit the login request when it is pressed:

[ 289 ]

*Adding Authentication*

8. Set the arrangement of the text fields and buttons using **AutoLayout.** If you are not familiar with AutoLayout, then think of it as a way to arrange UI components in the app such that they will adjust to different screen sizes of different iOS devices. Here, we set the top, left, and right margins to be 16 pixels for the email text field.

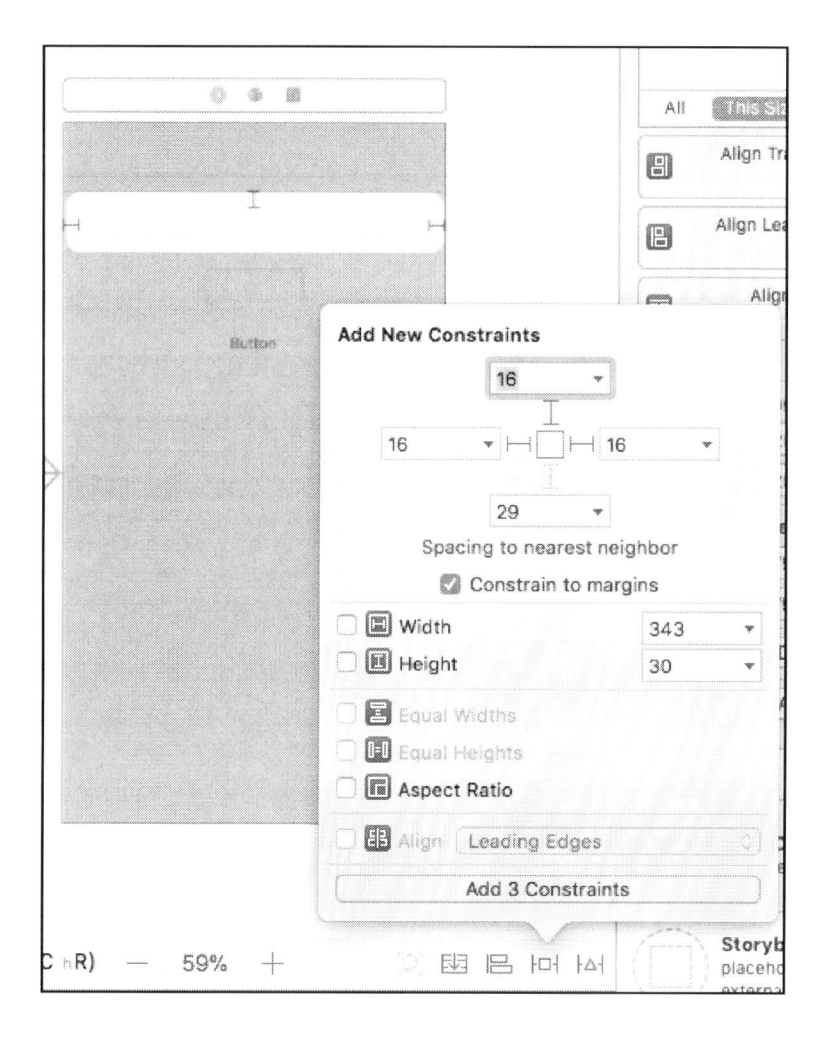

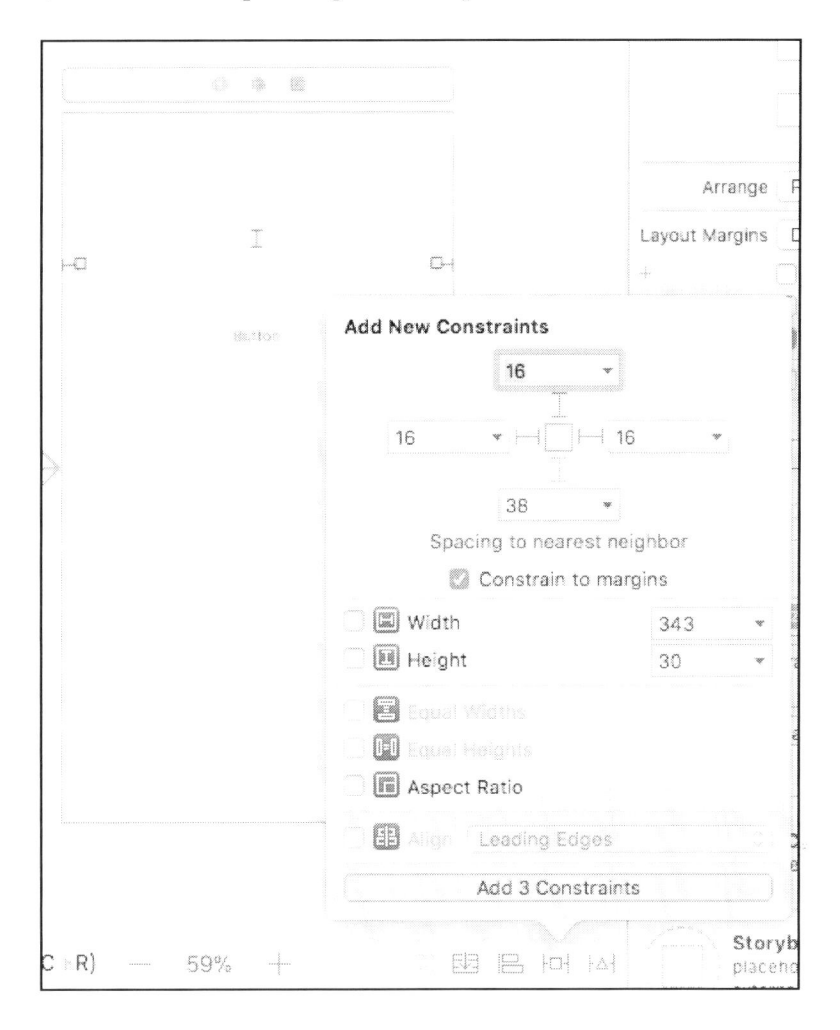

9. Next, set the same 16px margin for the password text field:

*Adding Authentication*

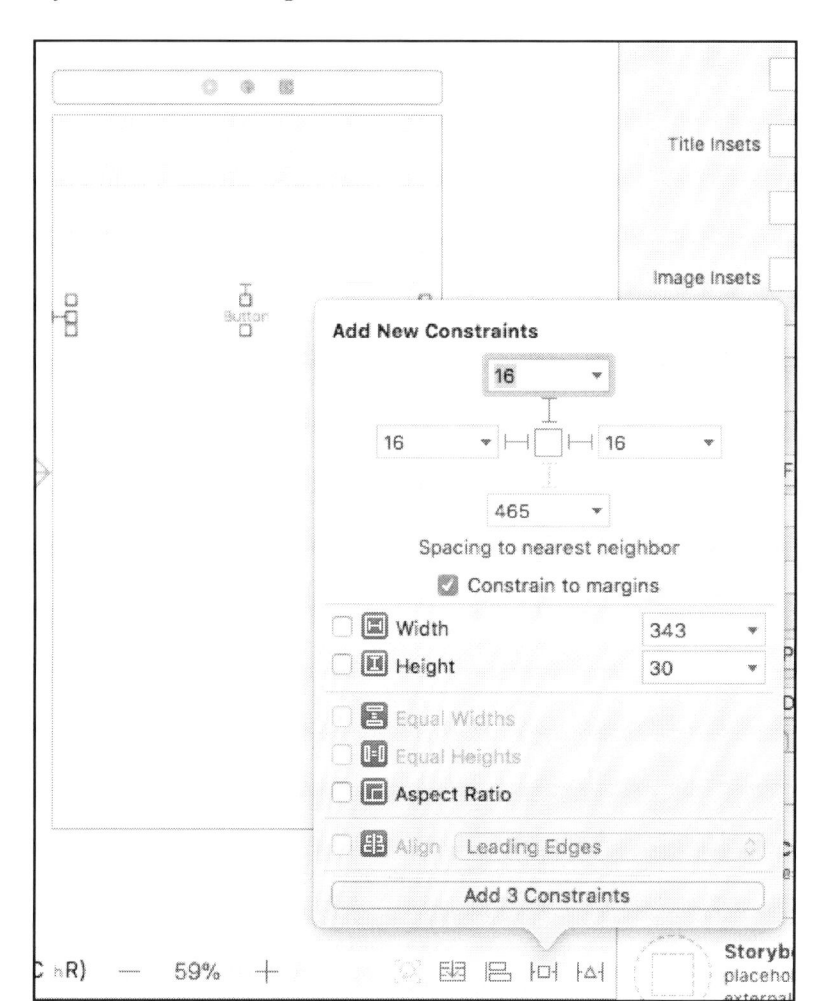

10. Finally, set the same margins for the button:

11. Select the first Text Field and set the Placeholder to be Email. Placeholder can be found inside the **Attributes Inspector** inside the right panel.
12. Select the second Text Field and set the Placeholder to be Password. Also, check the **Secure Text Entry** checkbox so that it does not reveal the password as a plain text.
13. Rename the Button to Login.

14. Now, press Control and drag from the **LoginViewController** to the Email Field and select **emailField**:

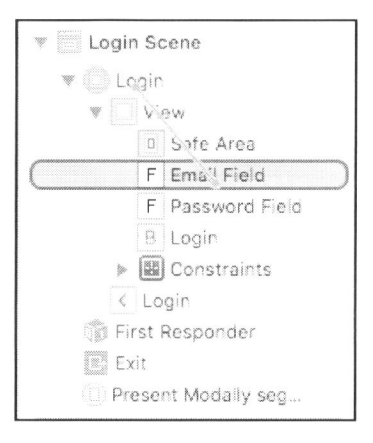

```
▼ Login Scene
    ▼ Login
        ▼ View
            Safe Area
            F  Email Field
            F  Password Field
            B  Login
          ▶ ▦ Constraints
            < Login
        First Responder
        Exit
        Present Modally seg...
```

15. Similarly, press Control and drag from the **LoginViewController** to the Password Field and select **passwordField**:

```
Outlets
  – emailField
    passwordField
    view
```

16. Now, drag from the Login button to the **LoginViewController** and select the **didSelectLoginButton:** method:

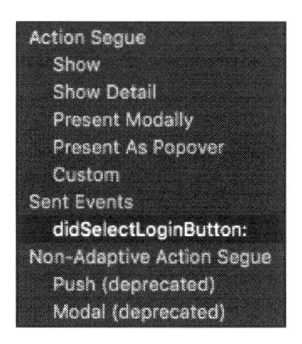

```
Action Segue
    Show
    Show Detail
    Present Modally
    Present As Popover
    Custom
Sent Events
    didSelectLoginButton:
Non-Adaptive Action Segue
    Push (deprecated)
    Modal (deprecated)
```

## Adding Authentication

17. Now that we have `LoginViewController` configured, we need to create a segue between our `LoginViewController` and the `Navigation Controller` of the Shopping List. This is easy to do by pressing Control and dragging from the `LoginViewController` to the Navigation Controller of the `Shopping List Table View Controller` as such. In the segue, select **Present Modally**:

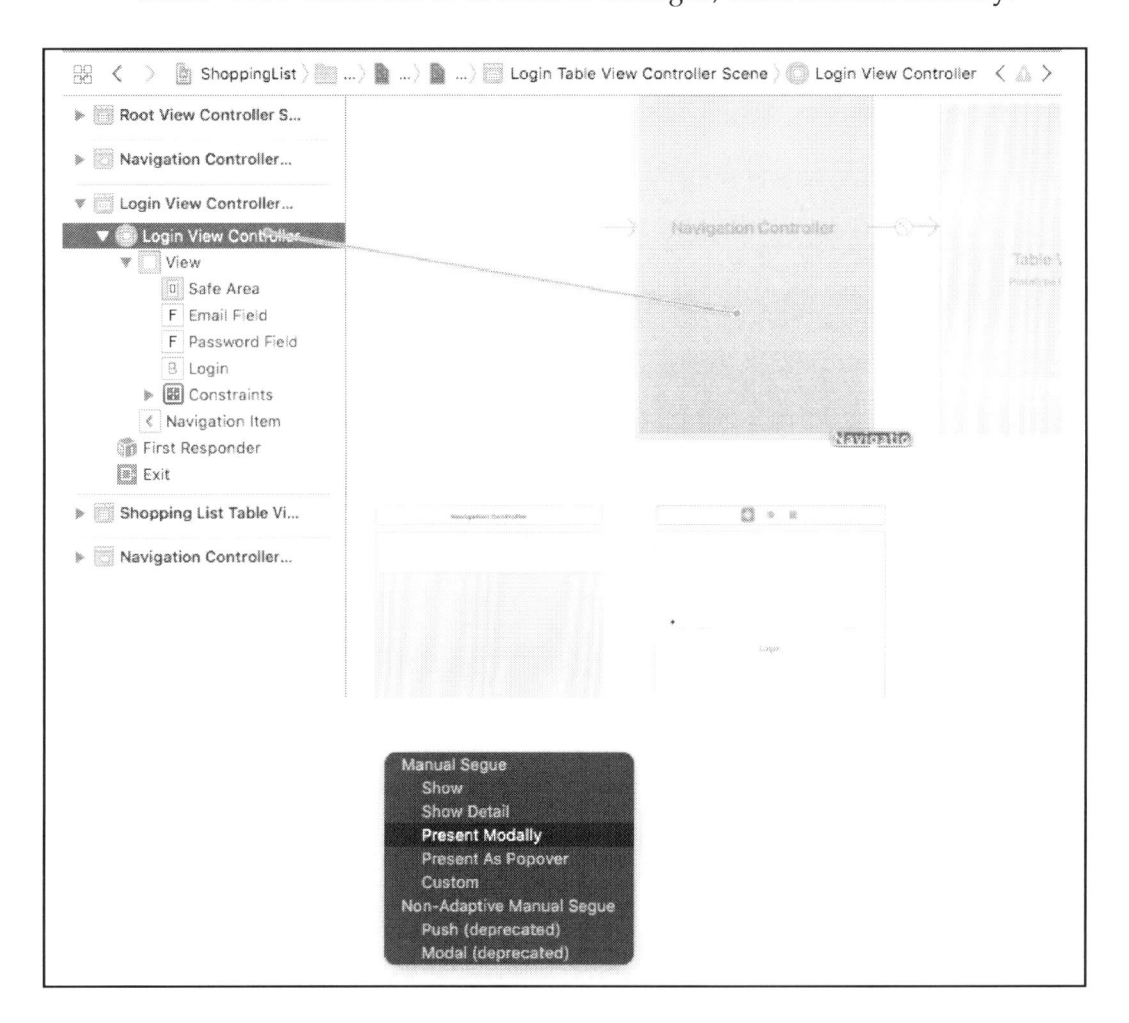

[ 294 ]

18. Now, click on the segue, and inside the Attributes Inspector, set the **Identifier** to `showShoppingList`:

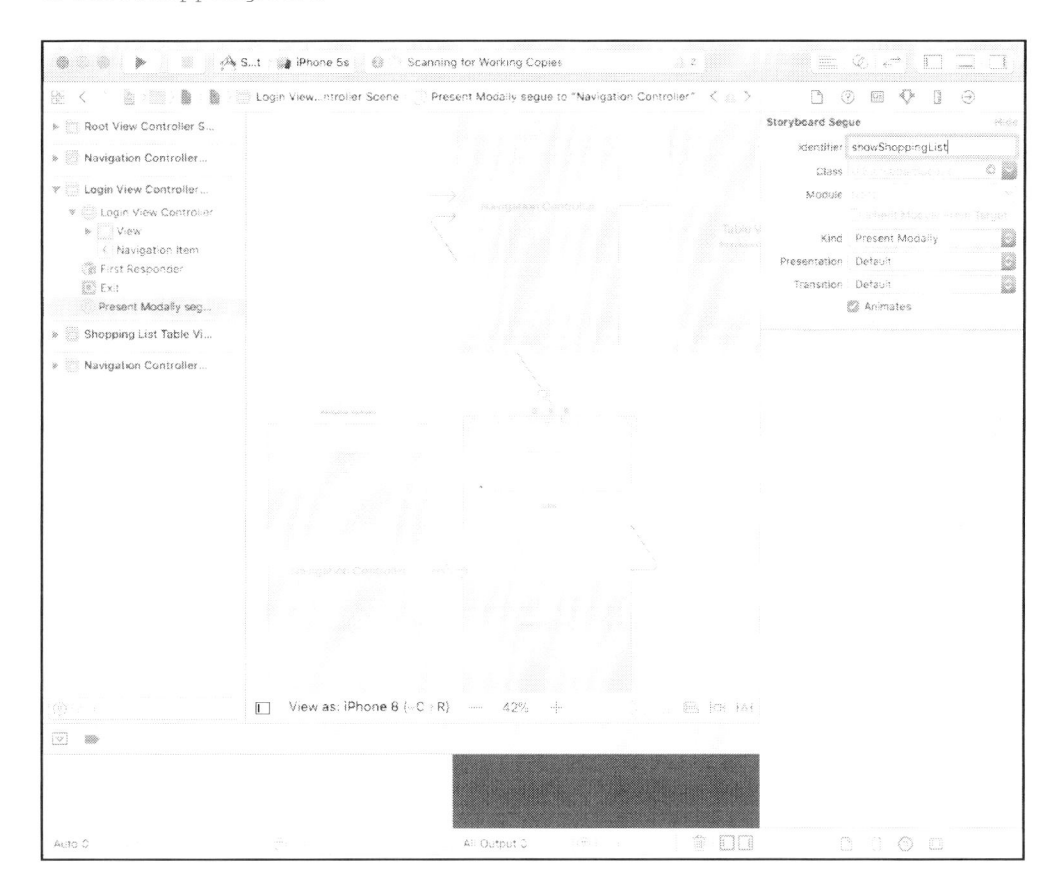

*Adding Authentication*

19. Drag a Bar Button Item and place it on the top-left corner of the Shopping List Table View Controller:

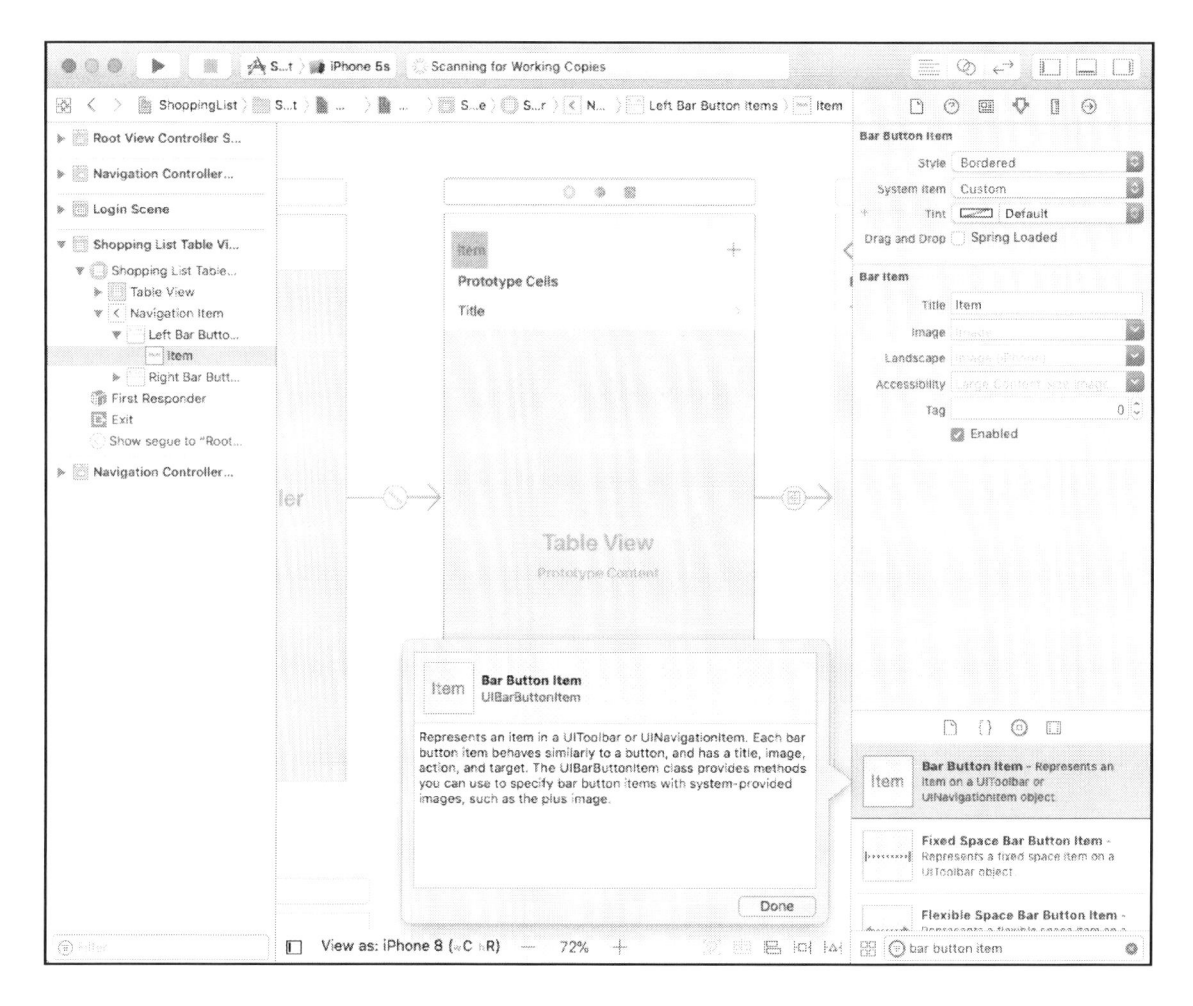

20. Rename the button to **Logout**, and press control and click and drag the button to the Shopping List Table View Controller and select the **didSelectLogoutButton:** method:

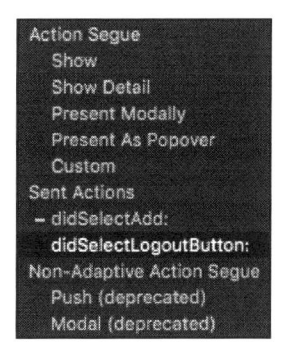

```
Action Segue
   Show
   Show Detail
   Present Modally
   Present As Popover
   Custom
Sent Actions
 — didSelectAdd:
   didSelectLogoutButton:
Non-Adaptive Action Segue
   Push (deprecated)
   Modal (deprecated)
```

21. Set the **Title** of the **Navigation Item** in the `LoginViewController` to **Login** and **Prompt** to `Shopping List App`:

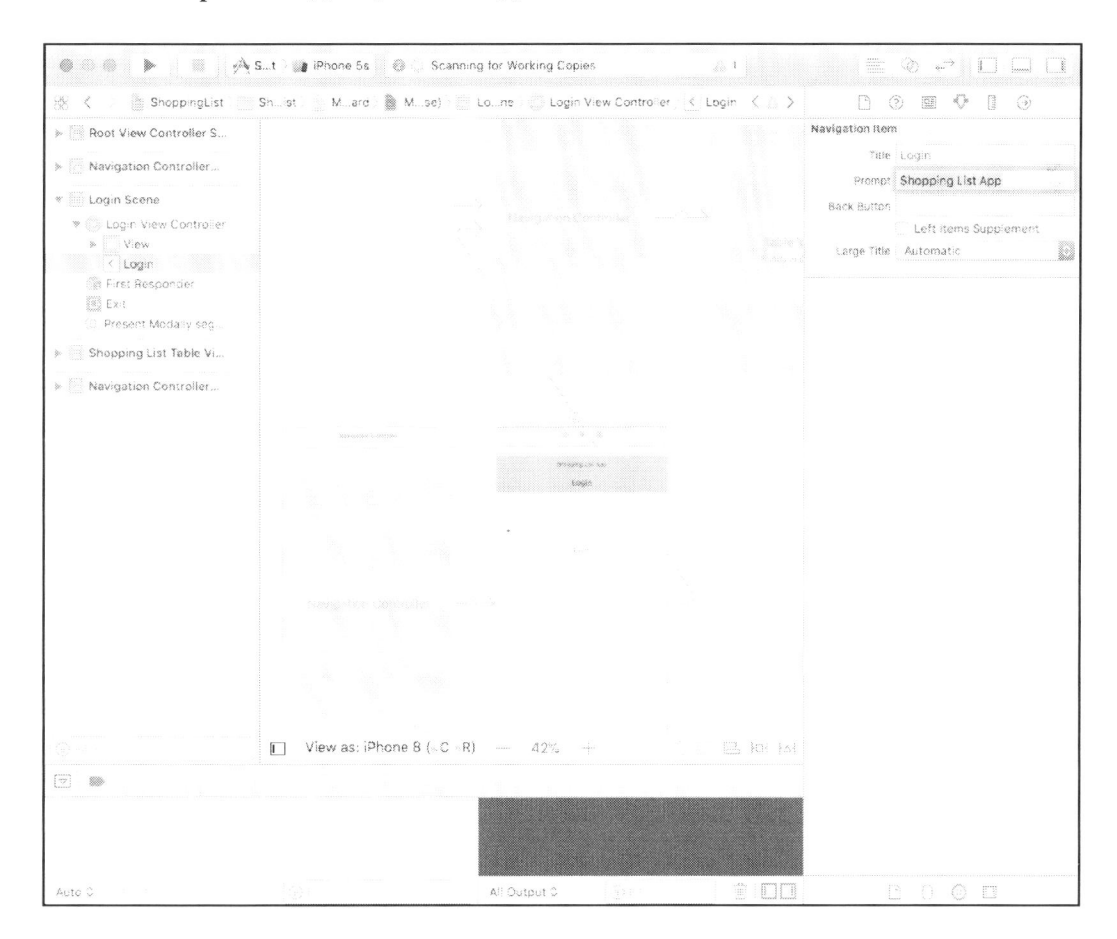

## Adding Authentication

22. Finally, drag the Storyboard Entry point to point to the **Navigation Controller** for the **LoginViewController**, and build and run the app:

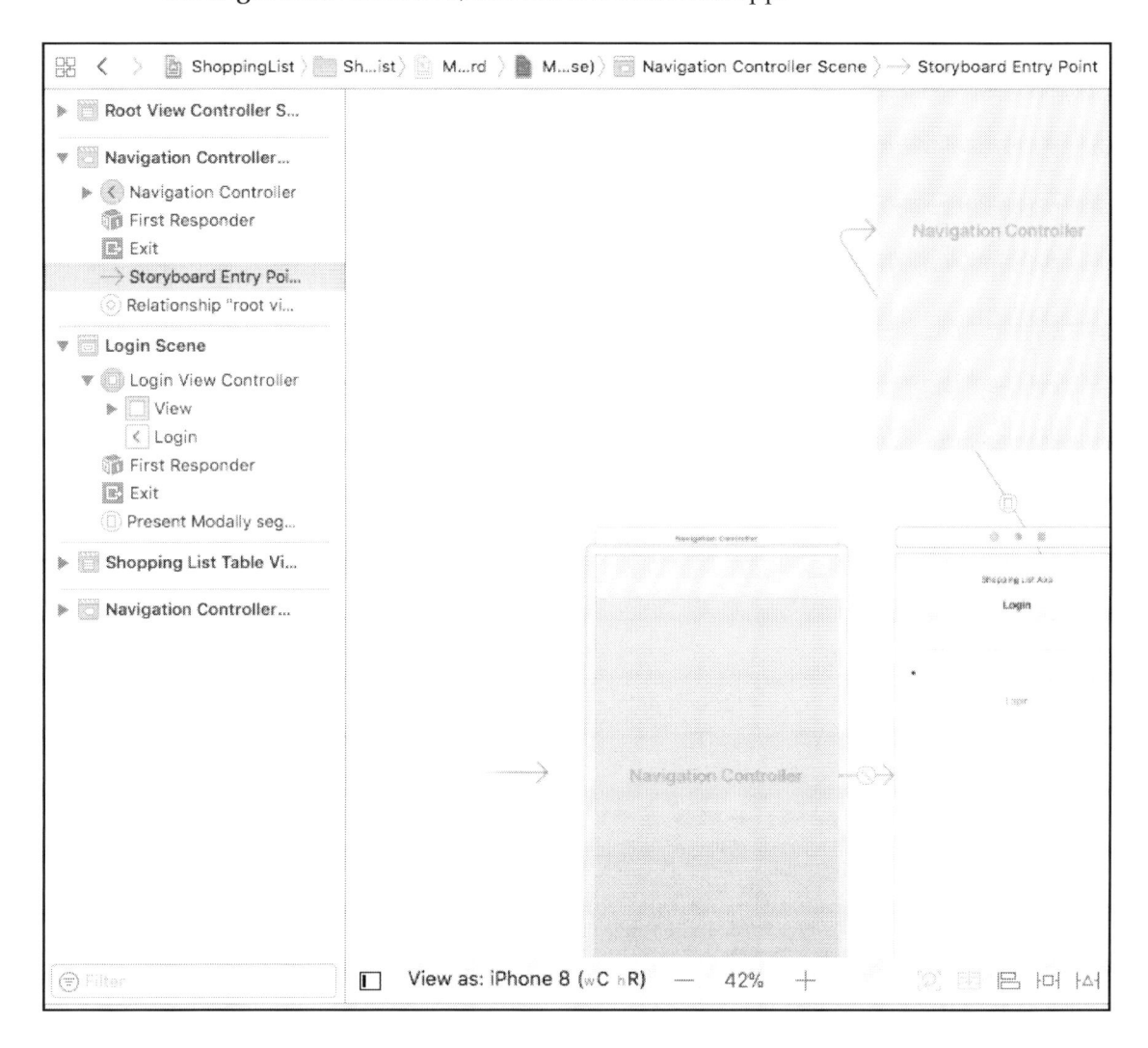

Great job! You can now build and run the app, and everything should work. Awesome! We can now log in using our user account and only see Shopping Lists belonging to that user. We can also edit, delete, and create new Shopping Lists and items that the user owns. We just converted our single user app into multiuser simply by adding a user model in the backend. Thanks to Vapor's `AuthProvider`, all we have to do was set up some routes to handle the authentication for us:

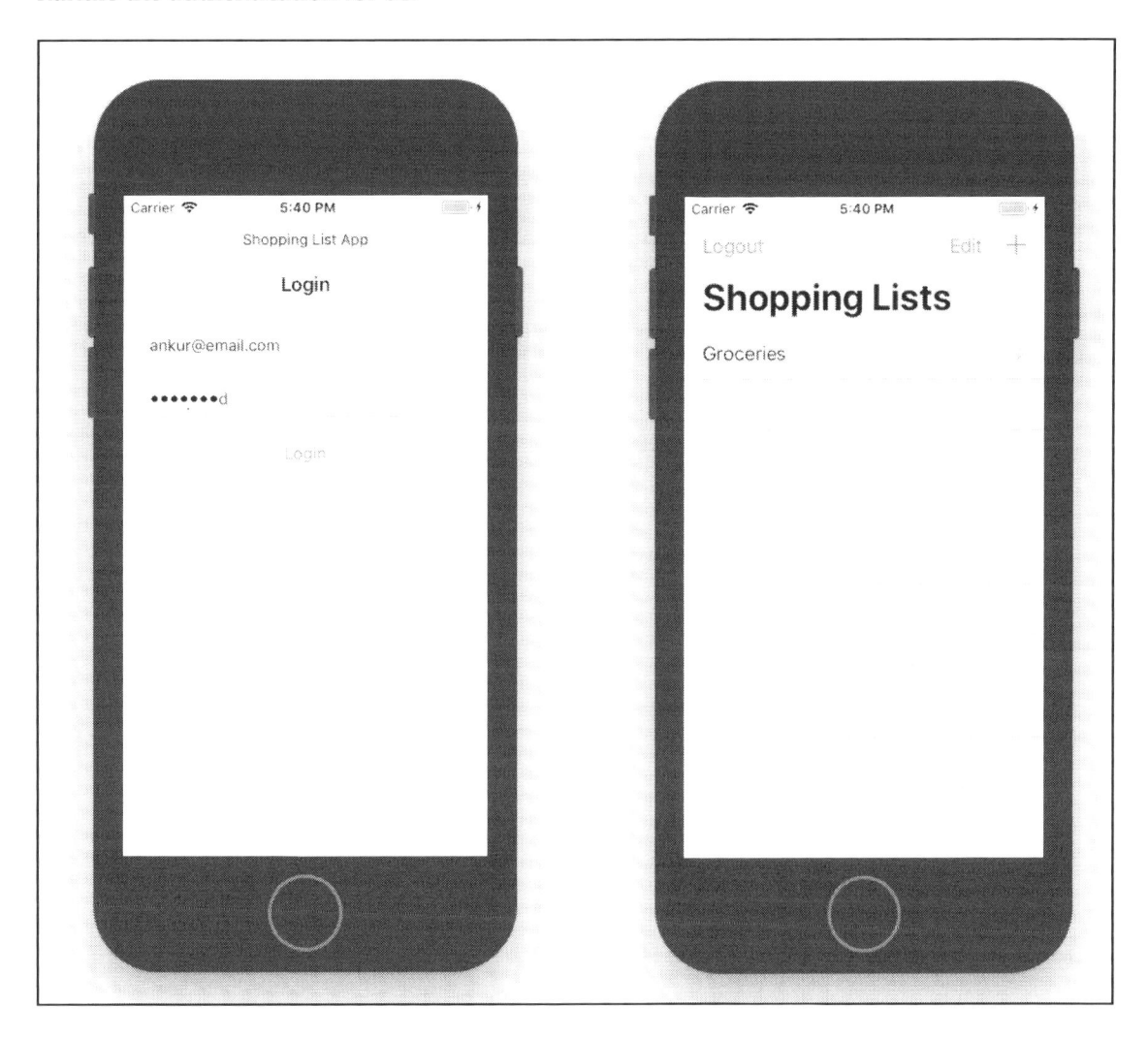

## Summary

In this chapter, we covered a lot of topics. We not only transformed our backend, but also both our web and native iOS frontend views that communicate with the backend. By now, you should have a good understanding of how to add User model to a Vapor application to make the app multiuser. You should also have a good background on how to store user information, including passwords, and how the authentication and persistence of session works in the browser after authentication. Lastly, you should know how to add token-based authentication to a Vapor app and how the token-based authentication works and the steps involved in it. In iOS land, we also covered how to conditionally load a Login View and store and make requests to the server using the token. There are still few things we did not cover, which include adding a registration view in the iOS app to register if a user does not have an account already, but you can implement it as an extra credit exercise.

In the next chapter, we will end the book by building on top of the same app but by making a tvOS version of the app. We will see how easy it is to build a tvOS version of this app with maximum code shareability. Developing an app nowadays is not just about building an app for iOS or Android. It is about building an ecosystem of apps across different platforms, and here we have an app that runs on iOS, on the browser, and, in the next chapter, we will have it build on tvOS, all using Swift.

# 11
# Building a tvOS App

You made it to the final chapter! By now, you should have a good understanding of both native iOS development and full stack web development using Vapor. We have covered several topics in the previous chapters regarding adding authentication and authorization to both our backend and to our iOS app. In this chapter, we will end the book by extending our app to work on the tvOS platform. As we learned before, building a product is more than just building an app. It involves building several apps across different platforms. Using Swift, now, we are able to build for different platforms, improving productivity and code shareability. This productivity gain helps a small team of iOS developers build an entire ecosystem of the application by themselves and compete with large companies.

In this chapter, we will finish off our app by building a tvOS version of it. Doing so, you will learn how easy it is to build a tvOS app from an existing iOS app and how we can share code across both of the apps, helping us build an app for another platform without much effort. In this final chapter, we will cover the following topics:

- How to create a tvOS target for our app
- How to make the code base work with both the tvOS and iOS platforms
- How to configure a tvOS storyboard such that it works with both the iOS and tvOS platforms

So let's get started and take a look at how to build a tvOS version of our Shopping List app.

## Shopping List app on tvOS

After the announcement of tvOS, Apple TV became another platform that Swift developers could build apps for, just like iPhone or Mac. tvOS is the operating system that runs on Apple TV, and it has a lot more similarities to iOS than macOS. tvOS uses the same frameworks used in iOS, making it more of an extension of an app on the TV platform.

# Building a tvOS App

For our Shopping List app, we will build a tvOS target, which will run on Apple TV. This app, just like the iOS version, will prompt the user to log in if they are not already logged in, and if they are, then it will take them to their shopping lists. The best part of making this tvOS app is that we will be able to use almost all from the code of our iOS app. All we need to do is configure the UI for the tvOS app in the tvOS storyboard. To see this in action, let's start building the tvOS app using the following steps:

1. Open the `ShoppingList` workspace in Xcode, and select the `ShoppingList` iOS Project. Inside the **TARGETS** section, click on the **+** icon to add a new target:

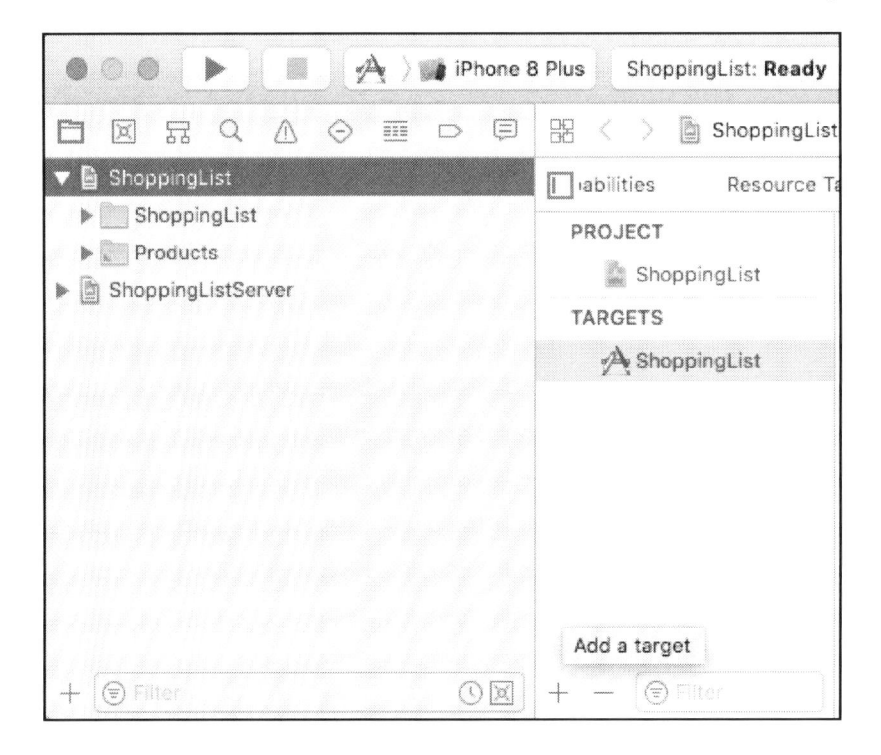

2. In the new target modal, select **tvOS** as the platform and then select **Single View App** and click on **Next**:

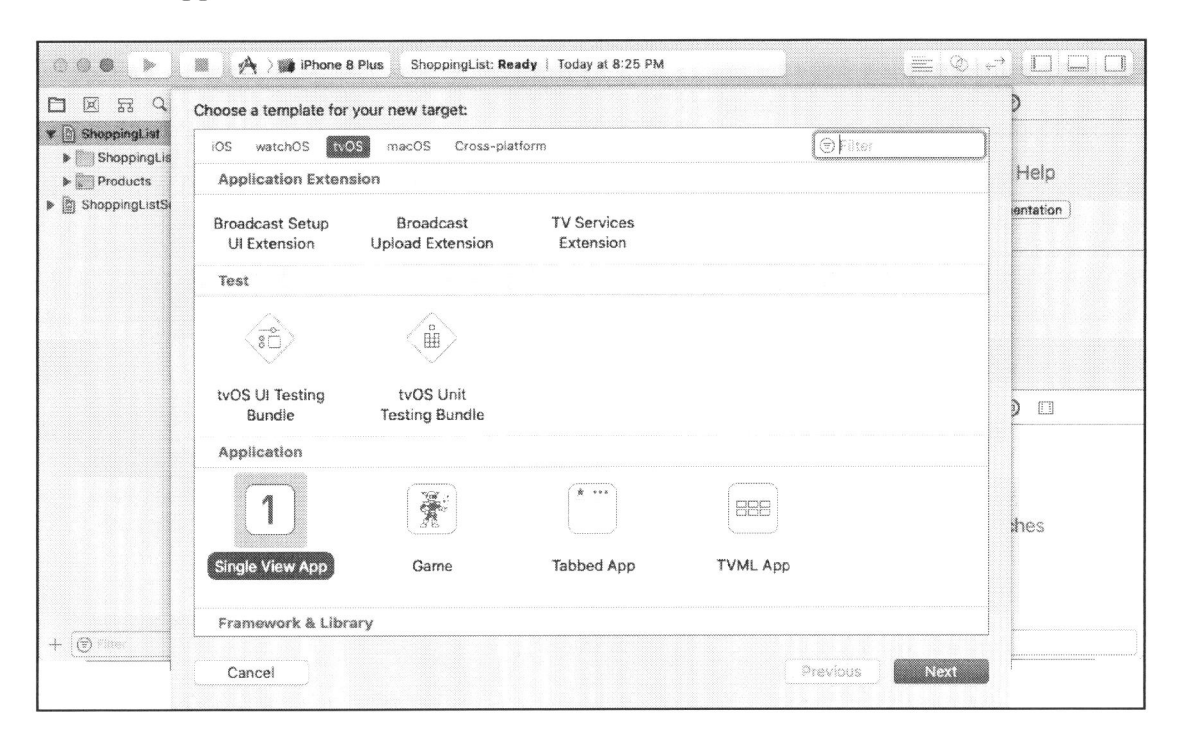

*Building a tvOS App*

3. Set **Product Name** to `ShoppingListTV` and click on **Finish**:

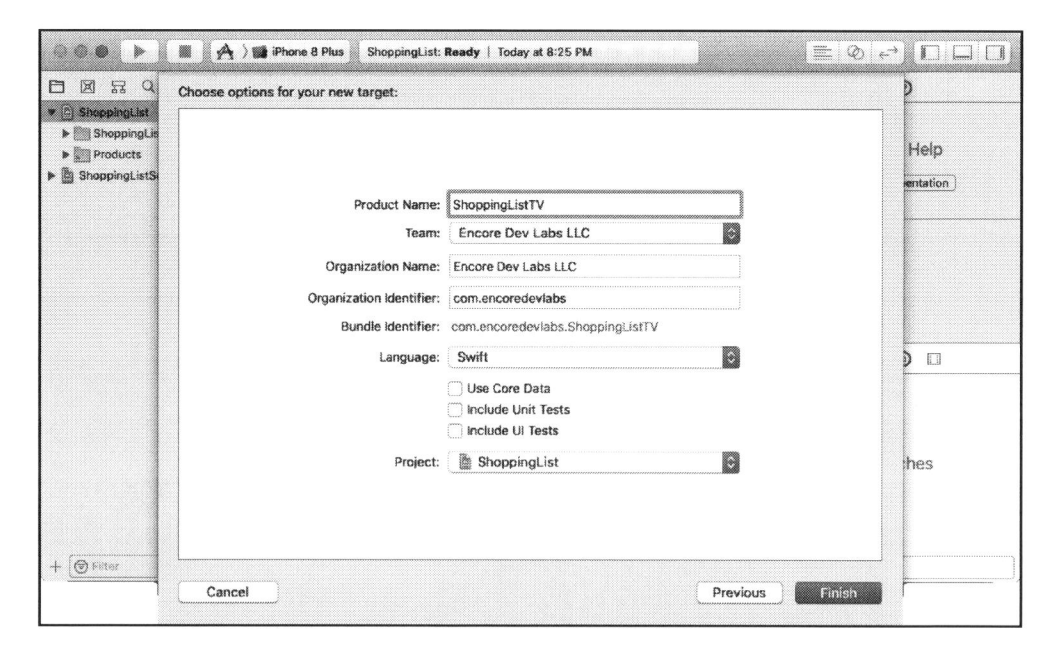

4. This will create a new ShoppingListTV target and also add a new `ShoppingListTV` folder, which will contain boilerplate code for our tvOS app:

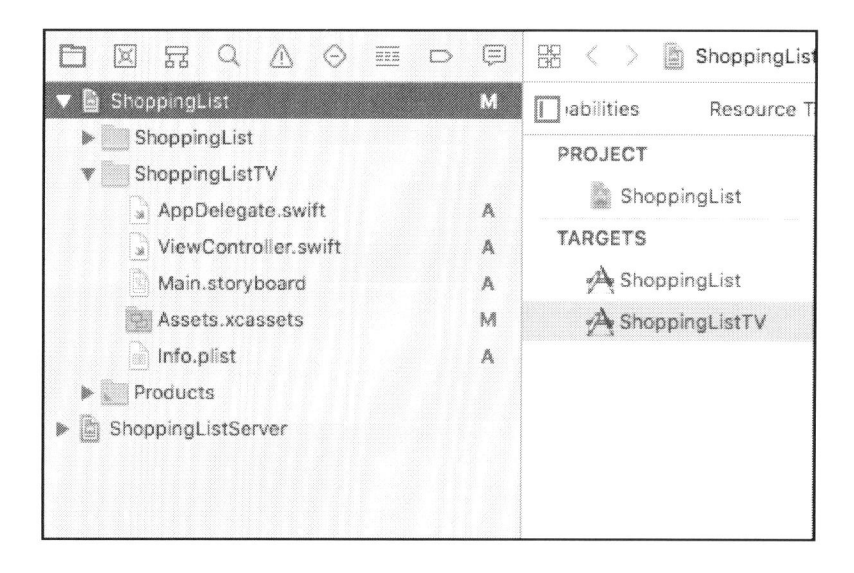

*Chapter 11*

5. You should now see a new scheme to run the **ShoppingListTV** app. Select the **Apple TV 4K (at 1080p)** simulator and run the app:

6. The app should start running on the Apple TV Simulator, and you should see an empty screen similar to the following:

[ 305 ]

# Building a tvOS App

Awesome! We have just created a basic Hello World version of a tvOS app. To understand why we see this screen, we will need to open up `Main.storyboard` inside the `ShoppingListTV` folder. You will see an empty **View Controller**, which is set as the entry point of our app:

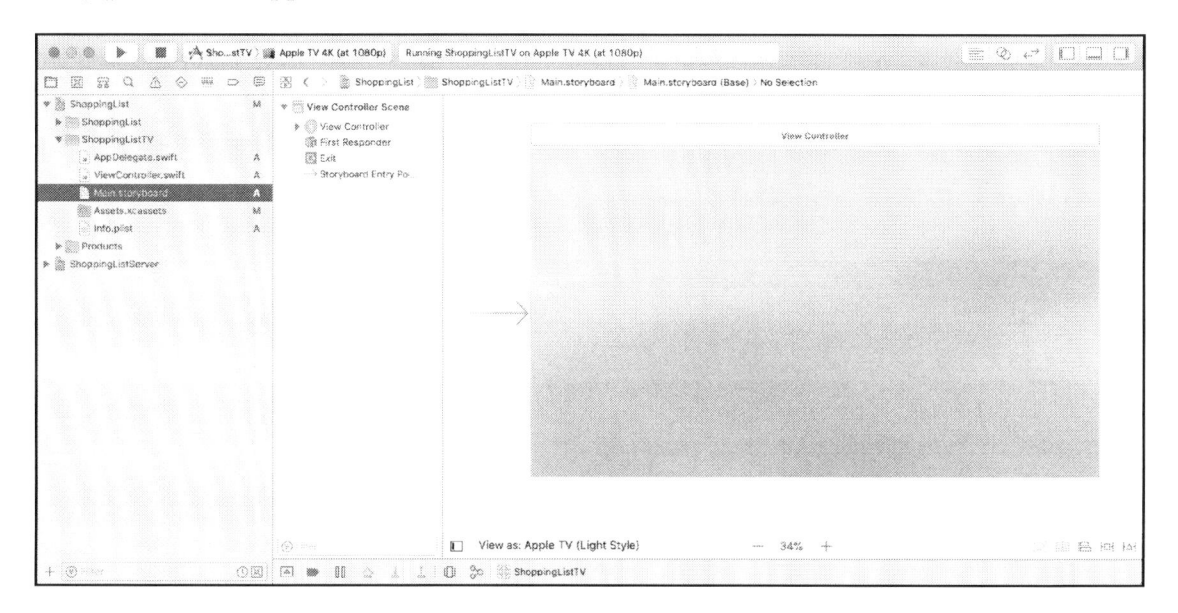

# Sharing code between iOS and tvOS

To share code between our iOS and tvOS app, we will need to let Xcode know the Swift files that need to be shared across different targets. This is easy to do by simply checking the targets a Swift file should be part of when compiling and building the product:

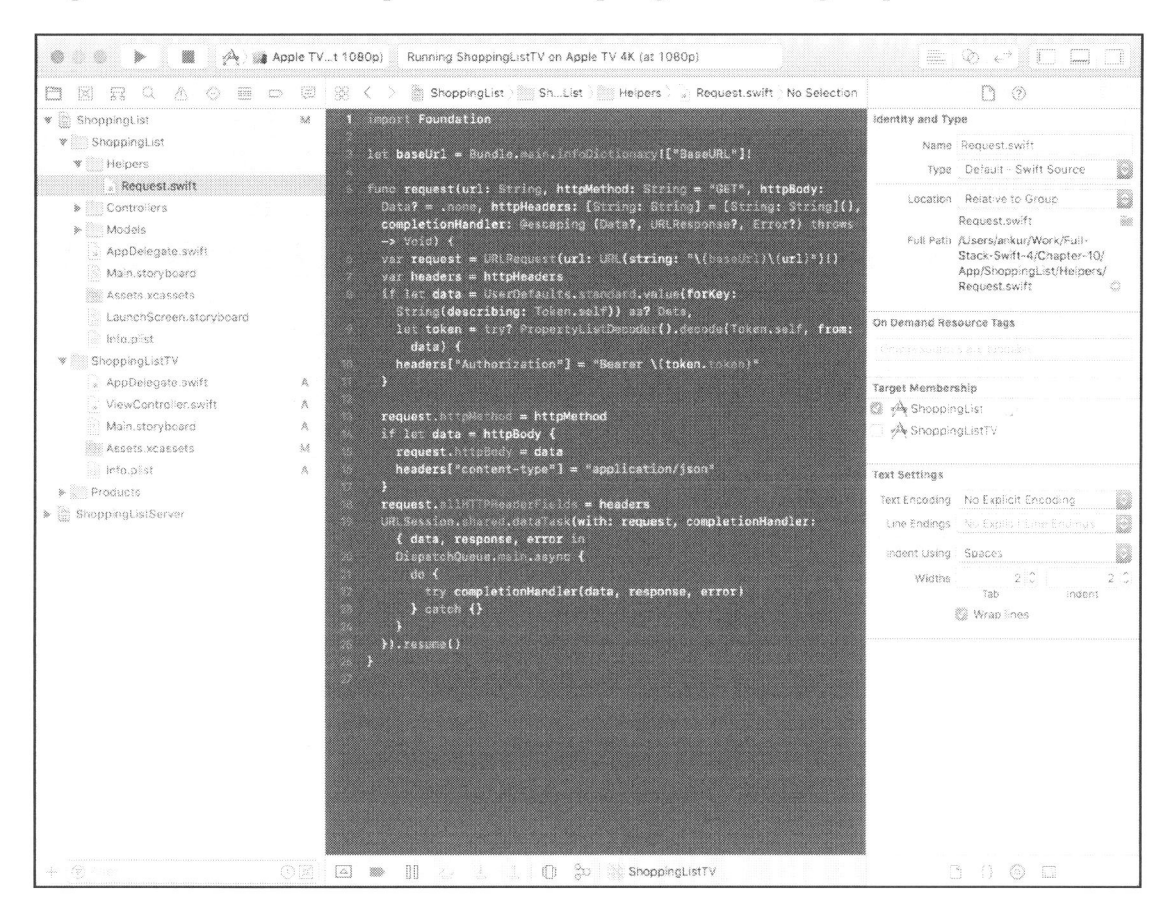

# Building a tvOS App

Select one of the Swift files inside the `ShoppingList` app folder, and you should see `ShoppingList` and `ShoppingListTV` under **Target Membership** inside **File Inspector** on the right side of the screen. Check the `ShoppingListTV` target. Now, go through the remaining Swift files inside the ShoppingList iOS app, except for `AppDelegate.swift`, and check the `ShoppingListTV` target, as we will share all of this code with the tvOS app. Once you are done, try building the app. You should encounter a bunch of errors, as our code will not work with tvOS just out-of-the-box. We will need to tweak some lines of code, as some APIs available in iOS are not available in tvOS. One such example is the usage of `prefersLargeTitles`, which is a new property added to the navigation bar only available in iOS 11:

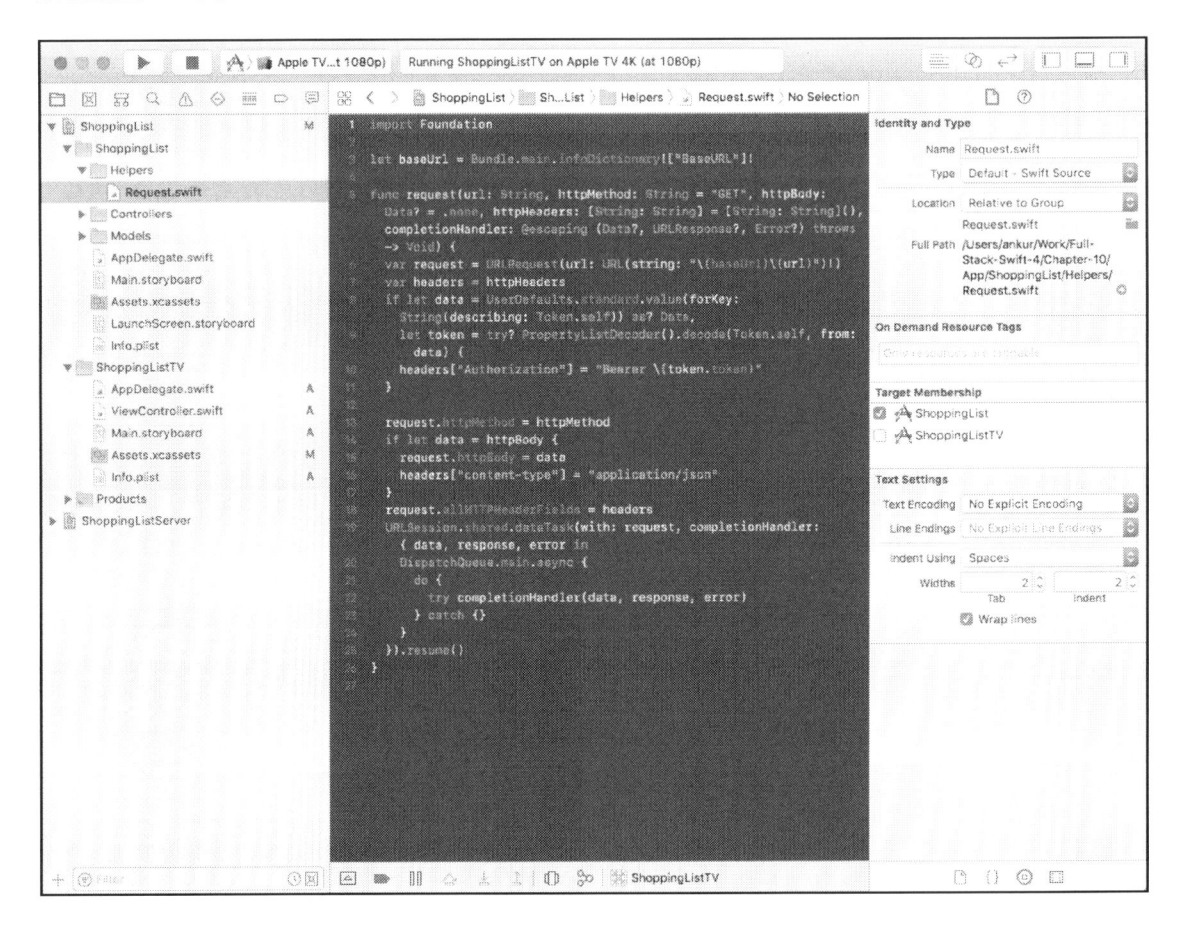

# Making code work with both iOS and tvOS apps

To make this work in tvOS, we will need to use the same strategy we used for server-side Swift to support macOS and Linux platforms. Using directives, we can specify the compiler to omit some lines of code on the tvOS platform or include some code only for the tvOS platform. Let's take a look at how we can fix our code by following the steps:

1. Open the `ItemTableViewController.swift` file, and go to the line causing the error inside the `viewDidLoad` method. The error is thrown because `prefersLargeTitle` is not available as a property on `navigationBar`. To omit this line of code on the tvOS platform, we can wrap the code with the `#if TARGET_OS_IOS` directive, as follows:

    ```
    #if TARGET_OS_IOS
    navigationController?.navigationBar.prefersLargeTitles = true
    #endif
    ```

2. Next, open the `ShoppingListTableViewController.swift` file and wrap the `prefersLargeTitles` and the `UIRefreshControl` inside this directive as it is not available in tvOS. Make sure that you keep the line of code to add `editButtonItem` outside the `#if` block:

    ```
    #if TARGET_OS_IOS
    navigationController?.navigationBar.prefersLargeTitles = true
    refreshControl = UIRefreshControl()
    refreshControl?.addTarget(self, action:
    #selector(didPullDownForRefresh), for: .valueChanged)
    #endif
    ```

3. To trigger a refresh of data on tvOS, we will add a refresh button to the navigation bar in our tvOS storyboard. We will also need to add the following method to our controller so that we can trigger this method when the refresh button is pressed from the tvOS remote:

    ```
    @IBAction func didSelectRefreshButton(_ sender: UIBarButtonItem) {
      loadData()
    }
    ```

[ 309 ]

4. Next, let's wrap the `didPullDownForRefresh` method with the iOS platform directive so that it is excluded from being included in our tvOS build:

   ```
   #if TARGET_OS_IOS
   @objc func didPullDownForRefresh(_ sender: UIRefreshControl) {
     loadData()
   }
   #endif
   ```

5. Also, add the iOS platform directive to the `endRefreshing` method, calling on `refreshControl` inside the `ShoppingList.load` closure function:

   ```
   #if TARGET_OS_IOS
   self.refreshControl?.endRefreshing()
   #endif
   ```

6. The last thing we will need to do is copy the two configurations from our iOS `Info.plist` file to the tvOS `Info.plist` file. Simple, right-click on the `Info.plist` file in the `ShoppingListTV` folder, and navigate to **Open As** | **Source Code** from the menu. Add these two configs toward the end of the file inside the **plist** | **dict** tag. This will allow our tvOS app to make a network request and also make a request to our localhost API endpoint:

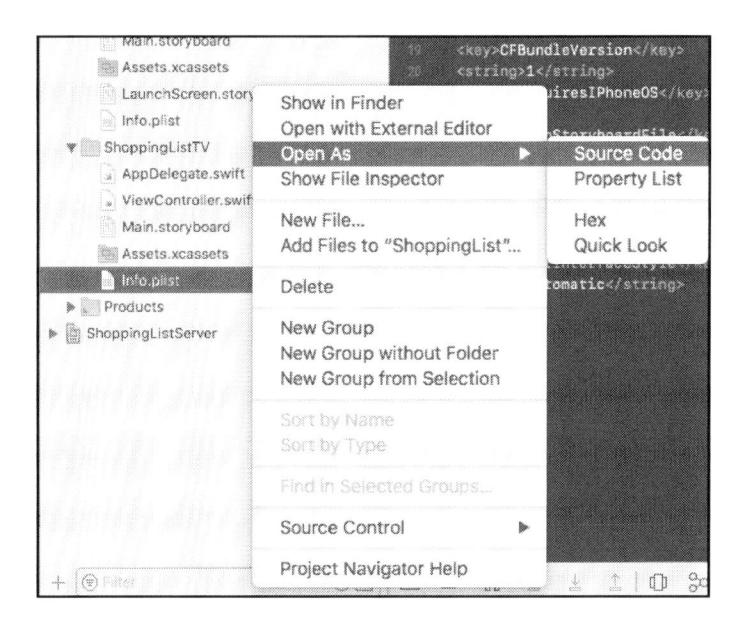

```
<key>NSAppTransportSecurity</key>
<dict>
  <key>NSAllowsArbitraryLoads</key>
  <true/>
</dict>
<key>BaseURL</key>
<string>http://localhost:8080/api</string>
```

That is it for code changes, and now we can build our app; it should compile without any errors. It will still not work when we run it, as we have not configured the Storyboard yet. In the next section, we will discuss how to configure the tvOS Storyboard.

# Configuring the tvOS storyboard

To get our tvOS App to show the Login, Shopping List, and Item screen, we will need to add these view controllers to our tvOS storyboard and link them using segues, as we did in our iOS Storyboard. We will also need to link the IBAction, which are methods that the view calls on the touch of certain UI controls, such as UIButton or selection of a table view cell. We also need to link the IBOutlets, such as the email and password fields, so that we can reference them in our controller and get the value that was entered by the user. So, let's wire up our Storyboard and get our tvOS App working by following these steps:

1. First, inside the `ShoppingListTV` folder, delete the `ViewController.swift` file, as we will not be using that. Just move the file to trash if prompted.

*Building a tvOS App*

2. Open the `Main.storyboard` of the tvOS app and select the **View Controller**. Then open the Identity inspector and change the **Custom Class** to `LoginViewController`:

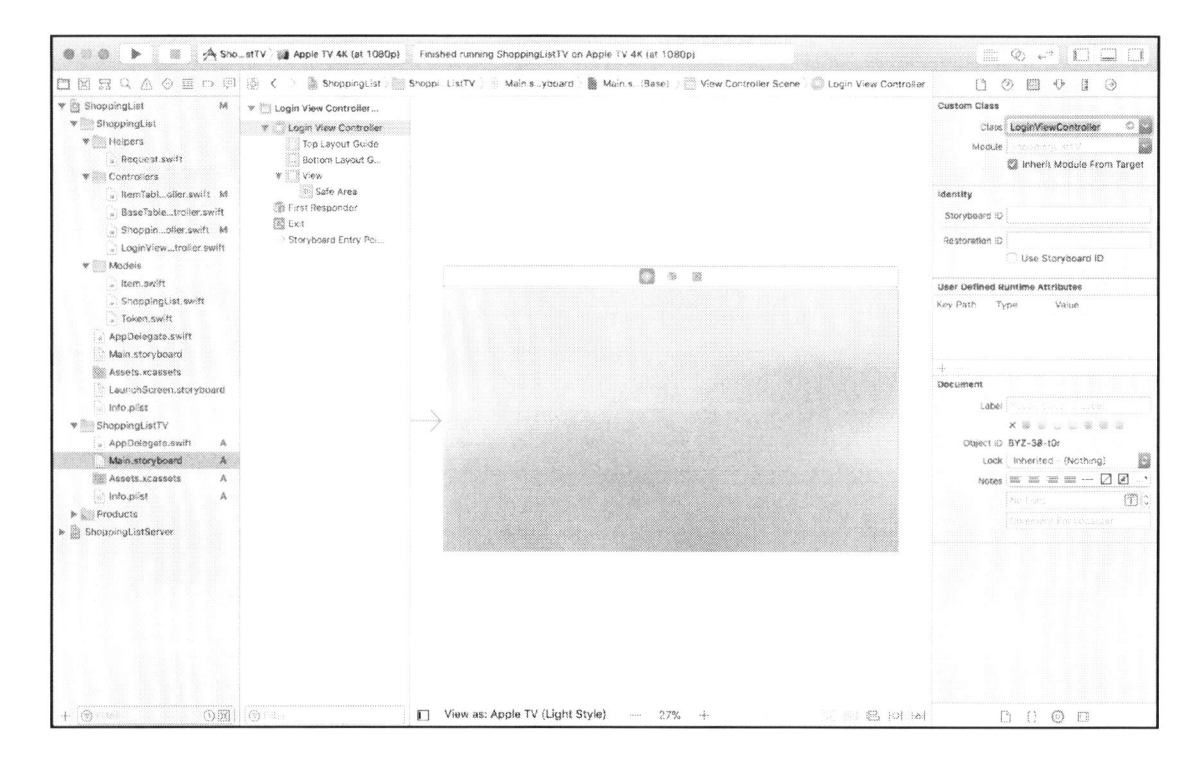

3. Next, drag the **Navigation Controller**, which will add a **Navigation Controller** and a **Root View Controller** to the storyboard:

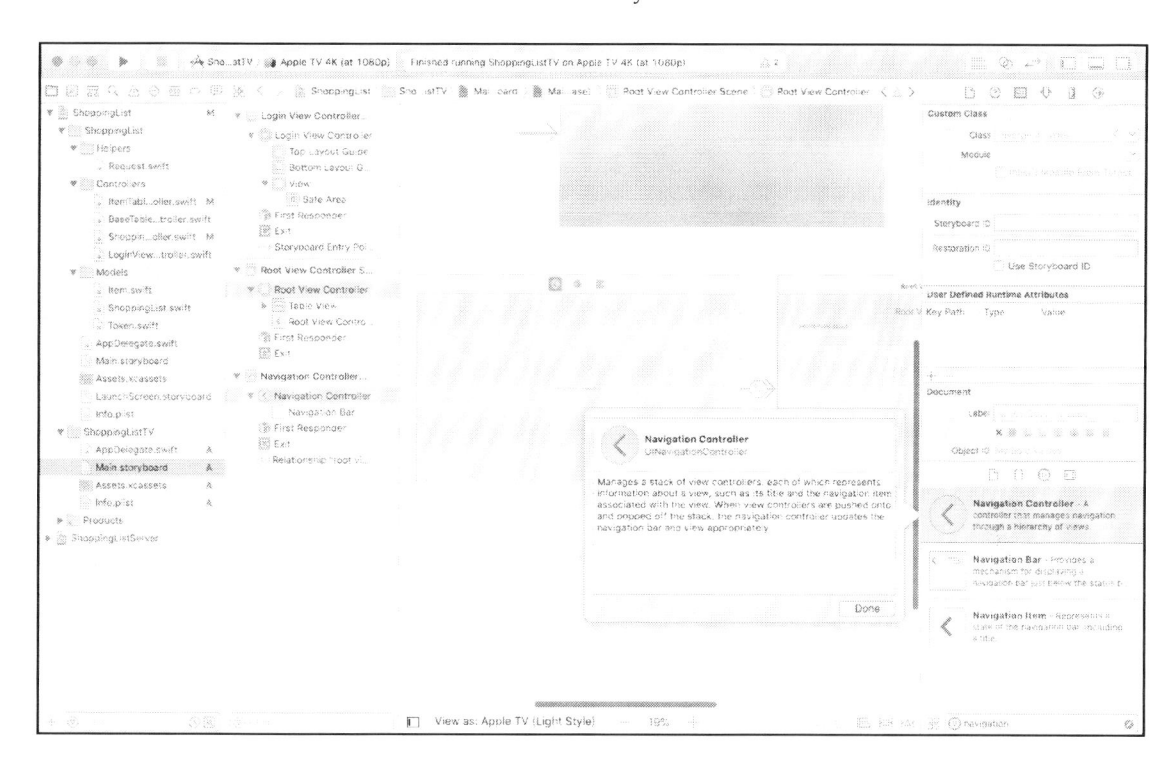

4. Now, hold *Control*, click and drag from **Navigation Controller** to the **Login View Controller** and set it as the **root view controller**:

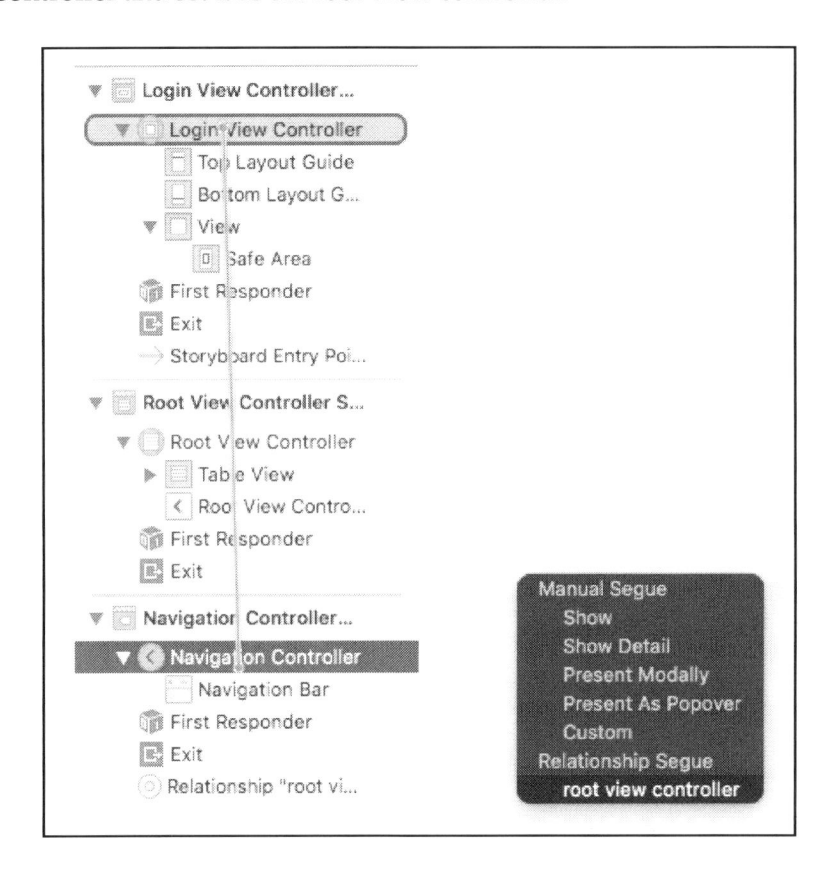

*Chapter 11*

5. Select the **Root View Controller**, which is the Table View Controller, and change the **Custom Class** to `ShoppingListTableViewController`:

*Building a tvOS App*

6. Also, click on the **Navigation Item** inside this **Shopping List Table View Controller** scene and remove the Title and press *Enter*:

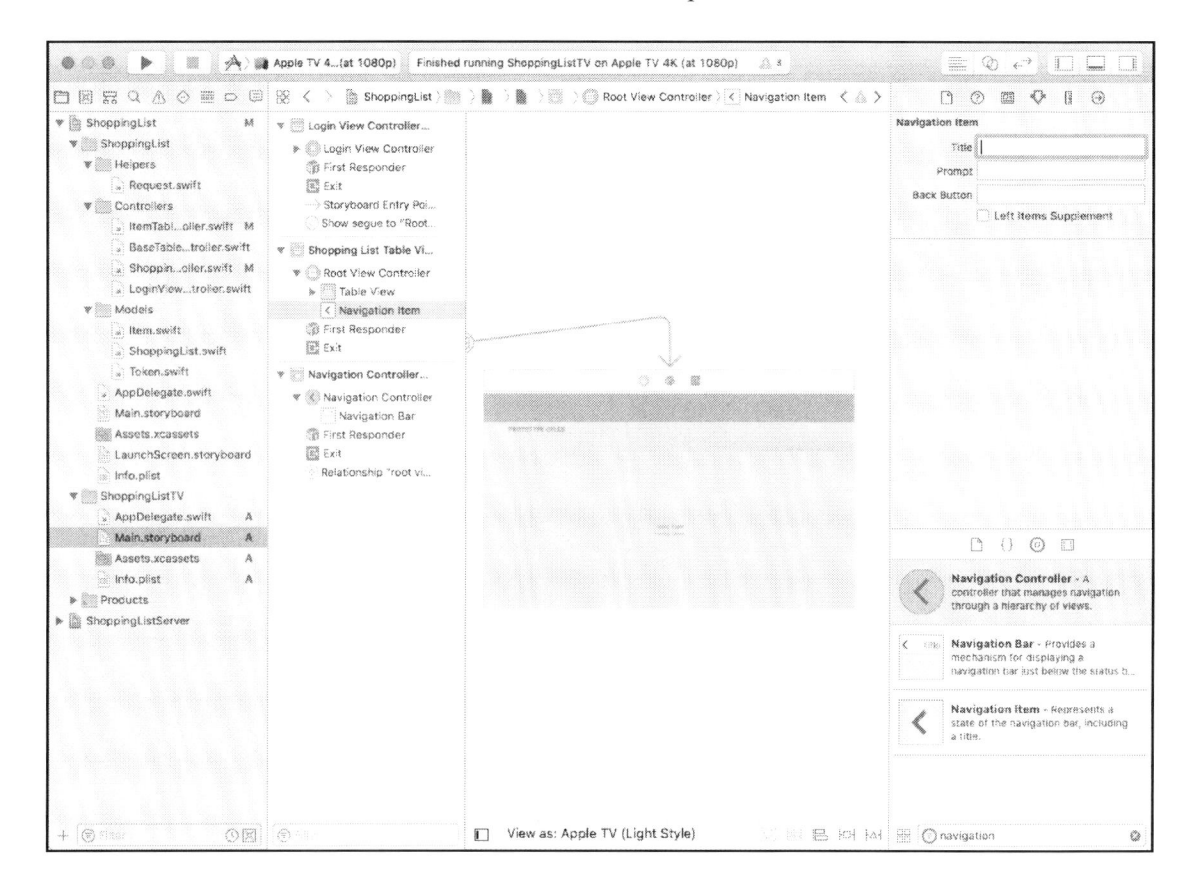

[ 316 ]

*Chapter 11*

7. Next, press *Control*, click and drag from the **Login View Controller** to the **Shopping List Table View Controller**, and select **Show** under **Manual Segue**:

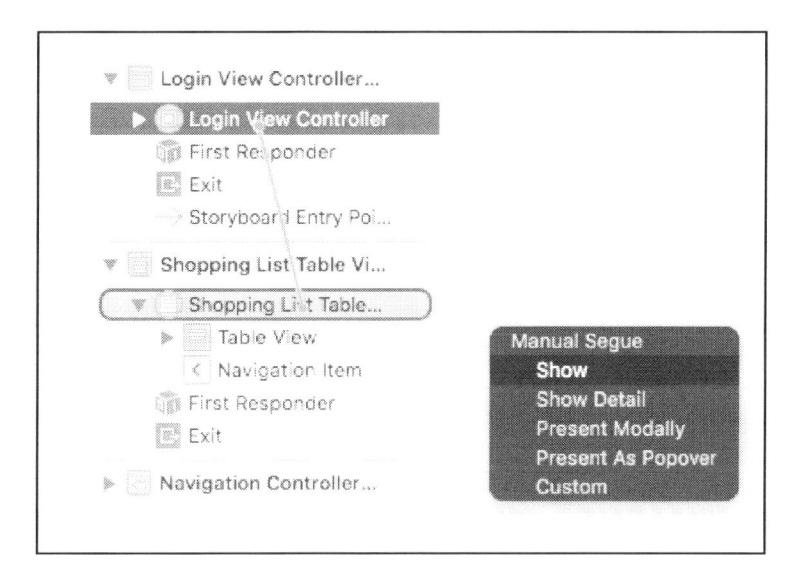

*Building a tvOS App*

8. Select the Segue that just got created and set the **Identifier** to `showShoppingList` inside the Attributes inspector:

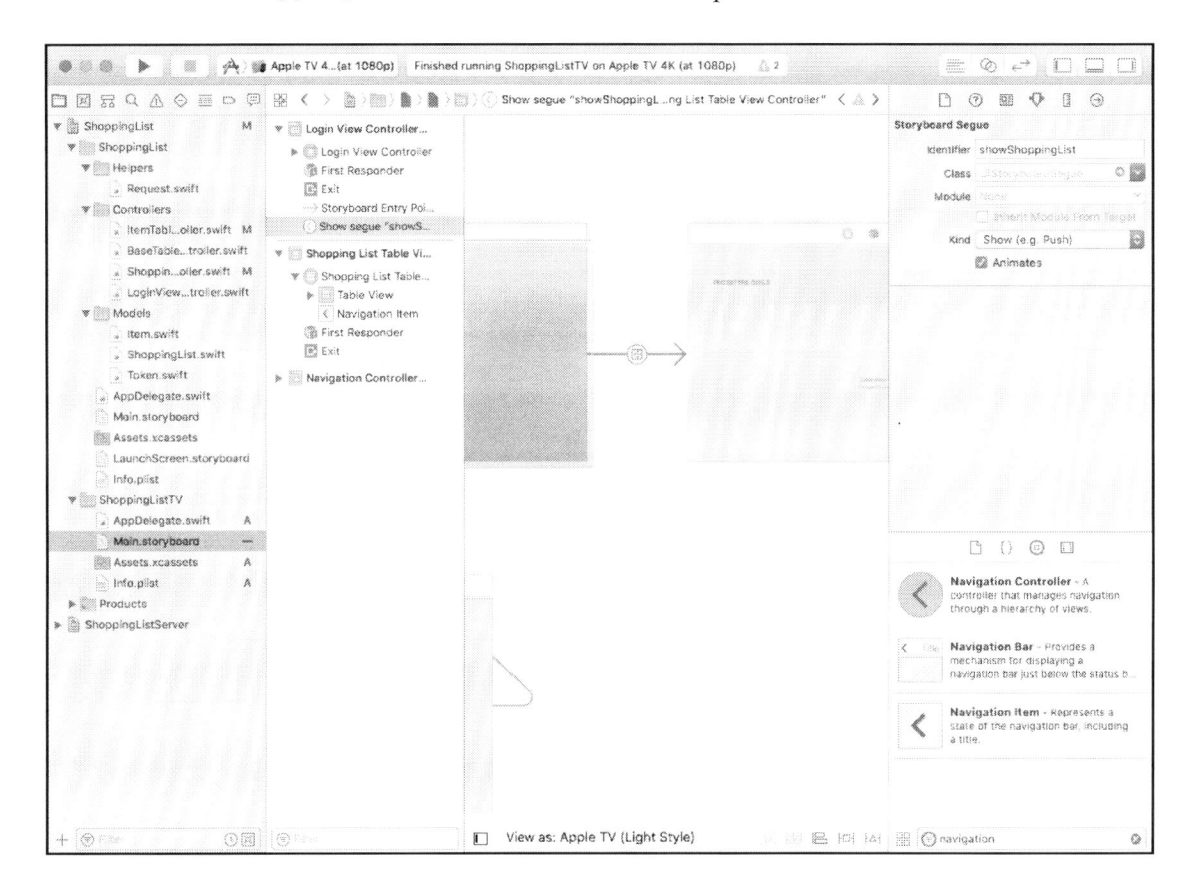

*Chapter 11*

9. Inside the **Shopping List Table View Controller**, select the **Table View Cell**, and inside the Attributes inspector, set the **Style** to `Basic`, **Identifier** to `ListCell`, and **Accessory** to `Disclosure Indicator`:

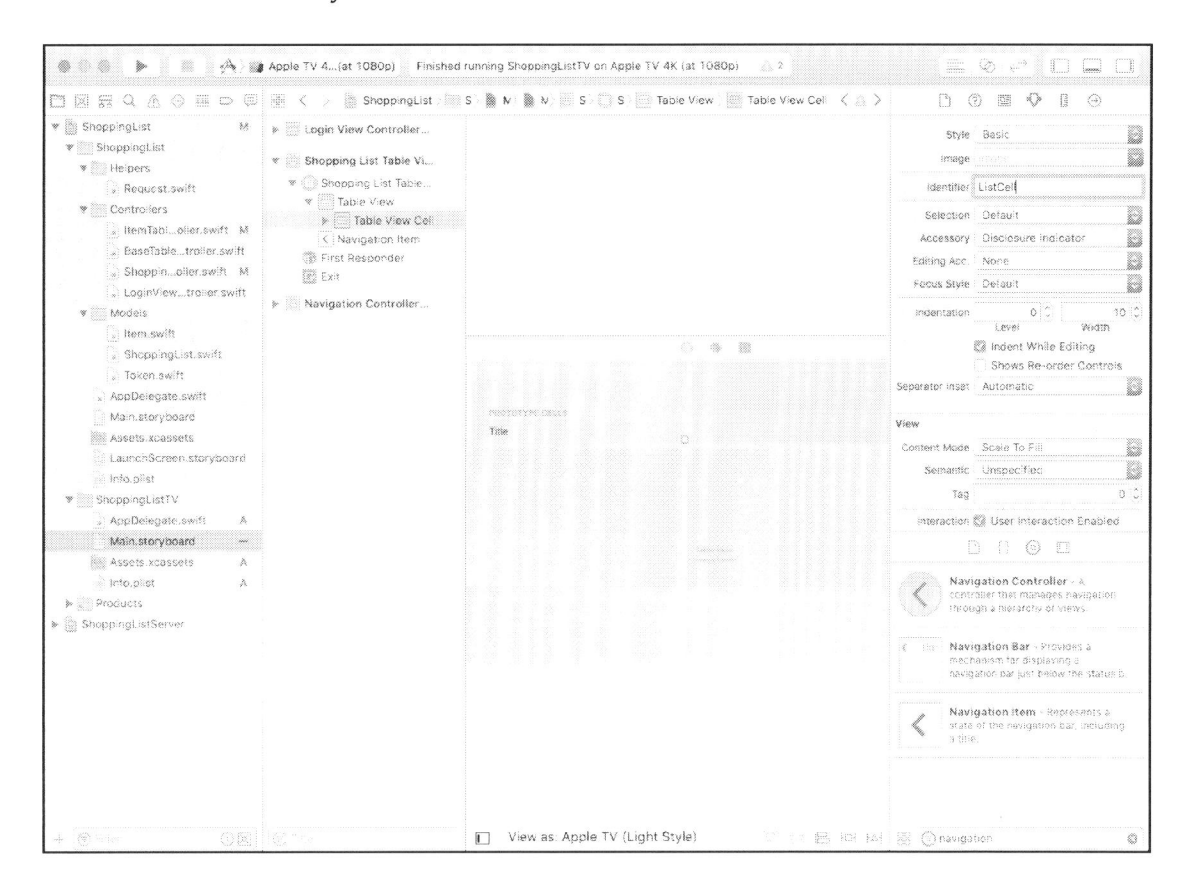

*Building a tvOS App*

10. Now, add a new **Table View Controller** by dragging it from the Object library.
11. Set the **Custom Class** to `ItemTableViewController`:

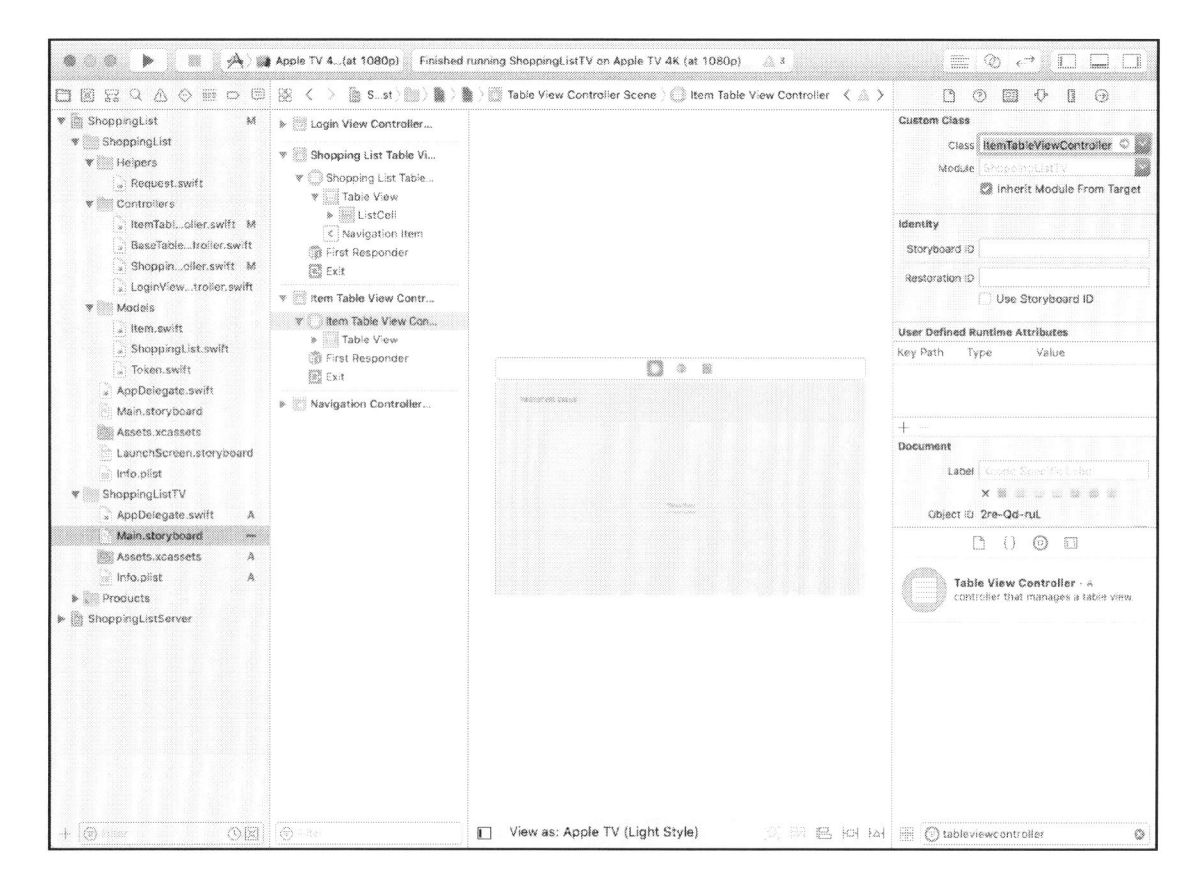

12. Similar to the Shopping List Cell, select **Table View** Cell from the **Item Table View Controller** and set the **Style** to `Basic`, **Identifier** to `ItemCell`, and **Accessory** to `Checkmark`.

*Chapter 11*

13. Now, press the *Control* key, click and drag from the **List Cell** to the **Item Table View Controller**, and select **Show** under **Selection Segue**:

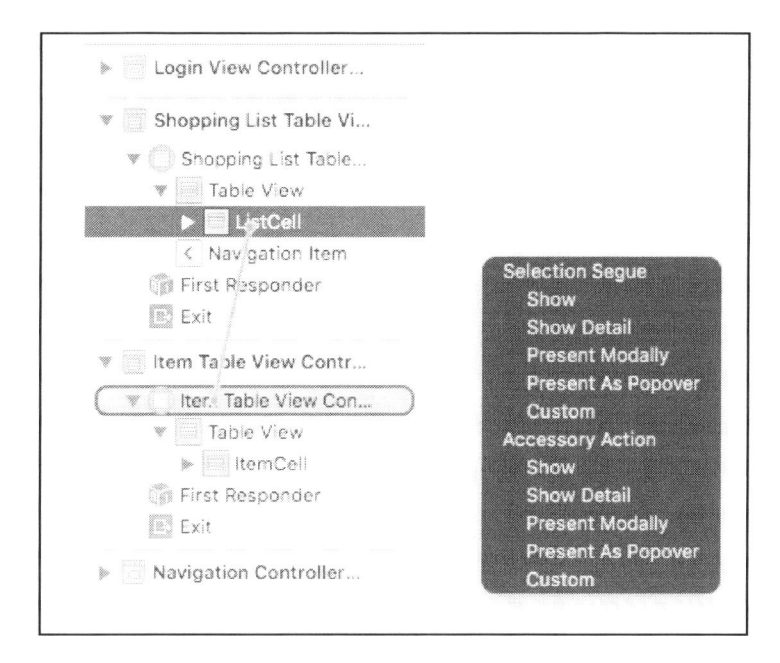

14. Now, return to the **Login View Controller** and select the **Navigation Item** inside it and set the **Title** to Shopping List Login.

*Building a tvOS App*

15. Now, drag two text fields from the Object library and place them in the **Login View Controller** scene and also drag a **Button** and place it below the two input fields. Just like the iOS app center, align the two fields and the button and change the text in the button to `Login`:

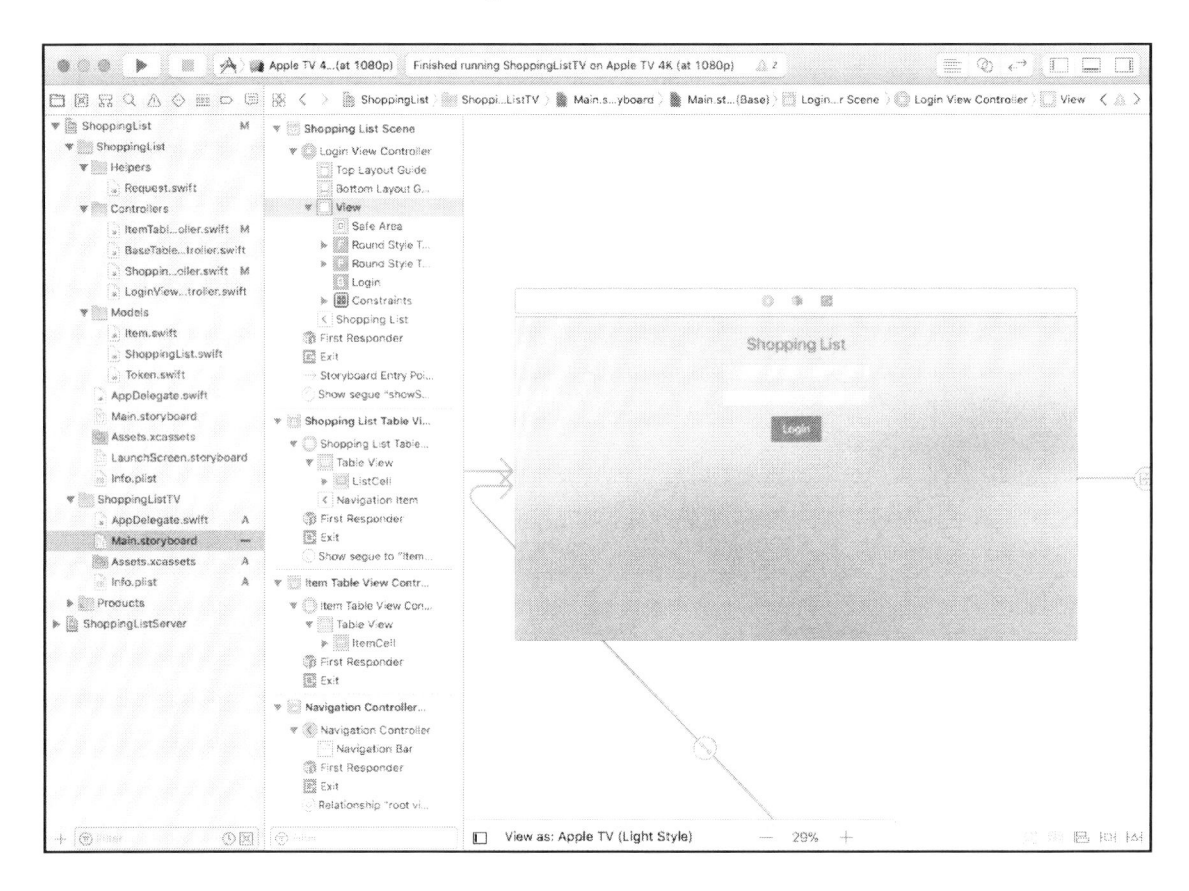

16. Select the first field and set the **Placeholder** to Email and select the second text field and set the **Placeholder** to Password, and check the **Secure Text Entry** checkbox inside the Attributes inspector.

17. Now, press the *Control* key, click and drag from the **Login View Controller** to the **Email** text field, and select **emailField**:

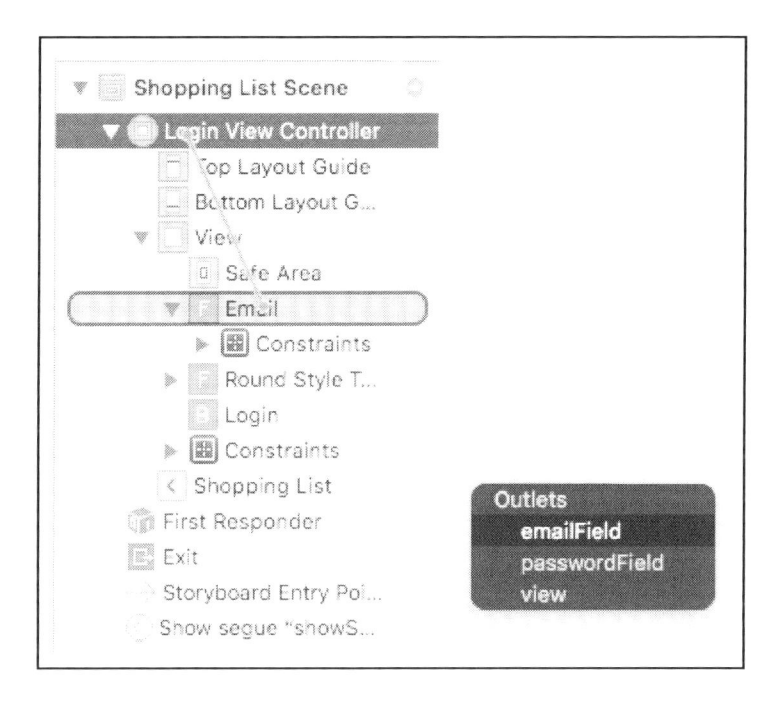

*Building a tvOS App*

18. Similarly, press the *Control* key, click and drag from the **Login View Controller** to the Password text field and select **passwordField**:

19. Now, press the *Control* key, click and drag from the **Login** button to the **Login View Controller**, and select the **didSelectLoginButton:** under **Sent Events**:

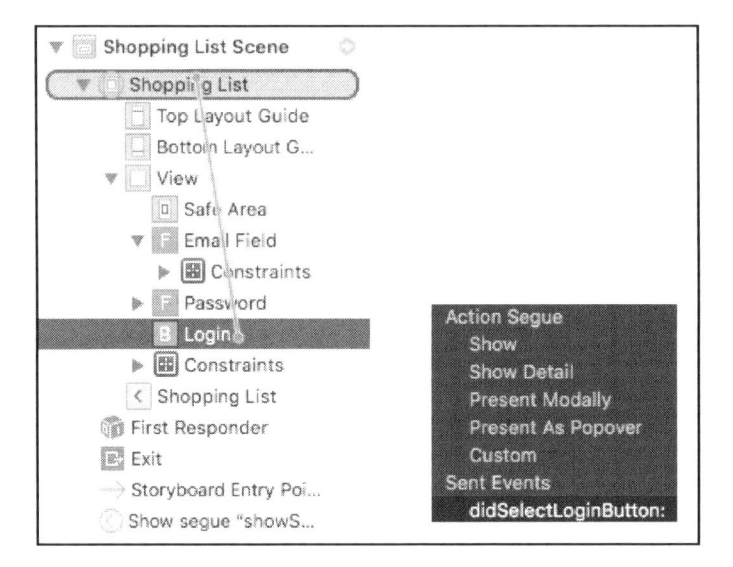

20. For the last part, we will now drag three UI Bar buttons to the navigation bar of the **Shopping List Table View Controller**. Drag one **Bar Button Item** from the Object library to the top-left corner of the Navigation bar. Rename the text of the button to `Logout`:

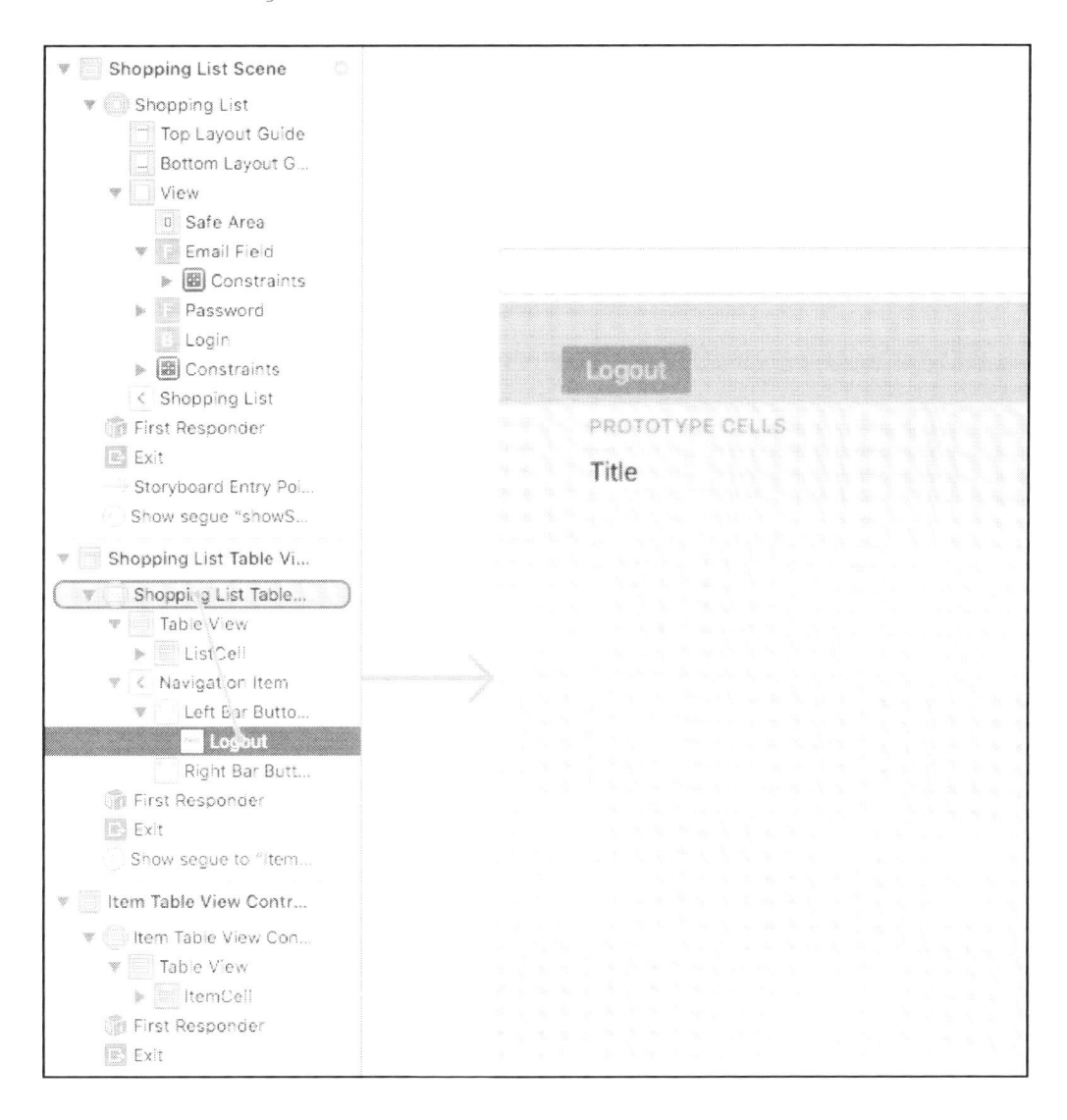

*Building a tvOS App*

21. Now, press *Control*, click and drag from the **Logout** Button to the Shopping List Table View Controller, and select **didSelectLogoutButton:** as shown in the following screenshot:

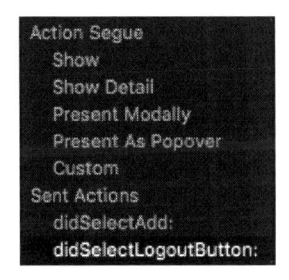

22. Next, drag a **Bar Button Item** to the top-right corner of the navigation bar. Select it and change the **System Item** to Add from the Attributes Inspector:

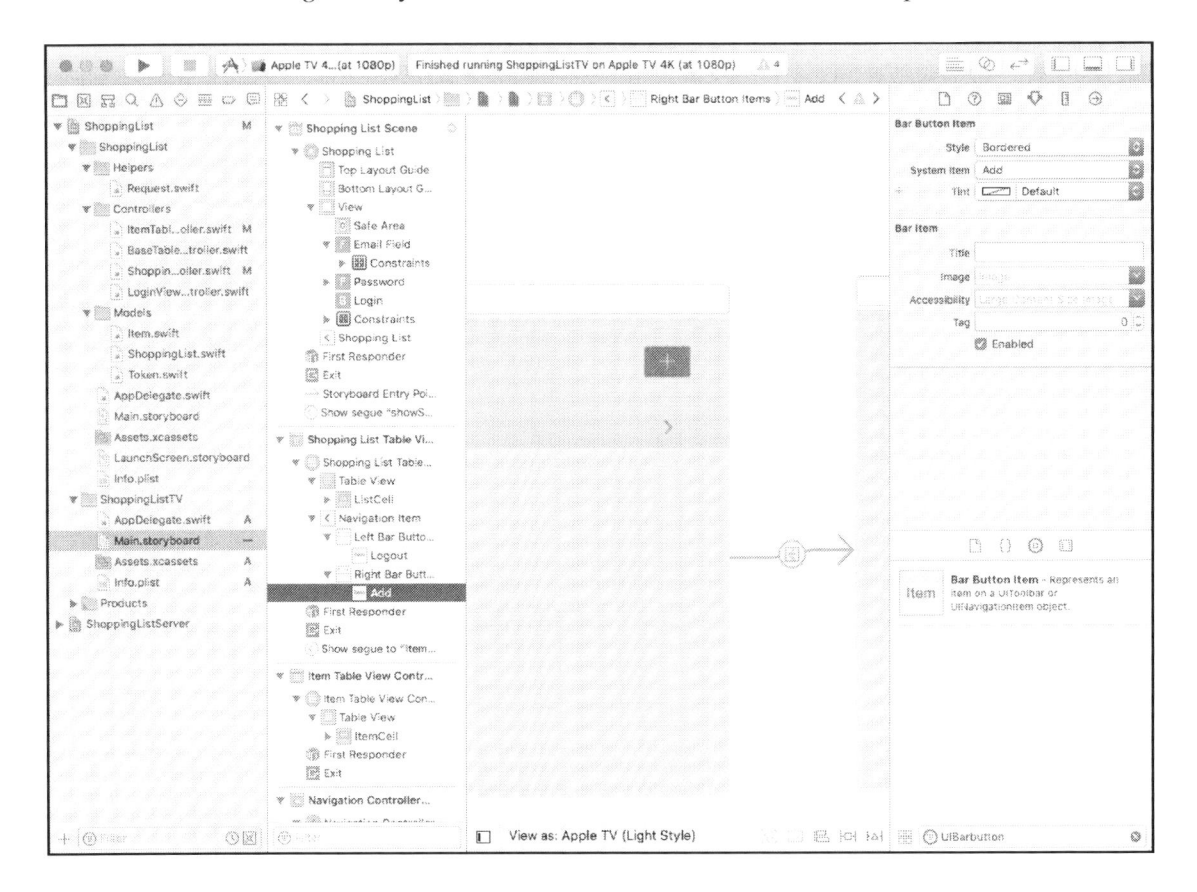

23. Now, press *Control*, click and drag from the **Add** button to the Shopping List Table View Controller, and select **didSelectAdd:** as shown in the following screenshot:

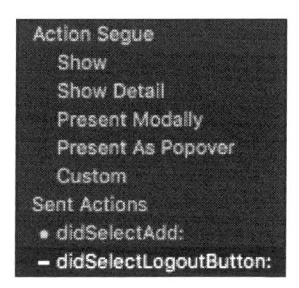

24. Now, drag one more Bar Button Item to the top-right corner of the navigation bar. Select it and change the **System Item** to `Refresh` from the Attributes Inspector.
25. Now, press *Control*, click and drag from the **Refresh** button to the Shopping List Table View Controller, and select **didSelectRefreshButton:** as shown in the following screenshot:

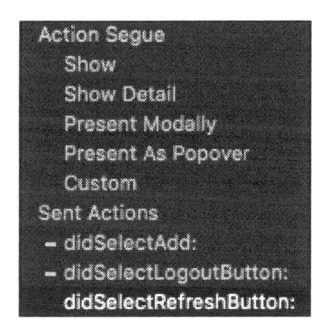

26. The last thing to do is move the **Storyboard Entry Point** to the Navigation Controller:

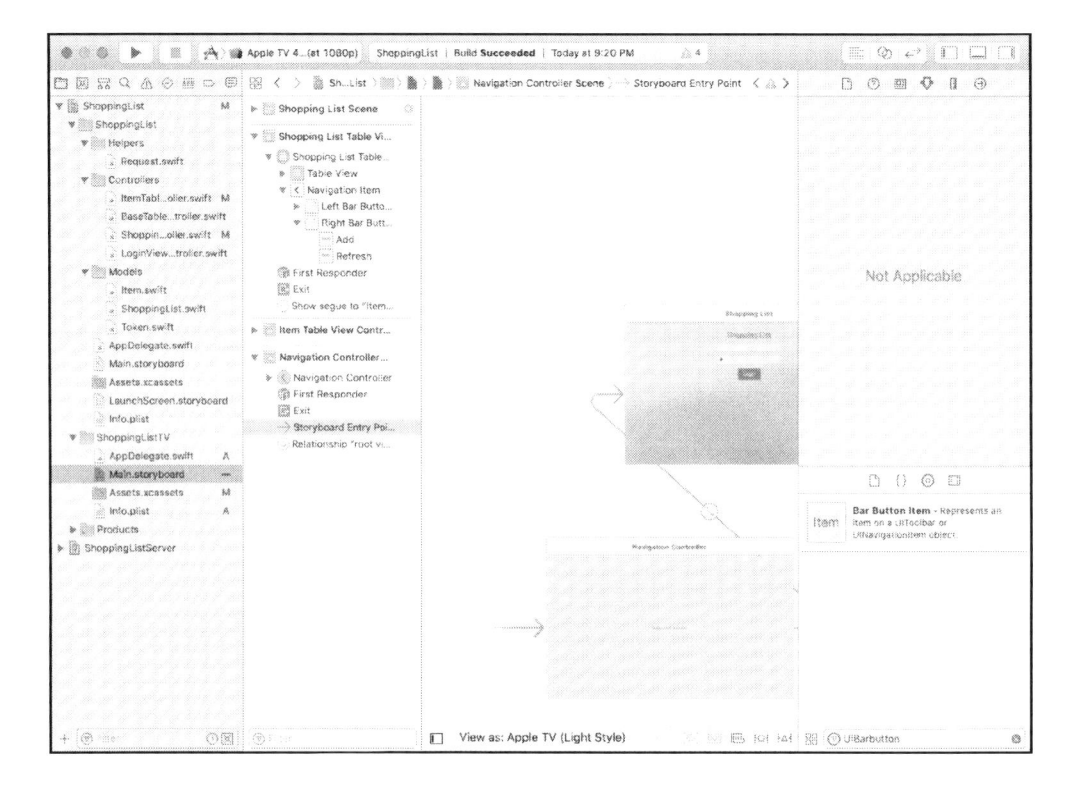

Awesome! Now, build and run your app, and make sure that you have the server app running. You should see the Shopping List App on Apple TV simulator now as a standalone tvOS App. After the app launches, you should see the email and password fields and a **Login** button:

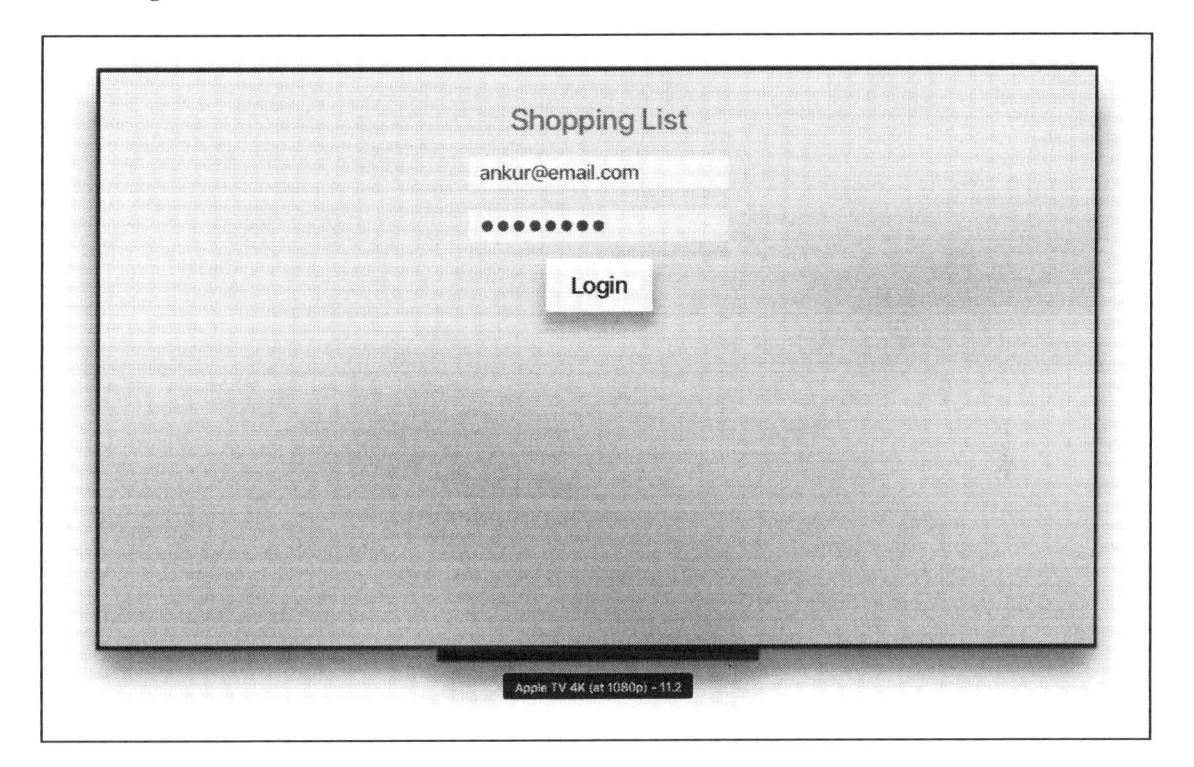

Once you log in, you should see your shopping lists in a similar table view format to the iOS app. You can delete a shopping list by selecting **Edit**, or reload by pressing the refresh button. You can also add a new Shopping List by pressing the + button:

Selecting a shopping list will show you the list of items inside of this list, and you can tap on the item to check and uncheck them. To return to the menu page, you can click on the **Menu** button:

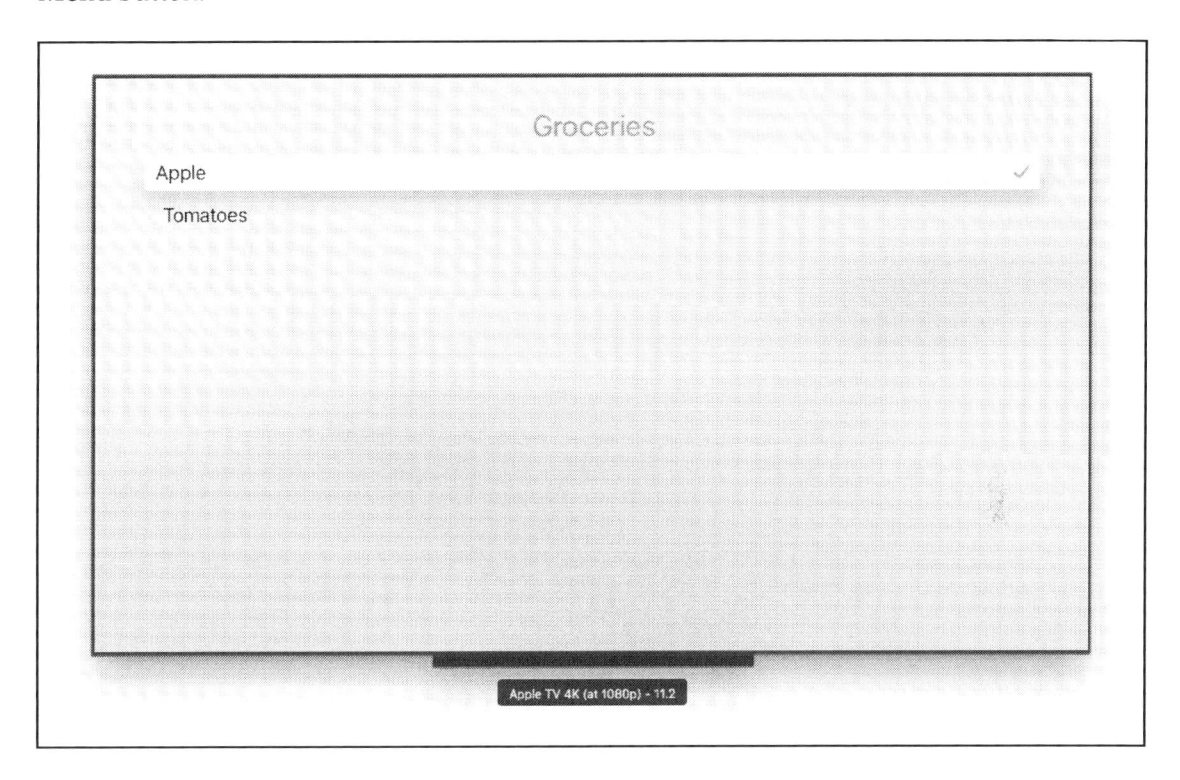

You should also be able to add a new shopping list by pressing the Add button, and it should show the prompt as a modal with a text field to enter the name:

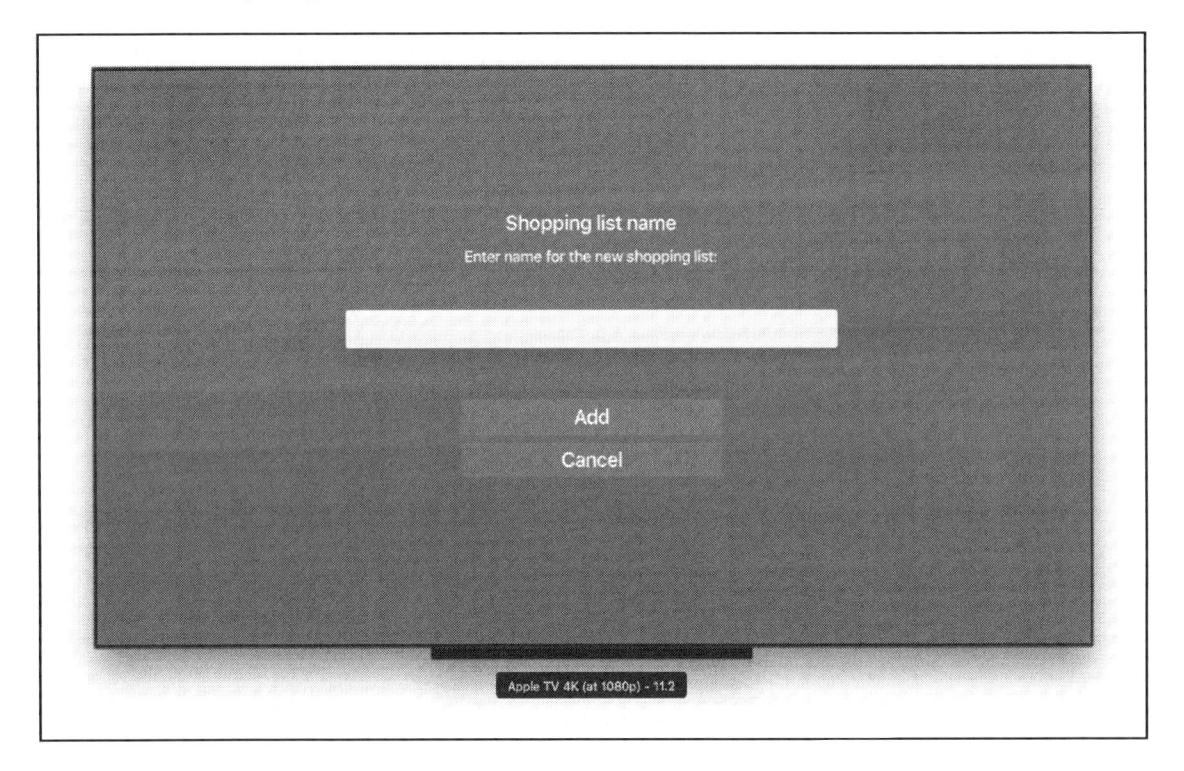

## Summary

Congratulations on making it through to the end of the book. You have gone through a developer journey of building a product across different platforms using one language by yourself. I hope this demonstrates the power of how one person can build not only a single app but come up with an architecture for a product and create multiple apps and services that communicate with each other to create a product, all using one language, Swift.

Swift, a language that was once announced as a new language in 2014, has quickly taken over different platforms, including Linux, which opens up the opportunity for developers to build not only CLI tools and services but servers using it. We have seen this in `Chapter 3`, *Getting Started with Vapor*, and dove into more detail in the later chapters. We have also seen how Swift and Apple advances in Xcode, and development practices have made it easy to build an app in pure Swift using the Model View Controller Pattern and Storyboard in `Chapter 3`, *Getting Started with Vapor*. We discussed how to build a RESTful API and a web server using Vapor, as well as how to integrate that API into the iOS app we build. We also discussed how to extend this app support to multiple users, and the ability for users to register and authenticate themselves both on the web using sessions and on the iOS app using tokens. Lastly, we touched upon how to build a tvOS app that makes our Shopping List product a multiple platform app, with maximum code shareability with our iOS app.

Besides these high-level topics, now, you should have a better understanding of how to build a full stack web application that can render HTML and JSON responses. Topics such as database providers, preparations, and relations were covered to help you understand the depth of the work involved in creating a backend for a frontend application. Also, we covered the best practices when it comes to web development, such as setting up an automated pipeline to run our tests and automatically deploy our code to a cloud service such as Heroku on a successful build and test run of our app.

We hope that you go on to new projects using Swift as your language, as you now have the toolset necessary to build a full stack multi-platform product using Swift by yourself or with a small team of people. It is sincerely hoped that this book demonstrated the power of modern Swift development, as well as building consumer-facing applications and backend services and servers using Swift and familiar tools such as Xcode to make development fun, easy, and enjoyable.

The following are a few resources that you might find useful in your journey of ongoing learning in the world of Swift:

- Diving deep into Swift: `https://www.packtpub.com/application-development/diving-deep-swift-integrated-course-0`
- Test-driven iOS development with Swift 4: `https://www.packtpub.com/application-development/test-driven-ios-development-swift-4-third-edition`
- iOS 11 Programming with Swift: `https://www.packtpub.com/application-development/ios-11-programming-swift-video`

# Other Books You May Enjoy

If you enjoyed this book, you may be interested in these other books by Packt:

**Mastering Swift 4 - Fourth Edition**
Jon Hoffman

ISBN: 978-1-78847-780-2

- Delve into the core components of Swift 4.0, including operators, collections, control flows, and functions
- Create and use classes, structures, and enumerations
- Understand protocol-oriented design and see how it can help you write better code
- Develop a practical understanding of subscripts and extensions
- Add concurrency to your applications using Grand Central Dispatch and Operation Queues
- Implement generics and closures to write very flexible and reusable code
- Make use of Swift's error handling and availability features to write safer code

## Reactive Programming with Swift 4
Navdeep Singh

ISBN: 978-1-78712-021-1

- Understand the practical benefits of Rx on a mobile platform
- Explore the building blocks of Rx, and Rx data flows with marble diagrams
- Learn how to convert an existing code base into RxSwift code base
- Learn how to debug and test your Rx Code
- Work with Playgrounds to transform sequences by filtering them using map, flatmap and other operators
- Learn how to combine different operators to work with Events in a more controlled manner.
- Discover RxCocoa and convert your simple UI elements to Reactive components
- Build a complete RxSwift app using MVVM as design pattern

# Leave a review - let other readers know what you think

Please share your thoughts on this book with others by leaving a review on the site that you bought it from. If you purchased the book from Amazon, please leave us an honest review on this book's Amazon page. This is vital so that other potential readers can see and use your unbiased opinion to make purchasing decisions, we can understand what our customers think about our products, and our authors can see your feedback on the title that they have worked with Packt to create. It will only take a few minutes of your time, but is valuable to other potential customers, our authors, and Packt. Thank you!

# Index

## A

app
  debugging 182, 185
authentication flow
  adding, to iOS application 281, 283, 285, 288, 289, 290, 292, 295, 297, 299
automated testing pipeline
  about 237, 240, 242, 243
  Travis build check, enabling on Pull request 244
Automatic Reference Counting (ARC) 8

## B

BaseResourceController
  creating 213, 215, 218
basic HTTP server
  building 78, 79
BCrypt 262

## C

children 122
code
  sharing, between iOS and tvOS app 307
  working, with iOS and tvOS app 309
Continuous Deployment (CD)
  about 247
  setting up 257, 258
Continuous Integration (CI) 237, 247
Controllers 99
controllers
  in Vapor 150
  RESTful Controller 150, 152, 153
  Shopping List controller 154, 155
Create, Read, Update, and Delete (CRUD) 120

## D

data
  fetching, from server 177, 178, 179, 181
database management system 112
databases
  about 112
  MongoDB 113
Directives 28

## E

Entity protocol 141

## F

flow of application
  controlling, View Controller used 39, 42
Fluent
  about 115
  in action 115, 117
  item finding, filter used 119
  item, counting 120
  item, creating 118
  item, deleting 120
  item, finding 119
  item, obtaining 119
  item, updating 119
  many to many 123
  one to many 122
  one to one 121
  relations 120

## G

Generics 209

# H

Heroku
  app, priming for deployment 251
  deploying 248, 250
  MongoDB Heroku addon, adding 255, 256
  Vapor, configuring 251, 253
  Vapor, deploying 251, 253
Horizontal scaling 248
HTML formats 209
HTTP methods 134
HTTP request 21
HTTP response 21

# I

item
  adding 221
  adding, to list 51, 52, 53, 55
  checking 223
  deleting 222
  unchecking 223

# J

JavaScript
  adding 219
  item, adding 221
  item, checking 223
  item, deleting 222
  item, unchecking 223
  Shopping List, creating 220
  Shopping List, deleting 221
JSON
  serving 209
Just-In-Time (JIT) 8

# K

Kitura 29

# L

Leaf 200, 201, 203
Leaf Provider
  adding 204, 205, 206, 208
List Cell 321
list
  editing 55, 57, 59
Low Level Virtual Machine (LLVM) 8

# M

macOS 28
middleware
  creating 209, 210, 212
mobile application
  data, requesting 21
Model View Controller (MVC) 75
modern app development 8
mongo 125
Mongo config 126
mongodb services 238
MongoDB
  about 113
  connecting 125
  executing 113
  Fluent config, configuring 125
  installing 113
MongoProvider
  adding 127, 129, 131
multiple lists
  about 62
  share code, refactoring 62
  Shopping List Model, blueprinting 63, 65
  Shopping List Table View Controller 66, 68, 71, 72

# N

network configuration 174, 175
network requests
  creating 173, 175

# O

object-relational mapping (ORM) 114
operating system (OS) 9

# P

parent 122
Perfect 29
Procfile 251
Providers
  about 104

[ 340 ]

adding 110
building 104, 107, 108
exercise time 109

# R

relational databases 112
Representational State Transfer (REST) 99
REST API
  in action 156
  items, creating 160, 162
  Shopping List, creating 156
  Shopping List, deleting 160
  Shopping List, obtaining 157
  Shopping List, updating 159
RESTful routes
  Shopping List, creating 233, 234
  Shopping List, deleting 234
  Shopping List, fetching 232
  Shopping List, updating 235
  testing 231

# S

segues 285
server side
  debugging 182, 185
server-side Swift
  benefits 10
server-side web frameworks 28
servers
  building, Vapor engine used 77
SHA-256 262
sharding 113
share code
  refactoring 62
Shopping List API
  Vapor application 102
Shopping List app
  auto-saving 60, 61
  features 33
  loading 60, 61
  on tvOS 301, 303, 304, 306
Shopping List item model
  blueprinting 37
  example 39

Shopping List Item
  adding 192, 193, 194
  checking 196, 197
  deleting 195
  unchecking 196, 197
Shopping List Model
  about 142
  blueprinting 63, 65
Shopping List Table View Controller 66, 68, 71, 72
Shopping List
  about 268, 269
  adding 186, 188, 189
  creating 220
  deleting 190, 192, 221
  example 192
static file server
  building 80
structured query language 114
Swift package manager
  about 11
  building 12, 14, 15
  consuming 16, 17
  package's executable, installing 19
  publishing 15
Swift's evolution
  about 8
  open source 9
  server-side Swift 9
Swift
  web server, building 24, 26, 28

# T

Table View Controller 40, 47, 48, 50
token-based authentication
  about 277
  adding, for app 276, 278, 280
  testing 281
Travis build check
  enabling, on Pull request 246
Travis CI 237
tvOS storyboard
  configuring 311, 314, 316, 319, 320, 324, 326, 327, 331

# U

User model
  about  264, 265, 266, 267
  creating  262
  password storing, best practices  262
user specific Shopping List
  displaying  275

# V

Vapor application
  building, from scratch  85, 86
  deploying  247
  Leaf  200, 201, 203
  test environment, setting up  226
  testing  226
  tests, executing  227, 229, 231
  view rendering  200
Vapor engine
  basic HTTP server, building  78, 79
  static file server, building  80
  used, for building servers  77
  WebSocket server, building  82, 84
Vapor folder structure
  about  93
  config  94, 96
  Controllers  99
  droplet  96
  Views  98
Vapor Model
  about  141
  Item Model  147
  JSONConvertible protocol  145
  Preparation protocol  144
  ResponseRepresentable protocol  146
  Shopping List Model  142
  Updateable protocol  146
Vapor toolbox
  about  87
  commands  88, 89
  installing  87
  used, for creating Vapor application  90, 92
Vapor
  about  29, 76
  controllers in  150
  dynamic routing  138, 139
  HTTP methods  134
  nested routing  138
  parameters, routing  140
  routers  135, 137
  routing  134
  URL  29
  wildcard routing  140
View Controller
  about  312
  used, for controlling flow of application  39, 42
view
  wiring up  42, 44, 46
Views  98

# W

web page
  login, adding  270, 272, 273, 274
  registration, adding  270, 272, 273, 274
  user requesting  19
web server
  building, in Swift  24, 26, 28
  working  19
WebSocket server
  building  82, 84

# X

Xcode app
  creating  34, 36
Xcode Workspace  166, 168, 170, 171, 173

Printed in Great Britain
by Amazon